HEAR US OUT

BETWEEN MEN ~ BETWEEN WOMEN ■ LESBIAN, GAY, AND BISEXUAL STUDIES

TERRY CASTLE AND LARRY GROSS, EDITORS

RICHARD CANNING

[CONVERSATIONS WITH GAY NOVELISTS]

HEAR US OUT

COLUMBIA UNIVERSITY PRESS ▪ NEW YORK

COLUMBIA UNIVERSITY PRESS

Publishers Since 1893

New York Chichester, West Sussex

Copyright © 2003 Columbia University Press

Library of Congress Cataloging-in-Publication Data

Canning, Richard.

Hear us out : conversations with Gay novelists / Richard Canning.

p.   cm. — (Betwen men—between women)

Companion volume to: Gay fiction speaks.

ISBN 0-231-12866-5 (cloth : alk. paper) — ISBN 0-231-12867-3 (pbk. : alk. paper)

1. Gay men's writings, American—History and criticism—Theory, etc.

2. Homosexuality and literature—United States—History—20th century.

3. Homosexuality and literature—Great Britain—History—20th century.

4. American fiction—21st century—History and criticism—Theory, etc.

5. English fiction—21st century—History and criticism—Theory, etc.

6. Gay men's writings, English—History and criticism—Theory, etc.

7. Novelists, American—21st century—Interviews.

8. Novelists, English—21st century—Interviews.

9. Male authors, American—Interviews.

10. Male authors, English—Interviews.

11. Gay men in literature. I. Title. II. Series.

PS374.H63C364 2003

813'.54099206642—dc22

2003060761

Designed by Lisa Hamm

c   10   9   8   7   6   5   4   3   2   1

p   10   9   8   7   6   5   4   3   2   1

CONTENTS

INTRODUCTION

WELCOME to *Hear Us Out*. I hope some of you will know—or will get to know—my previous collection, *Gay Fiction Speaks: Conversations with Gay Novelists* (Columbia University Press, 2000). In some respects, *Hear Us Out* aims to pick up the story of contemporary gay fiction where that book left off. But if you're a new initiate—don't panic. *Hear Us Out* is presented as an autonomous work. You don't need to bring anything with you.

Gay Fiction Speaks contains conversations with twelve of the most revered gay novelists writing in English—Dennis Cooper, Patrick Gale, Allan Gurganus, Andrew Holleran, Alan Hollinghurst, David Leavitt, Armistead Maupin, Ethan Mordden, Felice Picano, James Purdy, John Rechy, and Edmund White. (I've tended to use the words "interview" and "conversation" indiscriminately here, though I do believe the latter better reflects the mood and circumstance in which they were undertaken.)

In the book's introduction, I sketched out a list of aspirations for what was—and remains—a larger series, one that I hope will run to a (future) third volume. That account included some rules of thumb as well as a few reflections on the experience of charging across several continents one winter with almost no clothes, a tape recorder, at least two hundred "must reread" novels in my suitcase, and—it transpired—a desperately ill boyfriend at the end of the phone line (but that's another story).

I won't repeat everything I wrote there. Here I'll consider instead the relationship between this book and its predecessor, note some commonalities and divergences, and offer a few thoughts on what seems most significant in the conversations you find here. *Hear Us Out* involves some chronological overlap with *Gay Fiction Speaks*, but broadly aims to complement it by detailing—in loose, nonprescriptive form—the "next chapter" in gay fiction writing. Its subjects are a number of very different novelists whose work was in part enabled by the emergence of the authors featured in the earlier volume. It's a debt they acknowledge, one after another. Happily, meanwhile, all twelve contributors to the original volume not only survive but thrive. Many are producing the most celebrated and vital work of their careers—from Edmund White's poignant study in grief (*The Married Man*) and Allan Gurganus's fine novella collection (*The Practical Heart*), to Armistead Maupin's wrenching *The Night Listener* and Dennis Cooper's intricate *My Loose Thread*.

A university colleague warned when I began this project that I shouldn't expect it to be taken seriously. The thousands of hours devoted to transcribing, editing, fact-checking, revising, and so on, would, he averred, bring few rewards or acknowledgments. As he was drawing on his own experience of publishing two volumes of literary interviews, I took this caution rather heavily to heart.

I needn't have—though he was certainly right about the unimaginable time a project like this can consume. The academy's view of the book I'll leave to one side. I can't say yet that I know what it is. As for the lay response, I couldn't have been luckier. What many writers have long hoped for turns out to be true. Gay readers are invariably rather special readers—especially motivated, especially diligent; especially engaged; and especially suggestible. The reach and feedback I've had for a book of this kind has felt nothing short of miraculous—and profoundly moving. I'd like to record my gratitude here to everyone who got in touch, and I hope more of you will do so.

I always had recklessly high hopes for the project. I had to. Even the most well-meaning interviewee invariably adopted a quizzical expression on hearing that a university lecturer proposed to take the works of around forty writers of contemporary gay literary fiction seriously. Many were used to the sorts of questions which emerged from interviews on the usual publicity circuit. Some weren't just tired of being asked ad nauseam whether they supported gay marriage, or whom or how they'd like to get laid. Often, I suspect, they had come to expect and anticipate being asked only such "lifestyle" questions. As David Bergman put it in his foreword to *Gay Fiction Speaks*, on such occasions "the work seems secondary." Indeed, if there's a single aim to these books of conversations, it's to consider gay literature and those who write it *in the context of literature*. Bergman generously describes my approach as involving taking these writers "seriously as artists." That's certainly the hope— as well as to encourage others to see the point in doing just that.

I thought people would buy it—the idea, as well as the book—and was most fortunate that Columbia University Press shared the hunch and my enthusiasm. There's an opportunity here to note how vital it surely is that university presses, universities generally, and gay and lesbian scholars particularly, devote themselves to promulgating works of interest and passion which not only *could* attract lay readers but isn't shy of addressing them in their own language—that is, in everyday language we all share. I was as thrilled as anyone when, through the 1980s and 1990s, shelf after shelf became filled with intellectually distinguished tomes on so many aspects of gay and lesbian literature, culture, society, history, and politics. How many, though, were clearly and accessibly written?

Too many academics in our field have preferred to write voodoo prose, unaccountably egged on by an ever-dwindling number of colleagues to ever-more-intractable acres of prosaic purple. It's heartbreaking to teach literary prose of the quality, say, of E. M. Forster, and to witness how the worst sort of criticism can turn an honest, receptive, but untutored mind into a sort of "howling machine" of theory-born injunctions, objections, declamations, and obsessions. Enough! Enough, especially, of cries about what a certain author didn't manage to do.

Books are hard to write; harder still to publish! What *did* they achieve? I'm not ashamed of being unfashionably celebratory in the pages of *Hear Us Out*.

Still, it's little wonder that some writers I approached were initially wary in dealing with an envoy from the Scylla of Academe. At the same time, each of these novelists has to some degree struggled—and occasionally triumphed—in the Charybdis of the literary marketplace in the United States and Great Britain. The relentless media-led quest for the young and the new makes it very easy for today's publishing sensation to become tomorrow's has-been. It's a truism among writers that most big fiction publishers in New York and London consider gay-themed books more or less unmarketable. However they try, moreover, they can't expect the leading newspapers, magazines, or journals to devote much space to gay writers, especially up-and-coming ones.

The niche market for gay fiction in the States, for example, is invariably held to be between 3,000 and 5,000 copies—perfectly viable commercially, incidentally. Most of the bigger presses determined in the mid-nineties, however, not to bother with authors whose works sold in such reliable, but relatively modest, amounts and/or appealed to an apparently finite set of readers. There were, and are, exceptions. At least two such authors feature in *Hear Us Out*. Michael Cunningham's *The Hours* won the Pulitzer—not only reversing common marketplace assumptions about gay fiction but, more precisely, demonstrating something heretofore unimaginable: that a novel about AIDS could be a bestseller. Equally, Stephen McCauley's shrewd romantic comedies, meanwhile, have steadily increased in popularity among women readers—the evident Shangri-la in sales terms. This seems to have been accomplished by way of a cute, old-fashioned force: word-of-mouth on a quality read. At the same time, McCauley's novels were flying off the shelves in France—that unimaginable literary landscape where there's no separate shelving of gay titles, black authors, "women's writing," and little or no idea of "niche" marketing. Sexually explicit or transgressive material is as likely to be given serious space in literary reviews as anything else. These things won't happen in the States or in Britain. But it's still fascinating to consider what might be possible if they did.

Such exceptions have sometimes only confirmed to the less fortunate gay writer the strength of enduring rules in the marketplace. It remains a difficult place and time for gay writers, notwithstanding an apparent proliferation of titles. Dale Peck beautifully understates it: "Career choices and money problems can change the direction of your writing." Gary Indiana likewise reflects on the paltry initial readership of Melville's *Moby-Dick*. Unlike the tenured academic, say, the novelist's bread-and-butter needs invariably can't accommodate the writing of—even—a work of that sort of genius, if "genius" means attracting the select few.

It's noteworthy that, while some periods of our literary past have overwhelmingly been colonized by a large number of gay and lesbian literary critics—the fin de siècle, modernism, the Renaissance, the Romantics—the field of contemporary literature (that of the last twenty years or so) continues to receive relatively scant academic attention. Why? My hunch is that as literary criticism in the field of sexuality reaches ever-less-imagined realms of prose creativity and/or neologistic invention and obscurity, it attains its own avant-gardism. It becomes au courant, or contemporary. Roland Barthes was sometimes asked why, if he loved the cultural avant-garde, he nevertheless chose to study canonical writers like Balzac or Sade. The answer in his case, and in the case of many gay and lesbian literary critics, relates in part to the difficulty, indirection, and necessary duplicity of pre-liberation works. This naturally appeals as a ready subject for intellectual endeavour. Closed oysters promise unclaimed pearls.

This tendency has—ironically—offered to many a critic the vital "What if . . . ?" proposition always beloved of fiction writers: "What if Jane Austen were really writing about . . . ?" "What if James at this moment was actually preoccupied by . . . ?" Colm

Tóibín, himself working on a novel about Henry James and steeped in contemporary academic Jamesiana, comments on the appeal of such apparent "moments of disclosure . . . the art of concealment, the danger of being found out" in writers of the nineteenth and early twentieth centuries. Whatever the cause, the result is that contemporary gay literature receives remarkably little scholarly attention—especially if compared, say, to ethnic or national literary "schools."

Let me return to the context of *Hear Us Out*. I've increasingly come to feel that much of the smartest, less feted, and—my guess—more enduring work in the interdisciplinary field of gay and lesbian studies is that written by historians, often cultural historians. The people I'm thinking of present their ideas in accessible prose and want—like most novelists—to be read by everybody. Their textual conventions and allusions conform to the higher ideal of reaching a large, interested, but potentially uninformed readership. It's in this spirit that I present *Hear Us Out*—as an attempt, I suppose, to write contemporary gay literary history and/or to encourage others in that writing. Felice Picano memorably once borrowed from Edmund White the title of a discarded novel—*Like People in History*. In assuming the twelve subjects of this book to be writers of distinguished literary talent, I'm seeking to secure already a place in literary history for them and their works.

In *Gay Fiction Speaks*, Edmund White cannily suspected that the "mainstreaming" of homosexuality (its increasing presence and visibility in our media, including films, however circumscribed; its ever-greater ability to defend and articulate itself) might spell the end of gay literary culture—or, at the very least, the importance of gay fiction as an aid to those readers coming to terms with their own homosexuality. His toying with this controversial question is echoed in this volume by Colm Tóibín. Could gay liberation paradoxically prove fatal for gay literature? According to this logic, as homosexuality becomes more readily portrayed and accepted in society at large, it at the same time negates itself as a subject worth articulating. I'm not going to deliver a verdict on this here, except to indicate that such propositions inform what I'll shortly be saying about gay novelists as contemporary historians.

The careers of the dozen interviewees in *Gay Fiction Speaks* necessarily spanned a much broader time period than those featured in this book. James Purdy and John Rechy were first acclaimed in the 1950s and early 1960s, whereas Alan Hollinghurst's fiction career began in 1988, making him very much contemporaneous to the writers in *Hear Us Out*. In *Gay Fiction Speaks*, I wanted the conversations to interrelate implicitly, to provide a sort of provisional oral history of gay fiction writing. At the same time, I relished the diversity which stark differences in age, background, geographical location, and publishing history all brought about. The contributors to *Hear Us Out*, by contrast, reflect the dramatic proliferation of gay novels in the wake of the emergence of the idea of "gay fiction" in the late 1970s. Ten of the twelve were born in the fifties, the other two in the sixties. They first saw publication within a very narrow time frame indeed—between 1986 and 1994. Six of the twelve were first published in a single year, 1990. Are they, then, "closer" to one another? I think not. First—forgive the obvious—writers rarely obey the protocols of "groups." The works written by this dozen contrast and diverge as fundamentally as you'd therefore expect.

In *Gay Fiction Speaks*, alongside ten American authors, I included two English writers whose novels had, to my mind, made a substantial contribution—Alan Hollinghurst and Patrick Gale. *Hear Us Out* happens again to feature ten Americans, complemented by the Irish Colm Tóibín and London-based English author Philip Hensher. Hensher, like Gale, is not as well known Stateside as in Britain, where he's also a prolific columnist and critic of art, literature, and culture. He is, I trust, very much on the American map now, after the publication by Knopf of his fourth novel, *The Mulberry Empire*. I hope his choice views on the subject of that novel (colonial attitudes toward Afghanistan), and their evident contemporary resonance, will send excited readers off to hunt out Hensher's earlier novels—just as David

Bergman did after reading the conversation with Patrick Gale in *Gay Fiction Speaks*.

The Colm Tóibín piece here neatly throws into relief, I think, many of the social and cultural assumptions of "Anglo-American" thinking. On several occasions, Tóibín put me right, saying something like: "In Ireland, it wasn't like that." One could equally, however, say the same of Jim Grimsley's implicit challenge to the middle-class orthodoxies evident in so much literary fiction—or the Yankee bias in much American publishing. West Coast–based Matthew Stadler has compelling things to say on this subject. Bernard Cooper digresses likewise on the significance of Los Angeles's geographical, ethnic, and social makeup to his own upbringing and literary work. In sum, here are twelve authors—and twelve very different self-portraits.

The conversations aspire to show this dozen "like people in history." At the same time, history preoccupies gay novelists as never before. Tóibín's latest project—*The Master*, a fictional study of Henry James—coincides with Edmund White's new novel—*Fanny: A Fiction*—a first venture into historical fiction. Of the many novels by authors in *Hear Us Out* which could be considered fine examples of historical fiction, I'll name just a few: Christopher Bram's *Father of Frankenstein* and *The Notorious Dr. August*; Philip Hensher's *The Mulberry Empire*; Paul Russell's *Sea of Tranquillity*; Matthew Stadler's *Landscape: memory* and *Allen Stein*. As Hensher suggests, however, a novel set five years ago can be "historic." The term comes to signify a point of view, or a certain determination to arrive at a point of view, above all else. Tóibín notes likewise that, however contemporary his writing feels at a given moment, by the time it appears it already addresses the past, if only the near past: "I can't work to the moment." Of course, in fiction, he can't. That would be journalism.

Many more novels by these twelve might fruitfully be considered "historic." Bram's *Gossip* historicized the latter-day political world of Washington, D.C. Gary Indiana's recent bravura trilogy—*Resentment*, *Three Month Fever*, and *Depraved Indiffer-*

ence—unsparingly documents the various corrupt agencies that shape and twist our sense of today's world-in-history. Peter Cameron's *The City of Your Final Destination* asks tough questions concerning our current infatuation with the "truth" of past lives in its account of the travails of a flawed biographer.

Is there space in this particular history for gossip? I mentioned its allure briefly in *Gay Fiction Speaks*. There are many kinds of gossip, however. David Bergman properly observed that the pursuit of artistic concerns in that book's conversations had led me to "avoid personal questions." That's true. It doesn't mean I didn't get some very personal, not to say highly individual, replies. I hope anyone interested in gay male fiction will find plenty of appealing "tell-all" here. I lost count of the times my jaw hit the floor during these sessions. Here are a few teasers. Which author calls the fact that his father is dead and so can't read his novels "good justice"? Who claims never to have heard of *To the Lighthouse*, and describes Virginia Woolf's writings as "shit"? Which of the twelve "hates" Proust? Who received a letter from the son of a famous astronaut, indicating that the plot of his novel pretty closely matched the letter-writer's life? And which New York–based author argues, apropos September 11th, that "it may even be laudable" that America's enemies "take out two of our biggest phallic symbols and a few thousand of our civilians"? I know from correspondence how much people chewed over much of the implicit debates and off-the-cuff moments in *Gay Fiction Speaks*. Dare I suggest that *Hear Us Out*, if anything, delivers the bigger punch?

A few comments on method are necessary. These conversations were taped, transcribed, and then edited for good sense. They were shaped in collaboration with the interviewees, who were allowed to edit further, and to add and delete. Since some time passed after the recording of most of the pieces and the publication of *Hear Us Out*, the authors agreed, where appropriate, to a short further session, usually to comment on their most recent publications. In all cases but one, I've documented both the date the conversation originally took place, when revisions to it were completed, and when the additional material—which invariably follows an asterisked break—was added. For the Chris Bram piece, we both elected instead to integrate the material from the two sessions entirely. The resulting transcript, then, effectively reflects Bram's views at the later date. In a couple of places, the collaborators offered further comments or reflections on what they'd previously said—usually in the light of unforeseen developments. These I've dated and appended as footnotes to the earlier text.

Although in some respects I have to offer the conversations themselves as historic—many took place around five years ago—I've come to see how this could prove advantageous. As I pointed out in *Gay Fiction Speaks*, the exchanges were always meant to contrast with those undertaken essentially for immediate, public relations purposes—to advertise a particular book. They therefore range across an author's entire output. Moreover, they have—and need to have—time for discursion, rumination, the occasional irrelevance, digression, contradiction, and general comment. As in the first book, I've tried to allow the interviewees, in general, to direct the subject matter. At the same time, I had a mental shortlist of a number of elementary questions I'd hope all could answer at some point.

Moreover, everything here has survived the retrospective editing by the interviewee. This means, I think, that things which in the moment seemed momentous but which have subsequently come to seem parochial or insignificant have been weeded out. I'm also hoping that there's a conversational flow to these pieces. Surprisingly little, often, has been changed or newly introduced—something like 2 or 3 percent of the whole. I've expressly tried to retain moments of mutual incomprehension and/or tension—the occasional "misfire." Thank God my interviewees often didn't agree with me. We'd have had nothing to say.

I acknowledged a number of modes of writing I'd decided to exclude from *Gay Fiction Speaks*. In *Hear Us Out*, I've stayed loyal to the admittedly sometimes nebulous notion of "literary fiction." In 2000, I especially lamented the dearth of nonwhite subjects. I noted then something that remains true now: that certain subgenres of fiction which I'd decided to exclude on grounds of coherence—the thriller, popular fiction, fantasy—currently attract a good number of talented nonwhite writers: Samuel Delany, James Earl Hardy, E. Lynn Harris, Michael Nava. At the same time, I noted the loss of a good number of nonwhite writers to AIDS, and the emergence of up-and-coming nonwhite writers of gay literary fiction with—to date—just one or two books published. As I believe the conversations only reach a sort of critical mass once there's a sense of career narrative in place—across, let's say, at least three titles—I've once again been obliged to wait before the writers selected can fully and properly reflect the exciting ethnic diversity still emerging in today's gay literature. It's regrettable that the subjects of *Hear Us Out* are all Caucasian, especially as a conversation with the wonderful Randall Kenan was originally slated for inclusion, but couldn't be completed in time. This isn't wholly a question of nonwhite American voices either. There are Australian, Sri Lankan, and South African voices I want to find room for. In all cases, I ask for your patience. Watch this space.

Finally, this is the place to record the thanks I owe: first of all, to each of the writers included here, all of whom devoted so much time and energy to the project. Whatever merits *Hear Us Out* has reflect, above all, their earnestness and generosity. I'm indebted to quite a few other people for help with practicalities: David Bergman, Terry Bird and Clark Lemon, Michael Bronski, Ron Caldwell (lots!), Nicole Campbell, Harlan Greene, Allan Gurganus, Andrew Holleran, Keith Kahla, Patrick Merla, Felice Picano, and Edmund White. Thanks also to Tarani Chandola, Max Manin, and Mark Osborne for high-quality friendship, and to Roger Hollinrake for occasional houseroom.

The conversations project began with a travel grant and period of leave given by my employer, the University of Sheffield, to which institution I again offer gratitude. At Columbia

University Press I owe a great debt to a first-class editor, Jennifer Crewe, and her assistant Juree Sondker; to Roy Thomas, a superb manuscript editor and generous friend; to Ann Miller, who commissioned and oversaw *Gay Fiction Speaks*; and to Lisa Hamm for the elegant book designs. My sincere apologies to anyone I may have omitted.

HEAR US OUT

ONE

GARY INDIANA

GARY INDIANA is the author of two story collections and seven novels: *Horse Crazy, Gone Tomorrow, Rent Boy, Resentment: A Comedy, Three Month Fever, Depraved Indifference,* and *Do Everything in the Dark.*

Indiana was born in New England in 1950. His first published book was *Scar Tissue and Other Stories* (New York: Calamus Books/Gay Presses of New York, 1987). This was followed by a book of three short stories, *White Trash Boulevard* (Woodstock, N.Y.: Hanuman Books, 1988). Indiana's first novel was *Horse Crazy* (New York: Grove Press, 1989). Next came *Gone Tomorrow* (New York: Pantheon, 1993), then *Rent Boy* (New York/London: Serpent's Tail, 1994). *Resentment: A Comedy* (New York: Doubleday, 1997) began a three-volume series based on real-life crimes—in this case focusing on the notorious trial of the Menendez—here "Martinez"—brothers. *Three Month Fever: The Andrew Cunanan Story* (New York: HarperCollins, 1999)—a "nonfiction novel"—considered the media presentation of the killer, and killing, of fashion designer Gianni Versace. Evangeline Slote, the heroine of *Depraved Indifference* (New York: HarperCollins, 2002), was based in part upon notorious murderess Santee Kimes. His most recent novel is *Do Everything in the Dark* (New York: St. Martin's, 2003).

Indiana's plays include *Roy Cohn/Jack Smith* (filmed by Jill Godmillow in 1994), *The Roman Polanski Story,* and *Phantoms of Louisiana.* Indiana has also been a prolific journalist—most prominently for the *Village Voice, Artforum, Details,* and *Rolling Stone* magazines. A collection of his nonfictional prose was entitled *Let It Bleed: Essays, 1985–1995* (New York/London,

1996). He has written essays for photographer Aura Rosenberg's *Head Shots* (New York: Distributed Art, 1996), artist Nancy Chunn's *Front Pages* catalogue (New York: Rizzoli, 1997), and for the exhibition catalogues of Roberto Juarez, Barbara Kruger, and Christopher Wool. Indiana is also the author of the BFI's guide to Pier Paolo Pasolini's 1975 film *Salo, or the 120 Days of Sodom* (London: British Film Institute, 2000), and has edited an anthology of writings on animals, *Living with the Animals* (New York: Faber and Faber, 1994).

Indiana divides his time between New York and Los Angeles. The interview took place on Friday, April 24, 1998, at Gary Indiana's apartment in New York. It was revised in June 2002, when the material following the asterisks was also added.

RC   When I read your review of Hervé Guibert's fiction in *Let it Bleed*, it struck me that there were similarities in style between his work and yours. *Horse Crazy*, a book that predates the appearance of Guibert's works in translation, has particular affinities. That might be because so few writers have avoided the traps of bourgeois narrative and sentimentality when they discuss AIDS.

GI   I could see a similarity there. Guibert wrote three good books on AIDS, out of the experience of actually having it. I'm not sure what he was trying to do, but I remember thinking he wanted to particularize his own situation and distinguish it from anybody else's. What I was trying to do was explode the sentimental narratives that were being produced about AIDS in the mid-eighties. That was one intention of *Horse Crazy*, as well as being the impetus behind the whole second part of *Gone Tomorrow*— to attack the kinds of novels that were being churned out. These were social realist books that followed a politically correct line. They had all these absurd myths—that illness ennobles people; that it makes them into better people; that kind of thing. That's one reason I liked Guibert's *To the friend who did not save my life* so much. He was looking at himself in the round, not depicting himself as some plaster saint for whom this was a particularly tragic fate. I liked the fact he had that character in it who was jerking him around with the promise of this new medication; who played God with him essentially. That's the real scandal—that your life or death can very well hinge on someone else's caprice. It happens all the time—not only in the justice system and the medical system but in everyday life.

There was so much craven behavior during the early years of the epidemic. There still is. There's this whole process when certain artists die: these vultures move in and suddenly become their best friends, their legatees, their executors. It's quite ghoulish. I know one person in New York who flapped around every prominent corpse there was. The Valentina character in *Gone Tomorrow* was based on somebody who did much the same thing around filmmakers and actors who died—not all of them from AIDS. She profited very handsomely from other people's misfortunes. Some of the novels written about AIDS were similarly ghoulish. We're not supposed to speak ill of the dead, so I won't mention the name of this particular writer, but it was comical that one of the most revered writers on AIDS had not one or two but three lovers who died of it—one after the other! As soon as one was dead, he went out and found another—and memorialized them all in his books. I thought: "You can do this once and it's tragedy. The second time it's certainly farce. The third time is just bad taste."

RC   Some people thought they had finally found their subject in AIDS.

GI   If you wanted to ennoble it, you could say it was very much like the Pre-Raphaelite intoxication with tuberculosis. I thought there was something ludicrous about it. I know a lot of people who, if the person they were with dropped dead or left them tomorrow, would be with someone else next week, because they can't deal with being by themselves for one minute. There's something pathetic about that. If that particular author had gotten to the ludicrousness of it, really explored his compulsion to feel "incomplete" without a partner he could then exploit in his writing, I suppose one could have respected him. But really!

RC   In *Horse Crazy*, you wrote of the way Todd acts: "Some people die like pricks." That book came very early in confronting the phenomena of

AIDS-related piety and self-interest. You said you were reacting to the kinds of stories coming out then. Have things changed?

GI   A lot of what I reacted to initially wasn't only what people were doing in fiction but what people were doing in real life—reacting to a very confused, confusing, and highly politicized situation with a lot of different responses. The one I found intolerable was piety. I don't like piety as a mode for anything. There were all kinds of pious notions about what people were entitled to in life, compared to what they were getting.

I always find it absurd when a little girl gets run over by a truck and people call it a tragedy. No—*King Lear* is a tragedy. It's sad that the little girl got killed, but it's not a tragedy. The conflation of pathos with tragedy was something I had in mind in the eighties. A lot of people I cared about very much died. The people I was close to didn't exploit themselves in the way so many people seemed to think was all right. What was hard for them, besides dying, was having this generic, almost impersonal death, which is what one has in an epidemic.

People like sentimental narratives, no question. The daily newspaper is framed in terms of sentimental and punitive narratives. The epidemic affected a lot of people in very different ways. Some people felt there was a prescriptive way of responding to a social crisis. This medical crisis became a social crisis, as well as an opportunity to ingratiate homosexuality into the culture by means of special pleading. That worked very well. You don't have to make any apologies for being gay anymore, especially if you're gay and just like everybody else—that's to say, if your difference from the norm hasn't led you to repudiate the values of the norm, apart from the way your difference is normatively viewed. What I objected to wasn't necessarily people's political actions and posturing, but the idea you could apply all this coercive piety to literature and art; that you could call something "good" because its heart was in the right place, or because you'd successfully borrowed the narrative conventions of the middle-class novel and transposed them onto novels about gay people.

That irritated me. My experience is that life isn't that neat and tidy. Whether it's different now in so-called "gay fiction," I couldn't say. I find the whole subject of homosexuality extremely boring. I don't even think it's worth writing about anymore—partly because it is OK now. All these cute homo comedies have come out of Hollywood. A lot of suburban girls and gay guys probably identify with that sort of mental and emotional mediocrity. Unfortunately, now that our urban areas have become sub-urbanized, probably a lot of urban gays do too.

It doesn't interest me. I don't pay much attention to what people do with the subject matter of gayness anymore. I suppose it has some utilitarian so-cial value. It lowers the risk of your getting beaten up by yahoos. People whose opinions come from the mass media—which is practically every-body—learn to behave themselves, not because they've thought anything out but because they want to be cool. It doesn't have any artistic value.

RC Does your objection to typical AIDS narratives, then, concern aes-thetic laziness, the idea that experience stands in for artistic criteria?

GI Yes. It's unfortunately true that when you have a hierarchy in socie-ty of which voices are considered important to amplify, anyone fair-minded would have to acknowledge that, in spite of everything, Anglo-Saxon patriarchal males are still the privileged voice. They own and control everything. Within this subworld of "culture," you start privileg-ing the voices of minorities. You can. Culture's a sphere where that's OK to do. It adds a certain spice to capitalist consumption. It doesn't much threaten real power relations, though, and even in the cultural sphere, the patriarchal voices still dominate. Certainly they control the money be-hind culture. That's by way of qualifying what I'm going on to say, which is simply that a lot of people can find their niche within "identity politics" or "identity culture." I've seen the kind of ghastly social climbing certain black writers have to do because of racism in order to win a place in the literary world or any cultural realm. What else can they do?

It's a little different with gay people. Their voices were always privileged in literature and the arts. I can't think of a time in Western history when they weren't. Our problem isn't that we were never heard. It's that we were never heard in such a leveling variety of unanimity before. In the past, we had this "secret." The public form of it was a rarefied sensibility associated with sophistication and connoisseurship. In that sense, homo-sexuals were a sort of clandestine aristocracy. Now there's no secrecy—and no sensibility either.

Because it's so difficult for a black writer to win any recognition, I can see that even very good black writers may have to be political in the way they run their careers. This can involve forms of behavior I find personally distasteful. Whether that's necessarily true for a good gay writer, I doubt it. If anything, it's all too easy. Some AIDS novels were written by people who should never have picked up a pen. There was a kind of intimidation involved in those people having a career: "Hey, I'm dying!" And they were considered on the basis of their sincerity—the true kiss of death for any art.

I read an interview with this rent boy who fancies himself a poet. He said: "I didn't think anybody would want to read anything like this until I picked up a couple of books by Dennis Cooper." I thought: "God, this guy actually thinks he's in the same league as Dennis Cooper—because he's done things Dennis Cooper's written about!" I'm very elitist about writing. I resent it when my work gets lumped in with people infinitely inferior to me as writers because they happen to be gay or have written about subjects I've dealt with.

Is it better now? I don't know. I think publishing moved on from really lousy gay novels to really lousy alternative rock novels, Prozac novels; things like that. I remember telling Gus Van Sant some people thought *My Own Private Idaho* would kick the door open for movies about gay men. He said: "No, Hollywood's really specific. It'll open the door for movies about male prostitutes." The market for certain kinds of gay novels has probably already dried up.

RC   When you speak of books that shouldn't have been written, the obvious response is: "Time will sort these books out."

GI   But I don't want to wait around. I'll be dead. What good will that do me? You can see a development from the kinds of bad AIDS novels to the really bad memoirs that have been the craze for the past five years. Anybody who thinks he was molested as a child, anybody who had a pimple, can write a memoir. Publishers pay a lot of money. Time supposedly separates out the wheat from the tares. As I'm alive now, I have to pick through what I'm going to read. If the public goes for stuff I think is shit, that's their business. What I do care about is when the critical assessment of those things affects me personally.

RC The trend toward experience-based narratives is worrying precisely because it's an assertion of the worth of a text based on the biography of an author—which jeopardizes the primacy of the imagination in writing.

GI Yes. Also, people wrongly assume that their experiences are authentic. In the culture we have, most people's emotions are manufactured. Their experiences are prefabricated. We don't usually think of novels as analytical. But basically they're analyses of experience; renderings of experience which also analyze. Unless people can add something to what they think of as their experience, and even include some epistemological investigation of why they believe something happened, I don't see the value of it.

Once I was having problems with a drug addict. Someone wise—artist Larry Rivers, actually—told me that every ex-junkie thinks he knows everything there is to know about drugs, and that that simply isn't true. A few years ago, a director asked me to look at a script about S&M, written by a woman we both knew who'd been running an S&M brothel for years. It was a completely unbelievable piece of shit. The thing you're supposed to be able to do as a writer is imagine what somebody else's experience is, not your own. You know what your experience is. But it's not interesting just to say: "This happened to me." What's interesting is to figure out how it happened to the other person. If I were to write *Horse Crazy* now, I'd tell it from the point of view of the drug addict. That's what literature is about—an imaginative restaging of experience.

RC When you look back on your works, do you see important schisms or differences between them—discoveries of craft, direction, or interest?

GI Not when I'm writing them. Usually the only thing I think of in relation to what I did before is: if I already did it, I don't want to do it again. I try to avoid writing the same book twice. If you've already figured out how to do something, rediscovering how to do it isn't a challenge, even though I usually forget how I did something after I've done it. Continuities obviously you have no control over. But you don't see them until afterwards.

RC   It's probably a bad career move—doing something different with each book.

GI   The most successful writers in America write exactly the same book every time. They do it every year. You may have noticed that almost every one of my books has been published by a different house. The problem for someone in my category is money. I have to go where people will give me the most. I don't want to write any more journalism to make a living. Invariably, if you go back to the publisher that did one book with another, completely different one, they're in a position to say: "We don't really know how to deal with this." Or they don't offer you enough money.

Pantheon was an experience I'd never repeat. No effort was made to market *Gone Tomorrow* whatsoever. My editor was much too busy chasing pussy to give it the slightest attention.

RC   You spoke of wanting to stop writing journalism. Are journalistic skills far from those of fiction writing?

GI   No. With *Resentment* I really tried to merge them. Writing journalism just takes time from what you want to do. It's good training for mechanical things. You learn how to keep a piece moving; how to depict certain things; how to edit yourself ruthlessly; how not to be a prima donna about cutting. You get that immediate hit of seeing your work go out into the world, though that certainly wears off. But there's an attrition built into journalism. If you do it too long, you develop tics that are almost impossible to get rid of.

RC   In one essay you commented on publishers running a whorehouse, not a charity. This tied in with a comment in *Horse Crazy* about the culture in which one writes—Western capitalism, I guess—leading to the selling of the inner life. The narrator says: "Everything that lives in me becomes something for sale." That admission isn't so far from the practice of marketing one's own tragedy or experience which we spoke of earlier, is it? How does one distinguish between the proper use of one's talent—what one feels comfortable with—and the ghoulish or exploitative?

GI   As a great man once said: "I too have to pee, but for quite different reasons."

RC   I want to ask about narrative approach. Your earlier short stories featured a range of narrative voices. With the novels—until *Resentment* anyway—you stuck with the first person. Why?

GI   I always think of Dennis Cooper when I think about how I'd approach writing a novel. Dennis and I don't do things the same way. But he must go through something of the same process I do. I always want to get at the stuff—whatever it is—that has to be gone through with real studied detachment towards who this narrator figure is. Until *Resentment* the main character was nameless, partly because it was this invented "I" or "me" figure. It could be me, but with things added to or subtracted from me. You could use things that belonged to you, but part of what you're doing when writing is discovering that it really isn't you. It belongs to this floating zone—where you're making something that will be received and interpreted by somebody else.

I always wanted to get a kind of breathless, Dostoyevskian quality into these people's accounts of themselves—one that would be both brilliant and idiotic. I had more fun writing *Resentment* than any other book except *Rent Boy*. I don't think I ever had a better time than with that. Every day was a challenge: "How ridiculous can you make this? How far can you take it?" *Rent Boy* was written in the same way Scheherazade would tell stories. I have an actress friend who'd come over every morning for coffee. I'd read what I'd written the night before to see if I could get her to laugh so hard she'd spit her coffee out. *Resentment* was a more sustained effort of keeping myself amused.

RC   I was thinking of the relationship between the tendency to move wildly between voices in some of the *Scar Tissue* stories, and the sense of your narrative voice becoming distilled in the novels, until the bricolage-type effect of *Resentment*. In *Rent Boy* there's a brilliant moment when Danny hands over the experience he's recounted as a document. He therefore suggests Jay is behind the aesthetic ordering of the material. That's a solution to a problem in your choice of material there—namely, how literate, how insightful, can you make the figure of the *Rent Boy* without making things incredible. The answer is: deliver the experience self-consciously to a writer; make the shaping and trickery self-conscious. That moment, arguably, is also the point at which the coherent first-person narrative that served you in *Horse Crazy* explodes into metafiction.

GI   The first-person voice is very hard to maintain. Thinking about the explosion of memoirs particularly, I think it's very hard to maintain the integrity of the first person. If you're any kind of person, then you're actually at least two or three people. One of them is your superego, watching you emotionally manipulate the reader.

Probably my experience of the kinds of modernism I grew up with is such that I can't take that "I" seriously. Also, as we view the first person as this most authentic thing, I've always gotten great pleasure in building that up for people, then knocking it down from underneath. I suppose you carry spores of things with you though. Joseph Conrad was always a great influence. I always liked the idea of Marlowe sitting round with a bunch of drunks in Surabaya, telling this story about Lord Jim. In my scheme of things, the narrator's getting it wrong; making himself look better. That's what's interesting—how you make yourself look better, but then reveal you're making yourself look better by lying. I like that undercutting of the authority of literature or of privileged "truth-tellers."

RC   Manipulating your readership and questioning the stability of the self does remind one of Conrad. It makes me think of a French tradition too—Flaubert, Baudelaire, Rimbaud.

GI   Certainly the French nineteenth century was important in my development. But the Russian nineteenth century was even more so. Lionel Trilling's *Sincerity and Authenticity* was an important critical work.

When I began, I probably did believe that writing was supposed to be a therapeutic effusion of my inner nature as a lonely little boy in New Hampshire. It takes a long time to get disabused of that idea—that you're carrying this kernel of wonderfulness that is you which you hand out to the readers out there. That isn't what writing's about. Important writers for me from this perspective are Samuel Beckett, Thomas Bernhard,

Louis-Ferdinand Céline, and Witold Gombrowicz—even Gertrude Stein. In this century there's been a tremendous demolition of language as a narrative vehicle.

RC   American fiction hasn't always participated much in theorizing over language. There's a tradition of unreflective loquaciousness, of sermonizing and rhetoric—from Melville's *Moby-Dick* on.

GI   Yes. There's a predilection for heaviness or ponderousness; thickness and gravity over lightness. It comes out of the Puritan tradition in part.

RC   It's still there in Thomas Pynchon and Don DeLillo.

GI   And sometimes it works—in a book like DeLillo's *Libra*, which I have great admiration for. With the mainstream writers in America—by which term I'd lump people like Pynchon and Philip Roth together—a lot of formal invention does go into their work. It's not so apparent because their subject matter is extremely bourgeois. The viewpoint is firmly middle-class and recherché modernist. Some of Roth's books are amazingly constructed. Nothing he writes interests me, but I've read several of his books. Structurally they're fascinating. You could pour some other content into these containers; use the same structure to do something much more interesting.

A lot of formal innovation has gotten watered down by this need for heavy, ponderous content—middle-class marriage saved; middle-class marriage failed. *Libra* is so good because of the crazy voice of Lee Harvey Oswald's mother more than anything else. A writer I find continually interesting who couldn't be more mainstream is Norman Mailer. I think he is and always has been the best writer in America. Even though he'd probably love to be as middle-class as Goethe, Mailer has this incredible, encompassing sensorium. He pulls everything out of his environment. *Harlot's Ghost* is amazing. The first chapter is one of the most extraordinary things any American writer has ever written. Mailer builds this house with language, and then burns it down.

Now there's somebody whose public image has been entirely rebarbative. Fran Lebowitz has this theory that John O'Hara will come into his own once everyone who knew him is dead. Maybe it's the same with

Mailer. He made himself odious in so many ways that people stopped taking him seriously.

RC   The size of Mailer's recent works makes me want to ask to what extent the germ of a book carries a sense of its length.

GI   I used to think I had some sense of whether something was short, long, or in-between, depending on what it sounded like in my mind. Now I don't know. The way I work has changed a lot. Right now, I have something prepackaged, preordained to do—the Andrew Cunanan story. It's ostensibly true, so it has to have certain things in it. And it probably has to be quite big.

A lot of my short stories are things that looked like the first chapters of novels, until I realized they weren't. Others I knew would be that short. With novels, you always figure it's going to take you a certain amount of time to get from point A to point Z. Sometimes you get a sense of that about halfway through.

RC   Is the ending still up for grabs when you start a novel?

GI   Not necessarily. I usually start with at least a handful of things I know I want to do; things I didn't do anywhere else. I have a sense that I want to get this person or story from here to there; to make something happen between this statement and that statement. With *Resentment* I knew I wanted somebody who has Tourette's syndrome to testify in court. I thought that would be funny. I knew I wanted to have a cocktail party at the movie star's house. I knew roughly who I wanted to be there. You have these events as markers. Everything else becomes a question of how you make things happen in a way that fits with everything else. It's more about a certain pitch or vibration of things rather than length.

RC   Are you ever surprised by a character's behaviour?

GI   Things just happen when you're writing characters. Something will occur to you about this person. They could conceivably do something you didn't anticipate.

When people talk about characters taking over a book, it creates a bit of a false image of what you do as a writer. But you do get fond of characters. So you want to give them more business—like you would an actor in a stage play. It's like: "He's already robbed a liquor store; maybe I should have him kill a few people."

RC I was thinking of links between books. The narrators of both *Horse Crazy* and *Gone Tomorrow* refer to an abandoned novel, "Berma."

GI I suppose that did occur to me at some point—that there could be a suggestion that the same person was narrating all the books. But it wouldn't be the same person from one moment to the next.

"Berma" was a joke based on the figure of Berma—Sarah Bernhardt— in Proust. It suggested some lost moment in time to me. Maybe with *Gone Tomorrow* I had some notion that this was the narrator of *Horse Crazy* a few years later, or at the same time but in a different incarnation.

RC You mentioned a particular, local audience for *Rent Boy*—a friend. Does a wider sense of readership impact on your writing?

GI Really *Rent Boy* had an audience of one. I was writing it to amuse myself. There happened to be another person regularly coming over to have coffee; I enjoyed making her laugh.

Writing's too self-absorbed an activity to think too much about who's going to read it. I know I get obscene pleasure from doing something I know will make a lot of people laugh. That's one thing maybe I can share with my audience—when I do something funny. When people talk about the scene in *Resentment* where the psychiatric expert witness has Tourette's syndrome, they don't tell me what a great writer I am, or how hard that was. They just mention it and laugh.

I find it terribly embarrassing to have most people talk to me about my work. I was never very good at absorbing compliments or observations. One thing that's always very disappointing is that in the case of most people, all I have to say is what's in the books. And I never think of *Gone Tomorrow* as a book that was very widely read. I'm much more used to people having read *Rent Boy*. It seems to be everybody's favorite. But some people have said to me in the last couple of years that *Gone Tomorrow* completely changed the way they thought about AIDS. That surprised me, even though it was probably my intention. It was wonderful to hear that from people I didn't know.

With *Horse Crazy*, people tend to talk in terms of identifying with being obsessively in love with somebody. The negative thing I wanted to say about journalism earlier was that when I used to do a lot of it, I'd write something topical—say, on animal rights—and suddenly I'd meet people who thought I naturally wanted to hear from them because they had the same interest in animal rights. I write about things to get rid of them, essentially. If I write about something, you can be pretty sure it's all I have to say about it. I'm not going to make a living talking about the same thing for the rest of my life. I might be interested to read somebody else writing about the same subject. But it's not necessarily something I want to talk about with everybody I meet.

In the same way, you construct these stories because then you don't have to tell them to people. So it's always very odd when people want to discuss my work. Also I feel very uncomfortable as the subject of anything. That's why my narrators are so de-centered. Of course when I went into this profession, I thought it was one where you did become extremely famous. But I'm glad you don't, in fact, become that celebrated. It must be utterly horrific to have a lot of personal attention on you all the time from strangers.

RC   You reviewed Gore Vidal's *Screening History*, which speaks of this.

GI   Yes. He was talking about the prestige of literature. It's indubitable that literature has no prestige anymore, except in a rarefied element. [Literary critic] Hans Magnus Enzensberger says that's good. He says it was a coterie or cultish practice for most of its years. Until late Victorianism, most people didn't know how to read. So literature has gone back to its roots. I don't think it's bad.

Sometimes when you read a book that gives you enormous pleasure, you wish there were a lot of people who'd get the same thing out of it. What's paradoxical is that mass culture is so banal that anything that becomes popular immediately becomes suspect also. So if something you thought was very good becomes this runaway success, you suddenly think: "Maybe it's not as good as I thought it was."

RC   What's an example of a popular work which remains great?

GI   *Moby-Dick.*

RC   It came into its popularity late.

GI   Fifty-seven copies sold in Melville's lifetime, I think.

RC   Something to aim for!

GI   Ten would be perfect. I can't just grab something else out of the air. Good things do sometimes become extremely popular. I think it's more common with movies.

RC   If mass culture is generally banal, does working in film have no interest for you?

GI   Sometimes it does; sometimes it doesn't. I like going to movies. I have two huge movie houses outside, and it's a way to get rid of two hours of your life.

RC   But you'd never write for movies?

GI   I don't see the point. You'd write for film if you had nothing else to do and you wanted to be able to retire.

RC   Why, then, do you share your time between Los Angeles and New York?

GI   Los Angeles isn't alluring to me because of the film business. I've nothing to do with that. One of the bigger ironies of L.A. is that it's so saturated with the industry, with its ruthless corporatism and the idiotic values of its culture of celebrity. I find it very endearing and relaxing somehow. If you're not part of it, it's just some dumb spectacle that doesn't touch your life much. One fun thing in L.A. is walking into a restaurant, sitting down next to Gwyneth Paltrow, and not necessarily recognizing her.

RC Many people describe New York and Los Angeles as opposites. You make them sound part of the same world of hierarchies, just in different contexts: literary/intellectual and cinematic/visual.

GI New York's very similar to L.A. in a lot of ways. You can be in café society here or in L.A. or you can be outside it. The differences most people construct between the two cities are spurious to me. I don't see New York as the great serious intellectual capital so many people do.

RC Is there such a place?

GI Of course not. Out in the heartland of America, you find a lot of interesting social constructions that are probably a lot more serious than these metropolises. In Oxford, Mississippi, you find a much more serious literary culture than here. That's one privilege of being a backwater—you can cultivate that.

RC With the use of the word "backwater," I feel I know why you're not living in one.

GI I suppose it's because, like Howard Hughes, I like to live in a place where I can get a sandwich at four in the morning.

RC Now, a leap. Who else do you read in contemporary fiction apart from Dennis Cooper?

GI Lynn Tillman certainly. Irvine Welsh is an extraordinary writer. I like a lot of contemporary writers: Matthew Stadler, Ann Rower, Robert Glück, Kevin Killian, Heather Lewis, Linda Yablonsky, Patrick McGrath; James Purdy, still going strong at whatever age he is. Bob Colacello, who wrote on Warhol's Factory, could write a great novel. He's amazingly sharp. Gore Vidal; Muriel Spark; Sapphire. Renata Adler's one of the

most interesting writers around, but she publishes less and less. I like
Marianne Wiggins and Luisa Valenzuela. Emma Tennant. Aldo Busi.
Michael Tolkin, one of America's best writers. His second novel, *Among
the Dead*, is one of the finest of the last thirty years.

RC   I'm interested in the wider relationship between reading and writing; other than fiction, where does your curiosity lead you?

GI   I read everything, basically. I tend not to read that much written after 1900. I read a lot of eighteenth- and nineteenth-century writers.

RC   Your satire relates more closely to some historic authors than to
contemporary fiction writers. I thought of Swift and Rabelais.

GI   Rabelais—yes; Swift's "Directions to Servants." I even like Tobias
Smollett, who can be unbearable. William Godwin, Mary Shelley's father,
who wrote *Caleb Williams*. I like Henry Fielding a lot. *Jonathan Wild* is
one of my favorite books.

RC   Are you cautious about what you read when you are writing?

GI   I've heard people complain about this. Truman Capote always said
he didn't read Henry James when he was writing because his sentences
would get too long. Maybe I don't read Beckett or Thomas Bernhard too
much when I'm writing because I can very easily fall into that rhythm of
theirs, which I actually indulge myself in quite a lot anyway.

I've less sense of caution now than when I was younger. My ultimate
model is Patricia Highsmith, though I'd probably never be able to write
the way she does. One lobe of my brain thinks the best way to write is in
these simple, declarative sentences that you just lay down. You get said
whatever needs to be said. Highsmith has never been recognized as a
great American writer, which is ridiculous. They put her books in the
mystery section. Most people who work in a genre deserve to be there,
but she doesn't.

The other figure is William Faulkner. I have a Highsmith lobe and a
Faulknerian lobe. I'm trying to get them to mesh. I suppose I have to

avoid reading Faulkner when I'm writing. The danger is I'll start reading *Light in August* and just give up. I think that way too about Jane Bowles's *Two Serious Ladies*—the perfect novel. You keep thinking: "If I'd written that, I wouldn't have to bother with any of this."

Highsmith is the American Dostoyevsky, if anybody is. The fact people don't recognize it is very funny, especially when so many people have tried to treat the subject of the sociopath; so many so-called "novelists." Highsmith's very accurate about urban people's psycho-pathology. It's not just the villains in her books—everybody's obviously so sick! It's very odd she isn't recognized as this great psychological novelist—here, anyway. She is in Europe.

RC There's a clear sense of the writer as moralist in Highsmith. Your own work is more readily described in terms of an aesthetic tradition, though the satire clearly has moral intent. How would you react to being considered a moralistic writer?

GI It's not very appealing. I'm not especially an aesthete either. The problem I have with the label is that I hate the word "morality" so much. I hate the way people throw it around. The real predicament—in America at least—is that people assume if you're a moralist, that you have the same morals they do. Most people that feel comfortable using the word "morality" are so full of shit.

RC I didn't mean moralizing. But the literary models for satire we mentioned have a sense of anger and vengeance on others who purport to pursue a moral line. To that extent, satire's a moral tradition, even as it's a counter-moralist one.

GI Yes. The only reason it's problematic to call it moral is probably because in the end anything that can be configured as a moral point of view in American society today is both hypocritical and absurd. People are always talking about values. It's suffocating. Of course, the ultimate moral judgment is simply that these people are hypocritical monsters. You end up going back to whether, from your point of view, you believe most people in their wisdom can see through the crap we're surrounded by or not.

I suppose somebody like Fielding had more of a sense of outrage about injustice. He was a magistrate. I suppose he felt that somewhere there was justice. I don't see that in the world we have. If justice happens, it's completely accidental. When people talk about writers being unjustly neglected, I think: "What are you talking about? What does that mean? According to what?" They're probably justly neglected in the times we live in.

RC The hostility to prescribed moral positions connects to the structure of your books. In *Resentment*, disparate elements of plot are deterministically woven together. The implied author, then, is insisting upon the interrelatedness of the various situations described. Presumably what you're objecting to in the idea of "morality" is whenever the term suggests something absolute or immutable. Your work, in both content and form, insists on the relative nature of truth.

GI The usual thing that's said here, especially by the people you see on television every night splitting all these hairs, is that none of us can really cast the first stone, that nobody's in a position to judge; but that as a society we have to draw the line; we have to do this and that. I just think: "Wait—why do we have to? We know it always gets drawn in the wrong place. Why do we have to?"

Somebody in Dostoyevsky's *The Brothers Karamazov*—Ivan or Dmitry—says each of us is guilty of everything, and if we knew that, we'd have paradise on earth. But we don't. The idea of the United States kidnapping Pol Pot to hold him accountable for this genocide we started is too rich! Henry Kissinger and Richard Nixon are responsible for the Khmer Rouge coming to power in the first place.

RC Clinton always seems to be apologizing for American foreign policy—for the failure even of his own initiatives in Rwanda or Bosnia.

GI I tend to give Clinton the benefit of the doubt in terms of his intentions. Look at how he staffs the White House. He has lesbians and blacks and every other kind of person in government jobs. This guy isn't uncomfortable with difference. You can measure him by the rottenness of the people who make a living attacking him; these cunts on the evening talk shows who want to cram their medieval nonsense down everyone else's throats. Big deal—he fucked an intern. I'd like to see who some of these assholes are fucking.

What annoys me about the constant barrage of appeals made to "values" and "morals" is that I don't see the morality of an overpopulated world, or the morality of taxing individuals like myself to pay for the education of other people's children. I don't know why people should be rewarded in any fashion for having too many children. If we have no birth control policy, I become a slave. I have to pay taxes to support other people's kids—to send them to schools where they don't learn anything.

RC This sounds libertarian. It could be a philosophy of the right as much as of the left.

GI With temporary wealth has come a certain amount of conservatism on my part in terms of what I want to pay taxes for. I object to the way these bulwarks are always being drawn up: the defense of our civilization that's supposedly represented by being a "moral" person, respecting values, the institution of the family, and so on. What people lose sight of is how arbitrary that all is. This is why you can have your "morality": because over there, in Bikini Atoll, where you put all your garbage, these little natives are still waiting after fifty years to go back to the homes you A-bombed twenty-five times. We can have ecology as long as the rest of the world takes our garbage. The lack of analysis is disturbing. Why do we have conditions that create these problems? There's no systemic analysis. One thing that distressed me around the AIDS crisis was how limited the alliances were between poor blacks and AIDS activists. There were specious attempts to link some problems. But the analysis never cut deep enough.

RC At the same time, a counter-movement objecting to the "de-gaying" of the syndrome kicked in.

GI A lot of people will find themselves disenchanted with the whole idea of being gay in the future. I was born in the 1950s. I've lived through the entire development of American gay society, from a time when it wasn't visible—when, if you were openly gay, there was no support anywhere. When I grew up, it was like in Genet. Every faggot was every other faggot's bad smell. There was no sense of community. Through all this evolution, what's finally arrived is what Daniel Harris describes in *The Rise and Fall of Gay Culture*—that there's no gay culture anymore. You don't have a club if everyone can belong to it. And the opportunity to connect the disadvantages gay people shared with other peoples was lost. That was the only thing that would have been useful, that one would have wanted to identify with.

RC   Gore Vidal always articulated something similar to this—a political alliance of the disenfranchised.

GI   Yes. He wasn't particularly indexed by the loudest voices in the eighties. It's a little hard to assimilate Vidal. When I was growing up, he was one of three homosexuals in this country. Back then, he didn't feel it necessary to tell you all about his patrician background every time he opened his mouth. He does now. It turns a lot of people off.

RC   When people talk of progress in gay affairs from the 1950s until now, does the very idea fill you with horror? Do you somewhat admit the premise behind it—that things have, to some extent, improved?

GI   My biggest problem is that the world—period—fills me with horror every day. They jumble the contents around; it still turns out pretty hideous. I don't see how anything can change till the whole order of things changes—if it even could. Some things do get better for some people, obviously. Some things get worse for others. But as long as we have this kind of capitalism without protection for people . . . I mean, what's the good of having this highly organized society—one that can make so many things, cure so many illnesses, develop so many technologies to help people—if it can't lift the whole human race up to some tolerable condition of life? I'm no Marxist, but I don't see why that should be impossible.

Why does Bill Gates have to have forty billion zillion dollars? Why is somebody permitted to have that kind of wealth? Isn't one billion dollars enough for any human being? The social retrenchment we have in this country is bizarre. At the turn of the century, when Carnegie had these monopolies producing conditions of ghastly inequality, they had antitrust laws passed that put some limits on such people's activities. There are none anymore.

We have a system of incredible worldwide peonage. There are countries where we send our shit, that make our footwear, our clothing. Most of what we have on is probably made by a thirteen-year-old in Mexico. Why? I see that as something really fundamental that needs to be changed in human life before we can celebrate the fact that we or the blacks are better off than in the fifties. If you have cancer, it doesn't matter whether you have a beautiful complexion. That's what I feel about the country and world I live in.

RC   It's a running theme through the books. It comes back to capitalism quite explicitly, doesn't it? Your books criticize capitalist hegemony—but what's next?

GI   *Rent Boy* was originally going to be called *Hatred of Capitalism*. Then I realized that wouldn't sell too many copies. I've always been attracted to subjects that in some ways embodied those contradictions. I'm interested in Cunanan because the only meritorious thing anybody seemed able to say about him was that he was a social climber.

RC   His is a story about class, which is the last way anyone wants to read it.

GI   Cunanan's is a complicated story about class. I never wanted to reach for a simple analysis. In *Rent Boy*, I put what would probably speak for me in this respect most clearly in the mouth of a lunatic. I can't take myself that seriously.

But take the fact that Versace made his empire out of making upper-class women look like whores, and that Cunanan was someone continually identified as a male prostitute. That in itself is hilarious. At the same time, a story like Cunanan's doesn't reduce itself simply to the problems of class and sexuality and the other things you find in it. By the same token, a Marxist analysis of global capitalism doesn't completely account for the problem of evil. Just because we exploit and kill other people does-n't mean they're not talented at exploiting and killing each other.

The great metaphor of capitalism is prostitution. It's a system that makes everyone into a whore. All we have are levels of whoredom. You can fill various roles: a fancy courtesan, a street whore. These are the roles we're allowed. I find a lot of humor in that. I feel like I live in a big bor-dello. Every day I look at all the whores striking noble poses about how they're a different kind of whore than the next person, whom they despise. It's like: "I swallow cum, but I won't eat shit"; "I eat shit, but I won't eat shit for less than a thousand dollars." Whatever. This block of my street—despite our fascist mayor's cleanup—has been a center of prostitution for decades. I've seen male prostitutes I know from Times Square come here and service gay guys in this building. At the same time, their clients go to a community meeting to get the whores thrown off the block. We live in a system where you can't even necessarily view that as a contradiction.

RC   Did the Cunanan story jump out as suitable for you immediately?

GI   Yes—even before he shot Versace. He'd killed a couple of people in Minneapolis and this rich man in Chicago. At that point I was hooked. He was then in New York. I'd go to the Times Square bars to spot him. I never managed to. But I thought if he'd talk to anybody, he'd talk to me.

RC   I'd like you to say something about working methods. What is the process of revision like for you?

GI   There's usually not a lot of fat in what I write. I'm not prolific. I don't generate a lot more material than I need. I write every sentence, every paragraph, over and over, one piece at a time.

RC   Does journalism help with that swift self-editing?

GI   Probably. You've more room in a novel to go way off. Sometimes I have, but, in terms of getting a paragraph right, it's useful to have written for a paper like the *Village Voice*, where a piece has to go out every week and look a certain way or people aren't going to read it. I still dawdle incessantly. In the middle of writing *Resentment*, I went to South America for three months and left it here. It was due six months after I came back. But I couldn't stand it anymore.

RC   Had you hit a particularly difficult moment?

GI   I'd gotten to a place I didn't know how to get out of. Instead of just dealing with it, I decided I'd go to Macchu Picchu. As a writer, you can easily persuade yourself you need that experience to finish the book. It's true, actually, because you absorb everything that happens to you. I like novels more than stories for that reason. You live a long time while you're writing a novel, so you get the benefit of all the things that happen to you while you're writing. That's why I don't believe in writing a book every year. People who do that tend not to really live anything. They don't have lives; they're writing all the time. In some ways I admire and envy that. But I'm not put together that way. I don't have a million things I want to say. I get sick of writing, of my own voice. I have to go away. I've written almost nothing in the past year.

I tend to have to go somewhere I've never been, have things happen to me, and put myself in some sort of peril. I have to live through something that will shift things around.

RC   Do you write straight onto machine?

GI   I tend to more now. But I'm not comfortable doing it. I usually write in longhand, and type it up. I'm always trying to figure out different ways to work. I'm not very successful. Usually I can't write when I'm traveling. That's unfortunate. You'd think that would be one advantage of being a writer. But I'm too absorbed in what's around me. I don't want to go to this interior place. When I go away I feel the interior place is less real than it was when I was sitting in my apartment in New York or Los Angeles. I travel a lot in places where virtually nobody knows me. I tend to feel in those places that I don't really exist. By extension, why would my subjectivity be of any interest to anyone?

RC   I wanted to ask about what seems an inevitable paradox in your writing. On one hand you assault the breadth of hypocrisy that powers contemporary society. At the same time, that breadth is the great meat of your material. Were it to end, you'd lose your subject. So you're in a parasitic relationship with this foul, corrupt beast—the state; American society; culture. A better world is a less interesting fictional world, ultimately.

GI   We're not going to get a better world anyway, so there's no real problem for me. Anyway, I don't put myself above it. I'm as hypocritical as anybody. I don't think you can put people in front of a firing squad for living with a lot of contradictions. We're not capable of resolving them in ourselves or by ourselves. Supposedly, you'd resolve them in concert with other people. But, as we live in a world where self-interest is the ultimate value, that's not likely to happen, except maybe with small things, and sometimes big things through the mediated world of the mass media. For instance, Princess Diana is killed in a car crash, and that produces an accidental good result, like people giving money to charity. But the significant changes that make human life a little more tolerable tend to happen for stupid reasons.

RC   These things might make the aesthete in us recoil. The flowers for Diana outside Kensington Palace were beautiful. But the letters! I've never read so much bad poetry.

GI   Daniel Harris wrote two brilliant essays—one on the Versace funeral; the other on the Princess Di affair. He took things people had posted on the Internet and analyzed them—the bad spelling, and so on. The sensation of being in a world of complete idiots is staggering.

RC   Harris is an obvious kindred spirit. Regarding his comments on "The Kitschification of AIDS" in *The Rise and Fall of Gay Culture*, you'd got there first.

GI   It was great seeing that essay when it first appeared in *The Nation*. Such a slap in the face! I met Harris when his book was in galleys. He's very brilliant. It was very much what I was saying, but if anything, he was more pointed about it.

★　★　★

RC You've spoken of your most recent work, *Depraved Indifference*, as bringing to a close a trilogy of books based on real crimes, which began with *Resentment* and continued with the Cunanan book, *Three Month Fever*. At what point did the idea of the series come to you, and how and when did you know you should bring it to an end?

GI Like Doris Day, I'm a perpetual virgin: I thought mass manipulation had reached a kind of plateau with the Menendez trial, and that my own manipulation of that cultural effluvia dissected the whole organism. In fact it was merely the seed of a much more prodigious undertaking—the transformation of consciousness into a dream world of received ideas. I was interested in the Cunanan "story" before Versace was killed because it was paradigmatic of how the pathetic stereotype has come to stand in for actual persons. We're becoming interchangeable representatives of stereotyped groups, about which certain things are possible to say, and to whom certain things can be done without making much difference to people. Cunanan was "the dark side" of homosexuality, which is sex itself rather than the composite face of a benign minority group.

To put it more simply, everything heterosexual people fear about faggots could be expressed in the description of this particular individual. But the process goes even further. The construction of reality by mass media eventually produces a certain kind of individual who actually has no sense of reality: ergo Evangeline Slote in *Depraved Indifference*. She's this Nietzschean figure who can allow herself anything because she understands that consensual reality is an artifice, that everything she comes in contact with is already corrupt and dead. I had to stop writing books that engaged the full sprawl of this underlying rottenness because I believe life is worth having, and if our whole productive life consists in examining pathology you eventually drive yourself crazy.

RC Like *Resentment*, *Depraved Indifference* is a big book in many ways. It feels as if with each of these novels, you've forced yourself to occupy new territory—specifically, in the area of characterization. Evangeline's self-creation may have parallels in Cunanan's story, or in *Resentment*, but it's of a wholly new and monstrous order. Did you take more liberties with the real-life version of this story, knowing it to be the last, or was Santee Kimes a bigger self-creation in the first place?

GI Santee Kimes was—is—one version of a sociopathic personality I have encountered many times. I invented freely whatever I needed to paint an accurate portrait of this kind of person who is profoundly indifferent to the existence of others; in a curiously oblique way, I had a lot of material in my head about an entirely different real-life criminal that I needed to use, discharge, expunge, get out of my system, whatever. Santee Kimes and sociopaths in general are not exactly "self-creations" but montages with no "there" there—they're bits and pieces of other people they've constructed a simulacral being from, and behind this façade is nothing whatsoever except some primal damage that needs to express itself in violence and harm to other people.

RC Do you think now that there were especial difficulties relating to the "factional" approach in these books? Were there evident advantages over "pure" fictionalization?

GI These particular books dictated their own form. In many ways the "reality" from which they're drawn is not reality at all but a blending of narrative fictions about events or people considered "newsworthy." For each such story there are myriad stories that aren't being told; so you have to ask yourself: "Why these? What purpose do these stories serve?" Distraction from important public issues, yes, but also in being picked up as "news," they're being used to emit messages about human existence, about life—generally, negative messages about life outside the stereotype and the received idea. They reinforce notions about the virtue of conformity and obedience. All three of these stories are deeply engaged in a discourse about money: who should have it, who shouldn't, what the right way to get it is, what's the wrong way. What aren't they telling us?

They aren't telling us what money is, that money rules our lives, that money has become life in a certain sense. The callousness we demonstrate every day towards the millions of people in the world who don't have money is, in a sense, justified by this equation: the racism of money, the corruption of money, the obscenity of money is the great unspoken behind the privileging of these narratives in the so-called "news." Simply to embellish or expand on something of this kind that's dropped in your lap as a fait accompli, a "reality," is to accept the reality the media's constructing for you. So you have to tamper with it, disrespect it, and show that the alleged reality is itself a fictional creation.

RC You must have been asked many times to comment on September 11th, 2001. There's a sense of nothing being sacred in your books. Have you considered basing a book on the terrorist attacks? Some of the political reaction especially looks ripe for satire.

GI The novel I'm completing now—*Do Everything in the Dark*—concerns what we might call the great awakening and the great going to sleep that September 11th produced. For a little while, a window opened on the actualities behind the veil of Maya, and for a month—perhaps two—it was very hard for an American person to look at a billboard, say, advertising Calvin Klein perfume or the latest Disney film without a sense of revulsion and horror; without feeling that we have made a mockery of our own lives by turning ourselves into oblivious consumers and, when the time is right, statistical cannon fodder for the people who own the world. But that window got shut really fast, the rhetorical nonsense and warmongering and pandering to people's most craven fears quickly reduced most of the population to compliant, complicit zombies—somnambulists collaborating with their own annihilation. Now we see Christian fundamentalists, who have immense power in the new government here, joining forces with Jewish and Muslim fundamentalists, Hindu fundamentalists as well, for that matter, to bring about the Rapture. We've stepped into a different world, or regressed to a cultural condition of fear and trembling that feels very much like the 1950s to someone like me, who grew up with the threat of nuclear annihilation as the counterpoint to American affluence.

Strange to say, this next novel is not a satire in the sense that the previous three books are satires. The mental state of most people I know is not something I find much humor in. Of course, it's emerging now that a huge percentage of our tax dollars finance incompetent, competing agencies of government; we knew this, but September 11th has made it completely apparent even to people who prefer not to think about such things. Meanwhile the same corporate friends of the same powerful people are enriching themselves from the public trough, supposedly for our protection, and of course these people couldn't rescue a cat in a tree, let alone a country with millions of people in it. They don't care about us anyway.

Whatever I may personally feel about what happened on September 11th, and however personally I may have been affected by it—and I was considerably affected by it—it's pure hypocrisy for any American government to claim that this slaughter of innocent civilians is qualitatively any different than what Americans have perpetrated all over the Third World. From this point of view, it's understandable that the gross immorality and horror of this action takes the apocalyptic form that it does. The attacks were our own shit coming back on us, and there will be more of it, as America never learns anything from its own rotten behavior. Many more people than died in the attacks here—many more civilians—were killed in our retaliatory bombing of Afghanistan. If we do it, it's a triumph of some noble abstraction; if they do it, it's "terrorism." The hypocrisy of American foreign policy—ecology for us, and the rest of the world has to take our shit—cannot go on forever. Frankly, it may even be laudable that the people we oppress and whose resources we gouge and steal to maintain the pig-like, insensate consumption known as "the American way of life" take out two of our biggest phallic symbols and a few thousand of our civilians instead of burning their own houses down, as African-Americans, no strangers to terror themselves, have done in the past as a form of protest.

RC What form will the book take?

GI It's something like a collection of fragments, a series of overlapping stories about a set of characters—I can't say right now how many; I guess perhaps eight or nine people who are living at the same time, inhabiting certain worlds simultaneously, connecting or not connecting with each other. At this point, the book takes place over the summer of 2001, just before the attacks, and perhaps it will extend beyond September 11th, though I honestly don't know yet. I started with a particular idée fixe that I realized, after three hundred pages or so, was wrongheaded and artificial. For the past month I've been pruning the material I'd already written, and altering it drastically. I found it had an uncharacteristic redundancy about it, and a lot of filigreed prose that it didn't need. Mary Woronov, the painter and novelist, suggested to me at a certain point that perhaps I had too much rather than too little. After a couple weeks, that sank in and I realized it was true.

RC Thanks very much for your time.

TWO

BERNARD COOPER

BERNARD COOPER is the author of two collections of memoirs, *Maps to Anywhere* and *Truth Serum*, the novel *A Year of Rhymes*, and a collection of short stories, *Guess Again*.

Cooper was born in Hollywood in 1951. He attended the California Institute of the Arts, where he received his Master of Fine Arts degree in 1979. On graduating, he abandoned the visual arts in favour of writing, initially supporting himself as a shoe salesman. He next taught at the UCLA Writer's Program and, later, at the Creating Writing Program at Antioch University, Los Angeles. He is currently the art critic for *Los Angeles* magazine.

Cooper's short essays and memoirs have been anthologized in a number of volumes of *The Best American Essays* (New York: Houghton Mifflin); Brian Bouldrey, ed., *The Best American Gay Fiction 1996* (New York: Little, Brown, 1996); Thomas R. Cole, ed., *The Oxford Book of Aging* (Oxford: Oxford University Press, 1994); Robert Drake and Terry Wolverton, eds., *His: Brilliant New Fiction by Gay Writers* (Boston: Faber and Faber, 1996); and James McConkey, ed., *The Oxford Book of Memory* (Oxford: Oxford University Press, 1996). His work has also appeared in the *Georgia Review*, *Grand Street*, *Harper's* magazine, the *Los Angeles Times Magazine*, the *Mid-American Review*, *Nerve*, the *New York Times Magazine*, the *North American Review*, the *Paris Review*, *Ploughshares*, *Shenandoah*, and the *Threepenny Review*, among others.

Cooper's first book, *Maps to Anywhere* (Athens: University of Georgia Press, 1990; New York: Viking Penguin, 1991), with an introduction by Richard Howard, was published as a collection of memoirs; nevertheless, it won the PEN/Ernest Hemingway Award for Fiction. Cooper's first novel, *A Year of Rhymes* (New York: Viking Penguin, 1993), was followed by a further collection of memoirs, *Truth Serum* (New York: Houghton Mifflin, 1996), the title piece of which won an O. Henry Award. His most recent book, *Guess Again* (New York: Simon and Schuster, 2000), is a collection of shorter fiction.

Cooper lives in Los Angeles, where this interview took place on November 18, 1997. It was revised in August 2002, at which point the material following the asterisks was added.

RC I want to start by asking about your apparent renegotiation of the boundary between fiction and autobiography. One of your books is labeled a novel; another, a memoir, won a fiction prize; some stories have appeared as fiction as well as essays or memoirs.

BC Yes. That's going to require some explanation. Let's start with my evolution. I studied visual arts at the master's level, at what was and probably still is one of the most avant-garde art schools in the country, the California Institute of the Arts. It was around the time conceptual art had taken over. Distinctions between text and performance, performance and stand-up comedy, environmental art and sculpture, painting and assemblage had all become blurred—not always necessarily intentionally. There was an assumption that part of the endeavor of making art involved blurring boundaries, taking what you needed from different genres and recombining them in ways satisfying or meaningful to you.

So I came out of an educational environment where iron-clad distinctions between genres weren't that important. I'd always used language in my own conceptual art, and I'd always been a reader—particularly of poetry. When I started thinking of writing as the most interesting avenue for me, a lot of my reading involved blurred boundaries too. Sterne's *Tristram Shandy* was a favorite. A transforming experience during graduate school was reading the first international anthology of prose poetry, edited by Michael Benedikt. Here were pieces in prose which had the compression I loved in poetry. They read like fables, stories, or mini-essays. Everybody did what they wanted with the form. There seemed a tremendous amount of freedom. Thereafter I began writing some of the shorter pieces that appear in *Maps to Anywhere*. Although I was in a sense troubled by the fact that they couldn't easily be labeled, I resigned myself to the fact that that was a designation somebody else would have to make. I had to do what I wanted, keep my fingers crossed, and hope it was good, whatever it was.

I remember Amy Hempel once writing that I was one of the people who had intentionally tried to blur the boundaries between the short story, the essay, and poetry. I adore her and her work, and while I'm glad to be credited with just about anything worthwhile, that's not something I did intentionally. I did it because I needed to write about a range of subject matter in a particular way. I wasn't trying to push the envelope. And I never thought of it as experimentation, any more than anything any writer does is experimental.

I should also say here that my parents were second-generation Jews whose parents had come to America from Eastern Europe. They were very hush-hush about their background in certain ways. I didn't learn until much later, for instance, that my name had been changed from something I still don't know to Cooper. My parents either claimed they'd forgotten what it was, or actually had forgotten. That sense of the mystery of my past combined with an odd sense of anomie about being gay, about my view of my world as not fitting into what I perceived happening around me. These two things sensitized me, and made me interested in what's true and what's myth.

But I don't think my impulse to write things has ever been guided by the desire willfully to disrupt people's notions of what various genres can do. Anything I write takes the form it takes, and it's always some sort of hybrid of fiction and nonfiction.

RC   That hybrid can take many forms too. You don't present yourself in the third person in your fiction, for example.

BC   No. One thing I demand of the autobiographical writing I've done is that the self is at the center, but isn't the focal point. It's the eye that's doing the perceiving. That's why I've always felt a great kinship with poetry, which often has much to do with witnessing, recording, or interpreting phenomena. Annie Dillard's work is really important to me. She once said that when she wrote about collecting seashells as a child, she wasn't writing about herself as a child. She was writing about seashells, but the easiest way for her to access some sort of wonder, awe, or feeling about that was to recall that childhood situation. I agree. Some might say writing autobiographical work is by its nature self-centered or solipsistic. To some extent it is. But I'm also interested in the world around me, not just me as a persona, character, or presence.

One more thing regarding *Maps to Anywhere* particularly: I really did think of those pieces as species of nonfiction. It was only after I sent the work out to various literary reviews that they then began to publish them as short stories, fables, or prose poems. They made the categories. The University of Georgia Press and, subsequently, Penguin thought of the book as nonfiction too, but then it won the PEN/Hemingway Award for fiction. Carole Maso, one of the judges, had some pretty liberal ideas about what constitutes fiction. But I think they liked the book because it was difficult to categorize too. So part of the aura surrounding *Maps to Anywhere* in regard to its straddling different genres isn't something I had anything to do with. The book had an independent life.

A Year of Rhymes I based on personal experience too. It had an autobiographical core. But I added into it relatives who never existed and incidents that never happened. It's a much more conscious amalgamation than anything in *Maps to Anywhere*. And then *Truth Serum* was a series of memoirs, also based on real experience. Obviously, though, memory's fallible. That interests me. I've got to say the distinction between fact and fiction is less interesting than the way memory compensates for what's missing, or the way it changes or erodes things . . . makes them blossom into other forms.

RC   Memory does seem your theme.

BC   If I've been called on to speak about one theme more than any other, it's been memory, and the relationship between it and my work. I've been anthologized in the *Oxford Book of Memory*, edited by James

McConkey. At this point, I'm trying to move pretty far away from it. I've recently only been writing in the third person, which is fascinating and challenging, and writing stories about characters with lives and experiences pretty remote from my own. To date, all three books have toyed with the discrepancies between what's remembered and what's imagined. Now I've moved into something that is for the first time discernible as short fiction.

It's funny to talk about this. I'm forced to stand outside the medium in which I always live. Jean Cocteau said that asking a writer to talk about his writing was like asking a plant to talk about horticulture. But it's fascinating to try to articulate these things, which are so hard to define.

RC After a book is written, do you develop a certain indifference or dispassion to it, so that you don't mind how it is taken?

BC Well, in some senses I mind—in the same way, maybe, that an architect minds what sort of furniture's put in a house he or she has designed.

RC Or what kind of people . . .

BC That too—which one has no control over!

I feel that the process of writing—even though it involves a tremendous amount of passion—is finally a craft. During public readings for *Truth Serum*, quite a lot of people would say: "I so admired your honesty. You took so many risks with this." There was something about that that made me bristle. It was as if there was something so unsavory about my private life that I was taking a great risk in making it public. My answer, though, was that although maybe I am drawn to material that's a little touchy or is private to start off with, once you start forming that into sentences and thinking about how the sentence scans, about the connotations of every word, about how the sentences combine to make a paragraph, about how each paragraph makes the transition to the next, you lose any sense of it being raw or personal. It becomes the raw material you manipulate through your craft. There's a bit of dispassion involved there in getting the job done.

Flannery O'Connor, whom I idolize, and Raymond Carver are the two people who have written with the most incredible lucidity about the process of writing. They really demystified it. O'Connor once said that she was like the little old lady who doesn't know what she's going to say until she says it. I love that. And I feel that myself—that the process of writing is commensurate with the process of finding out what I have to say. I thrash my way through all this inchoate material to find that out. But the more you refine the work and worry about it, and carry it around with you day and night, and daydream about it—especially if you spend one to five years writing a book—oddly the material becomes almost invisible. You write it to see what's obsessing you, haunting you, moving you to write. You try again and again through the editing to clarify that. But you come up with something very hard to assess, something with a certain kind of invisibility.

Also, by the time you give readings or interviews about a specific book, you're actually onto something else. Paradoxically, that's the time you're called on to muster the most enthusiasm.

RC   I wondered whether you felt a degree of disengagement from readers of your work. Not critically—just in that the text, once it appears, forms certain impressions upon them that you're not privy to.

BC   I'd venture that a lot of writers—both of memoirs and fiction—feel that. People I don't know have come up and asked: "How's Brian?" They've read in *Truth Serum* about us being a sero-different couple. I'm moved by that. It's sweet. But I also think: "Who are you; how do you know about that?" The obvious answer is that I've told anybody who opens my book about it. But I keep myself a bit distant or protected for a number of reasons. One's that I have to work against any kind of self-consciousness. It would inhibit me in my writing. Also, I need to feel steeped in a kind of privacy in order to write, even if what I'm writing about betrays my privacy.

RC   I take it that you don't have much sense of a specific readership.

BC   The question of who you write for comes up with a fair degree of frequency. Until recently I've always felt there's something wrong with me for not having any idea. Rilke said he wrote to God. For me, and at the risk of sounding mushy . . . it's not God, but some listener in the world; someone who will listen. Who that is; what their demographics are—I've no idea. What preoccupies me far more than trying to appeal to a certain, preimagined audience is trying to get the sentences right—as incisive, interesting, communicative, and seamless as I possibly can. I know that sounds hopelessly pragmatic. But I hope the rest takes care of itself. I hope that kind of care will speak to a variety of people; that some kind of truth—whether it's the "actual truth" or an imagined one—comes through the language to appeal to a reader. That takes precedence over any conception I may have of who I'm writing for.

RC Perhaps it arises often now because of trends in publishing and marketing.

BC You're right. And it's been exacerbated by the popularity of the memoir in American writing. I love the memoir. But I'm not sure what the effects of its ascendance in literature are going to be. I'm a little worried. A lot of people write books about divorce so they can help a reader going through a divorce. There's a kind of altruism. For the same reason, people go on the Ricki Lake show to air their problems in the guise of helping the people watching.

RC Novels can get caught up in this. A novelist gets called on to testify to the authenticity of his or her fictional work—which can mean, simply, to admit that it all happened.

BC I remember once seeing Susan Minot read from a novel called *Monkeys*. It was about a family headed by an alcoholic father. Later an audience member asked whether her father was an alcoholic. She said—not defensively: "I don't want to answer that." It was of no interest to her. Somebody pursued it further, though, by asking what percentage of the book was autobiographical. Then Susan snidely said: "Two percent autobiographical on page one; 14 percent on page two." She made a mockery of the whole idea.

Oddly, when *Truth Serum* came out, some people responded to it not with questions about how or why I'd wanted to evoke these memories of sexual awakening. They'd ask me practical, talk-show-type questions, like: "What advice do you have for kids today who are coming out?" There are lots of things I could have said. But I wouldn't have presumed to have the expertise that would permit me to give my opinions with the intention of helping people solve their personal problems. I also started telling people who'd ask about the degree of veracity in *Truth Serum*: "I wasn't writing these memoirs to hold up in a court of law." It wasn't about getting the facts right; it was about getting to the truth. Toni Morrison wrote a beautiful lecture in which she made a powerful distinction between the facts and the truth, and about how the facts sometimes have nothing to do with the truth.

I'm interested in the tricks of memory as well as its possible accuracy. And I'm interested in artifice as much as in truth. I think artifice is a way to get to the truth.

RC Do we inhabit a culture that is unhealthily confessional in some respects?

BC Well, I'm so much in the middle of it that it's very hard to articulate. But American culture has talk shows where people commit all kinds of confessional excess in the name of "Let's-enlighten-the-world." It's horrible. Then there's that weird species the docudrama, where a real event is reenacted to show what really happened. Actors play the people to whom it happened, acting out what "happened." There are all these strange paradoxes.

Still, there seems also to be a form of cultural insistence on drawing the line between fact and fiction, while at the same time blurring it. We're obsessed with what's real and what's fictive. I become muddled thinking about it. I don't feel obligated, though, to have an answer as to the differences between fact and fiction. I think of Holly Woodlawn, one of Andy Warhol's drag celebrities. Years ago I saw her being interviewed by Dick Cavett. He was trying to pin her down about whether or not she thought herself a man or a woman. He said: "Holly, when you wake up in the morning, are you a man or a woman?" She said: "Who cares, as long as you're beautiful?" That's how I feel about my work.

RC   The public reception of poetry, since you mentioned that, seems especially germane. Someone like Sylvia Plath is invariably only read with reference to her biography.

BC   Then again, you wonder to what extent Plath cultivated the persona of the unsteady, slightly crazy mystic. Like Plath, an American poet named Sharon Olds made her mark by writing these scorching, powerful poems about incest and abuse. Not too long ago she revealed that they were written under a persona. A lot of people—myself included—were shocked. We'd assumed they were written out of personal experience. Although on occasion I'd used a persona or written through a mask in my poetry, usually the "I" in the poem was me. I was concentrating on the minutiae and subtleties of language, its shades of meaning. My interest in poetry is much more about essential aspects of language than about a way of playing with personae.

RC   I noticed in several places in *Maps to Anywhere*, you juggled first- and second-person narration, which is unusual.

BC   Yes, sometimes I did waver between the first and second person, or between second and third. My intention there probably goes back to my interest in the visual arts. There's one piece about going to get my haircut at a barber's. He gave me this calling card which had a wonderful little logo of a floating haircut. I used his telephone number in the piece. The idea seemed hilarious—making the piece an advertisement for this barber I'd had this experience with. That was very much related to the kind of art I was interested in in the sixties or seventies—by people like Robert Rauschenberg, or Tom Wesselmann. An artist might use an actual clock in a painting, so that the painting tells the time. There's the shock of something nonfunctional like a painting suddenly having a function. Some pop artists were blurring the distinctions between a rendered object and a real one.

One problem with the second person used consistently is it can be a little bit tyrannical—"you're doing this; you're doing that." There's something potentially authoritative about it. I used to throw the second person in occasionally to implicate or achieve a sort of sudden intimacy with the reader, to give the text a kind of liveliness or charge it might not otherwise have.

RC   I want to ask in this context about "English as a Second Language," which concerns the usefulness of art in tuition. An English teacher uses Auden's poem "Musée des Beaux Arts," but gets an underwhelming response.

BC   The reality of that story was a nightmare! I was hired to teach freshman English and composition at the Fashion Institute in Los Angeles. I've experienced the same thing at many schools during the long time I taught freshman composition. It's the horrifying experience I'm sure many teachers have shared, where you bring in things you love, and people start falling asleep. They look at you as if you should be locked up in a padded room for being enthusiastic. Part of my frustration at that led me to write that story.

RC   Can creative writing can be taught?

BC   I think ultimately I have mixed feelings about that. I've made my living as a teacher of creative writing. Because I'm teaching people who are really serious about it, in many instances I've seen people's writing change remarkably. Then the question is: Does someone achieving a kind of competence in creative writing make their work ultimately good? Can you influence someone to experience that essential spark that makes their work stand apart as unique or alive, in some way that distinguishes it from other work? I'm not sure you can. But you can help people toward that.

One thing that's very important—almost a personal crusade of mine— is to talk in class about things which aren't often addressed in creative writing classes: things like self-doubt; competitiveness in the literary world; the vicissitudes of publishing. If these people have decided they'd really like to commit their lives to this very difficult thing, art—which I don't necessarily recommend—I think it's a service not only to help them

find a direction to move toward in their work but also to get them thinking about the difficulties, about the expenditure of energy it takes to be a
writer or to commit to anything creative as your livelihood.

RC Are you preparing them for failure?

BC Yes, but failure's an experience of all writers. Joan Didion, another
one of my heroes, once said that the moment she wrote the first word of
a book, she knew it was a compromise. It was no longer the castle on the
hill she'd been imagining. The things one writes do fail.

RC And commercial failure?

BC Absolutely—especially now because dangled over everyone's head
are the very rare instances where people get enormous advances. What
happens to the great majority of people is disappointing compared to that
kind of financial and critical success, which is only for a few. It's an old
cliché, but writers have to be prepared for a lot of rejection. I've been so
lucky—not only in getting books published, but parts of those books excerpted, and so on. I'd never have dreamed even a fraction of the things
that have happened to me would have. Still, all it takes is one "no" to ruin
my week. I take rejection very hard, though in some ways I've developed
a thick skin. What I want to tell my students is that wherever they fall on
the spectrum between being tough or vulnerable, this is something you'll
constantly have to negotiate: getting ridiculed in a review; getting praise
sometimes that's so hyperbolic, it's nuts. You don't feel somebody's even
seeing what you've done when they're that positive. There are all kinds of
weird, dissonant feelings one is subject to with both success and failure.
Thinking about and negotiating those things is an ongoing struggle.

RC To some extent you're helping people find their way through to their
own expression, where the only experience you can draw on is your own.
To formalize any strategy—to introduce this poet you liked; that short
story—is surely in some way to shape other would-be writers according
to your own development. What of serendipity?

BC Well, until recently I taught at Antioch in what's called a low-residency program. It's very good for writers as they're only on the campus for ten very intensive days. They prepare for seminars by reading selections the teachers choose. The rest of the time they schedule their own reading material, which is approved by a mentor.

Otherwise, you're right. One of the great joys as a writer isn't when you feel you've done what you set out to do, necessarily, but when you realize that you're making a path through the world by your reading. That's the way to learn things you didn't expect. It's so vital, and you're right—it's very personal. One author will lead you to another, and so on.

The writers I use in my teaching are exemplars not only of good writing but of specific things. Let's say it's a class on memoir. So-and-so may have written something really personal without being self-indulgent or sentimental. That's part of what I feel a memoir should do. Or here's a writer who's talked about the father being abusive, not only without crying "victim!" but also with enough detachment to see the father's humanity, despite his cruelty. There are lots of things I want my students to see that writing can do. I hope what I bring into class leads them to other texts. It's not definitive. It's just a way to offer concrete examples of the kinds of things I'm trying to address. I also hope they'll be springboards for people to pursue more of that person's work, or other avenues of reading.

I don't think influence of any kind is necessarily a bad thing. If a teacher requires you to read author X for an entire year, that's kind of limited. But I don't think it's going to hurt you.

RC *A Year of Rhymes* contains great examples of writing which successfully negotiates the risks of sentimentality, or of trying to make language suggest too much. The resultant prose is very potent, rich, and resonant—and also very material. The metaphors are strongly material, as they are in *Maps to Anywhere*. How did you arrive at that materiality? Is it through revision, or is it something you struggle at line by line?

BC Both. I talk to my students a lot about the common mistake in writing a memoir, which is to want to exhibit your own emotions through the prose. Something that's very tricky about writing in general—and autobiographical writing especially—is that you want to convey the experience you had, but so that the reader feels the emotion, not the writer. If the writer feels everything, there's no room for the reader. Texts like that get very cloying, overwrought, and surprisingly distancing because of their emotionality. A funny translation has to take place. All the components of a scene—dialogue, environment, color, ambience, sound—everything has to work towards the reader becoming part of it. It's not just you the writer infusing the prose with emotion. It's writing a kind of prose that allows the reader to be engaged.

I don't mind writing with a touch of sentiment, however. Strong feeling has to be there. I like being moved in that quaint, old-fashioned way of being stirred or made melancholy by something a writer's doing. When the work gets sentimental, though, the writer's expecting the prose to carry too much. To invoke Joan Didion again—she once said something that's at the heart of how I experience my work. She talked about going to Berkeley to study literature. She doesn't consider herself an intellectual now, but was trying to be one then. In order to graduate, she had to write ten thousand words on Dante. She said she remembers nothing about what she wrote. What she remembers is the exact rancidity of butter on the train from her house to Berkeley.

You get the sense that she's the kind of person who clings to concrete detail. I'm so much that way. As soon as people start talking about theory or abstraction, I'm lost. I can't understand the world in those terms. But once they're made manifest in some sort of figurative or concrete speech, then I can. So, for example, you can say a woman's mad. But madness is really only an abstraction. But if you say: "She plucked at her hair as if she heard a sound in it." That completely conveys somebody's madness in a tangible way. That's the kind of spark I want my writing to have—where the net effect of the writing brings the world into sharp focus, but a focus that can embody abstractions without itself being abstract.

RC You suggested that you experience the world in this nonabstract way. Is it then a relatively effortless process to write in this way?

BC "Effortless" would probably be the last word I'd use! Someone once described writing sentences as like wrestling a bear. That was pretty good.

It's really hard. Some days a whole page, like a piece of ripe fruit, will fall from the tree into my hand. But that's so much the exception. I edit and revise a lot. The writer Evan S. Connell—who wrote *Mrs. Bridge*—said: "Words are all we have—and they'd better be the right ones." I feel that. The greatest responsibility I have as a writer is to create the right words. Some days that's easier than others; some passages are easier than others. But it's a lot of work. Often I wish I could sit down and write a book in a year. It doesn't happen that way. And, years later, I still have the impulse to change certain things that could have been better.

RC   Do you work at specific times of the day?

BC   My best time's the morning. I go down to my workroom with the world having intervened as little as possible. I drink coffee, eat my breakfast, and then am at it. Generally, I have a period of between three and five hours of intense concentration and some productivity. Some days I can come back after lunch and edit a bit. But producing the stuff is generally limited to a few hours a day. I try to be as consistent as possible, but that's hard too.

RC   Do you work on a single project?

BC   For the first time I'm now working on two books at the same time. I've always been superstitious about sticking to one thing until I get it done. There's a wonderful gay painter named Larry Pitman. He described the same thing. Generally, even if he can't do anything on a painting, he won't let himself do anything else. He'll keep beating his head against a wall till it's done.

One of the books is a collection of short stories, mostly in the third person, and all concerning things pretty distant from my experiences. Obviously, in fiction, everything's up for grabs. With a memoir like *Truth Serum*, no one can say: "I think you should make your mother a coal miner." With fiction, though, there's infinite flexibility.

The other book I'm imagining as a lot like *Maps to Anywhere*. It'll be a collection of difficult-to-categorize pieces. I'm interested in them having a single focus—which is the visual arts, and specifically my experiences in having gone to this avant-garde art school, spending years watching people do performances where they'd brush their hair for six hours and then fall asleep. That seems innately funny and appalling to me at the same time.

I'm trying to bounce back and forth between the two things. It remains to be seen whether that's a good way of working. But I'm enjoying turning to something else when I reach a real obstacle in one thing. I feel I always have something to work on. That's new.

RC Have you embarked on projects which simply haven't worked?

BC Sure. Not whole books. But I have uncollected material. There are lots of stories and essays that never quite came to fruition. Christopher Isherwood was one of the first writers to take an interest in my work. I sent him some poems first. Then I remember sending him what I thought was a really good story. It was about my father having been a lawyer for this case called the "Miracle Chicken." A farmer and his wife had beheaded a chicken which kept living. They charged people to see it. The SPCA wanted to kill it; they wanted to keep it alive—as a sign from God. My father defended the couple.

I'd never written prose before. It was horribly overstated. Isherwood called me up. He'd been so enthusiastic before about the poems. But he said: "I got the story you sent. You know, it's wrong; wrong; wrong." [*Laughs*] I was devastated. But he was right. Years later, I wrote the piece again from scratch and it became part of *Maps to Anywhere*. So there's a way in which some things get discarded forever, and other things get forgotten and ferment over time. Then suddenly it's the right time to work with that material again.

RC Could you summarize your own reading history?

BC My earliest reading was in poetry. Probably my life was forever changed by a teacher I had in high school who brought in an anthology called *Contemporary American Poetry*, edited by the poet Donald Hall. That was the first time I read Ginsberg to any extent. Also Plath, Howard Nemerov, and Anthony Hecht. Hecht was a powerful influence. He's written several kinds of poems. But he wrote a lot of strongly narrative poems—like stories with line breaks. The language was much denser than it would have been in prose. These were extremely dark, but funny at the same time. They involved all kinds of kitschy junk, like whoopee cushions. At heart, though, they were very unsettling. I loved the fact that he could balance those two tones, and that he told a story.

One of the first gay writers who turned my head was the poet Edward Field. His book *Stand Up Friend with Me* I found at a bookstore. The poems again were strongly narrative, accessible, and with a terrific gentle humor. They didn't seem academic at all. They had a loose, prosaic quality I responded to. They were frank about his sexual identity and the milieu he lived in in New York. He was my gay Robert Lowell—somebody who'd taken the material of his life and transformed it into poetry.

One remarkable thing about Michael Benedikt's anthology of prose poetry was that it opened my eyes to a whole genre I didn't know about . . . and not only the people who were pretty much the first to experiment in prose poetry—Baudelaire, and Rimbaud. There were a lot of Americans too—even people like Anne Sexton. I'd no idea she'd written prose poetry. In fact, I think they're very rarely collected. Michael Benedikt himself wrote some really funny stuff. Then there was a ripple effect. I began reading both poetry and prose; finally, just about anything.

Apart from their influence on this particular book, I don't know if I'd put these two writers in my ultimate cosmos, but tremendously influential to *A Year of Rhymes* were Denton Welch and Bruno Schulz. A friend gave me Welch's *In Youth Is Pleasure*. I was completely dumbstruck. I loved the fact that so little happened, yet the whole thing seemed charged with an amazing nascent sexuality. Everything had a sexual undertone. I kept thinking: "On the next page, he's going to have sex." But it never happened. And the events were all so trivial. One favorite moment occurs when as a young man the major tries to see if he can fit himself in the bureau drawer. It was so peculiar, and yet so provocative—this ordinary whimsical thing a kid might think of doing . . . It was completely riveting, even though nothing was happening. I loved the subtlety of Welch's work, and particularly the idea that a book can be charged with sexuality when the character, at twelve, was really too young, naive, or bashful to act on any sexual impulses.

Schulz was Polish. His work's an odd hybrid of autobiography and fiction. He was a great influence on the structure of *A Year of Rhymes*. I remember a quote of his: "Memories are like the filaments around which our sense of the world is crystallized." I thought of each section of *A Year of Rhymes* as one of those filaments. There was a central image everything seemed to congeal around—usually something that had a kind of hidden meaning I had to discover through writing it.

I'm crazy about Joan Didion's essays in particular. Though not many people find her funny, I think she's often hilarious, in a very bleak way. There's lots of work by Annie Dillard I've been really stirred by. Her stuff is unabashedly poetic—delicious and musical, full of alliteration and onomatopoeia. There's an American writer named Albert Goldbarth, a poet who also writes what he calls "poem-essays." He's not as well known as he should be but is constantly anthologized. He's a writer's writer.

One of my favorite gay writers is Allan Gurganus. I first came across his work with a really short story that was in *Paris Review*—"It Had Wings." It was brief, compressed like a poem. It relied on imagery. It was like a fable in its departures from the real. It was very exciting. I've been a fan ever since, particularly of the stories. I'm nuts about "Nativity, Caucasian" and "Condolences to Every One of Us," which I think are perfect.

RC *A Year of Rhymes* was compared to Truman Capote's *Other Voices, Other Rooms*, which surprised me. It seemed wrong formally; I associate *Other Voices, Other Rooms* with the gay tradition of elaborate, ornate, bejeweled prose. Perhaps people are really searching for thematic comparisons?

BC Yes. This is an odd phenomenon a writer has no control over. I think it was the publicist who wrote the jacket copy who first made that comparison. Then it filtered into reviews. Suddenly one person's assessment seemed like a unanimous critical comparison. *A Year of Rhymes* was also compared to J. D. Salinger. I think you're right—it's about theme. And at book readings, people always wanted to ask me about what it was like growing up gay, not about matters of form.

I guess the comparisons flatter. But it's like looking at yourself in a funhouse mirror. You know it's you, but the distortions make you feel incredulous. I don't think either comparison's right, whereas if somebody had said Denton Welch, I'd have felt they understood very accurately what I was aiming for.

This stuff happens and you take it in your stride—so long as they compare me to fabulous, famous writers! [*Laughs*] As far as ornate stuff goes, the writing in *Maps to Anywhere* was the most ornate mine has ever been. I was coming out of years of reading poetry, of being influenced by people like Anthony Hecht, who has incredible verbal agility. In my own way I was trying to imitate that. I love the richness of Nabokov's prose too.

You have to be interested in language to write—the same way a painter has to be interested in paint. How could you not be completely enthralled by your medium and still spend your life working in it? I feel really strongly, however, that, as much as I love ornate language in my reading, and as much as I've tried to produce it myself, I still want a certain kind of transparency in my work. I want the language to be in service of something said, something in the real world. I don't want it to be about itself. One contemporary literary movement that I'm completely baffled by is language poetry. It's solely a kind of formal experimentation. I want news of the world in what I read. And I do want a charge of feeling or sentiment in the work.

It's more likely that I'll be enamored, even envious, of writers whose prose is simple, because it goes against what for me is a more or less natural inclination—to approach language from a more skewed, aesthetic direction. So I love Raymond Carver. One of my other favorite American writers is Tobias Wolff. His prose is miraculously hard and clear, yet it always carries this plaintive or mesmerizing quality. I'm in awe of the lucidity of his sentences. Yet they always seem to be about something mysterious and ineffable.

I'm a little unsure ultimately where I fall on the tightrope between the ornate and the simple. I probably vacillate toward different extremes at different times. Something that does draw me to some degree toward the ornate, though, is that there's something slightly hyperbolic and complicated about the way I see the world. I think in part it has to do with being gay, and so never taking anything on face value when I was growing up. Everything seemed charged with innuendo. The world was supposed to be one thing, but there was a world beyond what was evident or obvious.

The other thing has to do with my being Jewish. That draws me to-wards the hyperbolic. There's a certain pitch of woe, of complaint or rib-ald humor, that characterized my growing up—in the way my relatives would talk to each other. You never had a problem. You always had "The Woyst Problem You Just Wouldn't Believe . . . " Everything was exagger-ated to this amazing pitch. So there's something authentic in the way that pitch captures my view of the world. There are a lot of Jewish-American writers where that kind of ornateness comes into play, like Cynthia Ozick or Stanley Elkin, who I think formally is one of the more adventurous American writers. Not only does he toy with language, but when things happen, they happen in this mad, slapstick way. I love that. It seems real to me—the way a child might draw a big orange blob with spokes on it, and that to him is the sun.

RC   How important is your Jewish ancestry to the work?

BC   In his introduction to *Maps to Anywhere*, Richard Howard wrote about something he found innate in my work: the flavor of second- or third-generation Jews. My parents were intent on assimilating. It was one of their big goals. But they were torn between two worlds. They spoke Yiddish, for example, but refused to teach it to me. In part, they wanted to be able to carry on discussions I'd know nothing about.

I remember very distinctly my mother advising me to tell people I was American when they asked who or what I was. She was very frightened—as she had reason to be—about how people might respond if I said I was Jewish. They were torn, like a lot of Jews of that generation. They were carrying on traditions with one hand, and shedding them with the other. I was barmitzvahed when I was thirteen. But I learned my speech pho-netically. I had absolutely no idea what I was saying. That says it all. It was a ritual my parents—superstitiously, perhaps—felt it was necessary to carry through, but not enough so that I knew what the hell I was doing. To be frank, all I thought was: "I'm going to get a lot of presents"—like the American consumer I already was.

I'm not very religious, which I think obviously has to do with my up-bringing. I have much more kinship with Jewishness as an ethnicity than a religion. What was most ingrained in me weren't religious precepts but things like Jewish humor, a way of talking. One thing I find most profound about Jewishness is that everything gets inflected into a question. Everything's doubtful. Even belief isn't so much about finding definitive answers as about figuring out the right questions. Those questions I feel are part of my soul, whereas the religious things . . . Well, I never know when Hanukkah is, for instance.

RC   Do you see any connection between the materiality of your prose and Los Angeles, your hometown—a place where, according to the cliché anyway, materialism and surface proliferate endlessly?

BC   One of the consistent elements I decided to pursue in this book of short stories is setting—I wanted them all to take place in or around Los Angeles. I'm very interested in the city's ambience. I do think the clichés about L.A. are true, but their opposites are also often true, too. I find L.A. a place of disturbing irrationality, of great mystery, of a kind of melancholy anonymity, in that people are very removed from each other. These things Joan Didion has certainly captured.

Something that makes L.A. ripe for the work I do is its superficiality. Pop art was the first aesthetic experience I ever had. It was profoundly transforming. Overnight I saw myself as an artist. One thing I've always loved about pop art at its best is that, though on the surface it's "about" surface, it can also address some really unnerving, complicated things. When Andy Warhol made two hundred Marilyn Monroe silk-screens, that was obviously about the superficiality of an image repeated ad nauseam. On the other hand, it was also about the way people become masks of themselves, which is both a sad and an amazing thing for a work of art to be about. The early work of Roy Liechtenstein took really loaded images of American clichés—clichés about heroism—and made them seem absurd and empty. That was earthshaking.

I've always loved the way the superficial—if dealt with interestingly—can lead to something more complicated and intricate. It's the way I've hoped to employ banal or superficial imagery myself. In a piece like "The House of the Future," where I talk about this almost laughable house at Disneyland, there's some sense in which all these plastic goodies speak to me about how impossible ideas of Utopia are—the way humans always strive for some glimpse of the future. It was the same with Anthony Hecht—he used articles about Marlon Brando from *Life* magazine to address some really stirring, often unhappy things. I love the resonance between what's supposedly superficial and what's deep or disturbing.

RC   In "If and When," there's a suggestion of the deep appropriateness of, or your own deep sympathy with, a very consumer-based engagement with art. Was that conscious? Or was it to introduce an element of irony or tension?

BC   I'm not sure irony's there. Andy Warhol said that the artist who truly expresses our times is the one painting flowers in his attic. In a way I find the fact that people have crappy reproductions of Rodin's *The Thinker* on their mantelpiece really touching and amazing. It speaks to me of the way people yearn for aesthetic experiences, and to understand things beyond their ken. We all do it. So I take kitsch very seriously. I'm fond of it in a way that isn't exactly ironic.

RC   "If and When" also features some very personal experiences of AIDS. Was that especially hard to write about?

BC   Absolutely. That's probably the most difficult thing I've ever written . . . not so much in setting things in language. There were extraliterary concerns that muddied the waters. One was that I was writing about someone I care for immeasurably. I felt a responsibility I've never felt before. It's one thing to try to reflect your own view of the world. It's another to do that for yourself and for someone you feel strongly about. That dual responsibility was difficult.

One of the really hard things—and I think I can say this without to the best of my knowledge being blinded by love—concerns the fact that, as most people who know Brian would tell you, he's remarkably resourceful. He's done everything he can to take care of himself. He's made sure that his health problems have not subsumed our relationship. He's also the most genuinely even-tempered person I know—quite different from the Jewish hysteric you're talking to!

I wanted to show those things—but accurately. I didn't want it to seem like some sort of crazy romanticization, or to make him seem somehow impervious to suffering, which of course he's not. I had to write about how he was. I wanted to write him in a way that captured his desire to live, simply put, yet wouldn't strike the reader as an attempt to make him more heroic than he is. Also, I wanted his approval. I knew at some point he had to read the piece, and if it wasn't OK with him, it wasn't going in. That had never happened before.

Also, we mentioned earlier how much of my writing concerns memory. This was really different. I was writing about it as it was happening. Not only that. Brian's health—as for a lot of people who have AIDS—can change dramatically from day to day. So it was like capturing something that was always changing. I wanted to let my emotion into the piece, but didn't want to be swamped by it, as happens quite frequently in my day-to-day life. I often feel overwhelmed by the gravity of his suffering. It may sound a little dramatic, but I'm bereft by the possibility of losing him. It's horrible. To find the right distance from the material was really hard.

One of the most incisive things anyone's ever said about my work was when Richard Howard read *A Year of Rhymes*. He said something that made me so grateful: "You know, this isn't at all a coming out story. This is about what it means to be in a body." I'd only been vaguely aware of that, but he was right on the money. The same is true with "If and When." One thing AIDS has made us all excruciatingly aware and hyper-vigilant about is the body. It may just be a carapace, but everything begins and ends there—the possibility of the greatest losses and salvation. Being able to continue to touch Brian, to experience his flesh—in one sense, this was the most superficial notion of a meaningful connection or romantic bond. But in the end, it was also the most profound thing possible. Everything began and ended with a small gesture on the surface of each other's body. It was there that the greatest depth of expression took place. And every time I felt despair about the possibility of losing Brian, the antidote was his physical existence. That, of course, made the possibility of losing him all the more frightening.

RC　It's like Brian's happiness at your testing negative. It's the tortuous circularity of AIDS logic.

BC That's a good phrase for it. My experience of being in a sero-different couple—and here comes the hyperbole—is that the fluctuation from one emotion to another is like being flung from one end of the room to the other. That's how violent it feels. These emotions chase their tails in a really ferocious way. What makes you happy simultaneously makes you sad because you risk losing it. Because you risk losing it, it's all the more important to you. There's so much of that. It's exhausting!

RC Who else has impressed you in writing about AIDS?

BC The AIDS texts that come to mind are the stories and nonfiction I'd read before I decided to write about it myself. I made a conscious effort not to look at other writings about AIDS when writing about it myself. I'd visited so many workshops for people with AIDS or sero-different couples—places where people were trying to write about this disease. But again, what allows me to write is a sense of anonymity or aloneness. So there was a conflict between feeling I was part of a community of people giving voice to an experience that's incredibly difficult and overwhelming, and trying to believe in the possibility that I had something unique to contribute.

I admire Paul Monette's *Borrowed Time*. I remember him giving an overwhelming reading of the poems from *Love Alone*. For the most part, people like Paul Monette and David Feinberg had contributed not only to a literature of AIDS but to the literature of anger. Their work was rousing and amazing. They harnessed this tremendous rage and weren't swamped by it. As angry and frustrated as both Brian and I have become, though, my writing's never been the place where I vent anger. I think if I tried, the results would be unreadable. I hope instead to try to chart certain paradoxes, certain odd, circular ways of thinking which lead to troubling aspects of human nature—things that are joyful and miserable at the same time. Also I wanted to offer humor. Gallows humor.

Sometimes I feel humor is like bread or sustenance for us. It's not just that we can laugh at the darkest possibilities. There's something genuinely nourishing about it. I find myself constantly making jokes with Brian. He makes them too, and they kill me. They come right out of left field. In my work, I try to use humor that seems particularly resonant, that make points about life and death that only a joke can make.

RC   Is AIDS a theme you've left behind?

BC   No. Some characters in the stories have AIDS. One thing that's been a little bit odd for me about this subject is that I grew up in a family with three older brothers, all of whom had died by the time AIDS hit. I have to say that AIDS seems like a really horrifying continuation of something that's always preoccupied me: a heightened sense of mortality and the impermanence of the body. One great sadness in my relationship with Brian—and maybe no love can do this—is that I wanted love to take that out of my life. But it put it in the center in a way I'd never have imagined, especially after going through all that with my brothers.

RC   Could you say something about the significance to you of the pre-AIDS sexual culture—what someone in "If and When" refers to as "Shangri-la"? Sex doesn't feature so heavily in your work.

BC   My own experience in the gay world was that I tried to find a place for myself in the Edenic 1970s. I took advantage of sexual opportunity. It was incredibly good for me. But I'd also lived with a woman for about three years romantically. My greatest thrills always seemed to be within the context of a relationship. I think I got the same sense of unpredictability, play, and adventure in an intimate relationship that other people might get from having different partners or exploring other avenues of sexual expression.

That's not a judgment. As for writing about sex, I like writing and reading about sex where there's some undercurrent of meaning other than just the experience of sex. A friend of mine said something brilliant—that writing about sex-that's-just-sex is like writing about chewing instead of about tasting food. That was perfect. Sex can be written about mechanically. That doesn't interest me. But the way sex can betray people's desperation or foolishness, or the extent of their hunger . . . That's interesting. As for my evolution as a gay man, I spent many years in a wonderful, slow process of coming out that involved a great deal of sexual exploration. But I'm more interested in exploring the complicated things that happen to people when they've had a lot of history together and a lot of things are at stake.

RC   What do you feel about statements regarding the appropriateness of sexual writing in gay literature?

BC   I don't feel persuaded by either extreme—the one that insists on excising sex from a work for the sake of propriety or whatever; or the other—using sex as an in-your-face way to get people to confront their feelings about gay sexuality. Nothing I write comes out of that. I do think about the repercussions of what I've written. But I don't write anything out of a theory. Generalizations don't work for me. I find them oppressive.

In the same way, there are lots of prescriptions about how people should write about AIDS—that you must be angry, or educate, or show safe sex, or have transgressive sex, or else you're erotophobic, or whatever. The supposition is that there are right and wrong ways to experience sex on the one hand, and grief on the other. I'm sorry, but I do it the best way I know how, which is sloppy and changes from minute to minute. I think one gropes through those experiences. It's the floundering, the trying to figure out what it all means that interests me.

RC   Is there anything you resist reading when you're writing?

BC   Right now I'm obsessed with reading short stories. That's all I can read. It's odd because I'm writing them too. Often I've felt when I was writing a novel, that I should read nonfiction; when I'm writing nonfiction, I'd read fiction, so I could feel there was a difference between my reading and writing lives. At the risk of sounding barbaric, though, in some ways it all seems the same to me . . . like different bodies of water. When you boil them down, you get salt.

RC   Do you still write poetry?

BC   No, though I still go to poetry readings and read a lot of poetry. One troublesome thing about writing poetry was that I got really stifled trying to figure out line breaks. Free verse is a lot more problematic than people give it credit for. Once I'd given up on the idea of trying to shape things into lines, my work became more expansive. I could stretch it. I was mobile in prose—flexible—in a way I wasn't in poetry.

RC   Have you ever wanted to write for stage or screen?

BC   No. In L.A., everyone asks if you're writing a screenplay. Plays and screenplays—as much as I admire them—don't offer what I love in prose: description. Sometimes I have an idle fantasy that I could make visual art again. But I have my hands full writing fiction and nonfiction. I'll probably be working with those forms for the rest of my life.

★   ★   ★

RC   Congratulations on the publication of *Guess Again*. You'd spoken of enjoying writing in the third person; I was surprised to find that the first story, "Night Sky," was not only one of three written in the first person but also that Sam, the narrator, casually reveals that he is HIV-positive. Did you hesitate before taking on this particular "I" voice?

BC   No. I welcomed taking it on. It was a way to immerse myself in a character whose HIV status is different from my own. It was a way, I hoped, to achieve greater empathy with a person who would be going through this threat to his mortality.

RC   In "Night Sky," protease inhibitors, which have so starkly changed circumstances for so many, are explicitly mentioned. Could you comment on the experience of writing so frequently about AIDS in these stories as the circumstances of AIDS treatment programs were changing so rapidly?

BC   Treatment programs are changing, but they change for every disease. What interests me is how people do or don't cope with treatment, how people do or don't learn to live with the degree of uncertainty that having a disease imposes.

RC   I assume you've continued to work on the proposed collection of memoirs concerning your experiences at art school. How has it felt moving back to autobiographical material after the hiatus of the very diverse fictional circumstances of *Guess Again*?

BC It's been a great pleasure writing about art—about the nobility and absurdity of the avant-garde, which interests me in the same way that notions of a utopian civilization interested me in the essay "The House of the Future" in my first book. I'm moved by how human beings have the capacity to imagine a perfect world, and at the same time to realize that those idealizations are fallible and will never be fully realized.

RC Thanks very much for your time.

THREE

CHRISTOPHER BRAM

CHRISTOPHER BRAM is the author of eight novels, including *Father of Frankenstein*, which was adapted into film as the Oscar-winning *Gods and Monsters* (1998), directed by Bill Condon; *Gossip*; *The Notorious Dr. August: His Real Life and Crimes*; and *Lives of the Circus Animals*.

Bram was born in Buffalo, New York, in 1952, but grew up outside Norfolk, Virginia, where he attended public school. He then studied at the College of William and Mary (1970–1974) before moving to New York in 1978. A first novel, "Gunny," dating from his first years in the city, remains unpublished. *Christopher Street* published Bram's short story "Aphrodisiac" in 1979; it subsequently appeared in Christopher Street, eds., *Aphrodisiac: Fiction from Christopher Street* (New York: Perigree, 1980). Bram meanwhile completed his next, and first-published novel, *Surprising Myself* (New York: Donald Fine, 1987).

Hold Tight (New York: Donald Fine, 1988), a historical novel set in New York during World War II, followed. Bram's third, *In Memory of Angel Clare* (New York: Donald Fine, 1989), concerned the impact of AIDS on New York gay life. *Almost History* (New York: Donald Fine, 1992), a long historical novel, moves between America and the Philippines.

Father of Frankenstein (New York: Dutton, 1995) concerned the last months in the life of cult British horror film director James Whale; for the 1998 film version of Bram's novel (*Gods and Monsters*), director Bill Condon received an Academy Award for his screenplay. Bram's sixth novel, *Gossip* (New York: Dutton, 1997), is a contemporary political thriller set in Washington, D.C., while his seventh, *The Notorious Dr. August: His Real Life and Crimes* (New York: Morrow, 2000), returns to more distant historical material. It tells the life story of one Augustus Fitzwilliam Boyd, a musician. Beginning in the American South of the Civil War, it ends in Harlem in the 1920s, with interludes in Germany, Turkey, and Coney Island. Bram's latest novel is *Lives of the Circus Animals* (New York: Morrow, 2003).

Bram has written several screenplays, including the scripts for two short films directed by Draper Shreeve. He has reviewed movies for the *New York Native* and *Premiere* magazine, and books for *Christopher Street, New York Newsday,* and *Lambda Book Report.* His many essays include a portrait of his neighborhood, "Perry Street, West Village," published in John Preston, ed., *Hometowns: Gay Men Write About Where They Belong* (New York: Dutton, 1991); "Mapping the Territory," an overview of gay male literature that introduces Robert Giard's book of photographs, *Particular Voices: Portraits of Gay and Lesbian Writers* (Boston: MIT Press, 1997); "Faggots Revisited," in Lawrence D. Mass, ed., *We Must Love One Another or Die: The Life and Legacies of Larry Kramer* (New York: Palgrave Macmillan, 1998); and "Slow Learners," in Patrick Merla, ed., *Boys Like Us: Gay Writers Tell Their Coming Out Stories* (New York: Avon, 1996). Bram also wrote an introduction to Richard Labonté, ed., *Best Gay Erotica 1998* (San Francisco: Cleis Press, 1998).

Recipient of a 2001 Guggenheim Fellowship, Bram continues to live and work in New York City. The interview took place on two occasions—Monday, April 20, 1998, and Wednesday, February 6, 2002—in his office. It was substantially revised and updated in June 2002.

RC Why do you work in an office?

CB Well, it's New York City. My boyfriend and I have a very small three-room apartment in the West Village. Draper is a graphic designer and filmmaker. We both worked at home. So when I got a little money for the movie of *Father of Frankenstein*—and it was a low-budget movie, so it wasn't much money—we decided I should get an office. As you can see, it's not much of an office: a big white cube with a window. My books are still in boxes stacked against the wall; I still need to buy bookcases. That duck decoy on top of the filing cabinet was carved by my father. Dad took up woodcarving after his retirement from the farm chemical business.

There's a therapist in the office next door; a realtor on the other side. Around the corner is a man who trains security guards. Down the hall is a jewelry designer. Our landlord is an accountant who chucked it all a few years ago to become a yoga instructor. It's a funkier, more laid-back New York than most people know.

RC   But you're not originally from New York.

CB   No. I grew up in Virginia, in the Norfolk–Virginia Beach area. I went to the College of William and Mary down there, on an ROTC scholarship. I didn't come here until 1978, when I was twenty-six, ostensibly because I thought all writers needed to live in New York, but actually so I could get away from the straight guy I was in love with. And to meet some real gay people and to get laid. I spent a year with the Social Security Administration, then seven years at Scribner's Bookstore, which was my equivalent of grad school.

Meanwhile I was writing. I have always thought of myself as a writer.

RC   How would you describe yourself as a novelist?

CB   Oh lord. All over the place. Polymorphous. More polymorphous than perverse. I'm something of a realist, but I like to try new things: different subjects, voices, genres. It's hard to say what kind of identity or unity my body of work has. There are themes, I suppose.

I'm known as a historical novelist. But of the seven novels I've published, only three are set in the historical past: *Hold Tight*, *Father of Frankenstein*, and *The Notorious Dr. August*. The others are set in my lifetime, if not limited to my experience. In *Almost History*, for example, the State Department protagonist, Jim Goodall, comes from a different generation than mine, but his niece Meg is my age. In fact, I gave her my family and some of my college experience.

Maybe if we separate my historical novels from the nonhistorical ones, we'd find two different novelists. But the truth of the matter is the historical novels are about contemporary issues: sex, gender, and race. I find race easier to write about when it's set in the past. And the contemporary novels are all embedded in a historical present, a similar case of time and custom. In the middle of writing *Gossip*, which was aggressively set "now," the Republicans won control of Congress. It radically changed the Washington I was writing about. So even when I write about the present, it becomes historical. Maybe I write historical novels about the present.

I suspect I'm known as a historical novelist only because so few other gay novelists visit the past. I'm the low-rent Gore Vidal. But I like to tell stories. Working in the past just gives me a bigger lake where I cast my net and fish out more stories.

RC   You don't draw immediately upon your own life, however?

CB   I do, but it's heavily disguised. My books are full of emotional auto-biography—private little allegories, conscious and unconscious. It would take a couple of very close friends and a really good psychiatrist to translate them.

I'm not sure why I don't write more overt autobiographical fiction. But I don't find my life all that interesting. And I don't trust my judgment writing it. I can't be as objective about it. Also, I've been with Draper for twenty-plus years now, which creates privacy issues. Besides, it's more fun trying out new stories, new experiences, lives I've never lived. Pieces of myself can't help but turn up anyway, only changed, like in a funhouse mirror.

Plus I have this horror of being bored, which might also be why I keep trying my hand at different genres.

RC   What do you consider your themes?

CB   I was hoping you'd tell me.

Let's see. I like moral dramas. I like to let my characters paint themselves into moral corners, and see what they can do to get out. I'm addicted to ambiguity. My good characters are always behaving badly, and my bad characters sometimes behave well—which I find drives some readers nuts. They want their categories neat—I guess to assure themselves that they could never slide into bad behavior.

I think in terms of families—conventional and unconventional families, including families of friends. They're forever falling apart in my novels, then coming back together as something new.

One subject, I notice, that recurs again and again, is the life of the artist. It's rarely writers, but everyone else. I've done filmmakers, musicians, actors, a failed poet in *Gossip*, a woman historian in *Almost History*. The novel I'm working on now is about New York theater, so it's packed with actors, directors, playwrights—successful or otherwise—and a theater critic from the *New York Times*. *Hold Tight* is probably my only novel where no real artist is present.

I write about artists chiefly because I love the arts: movies, music, books. But I'm also fascinated by vocations—careers and work. As Freud said, we find satisfaction in life only through love or work. One gets tired of writing about love all the time. I don't know enough about banking or business to imagine a character in those trades, but I do know something about movies and theater.

I also like to write about politics, but only when I can find a story where the personal taps into political institutions and ideas.

RC   You write more about politics than any other gay writer I can think of, except Sarah Schulman perhaps.

CB   But Sarah's politics tend to get narrow and sentimental. It's all good guys and bad guys, the damned and the saved, without the messy gray zone of choice and compromise where most political life takes place. That's where the politics of my novels happens, but I'm not the only one. Michael Nava does it in his Henry Rios novels. The books are mysteries, but his protagonist is a lawyer at work in a real world. There are always trade-offs and choices. Mark Merlis is a very political writer too—first in *American Studies*, where he explored a McCarthy-era betrayal. Then in *An Arrow's Flight* he produced an even better novel with a larger political meaning, a comic allegory about war and the State and gay men's lives.

RC   I noticed how often you move between first- and third-person narrators from one novel to the next. Has there been a pattern?

CB   Not really. I just choose whatever tells the story. First person is wonderful for the way it immediately plunges you in a character's life. But then you're stuck there. In my first-person novels often I get restless and find myself playing with devices—letters, journals, newspaper articles— just to vary the voices.

But the decision to write in first- or third-person isn't nearly as important as many people think. After you've worked both sides of the aisle, you learn it's the least of your problems in telling a story.

RC   What exactly do you have when you start a novel?

CB   A situation and a couple of characters. I'll think about it for a few months, and then start making notes. It's a sketching phase and can last a month or so. Sometimes the notes will turn into scenes. Sometimes I'll sketch out most of the story, although I never know exactly how it will end. At some point during this messing around, I'll hit upon a scene and realize: "This is the beginning." Then I'll start writing. I write steadily from the beginning of the novel to end, but will continue to sketch scenes up ahead as I go.

For the very first novel I wrote—my unpublished novel—I did an outline. I plotted it out and knew exactly what everything would mean. But then writing the book was a chore. I already knew how it would end. From *Surprising Myself* on, I leave things open. I need to write the book for myself in order to find out how things turn out.

RC   I suppose that's even reflected in the title. Has it always been easy to find an ending?

CB   Well, I always found the ending I needed. There have been times when I wrote past the ending—when the novel went on an extra scene or two. But a surprising number of my books end with epilogues, as if I'm reluctant to say goodbye to my characters.

RC   Then there are your open endings, such as the last line of *Surprising Myself*: "We weren't finished yet."

CB   It's an open ending to an epilogue. Draper complains about my long goodbyes with real people too. He says I have a separation anxiety.

I rewrote the epilogue of *Surprising Myself* more times than I care to remember. Basically I was trying to come up with a plausible happy ending for a gay novel. Back in those days, gay novels always seemed to end with one of the lovers dying or disappearing. I wanted my two men to stay together. Earlier drafts sounded a bit too "yippee!"

RC   Rereading *Surprising Myself*, I wondered if there was a danger of Joel, the gay narrator, becoming too good to be true. In trying to invert the earlier, negative gay stereotypes, there must be a danger of going too far.

CB   But Joel can be a selfish jerk. Originally, when the book was longer, he was even more of a jerk. He didn't come out until page three hundred. My original idea was to create a prickly, difficult, closet case where even straight readers would want to see him come out. Being gay would make him human. There were chapters about the lies he tells himself and how badly he treats Corey after they first go to bed together. And so on. All that got cut or telescoped when I rewrote the book. It was much too long—seven hundred pages. I heavily cut the first half—the coming out story, which other people had already written. I kept the second half—the living together story, which nobody had told yet.

The world was already full of tragic, self-destructive gay romantics. I wanted to create something different.

RC   I noticed that the fatalistic, self-destructive character in *Surprising Myself* was the heterosexual, Kearney.

CB   You're right. I hadn't thought of that. He's an army officer and treats Joel's sister very badly, but then goes AWOL in pursuit of her, which is the end of his career. It's a brash, romantic gesture . . . not least because she no longer loves him. The marriage is over.

RC Do you still heavily cut your novels when you revise them?

CB No. After *Surprising Myself*, I've usually had to add. There's almost always a scene or two missing in the middle. As I said, sometimes I write a scene or two past the ending though.

With *Father of Frankenstein*, I originally wrote an epilogue I couldn't make work. But then Bill Condon was writing the screenplay and he wanted something stronger for the ending. I told him about my failed epilogue, in which Clay Boone, years later, is married and a father. He wakes his son up in the middle of the night to watch *Bride of Frankenstein* on the late movie. Bill said, "Do you mind if I try something like that?" "Go ahead. Maybe you can make it work." And he did. He needed less explanation and setup with film. And he added Brendan Fraser's wonderfully spooky walk in the rain, which I still find extraordinary.

Incidentally, Clay was one of the hardest characters for me to write—a straight man in the 1950s. There would be none of the doubt or self-awareness that you find with straight men today. He'd seem like a complete asshole. But then I made him an outsider. He sees himself as a loser, and insists he's a rebel, but there's nothing very rebellious about him. But he's not married and has no children, so he sees himself as a failure, even though he's only twenty-six.

RC A nice irony is that, in gay terms, he gets treasured for the very things which make him feel redundant in the straight world. To be in your mid-twenties when you're gay means to be starting out on a journey, whereas to be straight at twenty-six . . .

CB Yes. In the 1950s especially. You needed to be established by the time you were twenty-six if you were "a real man." Straight people have become more like gay people over the past decades.

RC In plot terms, the idea of someone inviting their own death at the hands of a murderous lover bears comparisons with Muriel Spark's *The Driver's Seat*.

CB I don't know that book. But it's certainly a well-established, well-worn trope. It's such a strong trope that I was often afraid of it while writing *Father of Frankenstein*. The ultimate rough trade fantasy: a gay man wants to find a real man who will kill him. Usually out of guilt. James Whale has other reasons, but there was always the ghost of that old fantasy hanging over the plot twist. I'm glad to hear there's a heterosexual version of the myth.

But see? I try to escape the old fatalistic, self-destructive gay myths, but they're always still there. They're potent.

RC   Some writers don't engage with the process of their work being turned into film. Presumably with *Father of Frankenstein* and *Gods and Monsters*, you did.

CB   Oh yes. I told Bill Condon early on: "This is your baby. I know I have no control over it. But if you want to pick my brain or bounce ideas off me, please do." And he did. He used my failed ending, but made it his own. He asked me for casting ideas and showed me drafts of his script. He used my good ideas and ignored my bad ones. But he worked very closely to the book. He trusted it. He knew that I'd done a lot of the work already. The book was halfway to being a screenplay. He didn't feel that he needed to put his fingerprints all over the project just to make it his. He used a lot of my dialogue. And he knew what to leave out—which I didn't.

It was a wonderful experience from beginning to end. It's not supposed to be. It didn't hurt that I've written screenplays for short films that Draper directed. So I already knew that what's in your head when you write won't be what appears on the screen. All that really matters is that it works. And *Gods and Monsters* works.

RC   Perhaps it helped that Bill Condon both wrote and directed the movie.

CB   There were fewer cooks in the kitchen. But there were still producers—the money men—and Bill had to explain to them again and again the dynamics of the story. First they feared that Whale was a homophobic stereotype and needed to be softened. Then they feared that Clay was too negative and should be "a straight role model"—as if there's a shortage of those. Bill had to explain how each man was a mess and they needed each other. If you screwed that up, you threw the story out of balance.

RC   In *Father of Frankenstein*, you played with the story's chronology slightly. With *In Memory of Angel Clare*, however, there was a much more radical playing with time. I felt you solved one problem for novels concerning AIDS in those days—the sense of a closed narrative, one that must end with death or loss. You played around that, in the chronological disorder, while not being untrue to the bleak realities of the subject.

CB   You're right. And it wasn't accidental. It's what enabled me to write the book in the first place.

I wanted to write about AIDS. I needed to write about it—not for political reasons but for selfish ones. I wanted to address the pain and fear that was suddenly filling the lives of my friends and myself. But AIDS in the eighties dictated one simple brutal story: you get sick and die. I didn't know how to tell that story without drowning.

I started hearing stories about a particular young man whose older lover had just died of AIDS. First I heard from one friend how badly this boy behaved when his lover was sick. A few months later, however, after the man died, another friend met the boyfriend. He'd become the classic widow. His apartment was a shrine. All he could talk about was his grief for the man whom he had treated obliviously while he was still alive. I wondered: "Who is this person?" So that's where I started the story. It's one year later and Michael, the young widower, has inherited not only his lover's money but his friends. As I needed to explain things to myself or the reader, I'd step back in time, circling and circling the dead man, who we keep hearing about but never meet—not until the next-to-last chapter. I was building up suspense, but also needed to work up my nerve to write a scene from the point of view of a PWA.

I never met the source of the story. I might not have written it if I had. After the book came out, however, people kept asking me if Michael were based on this person or that person. It was always someone different.

RC   Both *In Memory of Angel Clare* and *Father of Frankenstein* are about filmmakers. Angel Clare is a frustrated director whose only movie was a cheesy horror film.

CB   Yes. That was a complete accident. Not until I was in the middle of *Father of Frankenstein* did I realize that James Whale is a successful

"Clare." I'm not sure what that means, if anything. As I said, I like to write about artists, so long as they're not writers. Through Draper I know about Clarence's world of film gypsies. In fact, Clarence's movie—*Disco of the Damned*—is the kind of cheap, sleazy first feature we used to joke about making.

Another connection I didn't recognize until later is that *Father of Frankenstein* is also an AIDS novel. Whale fought in the First World War, when half of his generation perished. He survived. Only now, forty years later, does he find himself mourning the friends he lost. So the novel is full of things—illness, grief, survivor's guilt—that I wouldn't know or need to think about without AIDS.

RC   In all your books, in fact, characters are asked to cross certain borders, and then justify it. In *Gossip* that border is more obviously one of ideology. I wondered how the problems with the characterization of Clay compared to those of the right-winger Bill O'Connor in that book.

CB   Bill was a challenge. I needed to make him round and human enough so that my leftist narrator, Ralph, would find other attractions in him beside the thrill of "sleeping with the enemy." I like to think that, given time, Bill could have become a sane, decent person. But he gets trapped in Republican success, and then killed. But there's a naive quality under all his noise—a hunger for affection. Ralph says at one point that he was a better man in bed than in print.

I like to mix things up. I like to throw different people together in a novel just to see what happens, and also to challenge my own assumptions. That's almost an ideology for me . . . or an aesthetic.

RC   *Almost History* must be at least 50 percent longer than the other novels. How much does a story dictate a book's length to you?

CB   There are fat books and there are lean books. *Surprising Myself* was first conceived as a fat, friendly, nineteenth-century novel, but I had to cut it down to a trimmer yet husky tome. The next two books, *Hold Tight* and *In Memory of Angel Clare*, are fairly short at 250 pages each. I still wanted to write a fat book. *Almost History* was first imagined as a family chronicle about a brother and sister. But the brother, Jim Goodall, a gay

Lord Jim in the foreign service, took over the story before I wrote a word. His sister's daughter, Meg, then became the second protagonist, a young woman my age who becomes a historian. The novel spans thirty-plus years. It was wonderful to work in that kind of space. Afterwards, however, I was exhausted; drained dry. And to be crass: it's harder to sell a fat novel than a lean one. I swore I'd never write another fat one again.

Nevertheless, a few years later, I started to think about writing a picaresque novel about a clairvoyant pianist. He was inspired by Francis Grierson, also known as Jesse Shepherd, a real-life musician and writer described by Edmund Wilson in *Patriotic Gore* and David Bergman in *Gaiety Transfigured*. But I knew it would be a fat book, running from the Civil War to the 1920s. I delayed writing it, and while I delayed, it grew in my head. My clairvoyant pianist falls in love with an ex-slave. (Grierson was gay, but his lover was a Polish tailor from Chicago.) The ex-slave falls in love with a white governess. It could be like Huck and Jim stumbling into a Henry James novel. And then I saw a wonderful documentary called *Coney Island: City of Fire*, which ends with the Dreamland amusement park fire of 1911. So I had my ending. I had no choice now but to write the damn thing: *The Notorious Dr. August: His Real Life and Crimes.*

RC You don't obviously owe a structural debt to any nineteenth-century novelist, however. Your longer books don't feel Victorian.

CB No? You say that as if "Victorian" were pejorative. But you're probably right. Even in *Dr. August*, it's still my voice, with a slightly different beat and vocabulary. There were so many wonderful words I was suddenly free to use: *bombazine, flapdoodle, prevaricate.*

Now that I think about it, though, Victorian novels aren't always fubsy or archaic in their diction. Look at Henry James in *Daisy Miller* or *The Bostonians*. And there's a sort of post-Victorian Victorian novel that combines Victorian scope with modern storytelling—books like Thomas Mann's *Buddenbrooks* or Arnold Bennett's *The Old Wives' Tale*. That's the right period and feel for *Dr. August*.

RC I wanted you to comment on the analogy that Fitz makes between his narrating and his improvisational composition of music. Do you see novel writing in those terms?

CB   Absolutely. I believe the best storytelling is improvisational, with the first draft anyway, and the draft before that—the one in your head. As I said before, I write my novels in order to find out what's going to happen, much as Fitz plays around at the piano in order to find out what he thinks or feels about something. Not until I was deep into *Dr. August*, however, did I realize how much he and I had in common. I don't mean only in our experience with "art" and imagination. There's a good bit of that unconscious autobiography I was talking about earlier.

RC   You introduce a number of encounters with real-life composers. Fitz meets Brahms in Baden-Baden; he attends the Wagner festival at Bayreuth. Did these opportunities present themselves through research?

CB   Yes. Brahms really was in Baden that summer, visiting Clara Schumann. If history gives you something interesting, you should use it. If it doesn't, you can make something up. But I try to keep to the facts when possible.

I love Brahms. I was tickled I could include a performance of his Piano Quintet, one of my favorite pieces of music. It was composed just a few years before Brahms meets Fitz. One of the pleasures of writing the book was that I could indulge my love of classical music, explore new recordings, and imagine how it sounded back when it was new—before it was "classical"; when it was just another piece of the music scene.

RC   In the "Author's Note," you acknowledge a number of historical and reference works. But you also mention visiting Istanbul. Did you need to do that for the book?

CB   Actually, Istanbul was a happy accident. The whole Lady Ashe–Freddie episode was originally going to take place in Venice. But everybody does Venice. It's been done to death, so to speak. But then Draper and I went with friends on a trip to Turkey. I discovered the European section of Istanbul, Pera, which is an imitation Paris built around 1860. When I got home, I did some research about the European community there, saw that Lady Ashe could be part of it, and so Venice was replaced by Constantinople.

RC I was interested in the conceit of Tristan, the "recording angel" of the book. The novel is in first person, but Fitz is dictating his story to Tristan, whose role expands as it goes along. Toward the end he takes on more definite qualities. A rather rarefied, second-person voice emerges. How did your understanding of Tristan alter during the writing of *Dr. August*?

CB Right from the start, with Fitz talking to an invisible "you," I liked the fact that the novel was a conversation between two people, but where you only hear one side. I hoped Tristan would grow—and he did. As the story went on, I found I could play more and more with this person who wasn't there. And it was fun to reveal things about him. Not until a third of the way through the novel do we learn that Tristan is the son of Isaac. Since Isaac is Fitz's lover at this point, we wonder how that happened.

But I continued to discover things about Tristan myself as I wrote. I didn't realize he was gay until just before Fitz found out. It came out of the material. It made sense. And it made good trouble—how would his mother Alice respond?

I'm still intrigued by Tristan. I'd love to write a whole book about him. I'm not yet ready to let him go. That's my separation anxiety again. I'm often reluctant to say goodbye to characters in a novel and hope to write a sequel. I haven't done that yet, but maybe I will with Tristan.

RC He fulfills a role as inheritor of the story which commonly, in historical or dynastic fiction, falls to the offspring of the main characters.

CB Yes, and that can't happen in gay fiction that spans large periods of time. But we can use nephews and nieces, uncles and aunts. I do it with Tristan here. I did it with Meg in *Almost History*. Dorothy Allison plays with similar ideas in *Bastard Out of Carolina*. Gay and lesbian writers have this whole other territory to explore—auntdom and uncledom. We get to have children, even if they're only half shares of your actual chromosomes.

RC Fitz describes himself as "pure mountebank" at one point. Are figures who practice deceit innately interesting?

CB   Sure. They're mysterious. All mysteries are interesting. Fitz is a char-latan, but he's not corruptly corrupt. He's not malicious. His deceptions are all benign. He's like a good actor. He captures a kind of truth by make-believe, by lying. He even helps people with his lies. He's like a good novelist.

RC   There are some bold uses of hindsight in *Dr. August* which seem intentionally to startle the reader out of the book's historic present.

CB   Yes. The past has its own past, and its own future. Fitz tells his story in 1925, so he can suddenly leap forward from the "present" of 1864 to Einstein's theory of relativity. His long life is a lens through which he—and the reader—can see the past enlarged and sharpened. It was fun to play the time card, but I was careful not to do it too much. One thing that drew me to Fitz as a character early on was the idea of somebody who has lived from 1850 to the 1920s—just how much their world has changed. That collision of the old and the new fascinated me.

RC   In general, it's clear that reading has been very important to you as a writer.

CB   As a writer, yes—but also in every other part of my life. Reading is very important to me as a gay man. I mean, I read my way into homosexuality. I wrote an essay about it last year, "A Body in Books: A Memoir in a Reading List," exploring all the books I read.

Looking back on it, I'm amazed by the authors I stumbled on without knowing they were gay—and even before I knew I was gay: Thomas Mann; James Baldwin; E. M. Forster. Early in high school came Thomas Mann—the scope; the ambition; the sheer literariness. As a side benefit, there were all these male infatuations. Mann treated them as perfectly normal. Now we know the truth about him—that his own infatuations were not just adolescent. I recently reread *The Magic Mountain* in a new translation. It's such a proto-gay book. Settembrini is just a garrulous queen—clucking at passing servant girls, sure; but the way he courts the two cousins is like an older gay man.

One of the strangest, happiest accidents was the summer when I was working as a counselor at Boy Scout camp. Another counselor left out a copy of *An End to Innocence* by Leslie Fiedler. What an appropriate title! The book includes Fiedler's famous essay "Come Back to the Raft Ag'in, Huck Honey," where he argues that a major theme of American literature is the flight of the white male into the arms of his black lover. I was stunned. I read it with my mouth wide open. Here I was, sixteen years old, learning that my crushes on other counselors weren't a perversion. They were as American as Huckleberry Finn.

Years later, while working on *Hold Tight*, I realized how much Fiedler was in there, unconsciously. The main characters are Hank Fayette and Juke. Juke sounds a lot like Huck, but starts with a "J" like Jim. Hank Fayette has the same initials as Huckleberry Finn. It all takes place in Gansevoort Street, a haunt of Herman Melville when he was working at the New York Customs House. I saw this about halfway through, and played these aspects up a little. At one point I was jokingly thinking of dedicating the novel to Fiedler.

RC   People sometimes claim this form of "gay liberation"—this journey to self-realization through literature—isn't necessary anymore, now that there's widespread representation of homosexuality in the visual media—in advertising, film; more immediate forms.

CB   Well, things have changed. But a book is still a good, private place to explore your sexuality and try out fantasies about sex and love. A book's like a portable closet—at least without a jacket. With the jacket, it can become a little billboard or handheld placard. But books still offer far more colors and shades of gray than movies or TV. There's more variety, more flexibility.

RC   You clearly have a love of films, though—the very things which some writers fear threaten the novel with obsolescence.

CB   Yes. Sometimes I think of myself as a failed film director. Or not failed, just distracted. In college my ambition was to make movies. The short stories I wrote often began as ideas for a movie. But screenplays are such a bastard form. A screenplay doesn't really exist until it's made as a movie. So I thought I'd write the thing up as a short story instead. By the time I finished college, I was enjoying that much more than I would have enjoyed making movies. For one thing, you can do it without half a million dollars. Also, I don't have the temperament for movies. I'd rather write novels.

I went to college in the seventies, which was a golden age in movies. People were experimenting with new subjects. They said: "Let's do something real!" There was an electricity and excitement about it all, which there very rarely is in movies today. There still is that in fiction. So, for me, the novel has taken over the role movies had in the seventies, and that foreign films had in the fifties and sixties.

RC   In your introduction to the 1998 volume of *Best Gay Erotica*, you talk about the importance of strong sex writing in your development of a gay self. Did it also influence you as a writer?

CB   Definitely. Writing about sex is the most primal kind of writing. Immediately after college, I began to stumble upon good fiction about sex that went beyond porn, that showed how dramatic and expressive the sex act really was. And it wasn't always the usual suspects. One writer was Harold Brodkey. This was around 1974. He was publishing chapters of a work-in-progress, *A Party of Animals*, in the *New American Review*. One—later published as the short story "Innocence"—was a forty-page description of a man trying to bring a woman to orgasm. What I found exciting was that Brodkey was writing through sex to a hundred other different things.

Then there was *The Story of Harold* by Terry Andrews. This is the fictional diary of a children's writer, Terry Andrews—now said to be the pseudonym of George Selden, author of *The Cricket in Times Square*—who loves men and rough sex. What excited me was how the book embedded sex in real life and real emotions. It could juxtapose a lush, lyrical description of fisting a doctor with the account of an evening spent taking care of a sad little toddler.

Other good, strong sex writing followed—sometimes gay, sometimes straight: *Endless Love* by Scott Spencer; *The Family* by David Plante, where a young Catholic boy has an erotic vision of Christ while looking through his father's copy of *Health and Fitness* magazine. Books like these encourage you to take risks. They give you permission to write similarly. They're little keys that unlock your imagination.

RC   What other writers have influenced you in your work?

CB   Influence is hard for me to talk about, simply because I love to read. The variety of my loves dilutes the influences.

There are writers I worship, but I know I write nothing like them. I mean, for me, the four giants are Henry James, Marcel Proust, Virginia Woolf, and Vladimir Nabokov. These are people I read and reread constantly. I'm as fascinated by their lives and careers as I am by their books. And I'm sure I've learned things from them, but I don't write a bit like any of them.

James is a dramatist—as I am, I guess. I don't mean that he's a playwright or plot-driven, but that he needs to dramatize his ideas; bring them to emotional life. He looks for dramatic situations that will enable him to explore his subjects. For the sake of the drama, he can be remarkably generous to his characters, even when he disagrees with them—even when he writes about anarchists. Compare James's radicals in *The Princess Casamassima* to Conrad's in *The Secret Agent*.

Nabokov's a great storyteller, too, which people often forget. His prose style is so glorious that we don't always notice how strong his stories are. He's also the great literary seducer, using language to make readers complicit in the most alien dramas. He, too, is remarkably generous to his characters, with an astounding range of sympathy. His mixture of cruelty and pity is amazing. In an early draft of *Father of Frankenstein*, I toyed with a pesky Nabokovian author-narrator, but I couldn't make it work. It went against the grain of the story. But maybe—and I just thought of this—that laid the groundwork for some of the narrator games I play in *Dr. August*.

Proust isn't just a novelist, but a philosopher, with a complex view of being. He sucked the memory business dry—you can't copy it—but his feeling for social texture and comedy is wonderful. He also wrote great party scenes. He's usually present in any fictional party I create, such as the George Cukor party in *Father of Frankenstein*.

And finally there's Virginia Woolf. I don't think there's a trace of her in my work, even when I've tried to include it, as in *In Memory of Angel*

Clare. I love her quickness; the sharp jumps in her prose; her wild mix of humor and poetry—the heady combination of the lyric and the comic which all of these writers use.

RC   Which nineteenth-century writers have you enjoyed? How about Trollope? I noticed that Ralph in *Gossip* reads the Palliser novels.

CB   I wanted to juxtapose the craziness of contemporary Washington with the quieter, frock-coated craziness of Victorian politics. And I wanted to read more Trollope. But I have a Trollope block. Maybe because a teacher back in college told me I wrote like him—meaning only that I wrote steadily and regularly. I had that reputation even then. Despite my intentions for *Gossip*, I gave up on Trollope again and read George Eliot's *Daniel Deronda* instead—a glorious, exciting mess of a novel.

I love Eliot, especially *Middlemarch.* Her prose can get awfully tangled, but it doesn't matter. The emotion keeps punching through. Tolstoy was my first great love as a writer. I keep moving on but falling back in love with him again. But you can't learn how to write from Tolstoy. He's his own creature. The same's true of Dickens, who I also adore, but there are no lessons there—nothing another writer can build on.

It's the usual suspects. The only odd note in my reading is Thackeray. He writes great dialogue. It doesn't sound stagy, as Dickens's and Eliot's do, even at their best. And there's a wonderful improvisational quality to his writing. You never know from page to page if you're going to get good Thackeray or bad. He can be very bad, or wonderfully wasteful, giving his best lines to minor characters. That makes his novels lifelike.

RC   What about the gay writers you read? You mentioned Terry Andrews and David Plante. What about Christopher Isherwood?

CB   I love Isherwood now, especially *Prater Violet* and *Down There on a Visit.* But he was a little too pure for my tastes back in my twenties. I had to get older to appreciate him.

Somebody I read early on was Jonathan Strong, who wrote a collection of stories called *Tike and Five Stories* back in 1969. One, "Supperburger," concerns a nineteen-year-old, working-class Italian boy who falls in love with a married composer, Arthur Supperburger. He's then passed on by the composer to his college-going nephew Louis. I read that in freshman year and fell totally in love with it. I'd just read and reread it. Part of it was the link to my own experiences. With the other gay books I'd been reading—James Baldwin, John Rechy—it wasn't my world at all, or one I wanted to live in. It was a gothic realm, whereas Strong wrote about an everyday world I knew, albeit through this romantic voice.

RC   How significant were 1970s gay authors like the Violet Quill group?

CB   I've read lots of Edmund White and Andrew Holleran, if that's what you mean. I'm baffled, though, when people talk about the Violet Quill as if it signified something. It's two first-rate writers—White and Holleran—who we'd be talking about whether they met each other or not. And two good writers—Robert Ferro and George Whitmore—who died before they could prove themselves. Otherwise the label is air. These men did not influence or shape each other. The name doesn't even suggest a shared sensibility, the way "Bloomsbury" does. And there's the assumption that the Violet Quill "invented" gay literature as we know it, which is nonsense.

If you want to discuss the rise of post-Stonewall literature, you should talk about Charles Ortleb and *Christopher Street* magazine. Ortleb made enemies later with the *New York Native* and his theories about AIDS. But what he did for gay fiction in the 1970s was remarkable. He and his editors Patrick Merla and Tom Steele did terrific work. I first read White and Holleran and a hundred other gay writers in *Christopher Street*. And I was eventually published there myself, so maybe I'm prejudiced. But I do believe they deserve far more credit than they get.

RC   So did White and Holleran influence you as a gay writer?

CB   Yes and no. They're not like father figures but older siblings. I was already developing my own identity as their books appeared. But their best influence on my work was simply: "These gay men are writing fiction about their lives. I can write about mine too."

I liked Holleran's *Dancer from the Dance* when it first came out, although I wasn't sure why. It doesn't work like a novel. It's all mood and voice. The chief event is what doesn't happen—Malone's ex-lover doesn't kill him. I recently reread it, however, and loved it. It still doesn't work as a novel, but has become a wonderful scrapbook about New York in the seventies—and not just gay New York either. And it's all mood—but what wonderful moods! I remembered the book being soaked in F. Scott Fitzgerald, but now I'm better read and I hear other voices: Capote, Proust, even Firbank.

As I get older, I find myself getting fonder of Holleran's books, for all their weirdnesses. You know, there's always that "Woe is me" note in his work, even before AIDS. He's always been writing elegies: "Oh look at that beautiful boy over there. He'll never look at me. Or if he does, he'll never go to bed with me. Or if he goes to bed with me, he won't call the next day." He's the Eeyore of gay literature. But I find myself enjoying him more and more as I get older. I also find I identify more with Eeyore.

RC   And Edmund White?

CB   I've read White ever since I picked up the Seymour Kleinberg anthology *The Other Persuasion* when I was still in Virginia. It included a short story, "The Beautiful Room Is Empty"—no relation to the later novel. When I started writing for *Christopher Street*, the editor—Patrick Merla— gave me a stack of back issues with the articles that were the basis for *States of Desire*. They were wonderful. I especially liked how White could start with a gay point of view and then capture and characterize an entire city. Then came the short story "First Love," the first chapter of *A Boy's Own Story*, which was published in *Christopher Street* and then in *Aphrodisiac: Fiction from Christopher Street*. I read and reread it. I couldn't wait to read the rest of the book. When it was finally published, however, it wasn't what I'd expected. It felt too episodic and detached. Then I realized that the book I wanted to read was the one I was writing, *Surprising Myself*, so I was re- lieved. Now I can go back to *A Boy's Own Story* and admire it for what it is.

I find something to admire and enjoy in almost all of White's fiction— even the books that don't entirely work. The only book I don't like is *Noc- turnes for the King of Naples*—a silly book—the *Last Year at Marienbad* of gay fiction. I'm baffled by the people who praise it, usually in the course of trashing his later, better, more open books. For me it's a throwback— a tony piece of stoner closet fiction.

The Other Persuasion, by the way, was also where I first read the Jane Rule short story, "Middle Children." It's about two women who become lovers in college. Basically they want to balance their private and public lives together—that is, how much they should live for each other, and how much for the world at large? At that point I think I needed to be told, both as a person and a writer: "You can be gay and it doesn't have to take you out of the world. You're still in the world."

RC   What about Armistead Maupin's *Tales of the City*?

CB   I enjoyed *Tales*. It was like a great comic strip in prose. I love a good comic strip. But it worked even better on film than it did on paper, when you had actors to flesh out the world of the books. I like Maupin's last novel—*The Night Listener*—far more. It's a wonderful novel. It doesn't need actors. It's fully there.

RC   And then there's Larry Kramer. You wrote a generous essay about *Faggots*, arguing that we should listen to the tale and not the teller.

CB   Yes, well, Kramer is a better playwright than he is a novelist, but *Faggots* is not the one-dimensional screed that his enemies or even Kramer said it was. It's as if he believed the attacks and no longer noticed what's in his own book. *Faggots* is actually a very good novel folded up inside a bad novel. The good novel is full of wonderfully dangerous, mixed feelings about sex and love and community, but Kramer can no longer admit that, now that he's become the village scold.

RC   Which other contemporary gay writers do you read?

CB   Well, Alan Hollinghurst. I've read each of his novels twice, despite his cool indifference to story. He will get three or four balls of plot up in the air, and then drop them and toss around a single new ball at the end. But it doesn't matter. I enjoy the prose and sex and texture of his world.
   Allan Gurganus is amazing—as brilliant and inventive as Tony Kushner, who also awes me. There are two stories in *White People*—"Adult Art" and "Blessed Assurance"—that I count among my favorite life-changing works of fiction. Stretches of *Oldest Living Confederate Widow Tells All* offer some of the best American prose since *Moby-Dick*. The ending of *Plays*

Well with Others is stunning: a vision of heaven that is both comic and chilling after the AIDS deaths that precede it.

And then there's Paul Russell, who's a friend, but we became friends because we like each other's work.

RC   Both Russell and Gurganus are fascinated by breadth.

CB   They both love to swing from the macro to the micro. The scope of Russell's *Sea of Tranquillity* is extraordinary, ranging from two teenagers fucking in a basement to the astronaut father of one walking on the moon. His next book, *The Coming Storm*, is utterly earthbound, with four protagonists in the very real world of a prep school: a sexually repressed headmaster; his wife, who understands him better than he understands himself; a young, new teacher who's gay; and a fifteen-year-old boy discovering sex. Each time you're reading one of those characters, you want to stay with him or her.

All three writers—Gurganus, Kushner, and Russell—have capacious, generous imaginations. They want to write it all, gay and straight, but from a gay perspective. Michael Cunningham is like that, too. I especially enjoyed *A Home at the End of the World*.

These are exciting works. They start with a gay point of view, but go on to take in the whole world. This isn't to dismiss ghetto writers. I don't think even ghetto writers are sealed off from the rest of the world. The world can't help spilling in.

The frustrating side of all of this is the mainstream doesn't want to be seen through our eyes. They get very uncomfortable when gay people write about straight people. Read some of the reviews that Cunningham got for *Flesh and Blood*. There's this indignant note of "How dare a gay man talk about us?"

RC   Isn't there something implicitly political about granting gay experience some importance alongside heterosexual lives too?

CB   Definitely. Straight people have far more in common with gay people than they care to admit. The critic Michael Bronski was at a symposium several years ago when the question came up: "Are gay people different from straight people?" He surprised everyone who knew his politics by saying: "No. They're the same. It's just that straight people lie about it."

Back in the early sixties there was a slew of attacks on Edward Albee and Tennessee Williams. They were claiming: "These are gay men, and they're writing about gay life under disguise. They're not really telling us anything about us." Yes, they are! Nowadays, we have gay writers saying: "We're gay, and we're going to tell you about us—and about you."

RC   Despite the number of books being published, you don't sound too optimistic about the future of gay-themed literature.

CB   Not this week. A few years ago I thought: "It's going to happen soon. The breakthrough's around the corner. They will read our books as naturally as we read theirs." But I'm getting impatient. Even Michael Cunningham, after the success of *The Hours*, said in an interview: "I can't help noticing that as soon as I write a novel without a blowjob, they give me the Pulitzer Prize."

RC   It's weird to think of where we've come in twenty-five years. There used to be straight novelists writing about gay experience—Iris Murdoch, say. Maybe the appearance of identity categories makes other writers think they shouldn't write about gay characters.

CB   But Murdoch was an exception. Some of her gay men are actually better than her women. She was quite pansexual herself.

Things are changing, just not as quickly as I'd like. Nowadays there are several good straight writers who include gay people in their worlds. Peter Carey in *Jack Maggs*, his twisting of *Great Expectations*, has a gay Pip and a gay footman. An Israeli novelist, A. B. Yehoshua, wrote a terrific novel called *Late Divorce*, with a gay son and the son's lover. The lover is likable, and he and the father become friends. The son's a shit—not because he's gay but because he's too much like the father.

The writers are smarter than the reviewers. I like to think the readers are smarter, too, but they haven't caught up with the books.

RC   You seem to read very widely.

CB I'm very promiscuous. I read lots of contemporary fiction. I'm always hungry for news. Russell Banks; Nadine Gordimer. A few years ago I read all of Gordimer, looking for ways to write about politics. Then Mary Gordon, especially *The Other Side*, which is like a *Mrs. Dalloway* set in Queens. Bharati Mukherjee, an Indian-American writer. She grew up in India but went to college in Iowa and has been in the United States ever since. She wrote an incredible book, *Jasmine*. The first chapter's about being an eight-year-old girl in a village in the Punjab. In the second, she's twenty-six and married to a banker in Nebraska. The rest of the novel is about how she got from one place to the other.

And Yehoshua, who should be a household name. He seems to be able to get into the skin of anyone—male, female, young, old, Jew, Arab. More recently I read all of Charles Baxter, a great short-story writer who has also written an amazing novel, *Feast of Love*. He too includes gay men and women in his world. I'm not saying that's required, but I've noticed that writers I like will eventually write about gay men and lesbians. After all, we're a great subject.

I read a lot of history and, more recently, tons of biography. I'm not sure why I'm suddenly addicted to biography. Maybe it's middle age. I want to know what shape a life might have. I read some poetry, some philosophy—just enough to get me in trouble. I read more literary criticism than is probably good for me.

RC You don't find it useful for your craft?

CB Not really. Literary criticism is all about meaning, not about how to achieve meaning. And it's full of things that a writer has to unlearn—those clever systems of metaphor we used to hear about in New Criticism, or the abstract anti-meanings we get in post-structuralism. They just get in the way when you try to do them deliberately.

The most useful critic I ever read—the one who taught me the most about storytelling, and something about life too—is Pauline Kael, the film critic. She was wonderful about story construction and the games we play with genre—how you can achieve serious ends by playful means. She was not afraid to bring her own life into her criticism of a movie—just as a reader brings his or her own life into the reading of a book. And she wasn't afraid of sex or humor. She loved their complications. She understood how the disruptive energy of lust can feed a work of art. Draper and I own all her books. She takes up a whole shelf at home, under my volumes of Edmund Wilson. But I reread her more often than I reread Wilson.

I reviewed movies for the *New York Native* back in the eighties, and quickly learned there was too much Kael in my voice. I experienced more anxiety of influence over her than with any other writer. That might be why I stopped reviewing movies.

A few years ago, Draper and I got a chance to meet her. We drove up to Great Barrington, where Kael lived in a big Victorian gingerbread monstrosity. We took her out to lunch. She was a short, friendly, feisty, opinionated old lady. As Draper said afterwards, she was like a grandmother, but one who said "shit" and "fuck" a lot.

RC   Now, a leap. Are you able to support yourself as a novelist?

CB   Usually. I haven't had to take a full-time job since I sold my second novel back in 1987. But I've done most things writers do to make ends meet: teaching, freelance journalism, even some screenwriting. Screenplays are all structure and dialogue, the two things that come easiest to me. The hard stuff—character, psychology, description, texture—are added by the actors and director. It pays better than novels. On the downside, most screenplays never get filmed and are read by only four people.

I enjoy teaching too. I've been writer in residence at a couple of schools, including my own alma mater, William and Mary. But I can't write while I teach. It seems to draw on the same performance side of my brain. Also, you find yourself being very wise and all-knowing with students, only to find when you sit down with your blank page that you're just as stupid as ever.

Oh, and I also edited porn for a few months as an associate editor for *Torso*, *Inches*, and *Mandate*.

RC   You seem to have been very prolific—especially in the early years.

CB   It looks that way, but it's misleading. I took seven years to write *Surprising Myself*. It went through three complete drafts. The next two books took about nine months each. It was like I had all this energy built up. I was overjoyed just to be writing something new. Looking back, I'm amazed I wrote both *Hold Tight* and *In Memory of Angel Clare* so quickly. *Almost History* took much longer. It's fatter. Also, as you get older, your energy goes down. You grow more self-critical. You explore things a little more slowly.

RC   But you've never been stuck for an idea for the next novel?

CB   Not yet. There's usually six months between the time I finish a book and start another. But I often have all this energy when I finish and immediately start making notes for the next project.

RC   Are you friends with other novelists? Are you part of a literary group?

CB   I'm good friends with several writers, but not many novelists. Even those whose work I admire—Gurganus and Merlis—I see rarely. I know them chiefly through their work. I've become close to Paul Russell over the years, but Paul's up in Poughkeepsie. We talk on the phone every month or so, but he rarely gets to New York.

On the other hand, there's my friend Ed Sikov, who lives just around the corner. Ed's a biographer, author of books about Billy Wilder and Peter Sellers. We see each other once a week anyway, and have a million other things to discuss besides our work. But we read each other's works in progress. There's Michael Bronski up in Boston, who's a culture critic and historian—incredibly well-read; the great unnatural resource of gay and lesbian letters. We talk on the phone regularly.

There are playwright friends—Craig Lucas and Tony Kushner—who I see rarely. They're often in my head. And there's Victor Bumbalo, an excellent playwright, author of *Adam and the Experts* and *What Are Tuesdays Like*. He moved to L.A. a few years ago, but we talk or visit regularly, and we recommend books to each other. He turned me on to Arnold Bennett.

I've met most of my peers, who can be interesting. But you usually get the best of a writer in his books. The first time I ever went to the baths—

I was shy back in the seventies—was in 1992 with Andrew Holleran. This was down in Miami at a literary festival. One night, a pack of gay writers went to the baths together. Andrew and I just sat on a bench in our towels and talked about books. Andrew would jump up now and then to see what was going on down the hall, but would return and resume conversation. I don't think either of us got laid that night. Well, I know I didn't.

RC   But you don't need the company of other novelists?

CB   I read them and hope they read me. Maybe that's company enough. But writing, like reading, is a fairly solitary activity. We like our myths about wolf packs of writers—Bloomsbury or the Violet Quill. But we all do our best work alone. Part of the appeal for me of filmmaking and theater as subjects for my novels is that these are highly social, collaborative worlds where you get lots of company.

More important than the company of writers is having a few trustworthy readers—good friends who can read a work in progress. I've accumulated five or six people over the years who I trust. One, Mary Gentile, I've known since college. The most recent is Paul Russell. We found that we not only liked each other's fiction, but could talk about raw work in a mutually useful manner. But the best reader doesn't have to be a writer. Mary used to teach at Harvard Business School but is now a consultant in diversity training. And Draper is an invaluable, ruthless reader, although his experience with film editing makes him a kind of writer.

I've also been lucky in my agents—first Eric Ashworth; now Edward Hibbert—and my editors and even copyeditors. I've hit upon some wonderful details or turns of phrase only because a smart copyeditor flagged a dubious sentence on my manuscript.

Gertrude Stein once said that she wrote only for herself and strangers. That might be why her writing became less readable as her career went on.

RC   You talk a lot about movies. Do you think you'd be happier as a screenwriter or a director than as a novelist?

CB   There are things I love about movies that you can't get in novels. Actors—God, I love actors. What they can express with a look or inflection! And I love good photography. And music. But it takes a million dollars to make even a small movie. And it can take years to convince a few un-imaginative people with money that your movie is worth making. With a novel it's just you and your brain and many, many, many hours alone. My only real complaint about novels is that there are more moviegoers than readers.

But it's all about telling stories. I just want to tell stories. Whatever medium tells the story is enough for me, no matter what the numbers are.

RC Bill Condon's screenplay for *Gods and Monsters* won an Oscar. Did your own career change as a result?

CB Not really. Alas. You'd think movie people would be snatching up my other books, but no. *Gossip* was optioned by a young producer, but that was before *Gods and Monsters*. Never underestimate the homopho-bia of Hollywood. Even now, even after the success of wonderful work like *Six Feet Under* or lousy work like the American *Queer as Folk*. They dislike gay material—especially the gay people in the business; even when they're out themselves. Very few are in the closet anymore. But they don't want to be seen as too gay, or narrowly gay, or politically gay. They want to be seen as universal. I often joke that I'd sell out in a minute, if only someone were buying. But being a gay writer has kept me honest.

However, I should add that the movie experience itself was amazing. You can't imagine how wonderful it is to hear your words delivered by people like Ian McKellen or Lynn Redgrave. Or what it's like to sit in a box at Lincoln Center during the New York Film Festival while a very smart audience of a thousand people catches every joke, every shift in emotion. And then it's over and they erupt into a storm of applause. Nov-elists don't get that. We don't get a thousand readers reading a book to-gether and finishing it at the same time—though maybe, just maybe, it's going on in secret, dispersed all over the world.

RC On that hopeful note, thanks very much for your time.

FOUR

MICHAEL CUNNINGHAM

MICHAEL CUNNINGHAM is best known as the author of three novels: *A Home at the End of the World*, *Flesh and Blood*, and *The Hours*.

Cunningham was born in Cincinnati, Ohio, in 1952 and grew up in Chicago, Germany, and—mostly—Los Angeles. He received his B.A. in English Literature from Stanford University in 1975, and then moved to San Francisco for two years. In 1978, Cunningham enrolled in the University of Iowa Writers' Workshop, and was awarded the M.F.A. in 1980. He was then resident author at the Provincetown Fine Arts Work Center for a year, before moving to New York, where he still lives. A number of short stories were published in the early 1980s: "Cleaving" in the *Atlantic Monthly* (January 1981), "Bedrock" in *Redbook* (April 1981), and "Pearls" in *Paris Review* (Fall 1982). Cunningham's first novel, *Golden States* (New York: Crown, 1984), followed in 1984.

Two more stories appeared in the late 1980s: "White Angel" in the *New Yorker* (July 25, 1988) and "Clean Dreams" in *Wigwag* (August 1990). The former later formed part of Cunningham's second novel, *A Home at the End of the World* (New York: Farrar, Straus, and Giroux, 1990), and was selected for Shannon Ravenel and Margaret Eleanor Atwood, eds., *Best American Short Stories 1989* (New York: Houghton Mifflin, 1989), and for Ethan Mordden, ed., *Waves: An Anthology of New Gay Fiction* (New York: Vintage, 1994). *Flesh and Blood* (New York: Farrar, Straus and Giroux, 1995), Cunningham's next novel, appeared five years later. In 1993, Cunningham was awarded a Guggenheim Fellowship, and in 1998 he received a National Endowment for the Arts Fellowship.

An essay on New York drag culture, "Slap of Love," appeared in *Open City*, no. 6. *The Hours* (New York: Farrar, Straus, and Giroux, 1998), Cunningham's most recent and celebrated novel, was in part inspired by Virginia Woolf's *Mrs. Dalloway*, and features the English author as a character. It won both the 1999 Pulitzer Prize for Fiction and the PEN/Faulkner Award for Fiction. It was subsequently adapted for film by screenwriter David Hare and director Stephen Daldry (2002).

Cunningham currently teaches in the Creative Writing Program at Brooklyn College, having previously taught at Columbia University. He wrote the introduction to the Modern Library edition of Virginia Woolf's *The Voyage Out* (New York: Random House, 2000), and to a reissued edition of Matthew Stadler's 1993 novel, *The Dissolution of Nicholas Dee: His Researches* (New York: Grove Press, 2000). *Land's End: A Walk Through Provincetown* (New York: Crown, 2002), Cunningham's account of the Cape Cod town, is his most recent publication.

The interview took place on November 3, 1997, at Michael Cunningham's home in New York. It was revised in October 2002, at which point the section following the asterisks was added.

RC   I didn't realize at first that your career had been in two stages, as it were—that there had been an early novel, *Golden States*, which came out in 1984.

MC   I don't think of it in terms of stages, but I do have a largely unacknowledged first novel which I don't mean to conceal. The book's not some kind of secret. I wrote it in a bit of panic. Without quite meaning to, I frittered away my twenties. I was looking at becoming thirty. I'd published some stories, and kept starting novels and then abandoning them. I was overwhelmed by the immensity of the work, and by my fears of just not being good enough—by my sense of the ghosts of everyone from Tol-stoy to Radclyffe Hall staring down their noses at me, wondering how I could dare to imagine that I could do something like this. I wrote *Golden States* in order to have finished a novel by the time I was thirty. I wrote it in about forty-five minutes.

It's not a bad book, but it's not good enough. It spurred me into action, so I'm very glad to have written it. That seems to me to have been its pri-mary purpose. Even at the time it came out, I was never anxious for it to have an extensive life in the world. Writers crank out too many books that aren't the best goddamn book they could possibly write—that don't con-tain much in the way of heart's blood. I feel like we as readers are all drowning in "OK books." I just didn't want to add another one to the stack. I don't mean by implication to make inflated claims for the subse-quent two books, but they were the best ones I could have written at the time. I don't feel embarrassed to offer them to the world. The first book felt like practice to me.

RC   Has the question of republication come up?

MC   Yes. It persistently comes up, now that the other books have done all right. But I'm adamant about that: it will not be reissued. It's done. It served its purpose. Jeanette Winterson has a book no one knows about—*Boating for Beginners*, her second. It's my impression that that book dis-appeared for similar reasons. Winterson simply didn't think it was part of a dialogue. Doctorow has a book no one knows of. I think it's a perfectly valid practice—simply to shoot down a book that you don't feel can make some kind of necessary contribution.

RC   I was looking at narrative approaches in *A Home at the End of the World* and *Flesh and Blood*. In the former, there's an elaborate series of first-person narrators; in the latter, you deployed third-person narration. It made me want to know what the trajectory was from the first book, and what your experience of moving between voices had been.

MC   To me those two books are part of a series. The series is now com-plete; it's those two books. What links them isn't so much a question of voice or scope or things like that, though those aren't uninteresting questions. Both books were written during the first ten years of the AIDS epidemic, and they're meant to be books for people who are mortally ill. I found myself wanting to write for the friends I had who were very sick and who had time to read only five, maybe ten more books. Many of these people—though they were intelligent, aware members of the species—were not the kind of dedicated readers to whom you'd take Plato, or even Chekhov. It was too late to start them on Henry James. They simply wouldn't have gotten it. I found that there weren't to my satisfaction enough books to take to gay men who were very ill. There weren't enough books about their lives, certainly, and there weren't enough books about gay lives that delivered something that felt emotionally true—books that weren't trash, but were accessible. You write a book for a lot of reasons, and this certainly wasn't the only one. But it was on my mind—that among the missing books in the world are books that have to do with the lives and passions of gay men, told in a fairly simple, straightforward way.

RC   You must be aware of the fact that some writers would run a mile from the idea of a dedicated readership, however hypothetical, or the idea of the impulse for a book coming from this almost ideological consideration.

MC   Well, that's simply how it worked for me with those two books. It's not true any more. While I was writing them, one of the real conflicts was the whole question of whether—in the middle of an epidemic, with a government doing nothing or very little—these were the years of Reagan and then Bush—it was morally defensible to be writing novels at all. I didn't have any particular illusions about Reagan or Bush walking into an office in the morning and saying: "I've just read this book by Michael Cunningham, and I've realized . . . "

Yet writing novels is what I do. It's what I'm best at doing. And the books aren't especially political. But I do think they represent in some way an attempt on my part to bridge the gap between my life as an artist, if that's not too unbearably portentous a phrase, and a life devoted to political activism. At the time, I was especially cranky about the idea that "my art is my contribution." I was like: "No, your contribution is storming the White House."

RC   As you suggest, that spirit of activism didn't enter the books so directly.

MC   Not especially, no. They're books for a lot of people, among them people with AIDS, that attempt to offer something of some depth about our lives during that particular period. Writing political novels didn't feel like the answer, partly because it's not something I can do. I'm not especially interested in political novels. At the same time, I felt a certain imperative to write a certain kind of book, in a certain kind of way.

RC   When did you begin to think of them as a series?

MC   It wasn't anything so self-conscious in the making as: "I'll now spend the next ten years of my life writing two books for people surviving the epidemic." I wrote one book; it didn't feel quite complete, and I wrote another. Now I feel done with it. It's intuitive. You have sated yourself.

RC   After *Flesh and Blood*, did you feel a new subject calling to you, or just that this subject was done?

MC   "Subject" is a slightly problematic term. This strategy felt done—the attempt to write very straightforward, accessible books for people who are by no means stupid, but don't necessarily read a lot of books. I wanted to write a very reader-friendly kind of book then. I'm not interested in doing that anymore. The one I'm finishing now—*The Hours*—is very different; much more complicated. I'm afraid it marks the end of cute boys coming up to me at the gym, telling me how much they like my work, which I'll miss. It's a triptych involving an imagined day in the life of Virginia Woolf as she was writing *Mrs. Dalloway*; a re-creation of Mrs. Dalloway as a woman in New York during the AIDS epidemic; and a day in my mother's life, during which the book she's reading is *Mrs. Dalloway*.

RC   You call the book a triptych. But do you think of it as narratively whole?

MC   Yes. It's these three days, told in alternating chapters, each one of which reverberates with the others.

RC   Your experience of AIDS in New York still features centrally though.

MC   Yes. That's my world, just as it would be crazy for Nadine Gordimer not to write about South Africa.

RC   It sounds as if in the case of the earlier two books, the form was shaped in some sense at will and from the outset, once you'd made the decision about accessibility. How much is generally determined of your novels at the outset?

MC   In retrospect, things usually feel more conscious and deliberate than they ever were at the time. I didn't begin *A Home at the End of the World* thinking: "I'll now write an accessible book for people with AIDS." But I did want to write something useful for particular people I knew. I always write for someone. That certainly directed the way that book went. As I was writing, I made decisions along certain lines that began to reveal themselves as having to do with accessibility. But one's intentions to some extent reveal themselves as one goes along. I didn't sit down with *The Hours*, saying: "Now I'll write a difficult book—one which people have to have read a great deal of Virginia Woolf in order to comprehend.

RC   When did the idea of the triptych occur to you?

MC   That developed later too. My original idea was to rewrite *Mrs. Dalloway*, set in New York today. I got a ways into that, and it began to seem like a parlor trick. I thought: "Why do something like this; something that was only interesting to me, and on some days not even sufficiently interesting to me?" I thought I was going to have to dump it. I thought: "Well, not every idea pans out." But I continued to mess with it, and to write notes about it. I started to ask myself: "Why, with your limited lifespan and energies, and a limited number of books to write, why *Mrs. Dalloway*, of all books?"

RC   You'd made the intellectual link between Woolf's fictional world and the impact of AIDS on New York?

MC   Yes. The whole notion of the contrast between Mrs. Dalloway, who has survived the war, and Septimus Smith, who hasn't really, reverberated for me—as someone who is HIV-negative, trying to minister to people who were not. That was a briefly interesting idea that lost steam. But then I went from Mrs. Dalloway to my mother to Virginia Woolf, and what it has turned into does feel like a book to me. It's moved quite a way from some kind of fool notion about just rewriting *Mrs. Dalloway*.

RC   In the course of writing, does the sense of a book's scale, even of its size, preoccupy you?

MC   Oh yes. I'm a size queen. I always want to write the biggest book I possibly can. There's scope and then there's size, though. I've been so very steeped in Woolf these last couple of years, I feel a great kinship at least now and probably forever with her determination; with her insistence upon finding the enormity in the parlor, as it were; with the idea that the movement of nations, wars, and religions—all the big subjects of literature—are present right here.

RC   She had a deliberately perverse relationship to narrative size in relation to size of theme, though. I'm thinking of trapping the First World War in the middle section of *To the Lighthouse*, for example. She could write things in either diminished or accelerated ways, not to diminish their impact but to render that impact on a deliberately limited canvas. Has that been influencing you?

MC   Absolutely. I don't know how it will affect subsequent books. But I've become increasingly interested in trying to split the atom, as it were;

to find the profound in the commonplace; to see what can be made of the world in an ordinary day in an ordinary life. Forgive me, Virginia Woolf, but *Ulysses* is of course the ultimate expression of this impulse. I feel more temperamentally aligned to Woolf, but Joyce produced the singular achievement in this area—the ordinary squeezed so hard that it finally explodes into something that feels like the galaxy.

RC   Does *The Hours* more resemble *Ulysses* in size?

MC   Well, my books are absolutely getting bigger in scope and, simultaneously, more compact. They're not getting bigger in terms of length or the time period they describe.

RC   The ending of *Flesh and Blood* saw you drawn to some very daring narrative moves. There were chapters of great concision and precision— but wide-opening scope. Can we see these as indications of the way you'll be moving away from the more immediate and accessible narrative elements of that book and its predecessor?

MC   Yes. *The Hours*, successful or not—I feel like I have to say that, in case something with leathery wings is flying overhead, listening for authors who are too confident about their books—is a huge step, in terms of experimentation; of pushing narrative voice, and seeing what I can make it do that has not yet been done.

RC   I want to return to your deployment of the third-person voice in *Flesh and Blood*. Presumably one of the challenges with *A Home at the End of the World* had been to perfect this range of very distinct voices. Why did you switch?

MC   This may be a disappointingly prosaic answer, but having tried it one way, one tries it another way. I think it might be as simple as that.

RC   Was the variety of voices in *A Home at the End of the World* hard to master?

MC   Yes and no. It *was* difficult . . . But everything's difficult. I didn't end that book thinking: "Phew, I'll never do that again! Now I've learned my lesson." This is all on a rather mundane level, but that's where this question resides for me. There are great advantages to writing a book in the first person, whether it's one of a series of voices or not. You can work with a much more inflected voice. You can perform pirouettes that would seem too mannered in the third person. You can go more effortlessly—more deeply—into the character's psyche and poke around at the soul, for the lack of a more precise term. But in the first person, you're also trapped inside that character's skull. There's something tremendously liberating about simply exiting those people's heads and writing from somewhere up in the ether.

RC   Moving between narrative "I's," though, must create especial difficulties. To produce a narrative structure like that, did you move between the voices with ease?

MC   Yes. It's essentially impossible to create life on paper. Then, once in a while, someone does. Once in a very great while. But it's essentially a doomed enterprise. Given that, as a writer, it seems to me you set yourself the most difficult possible task, then you have to find the easiest possible way to do it. It seemed most possible to write that book that way, using those different voices.

RC   When you talk in terms of "tasks," one crude way of thinking of the difficulties of writing fiction relates to the particular problems of narrative closure and endings. I wanted to ask two questions about the figure of Eric in *A Home at the End of the World*: first, given what you said about writing for and about people with AIDS, why was this figure not given a first-person "I" narration? The second was whether that book's close, with all its ambiguity, was conditioned by your writing of the novel, or whether it had always been clear.

MC   I had no idea how that would end as I wrote. I never do. I wouldn't want to. I think of something Flannery O'Connor said. In addition to being a remarkable writer, she said some of the smartest things about writing. I find myself quoting her all the time. She said: "How can there be any surprise for the reader if there hasn't been any for the writer?" I'd rather let it happen and see where it goes.

In the writing of *A Home at the End of the World*, what I originally set out to do was tell this story from the points of view of these two men, Bobby and Jonathan, using alternating chapters. That seemed the best possible way to scale them out. I knew it was going to be a long, ragged story that spanned a great deal of time, and one that was semiautobiographical. As I went along, I found these two voices became claustrophobic and almost cloying. There was this unarticulated love affair between the two men, one of whom isn't exactly gay. It kept veering too far toward sentimentality. I don't mind going very close to sentimentality, and even occasionally going over the line—at least, I hadn't minded with these books, but only up to a point. I was in New Orleans, where I went to live for a while, and it occurred to me that if a third character had a voice, then that person could train some kind of dispassionate eye on the relationship between the two men so that it would reverberate in a whole different way. Something really bracing and sour could come into the mix. So I gave Alice a voice—Jonathan's mother. That felt like the way forward. Then I went voice crazy, and everyone had a voice. There are discarded chapters in the voice of just about every character. Household appliances had voices in various drafts. It became cacophonous and unfocused, of course. There was a sense of having let all these people gather in a room and let them all talk at once about their lives and passions. That became unruly. So I narrowed it down to the four final voices—two men, two women.

RC   Did this involve rewriting certain episodes?

MC   Some. And the simple discarding of some tangents that had seemed germane at the time but in the end were much less so. There are voices for the people who are in love. Everyone's in love, complicatedly and with a number of people, but essentially it's four people in love with each other, and it's their four voices.

RC   You spoke of the genesis of the story with Jonathan and Bobby. It made me think of how people have reacted to the ending of the book.

Does it suggest, as some have argued, that there's no place for Clare? The book arrives at the last of hundreds of different models of family; Clare, it seems, withdraws from it.

MC   Yes. There were questions concerning what we were to make about my feelings about the fate of alternative families—as if I had definitive views on the subject, and as if I'd consider a novel the appropriate place to air them. It came up a surprising amount, too—which raises the whole question of why people read novels. As I said, I create the characters, zap them with enough lightning bolts to bring them to some kind of life, and then see what they do. I think if the book has a theme along those lines, it's simply this: traditional families don't seem to work very well. The idealized alternative families we create for ourselves don't seem to work very well either. Something's dark in human relations. As for our wholly admirable but partly deluded notion that "this time we'll get it right"—well, we do get it more right. I've been with somebody for ten yours. I'm more than happy. It's a much better relationship than any other I've had. But still there's a kind of idealization I resist.

With *A Home at the End of the World*, it's truly and simply the story of these particular people. There's a parallel universe in which Clare or someone not quite like Clare but in her position stays very happily, and they all live very happily, raise their child, and have an embattled but real, ongoing, family life: three adults and a baby. I don't count it out; it's just not what happened to these people.

One summons up the characters and tries to let them choose. Once you've got them going, it's like: "Wow, they're going to do that?" Sometimes it's not what you'd want them to do. They don't always make the ending that you'd necessarily want for yourself or for your characters. But it's the ending they make.

RC   Have the two novels had interest from filmmakers?

MC   Both books have. *A Home at the End of the World* has been optioned by somebody good—an actor named Tom Hulce. He's wonderful; very smart. He has a young playwright doing the screenplay.

RC   You wouldn't have anything to do with it?

MC   Actually I did rewrite the screenplay for *Flesh and Blood*, which was optioned by a big studio. It looks like it's going down in flames though. It's not the kind of book Twentieth Century Fox wants to make into a movie. But somehow they thought for a minute that they did, optioned it, paid a great deal of money to a screenwriter to try to adapt it. You don't want to know what he did to it. I tried to fix it, and didn't do a bad job, but I think it probably isn't tenable. It's just not—right. I have some kind of hopes for *A Home at the End of the World*. I don't know if it's any more conducive to film. It's going to lose a lot, but the people involved in it—who have no money and a great deal of passion—have managed to get something done.

RC   Back to parallels between the two books: they're both analyses of the family, from the fifties, and how families fall apart, real and invented.

MC   Yes . . . I clearly have some real kind of fixation on families, which is one of those things you begin to see as the books start to pile up. I certainly couldn't have told you that several years ago.

RC   You spoke of giving the third voice in *A Home at the End of the World* to Jonathan's mother. That was interesting because, looking at your books in terms of narrative, one of the striking things is the relationship between relational dynamics which are horizontal—between friends and peer groups—and those which are vertical: family affiliations and so on. Clare talks about how different she found the experience of becoming a mother, and how much stronger this vertical bond was than any horizontal one she had felt. You describe strong tensions between these two kinds of ties. That is, I suppose, obviously a rather universal tension, but it's something that many gay novels don't tackle honestly.

MC   That's true. One thing I've found missing in a lot of books about gay people is that they seem to take place in some gay corner of the universe where straight people barely exist. But it's been my experience that they exist in abundance and are quite intrusive, and are often difficult and often quite wonderful. It's always felt important to me when writing about a gay character to place him or her in context, in a world in which most people aren't gay.

RC   It's interesting that you use the word "context" here, rather than thinking of it as distinct, "nongay" subject matter. Often gay writers and readers assume an "either/or" position, where one chooses either "gayness" as a subject, or something else—the family; whatever. What you're suggesting is the impossibility of the one subject without the other.

MC   That's exactly right. I want to write about the biggest world I possibly can. I know what I know about gay people, but I know a lot of other things. [*Laughs*] It would be a shame not to write about those as well.

RC   Likewise, one could just as easily describe your novels as being about America or about the family as being "about AIDS." Thinking specifically of literature that considers AIDS, which other works have explored the subject in a similarly expansive canvas? Perhaps too easily, Tony Kushner's *Angels in America* comes to mind. It occurred to me when I reread *Flesh and Blood*. The space given to the father and his views in that book reminded me of Kushner giving space to his political antagonists in *Angels in America*. That seems to me the one work which has attempted a similar scope.

MC   I'm thrilled that you mention *Angels in America*. After I finished *A Home at the End of the World*, I was writing a piece for the *New York Times* about gay theater. It was just as a musical called *Falsettoes* was about to open. I went and saw anything being performed by anyone that had anything to do with being gay or lesbian. Everything was horrible. A friend of mine said: "There's this play at the National Theatre in London by somebody named Tony Kushner," who I'd vaguely heard of. He'd something produced here a few years before, which was supposed to have been remarkable. She got me his agent's name. I called the agent and said: "I've heard there's this great play which is supposed to come to America eventually. Could I possibly see a copy?" This was only *Millennium Approaches*, the first half. So it arrived. I read it and just thought: "Finally—thank God!" It's a remarkable play. There's a sort of greatness in it. It was the first thing about being gay during the epidemic in America that really thrilled me—that made me envious.

RC   The lack of many fictional works of similar ambition concerning AIDS might seem more surprising.

MC   It's surprising to me too.

RC   Subsequently, there have been attempts at an epic, "postwar" gay novel featuring AIDS . . .

MC   Yes. I think they're awful. It seems that this very interesting idea has been taken up by some of the least interesting writers. It seems to have become largely the province of gay hacks. The gay writers I think of as serious don't seem to want to do it.

Flesh and Blood and these books were often lumped together, which was horrifying to me. That's one of those things you can't control, though *Flesh and Blood* does have an obviously pulpy affinity with them. I hoped to work authentically with an essentially pulpy form. Then, lo and behold—all of these actual pulp gay romances came out! But the gay writers I'm really interested in, like Alan Hollinghurst, Dale Peck, Edmund White—these people aren't writing this kind of book. Edmund White's a great writer—though I didn't like *The Farewell Symphony* that much. He's the real thing, so by definition there'd have to be good things in it. I don't think he could keep them out. But it feels slightly like a book from an early era—from a time when "practicing homosexual tells all" was still an interesting notion, which it isn't anymore.

RC   These are writers, then, that you'd make an effort to read. Are there any other books on AIDS that have worked for you?

MC   Paul Monette's a problematic figure, in that I'm not especially drawn to him as a writer, but hugely as a force and figure. I'm really conscious of him writing those books as fast as he could because there just wasn't time. They feel that way, and they suffer as books, yet there's something tremendously compelling about the way he had to clatter them out. I guess it's a funny way to think of literature, yet I can't help it: they've been hugely useful books to people. I was asked by somebody to review his last novel, *Afterlife*, but I wouldn't do it because I knew I'd feel strange giving it a rave. It's not well written enough. But Monette's a serious artist who produced less serious art as he had to get as much down as he possibly could.

There's an awful lot I haven't read. What's piled around here aren't gay books. The new DeLillo's on the floor. There's the new Harold Brodkey, arguably a gay writer.

RC   Has he been important to you?

MC   Hugely. Even that unreadable novel of his I sort of love. I like Peter Cameron's books. But I don't make my decisions on the basis of sexuality. I don't choose books by "gay writers," or books on AIDS. If that's what happens to turn up, and I've reason to believe it may be great, I'll get it.

RC   Both Brodkey and DeLillo write prose of great ambition—again, always seeking the largest scale and canvas. DeLillo especially attempts the bravura statement.

MC   Yes. I seem to be mainly interested in that . . . I don't know how to put it. There's this intractable mystery of trying to create life on paper. Anyone who seems to be managing that, in whatever way. For me it usually involves some remarkable, magical voice—something unlike anything I've read before—so: Brodkey; DeLillo; Denis Johnson—whoever. The subject is secondary. It's not immaterial, but it's not what drives me.

RC   Let's go further back in literature. Who are the writers who made you want to write—or even the writers who made you think: "I can never write"?

MC   Often they're the same person. Tolstoy was hugely important to me. And Flaubert. I had a half-assed high school education, which was partly my fault. I could have insisted on a better one but didn't. I was lazy, and taking too many drugs. It wasn't until my senior year in high school that somebody forced me to read *Madame Bovary*. It knocked me out. It turned my head inside out. It happened to be that book. If somebody had made me read *Anna Karenina* or *The Mill on the Floss*, it would have been the same. But that was the first great book I came into active contact with.

RC   George Eliot features in *A Home at the End of the World*.

MC   I love Eliot.

RC   In an interview long ago, you were talking about the question of free will and the problems of introducing AIDS into a narrative. You mentioned *Anna Karenina* then. Now, though, you're into your third book with AIDS as a theme. Is it more manageable now? Have you learned new tricks?

MC   No. I don't think I can trick this subject. If anything, I've simply moved on to other battles. In *The Hours*, AIDS is a factor in one of three stories, rather in the way the First World War is a factor in *Mrs. Dalloway*. It's the event after which nothing's ever the same again.

If I live long enough to write as many books as I'd like, I won't want to write about the AIDS epidemic all my life. I don't want to have to write about it. I want it simply to cease to be a concern. At the same time, I can't imagine in some way not being haunted by it, even if I'm not writing about it directly. That's simply because AIDS seems to me to be for two generations or more of gay men, but certainly for my generation, a singular and transforming event, not just in the obvious sense—that it decimated our population—but in that it made a number of us realize, if we hadn't sniffed it out already, that we weren't in the picture, that we were considered expendable. There were meetings at which Ronald Reagan was present at which it was decided that this wasn't a priority. Well duh! And yet so many of us were white guys, with privileges and educations. I think we'd imagined things differently.

RC   I don't think I expected you to talk about this quite so much. I'm interested in the consequences for your potential readership. One response to your novels has been to position them as indicative of a sort of "post-gay" or assimilative sensibility. Yet the importance you're now placing on being coerced into treating the subject of AIDS through a sense of political solidarity made me wonder how you reacted to that. Does being considered a "universal" writer concern you at all?

MC   I've always wanted to be read as widely as possible. My main conscious concern—the reader I had most vividly in mind—was a gay man,

someone not unlike people I've known who were sick. But I also imagined the books being read by that guy's mother, and then her friend, and
then that woman's straight daughter—a chain of readers.

RC What about the father—your character Constantine, say, from *Flesh
and Blood*, as a reader?

MC I'd love to be read by Constantine.

RC But you've moved to the conditional tense . . .

MC Yes. I have somewhat more modest hopes along those lines. It's not
been my experience that a lot of straight men of a certain generation seem
to read my books, though I would love them to. It's tricky. Of course, I
want to be read by other gay people, and be true in some way to my experience—to our experience. At the same time, and certainly more im-
portantly, writing only about us or for us feels depressingly small to me.
It's just not what I want to do. Being gay, I know about certain things. It
seems crazy not to write about them. But the idea that that imposes some
kinds of limitation, that being gay arrives with a certain obligation to
write only about this and not about that . . . I reject that.

RC I was thinking in particular of the use of sex in your books. It seems
striking that everyone has a different take on the role of sex within your
narratives. There's sex depicted across the widest range of experiences—
different generations, genders, whatever. Does that happen by default? Or
do you consider the experience of sex especially revelatory or important
to the development of character?

MC Absolutely the latter. I think sex—the actual depiction of the sex
that transpires between characters—is overlooked by most writers, for
reasons I understand. It's hard to write about—partly because sex
seems the most idiosyncratic of experiences. What's sexy to me is just
going to leave you stone cold. And the English language actually deserts
you. There's no useful term for the female sex organ. "Vagina" feels a
little more clinical than you might want. "Cunt" feels derogatory. We're

literally deprived of language in the face of this. Yet it's obviously hugely important. It seems to me the one new area available to writers who are alive and working now. It just wasn't available to Eliot or Flaubert. But what happened to Emma Bovary and her husband in bed was actually still important. There's that thing Oscar Wilde said: "Everything in the world is really about sex—except sex, which is really about power." I try to be guided by that when I write about sex.

RC There's nothing inherently inevitable about including it in detail, though, is there? In *A Home at the End of the World*, you describe retrospectively in the exchanges with Eric how many people Jonathan had sex with. You don't go through them one by one. Similarly, one sex scene in *Flesh and Blood* struck me especially. The point at which the total resonance of a sexual exchange has been captured was the point at which you chose to move on. Presumably intuition guides you in this case.

MC Yes. And of course I can't remember who actually has sex in that book, and who gets near to it, and then doesn't. But it's intuitive. It's simply what feels germane. It was certainly important to me, obviously, in *A Home at the End of the World* to include sex for everybody—not just to go with the gay guys having sex. It was kind of a thrill to imagine my way into sex of all different kinds.

RC You've previously said that it's difficult. Is the writing of sex scenes slower, or subject to more revision?

MC Yes. As I said, you certainly don't have the language. There are no terms for the things; there's not much precedent either. We're kind of on our own with this. We have great examples of how to get characters through a dinner party, but almost nothing on how to get them through a fuck. Sexuality is so various and idiosyncratic too—to the point where gay, bisexual, and straight feel like useless categories, way too crude. I find it's more important to try to write about it in terms of power; to write in a way that feels true to sex—which is, after all, a lot of things, including a lot of fun—without trying to titillate. That feels doomed to me.

RC   Have you ever explored theories of sexuality—nonfictional works?

MC   Not with a specific eye toward writing about something, but I have read Freud and John Preston. The question of what human sexuality is interests me. Partly in spite of the fact that we now talk about it a great deal, it still feels like one of the ways in which we're particularly foreign to each other. I feel more confident that this coffee tastes about the same to the two of us than I do about our shared sexuality, which is fascinating.

RC   On the redundancy of categories of sexual identity: if the question of "what sex is" is that compelling, one can read the development of Bobby's character as a sort of fictional playing out of it, a removal of the categories that might be imposed on him.

MC   In *A Home at the End of the World*, though, I backed off from the sex, for the aforementioned reasons. I then tried to resolve them in *Flesh and Blood*. If I were doomed to write *A Home at the End of the World* again today, one thing I'd do is put more sex in. I couldn't find a way to do it then that felt authentic, and not forced and cheesy.

★   ★   ★

RC   Virginia Woolf as a subject has been written up biographically by many hands. You state in *The Hours* that you were seeking to render her—externally at least—"as accurately as possible," and you cite the many sources you consulted. Nevertheless, was it daunting to write her up as a fictional character?

MC   Yes, absolutely. It was just about the most difficult task I could imagine setting for myself. I mean, she's a person who actually lived; she's a woman; she's from another time and country; she was a great artist and a feminist icon. It was enormously daunting even to think about trying to write about her. And, you know, if you stand too close to a huge figure, you're likely to look even smaller than you really are. But then I thought: "Why would you want to do something you know you can do? What's the fun of that? Better to go down in big blue flames than to sputter out like a birthday candle."

Once I started, I found to my surprise that writing about her was neither more nor less difficult than writing about anyone, as long as I thought of myself as creating a fictional person named Virginia Woolf. There were of course facts about her life and character, but they didn't really speak to her essence, which I invented. The fact is, any person is daunting to write about, whether real or imagined. Woolf was neither more nor less deserving of my respect and caution and whatever skill I could muster than anyone else.

RC   Could you talk a little about your shorter fiction? Are the stories you had published in the 1980s ever likely to be republished? Do you still get a lot of ideas for shorter fiction?

MC   I hardly ever have ideas for short fiction. I hardly ever write short fiction. Really, since I was in college, I think I've written about ten stories, and that would be over a course of twenty-five years. Most of them were terrible. The ones that weren't terrible were all published. I love short fiction. I read it all the time. But I very seldom try to write it. I seem to need a bigger arc—more room to move around in. It's hard for me to make anything happen in ten or twenty pages. I tried to paint, many years ago, and wasn't good enough at it. But one of the things I learned from painting is, your arm tends to move in a certain way as you put paint on a canvas, and you either naturally paint small or large. It's idiosyncratic and almost purely physical. If you're a big painter you can produce small paintings, but they're likely to feel squashed and claustrophobic. If you're a small painter, your big paintings are likely to seem stretched and thin. I suspect it's like that with writing. I don't take naturally to compression.

RC   I was particularly intrigued by the essay "Slap of Love," which concerned Angel Segarra, a Puerto Rican kid from the South Bronx who became "Angie Xtravaganza," one of the drag queens in Jennie Livingston's documentary film *Paris Is Burning*. Angel died of AIDS, which is one possible explanation for your interest. But I found your emphasis upon his adoption of others in the drag world compelling, given our previous discussion about alternative families. You described him "mothering" those younger and more naive then he was. Of Dorian, one of your interviewees, you commented: "Everybody needs a mother. Some of us get one who loves us enough, who does more or less the right thing. Others of us decide to become the mother we didn't have." Could you comment further?

MC   That piece, which ended up getting published in *Open City*, was actually written years earlier for *Vanity Fair*. An editor at *Vanity Fair* called me up and asked if I'd like to write a sort of "Where are they now?" story about the people who'd been in Jennie Livingston's great documentary *Paris Is Burning*. I said: "Sure, I'd love to." So I wrote the piece, and the people at *Vanity Fair* claimed to love it. They flew in a photographer from L.A., rented a studio, brought in tons of wardrobe, and took the girls' pictures. I can't imagine what they spent on that shoot. It might have been close to six figures. And then they never ran the piece, and never really told me why. I suspect it was something like this: they'd been expecting high glam—more along the lines of Jaye Davidson in *The Crying Game*. They weren't expecting these big middle-aged things in glitter gowns and headdresses. I think it scared them too much.

Anyway, the houses that come together for the balls are absolutely family units—of a kind. And the house mothers are true mothers to the children in their houses.

RC   The piece goes on to discuss Angel/Angie's taking hormones to become transgendered. All the "legendary mothers" of the drag scene "live in a gray area between genders," you noted, by keeping their penises. It's a fascinating topic, which seems a very ripe area for a novelist. Were you tempted to turn the research into fiction?

MC   I did. She's called Cassandra in *Flesh and Blood*. She's taken fairly directly from the people I met when I was writing "Slap of Love."

RC   The sense of the piece is very much that the world of the bar Sally's II is a sort of throwback to or relic from an older gay culture. Then again, you note how mainstream drag culture has also become. Drag has also evidently become masculinized—if such a thing can be said. You wrote that "the drag queens are thinning out and the butch queens are multiplying." The consequences of gay culture's assimilation into the mainstream in so many respects are legion. Are they ever beneficial? I'm wondering especially what your opinion of the cleaning up of Times Square was. It wiped away so many places like that.

MC I suspect that the horror of gay culture assimilating into the mainstream is particularly rampant among those of us who already tend to benefit from the mainstream, and who enjoy at least some of its fundamental protections. If you're a white gay male, it's probably easier to insist on gay people as romantic outsiders than it is if you're a black man with breasts and you live that way, with all it implies in terms of how you're treated.

Still, one of the fascinating and unexpected things that came up as I talked to people on the ball circuit was the degree to which different generations disapproved of each other. Even there, the older members tended to get sniffy about young people who didn't appreciate the finer points, like never ever walking a ball without the bottoms of your shoes polished, and the younger people thought the old ones were drags—no pun intended. See, it happens to everybody, everywhere.

RC The piece also brought you into contact with black urban culture. Is this the first time you've written about that?

MC Yes. I've found that race is the most difficult barrier to cross in my fiction. I've never managed to do it. I can get into a woman's mind as easily as I can a man's, but the mind and desires and experiences of someone of another race? I've tried, and it always comes out as a white guy's well-intended attempts to understand what it's like to be someone else. That may be as much as most of us can do in our lives, but it's not good enough for fiction. I am firmly of the belief that any writer can write about anybody. If there are limits to who and what we're allowed to write about, I don't want to do it at all. But you've got to know, yourself—when you're full of shit and when you aren't—and if you can't write a character in a way that feels true, you'd better not write him at all.

RC   Near the end of the piece, you wrote: "After Angie died her ashes were sent back to the South Bronx, with the name Angel Segarra on the plaque. It seems that our pasts have a way of reeling us back in, no matter what we do or how far we travel. Still, our created selves, however short their shelf lives, can leave legacies behind. They are small legacies, but they're legacies nonetheless, and ones that we could never have offered if we'd just stayed home." The evidence is that one of the people Angel/Angie cared for—Hector—has survived, and thrives. An analogy occurred to me with the creation of fiction, and the need to write for posterity. Do you consider that one of the impulses behind your own decision to become a writer—to leave something behind?

MC   Sure. But I'm more interested in what happens while I'm still here.

RC   You still teach creative writing, don't you? What is the value of courses like the one you taught at Columbia and the one you studied under at Iowa?

MC   I've actually taken a new job, in the M.F.A. program at Brooklyn College. I find that a lot of people are skeptical of graduate writing programs, which always seems a little strange to me. We don't expect painters or pianists to just sort of noodle around on their own until they figure out the process, do we? It's only a demand we make of writers. I suspect that particular demand originates in the fact that until relatively recently, writers didn't have formal training. However, writers until recently tended to live in proximity to other writers, in a world that cared enormously about what they were doing. A young writer now likely as not lives a block away from a strip mall, and is the only person he or she knows who even reads books, much less is trying to write them. At the very least, an M.F.A. program offers young writers two years in a community dedicated to the notion that what they're doing is important. That's probably the main thing I got from studying at Iowa, and it helped me tremendously. I try to pass some of that along to my students.

RC   In the end, *The Hours* is the first of your novels to become a film. To what extent were you involved in the making of it? What do you make of the result?

MC   I like the movie a great deal, though I was surprised when I saw it to find that I couldn't really see it at all, any more than I can see something I've written myself. I could tell it had good things in it; I could tell it was beautiful to look at and remarkably acted, and that it had coherence and style, but beyond that? I couldn't say, just now, if it's a great movie or a pretty good movie or a flawed gem, or whatever. I may be the only living American novelist who's had a good experience with Hollywood. I didn't write the screenplay. David Hare did. But David, Scott Rudin, the producer, and Stephen Daldry, the director, were great about showing me things, asking my opinion, and listening to it.

I don't have that fixation on the "Sacred Text" that some writers do. Any novel of mine is simply the best I could do with those people and that story at that time in my life. Six months later, I'd do it completely differently. So if I'm lucky enough to have someone want to turn a book of mine into a movie or an opera or a situation comedy, and it's someone I respect and admire, I want to turn it over to him or her and see what'll get made of it—how this material can be pushed in some way I wouldn't have thought of. I don't want a faithful adaptation. What would be the point? Everyone involved in the filming of *The Hours* was a gifted, intelligent person trying to make the very best movie they could. I can't ask for more than that.

RC   What have been the consequences of the prizes *The Hours* has won?

MC   Apart from the prosaic but far from insignificant material differences it's made, it was difficult at first. I got depressed after it won the Pulitzer. For a lot of reasons, but the one I can talk about is the obvious one: "What do I do now?" I'd always written in a kind of fury, because I felt muffled—like I wasn't being paid sufficient attention and so I had to write a book no one could possibly ignore. Then, OK, that happens; what impetus do you write from now? But then, after I more or less came back to myself, I decided that if I'd been raised up to a level from which all I could do was disappoint people, I might as well work with that, and write the biggest, strangest book I could imagine. Which is what I'm doing.

There's another thing I should probably mention. The success of *The Hours* has been hugely encouraging, to me and a lot of my fellow crackpot writers, in that it's reminded us that there are people out there who actually want to read books that aren't the regular thing—that stretch in different ways, and that don't contain one single sex scene or car chase. Not that I don't love sex scenes and car chases.

RC   In your introduction to Virginia Woolf's *The Voyage Out*, you wrote about how both *Jacob's Room* and *Mrs. Dalloway* were "by implication antiwar novels." Woolf described the First World War as "a preposterous masculine fiction." America—and New York in particular—could be said to be in a rather belligerent mood just now. Does the example of Woolf's writing suggest that a writer's response to September 11th and its political consequences should remain similarly indirect?

MC   I'd never venture to say what writers should or shouldn't do. I know that for myself, for the kind of writer I am, it's better to separate, to some degree, fiction writing from direct political action—to engage in both, but to see them as discreet. I feel like as a citizen it's my duty to try and stop George W. Bush from bombing everybody and annihilating the environment, and as a writer it's my duty to try and understand what it's like to be George W. Bush. Because as far as I can tell, no one ever comes home at night, looks in the mirror, and says: "Nyah ha ha—another day's evil done!" Everyone is the hero of his own story. Everyone thinks they're doing good in the world. I feel like one of the fundamental values of fiction is its ability to take us into the souls of people who are, in essence, our enemies. And that doesn't in any way mean that, as citizens, we don't do everything in our power to stop them from fucking everything up.

RC   You wrote too of Woolf's reticence regarding sexuality. What do you make of the recent publication of a version of *The Voyage Out*, *Melymbrosia*, which its publishers have claimed is more sexually forthright?

MC   It's only marginally more sexually forthright. She just didn't write about sex—not directly. I do take a dim, if slightly ambiguous, view of this sort of literary tomb-raiding—publishing work by deceased writers who clearly and inarguably didn't want it published. It's disrespectful, and I don't want anyone rooting around in my discard pile after I'm gone. That said, I wanted to see *Melymbrosia* too.

RC Is it too soon to ask what direction your own fiction writing has been taking since the publication of *The Hours*?

MC I wrote a short nonfiction book, a sort of wacky travel book about Provincetown, called *Land's End*. I was asked to do it. It's part of a series of books by fiction writers about their favorite places, and it just came along at exactly the right time. I was so unsure about what to do next, and here, as if from heaven itself, was this call from an editor proposing this very finite, doable project.

Now, on to the *un*-doable. I'm about a third of the way through a new novel. I can't talk about it in much detail, but I can tell you it's three linked novellas, each in a different genre. There's a gothic horror story, set in the past; a thriller, set in the present; and a science fiction story, set in the future. Each involves the same three characters, but in each story a different one is the main character. And, to my surprise, Walt Whitman figures in each of the stories. In the first, he's simply himself, the visionary poet. In the second, he's a terrorist bent on bombing civilization back to its idyllic, Eden-like state. In the third, he's a mythic scientist who has disappeared with a crucial discovery. In short, it's another crackpot book.

RC Thanks very much for your time.

FIVE

JIM GRIMSLEY

JIM GRIMSLEY is the author of six novels, including *Winter Birds, Dream Boy, My Drowning, Comfort and Joy,* and *Boulevard.*

He was born in 1955 in eastern North Carolina, and grew up there in a poor, rural community similar to those described in his first novels. As a boy, Grimsley was confined to bed for long periods on account of his hemophilia, which he shares with the character Danny, who features in *Winter Birds* and *Comfort and Joy.*

Grimsley studied writing at the University of North Carolina before moving to Atlanta, where he held a clerical position at Grady Hospital from 1980 to 1999, when he joined the faculty at Emory University to teach Creative Writing. Grimsley's playwriting career was first to flourish. His first play, *The Existentialists,* was produced in 1983. In 1988 he won the George Oppenheimer/Newsday Best New American Playwright Award for his third play, *Mr. Universe,* which had premiered at the 7Stages Theatre, Atlanta. Grimsley has written over twenty plays, including a 1991 adaptation of Edgar Allan Poe's "The Fall of the House of Usher." He was awarded the Bryan Family Prize for Drama by the Fellowship of Southern Writers in 1993.

Grimsley's first published novel, *Winter Birds* (Chapel Hill: Algonquin Books, 1994), was a finalist for the PEN/Hemingway Award for Fiction and won the Sue Kaufman Prize for First Fiction. Its first appearance, however, was in a 1992 German edition. A 1994 French edition also preceded its appearance in English and won the Prix Charles Brisset. Algonquin had in fact originally refused *Winter Birds* in 1985.

Dream Boy (Chapel Hill: Algonquin Books, 1995), his second novel to be published, appeared the following year. It was nominated for the Lambda Literary Award for Fiction and won the American Library Association's Gay, Lesbian, Bisexual, and Transgender Fiction Award. *My Drowning* (Chapel Hill: Algonquin Books, 1997) was a Lila Wallace–Reader's Digest Writer's Award winner and also won Grimsley the 1998 Georgia Author of the Year Award for Fiction.

Comfort and Joy (Chapel Hill: Algonquin Books, 1999), a sequel to *Winter Birds* and actually the second novel that Grimsley wrote, first appeared in German, French, and Dutch translations before its emergence in English. An excerpt was published in David Bergman, ed., *Men on Men 6* (New York: Plume, 1996). Grimsley's latest novel is *Boulevard* (Chapel Hill: Algonquin Books, 2002).

Grimsley has also written a fantasy novel, *Kirith Kirin* (Decatur, Ga.: Meisha Merlin, 2000). He remains playwright-in-residence at the 7Stages Theatre, Atlanta, as well as at the About Face Theater, Chicago. Four pieces of drama were published as *Mr. Universe and Other Plays* (Chapel Hill: Algonquin Books, 1998). Grimsley's shorter fiction has appeared in *DoubleTake*, *New Orleans Review*, *Carolina Quarterly*, the *New Virginia Review*, and in Michael Lowenthal, ed., *Flesh and the Word 4* (New York: Plume, 1997). The story "City and Park" was published in John Gardner, ed., *Best American Short Stories of 1982* (New York: Houghton Mifflin, 1982).

Grimsley still teaches Creative Writing at Emory. The interview took place on Sunday, November 16, 1997, at his Atlanta home. It was revised in August 2002, at which point the section following the asterisks was added.

RC Let's start with the publishing history of your books. There's obviously something odd about how your first novel *Winter Birds* appeared.

JG Yes. It was originally published in German in 1992. I had some friends in Germany that I met through theater. One, Frank Heibert, was founding a publishing house over there. He became passionate about *Winter Birds* and published it even when it wasn't published here. In fact, he found a French publisher also, so it was published in French as its second language. Then he insisted Algonquin read it when they came to the Frankfurt Book Fair, so that's when they picked it up. So it came out with English as its third language. There's a fourth novel of mine—*Comfort and Joy*—that's out in Germany, France, and Holland, but not out in English yet. It wasn't the fourth to be written, though—it's the second, and a sequel to *Winter Birds*. It's about Danny many years later, with his gay lover, going home for Christmas.

I'm not altogether comfortable with publishing it. It's a lot more romantic than the other books I've written. Every time I've got ready for it to appear here, I've had another book ready, so I've gone ahead and done that instead. I think *Comfort and Joy* was weak from the conception in some ways. I wrote it when I couldn't get *Winter Birds* published. I wanted to write a gay romance novel because I could probably get that published. In a lot of ways that choice scarred the material. It took years to work the bad romance writing out of it. I'm not sure if I did get all of it out. Sometimes it feels too soft. It's the one I wish I could start over from scratch again and do a different way—a harder way. But then again, I don't think I'll ever be in a mood to write it again. But it's obvious to me that *Comfort and Joy* is weaker than the other things I've written.

RC Do you read the novels in the other languages?

JG I read Spanish. I don't read German and French. I can make my way through a French letter, but that's about it. But I read the Spanish edition of *Winter Birds*, which I liked, though I'm told by my Spanish literary friends that it's not a great translation. *Dream Boy* is about to come out in Spanish too.

RC You said you were relaxed about publication. Is one reason the fact that you still work in theater?

JG   It's nice to have both worlds, and to be able to move back and forth between them. The rhythm's so different with plays than books. The response is much narrower. As small as the literary world is, the theater world's even smaller.

RC   Do you philosophize about the difference between your theater work and your fiction? Is there a clear division of material?

JG   Yes. The novels are personal stuff, usually—not always my stories, but stories that feel very personal to me. In the plays I've worked a lot more with ideas and intellectual themes. I've written every kind of play I've seen. I'm a great imitator. If I liked a play, I'd write a play like that. So I've got plays in many different styles.

I enjoy plays because they're collaborative where the novels are private. You work on them by yourself. You have an editor, but that's rarely more than a voice on the phone or a fax. You're by yourself with the work, and you're there for a long time with the novel. A play is quick, collaborative, and you've got to deal with people from the start—producers, actors, all that. It's a lot more public than I'm used to being, but when I'm in the mood for that, it's perfect. When I'm not, I can retreat back into being a novelist.

RC   I was told that you work very closely with actors in rehearsal.

JG   Yes. This house is owned by my producers, so I'm their tenant. I'm definitely playwright-in-residence!

RC   Was the division of material planned?

JG   No. I think it grew out of the way both genres feel. I started writing plays when I was having trouble getting fiction published—during the time I was trying to sell *Winter Birds* in this country. I didn't stop writing fiction, but I started writing plays again because I'd got some early success with them and could make a bit of money. What evolved was that it felt very natural to work in this big, broad comic intellectual way in the theater, whereas I'd already developed what I wanted to do in fiction, which was with a much more personal voice.

RC   *Winter Birds* still has a copyright of 1984. Why is that?

JG   That reflects the date of the finishing of the book—the date printed on the copy the Germans used—so they listed it on their copyright pages. That's when I finished the book.

RC   So there were eight years of waiting before your first book came out?

JG   Yes, trying to sell the book.

RC   You said you were relaxed about it. But was that patience something you had to acquire?

JG   I guess I'm relaxed because nothing I've ever done to try to move my career ahead has worked. Everything that's worked for me has been accidentally, and over a period of time. Now I'm forty-two, I'm used to that. It really doesn't matter to me. My publisher and agent take care of that. Also, something's out there now. That makes a huge difference.

RC   *Winter Birds* struck me as such a complete, polished work. How did you arrive at that? What had you been writing beforehand?

JG   I'm very careful about what I'll publish. *Winter Birds* was much longer when I first finished it. Over time working on it, I saw that the part which was published as the novel was a discrete part of this longer, messier manuscript. In reading it over and over again, and with the help of some good friends, I finally understood that the rest of the book wasn't up to it. I'd hit on something in this section of the book that wasn't paralleled in the rest. If you read it, you didn't need to read the rest. So I had the good sense to cut, which a lot of young writers don't. It took ten years to do all that—to write it all, and then to realize how to clear it up, and to realize it would stand on its own in this smaller section. That was really the work that taught me my craft. It's the single most important thing I've ever done in terms of learning how to write.

RC   Has the discarded material been the basis for anything that appeared subsequently?

JG   Definitely. The fact that I can now do a book in two years rather than ten comes from *Winter Birds*—because of what I learned not to do. Also, the material of *Winter Birds* carries through into *Dream Boy* and *My Drowning*. Those three books are much more similar to each other than the book I'm working on now, which is called *Boulevard*. It's set in New Orleans and it's about a kid in his twenties. I'm trying to move away from rural settings. I'm trying to move into a city, to age the people I'm writing about—not to write about kids anymore. I've done that and liked it, but I don't want to go on doing it.

RC   In the process of being translated, you must have reflected on what translation might do to your very distinctive prose. My first thought was that your language might present fewer problems than with other writers. Now I'm not so sure.

JG   It was a big problem for the French translator. I know that because I worked with her. It's because it's deceptively simple. You think it's going to be easy to duplicate, yet there's a quality of poetry it has that is very difficult to maintain. What I do in that way is very delicate. I don't try to force poetry. I don't use poetic "technique." What I go for is much more what Hemingway did. But I'm a little more generous with language than he was. I think he's probably the person I'd point to, in terms of style that I most like. Or Virginia Woolf, when she's in a clear mood. Those are the people I emulate when I think about style. But Hemingway pushed the simplicity so far that it becomes monotonous—too much like a gimmick after a while. That won't sustain a novel for me—not my novel. I'm probably a little more fulsome than he is.

RC   It's one thing to mention people you revere; another to suggest emulation. You seem comfortable with the idea of talking about influences in that way.

JG Sure. You do emulate people when you're young. I don't now. I don't even read them anymore. When I talk about emulation, I'm talking about the people I was reading in college—that I wanted to write like, and whose style of writing I admired.

RC I haven't seen your work described in terms of other writers. There must be a tendency to make lazy thematic comparisons with writers whose style is very different—William Faulkner, perhaps?

JG Yes. Sometimes I'm Faulkner; sometimes I'm Flannery O'Connor; Tennessee Williams, when it's a play that's being written about. Not terribly original. I got compared to Dostoyevsky once. I really liked that. And to Henry James's *The Turn of the Screw*. I didn't like that so much. Although I like James, I don't want to write like him.

RC How does it feel to be compared specifically to Southern writers?

JG Well, it's a help, because Southern literature gets talked about. It's one kind of literature that people in America know has been written. If you're a Southern writer, you have a comfortable place already. It's also burdensome sometimes because folks in other regions think we're simple, stupid folk down here. If we can spell, it's kind of accidental. If we can write, it's even more accidental.

But it's what I am. Everything I write—even the plays—sounds Southern in terms of word choice and diction. So it's inescapable. And it's a help sometimes. There aren't many Southern gay writers, for instance—especially ones who still live down here. Most everybody's migrated someplace else.

I have had intelligent comparisons to other people—like Djuna Barnes's *Nightwood*, or Nathanael West's *Day of the Locust*—books that sustain themselves by tone. I love *Nightwood*. It's amazing—the wonderful crypticness of it. I could read the same page five days running and get five different stories out of it. It's not at all that she's writing vaguely. She's being incredibly specific. It's just that the language collides in such a curious way.

I'd say the same thing about *The Day of the Locust*. It's perfect. It's compact—compressed just beyond the point that you'd usually write a thing.

It's even denser and richer than usual. That's what I love about both those books. *To the Lighthouse* has that quality to me too—the wonderful clarity of every paragraph, in spite of the fact that it's such an inhuman point of view that Woolf takes. It's astonishing.

The reviews I've liked make comparisons like that—to simple things that aren't simple at all, which is really what I think I'm doing. As for the Faulkner comparison, any good Southern writer's going to be compared to him at some point, whether he bears any relationship to Faulkner or not. In fact, most bad Southern writers are going to be compared to Faulkner. It's how it is. Faulkner's great, but he wouldn't be my favorite Southern writer at all. He's got a lot of problems as far as I'm concerned. One is the ego with which he wrote. I don't want that kind of writing for myself. I don't want to write thinking what a great writer I am.

RC   Words like "poetic" or "lyrical" are often used in relation to works like that. But what one is really talking about also is ellipsis. In the case of *Nightwood*, the language is precise, as you say, but entirely unexpected. You get a sense of a thinking presence behind the book with bewildering ideas.

JG   In Barnes's case, the presence is so kinetic it's as if she might change the words right in front of you. She might decide today when you read it to have written something different. That's a wonderful feeling.

RC   Speaking of the genius behind a given work, have there been attempts to interpret your fiction as autobiography?

JG   I was very frank about *Winter Birds* being autobiographical in all the interviews about that book over here. Because of that I think everybody reads the other books the same way. I had people asking me if *My Drowning* was autobiographical. Well, no; I'm not a nineteen-year-old girl. I didn't grow up in the 1940s. Yes, these are stories I heard about from my family. But autobiography isn't that.

What they mean is: "Are you writing about your own life?" I think that means, especially in the case of *My Drowning*, that I'm doing what I'm supposed to do. To them it feels like I'm writing about my own life. Of course I'm not. Even in *Winter Birds* it's all fiction, even though it's based on fact. It's a hard process to explain to anyone, fiction writing—that you take a true thing and make a complete fiction about it. But it's true.

RC It's particularly a problem in relation to the emergence of a literature of confession recently.

JG It's weird. We assume people who write nonfiction are generally lying, and that people who write fiction are generally telling the truth, which is a curious double twist. I think people want to know, especially with books like *Winter Birds*, that you know what you're writing about; that you didn't make that stuff up; that you're not making them go through it for no reason. That's part of what made Frank McCourt's *Angela's Ashes* such a big book over here—that it wasn't made up; that people knew he was telling his own story. You want that much of a payoff if you're going to go through reading something as intense as that.

RC That must be frustrating though—that when something feels vivid to a reader, it's considered to reflect "true" experience, rather than to great writing.

JG Yes. I was frustrated with some of that stuff with *My Drowning*. People don't see how much work you've done to make the book. It's as if, if it happened to you, it must have been easy to write the book. That's not true. Things happen to a lot of people who aren't then able to articulate anything about them. The writing's always a different thing.

RC And to translate experience into language is already to fictionalize.

JG Yes; it's fictive, definitely. I've done some workshops here with reporters at the daily paper. We've talked about the fact that what I do has lots of parallels with what they do. There's an essentially fictive process going on in writing about any event. You can't really do it; you just pretend you do it. People's brains allow you to do it through convention. And it all falls apart if you look at it too closely.

RC Have you ever constructed a specific kind of readership in your head?

JG [*Laughs*] Large—millions. No more specific than that! No, I don't picture any specific reader at all.

RC Are you ever concerned about the reactions of real people from whom you've loosely drawn in your characterizations?

JG My family's been very good about that—I think partly because they wanted the story in *Winter Birds* told. My mother's family became the source for the portraits in *My Drowning*, and they were delighted. They aren't people who ever thought they'd see themselves in a book. They're those people—very poor people in eastern North Carolina. So the idea that their cousin would rise up and write a book about them was thrilling. I haven't had any problem that way. The only problem would have been with my father. He's dead, so he doesn't get a vote—which is good justice, I think!

RC Could you say something about the challenge of writing *My Drowning* using a woman's voice?

JG I moved into that novel with a good deal of trepidation. I had always wanted to write a book based on my mother's childhood, but knew that writing from her point of view would be a challenge. It's no longer politically correct for a male writer to write too freely from a woman's point of view. When I made the decision to write in the first person as Ellen, the job became even more daunting. Let me note that these fears had nothing to do with the writing since I was pretty confident I could do the girl's voice. I wish that a lot of ideas of what's correct or proper to write about would go out of my head, but you do have to pay a certain amount of attention to those requirements. I was very happy with the way that book came out.

RC When you introduced *Comfort and Joy* as the second novel you'd written, you shattered my very neat construction of your career in terms of the three different approaches to narrative in the three books published in English: second-person, third-person, first-person voice.

JG I don't like doing the same thing over and over. I don't see any reason that the books should feel like the same person wrote them necessarily. I think I can write in a lot of ways I haven't tried yet. That's what interests me about writing. With *Boulevard*, I'm trying to write from an omniscient point of view, which is very different to any of the voices I've used yet.

RC In the case of *Winter Birds*, the use of the second person is compelling. It's rare in fiction.

JG I found it after trying the other two points of view—first person and third person. I couldn't make them work. I fell into the second person through poetry, basically—where the poet would address an unnamed "you." It seemed to connect the writer with that person in a peculiar way. That fit what I was working on in *Winter Birds*.

I found a version of the first page that was done in the first person when I was getting something out recently. A few pages later in the same notebook, there's the same page written in second person. I can't remember exactly what triggered the shift. But what made it work and continue to work was the relationship between the writer and that character. It implied a version of Danny that had aged beyond that eight-year-old boy.

RC It implied it without confining your narrative. It allowed another inflection, so that during the hospitalization, for instance, the "I" figure doesn't intrude.

JG Yes. It allows me to cheat really; to know all kinds of things that the boy doesn't know, that I can claim to have found out later from the mother, or that can be inferred to have been known later through memory or through visualizing the scene from that later point. It was a very freeing way to write.

Most people will never be comfortable with it, quite. And I didn't want to go on and do another book that way. It wasn't a choice made to be daring; it was a choice that just happened. If I'd known the problems it would cause in terms of having it published . . . Lots of people told me this point of view would never work. It was: "We'd consider the novel if you would change it out of this point of view." There was that response, and then there was the "this story's so sad; no one will ever want to read it" response. Those were the two major reactions I got to that book through the years of trying to get it published. But to change the book out of that point of view was to write another book. I thought: "That's what I'll do, if I have to. But I won't change this." It felt to me that they were wrong—that this did work.

RC   A part of you dug in at that point and said: "I must be doing something right if everyone objects."

JG   Well, I don't like that kind of thought. I think it's the refuge of foolish experimenters everywhere. Very often, foolish experiments lead to works nobody can understand. But what I do believe firmly is that you should never accept anybody else's criticism of your work in such a way that would change the nature of it totally. If somebody gives you a suggestion that would cause you to write essentially another book, then that doesn't have anything to do with you. You don't have to listen to it. And I wasn't just concerned with getting something published.

In my twenties, when I'd finished *Winter Birds*, I thought I had plenty of time. I had the feeling that if I were patient, the book would be published. Toward the end of those eight years, it got to be old. At that point I had enough reactions to know that somebody wasn't getting the point. There were so many people telling me this was an extraordinary book, but they couldn't publish it. I thought: "Somebody somewhere is going to decide the other way." That's what happened ultimately. I was lucky to find my faith justified.

RC   Was writing in the second person especially hard?

JG   Not at all. It felt completely right. Frankly, it's a tone of voice I could write in forever. There's something about the sound of language it produces that I understand. It's very seductive to me—and pliable, especially done in the present tense. I don't know that I could do it in the past tense.

But I decided I'd never do it again, or rather that I'd fight like hell not to do it again, because I didn't want to be labeled as "that-person-who-always-writes-in-the-second-person."

RC   In the context of gay-themed fiction, I can only think of Edmund White's *Nocturnes for the King of Naples* written in second person.

JG   That's the only other one I like a lot. Jay McInerney's *Bright Lights, Big City* is in the second person. But it's really just saying "you" instead of "I." It isn't a change of point of view. A book called *Buffalo Soldiers* by Robert Connor came out a couple of years ago. It's basically the same trick. It's "you" instead of "he." It's not a true shift in vision. You have to envision the book differently if you're going to use "you." There has to be a reason; some connection that you want to make with one character in particular.

RC   And *Nocturnes for the King of Naples* worked for you?

JG   I think pretty much everything Edmund White writes works. There were times when I used to be impatient with him. All his books were about upper-class gay men. But that's who he is and what he writes about. I realized you can't always judge literature as bad because you're jealous of the upper class.

RC   I want to get a wider sense of how reading informs your writing. Do you avoid certain kinds of books when you are writing, for instance?

JG   I read by instinct. I imagine some of that comes into it—some resistance to certain books because of what I'm writing. But I'm not conscious of that usually. I am with *Boulevard*, though, because I'm reading a lot of history. Not about New Orleans, necessarily. I read a terrible book on the Battle of Britain that has nothing whatsoever to do with what I'm writing. But there's something about reading that narrative language of history that stimulates me.

RC   Do you also read poetry?

JG   Not as assiduously as I'd like. There's not time. I have to try and keep up with fiction, I feel. That's the most important thing. And there's so much to keep up with. But I read Adrienne Rich, Audre Lorde, Minnie Bruce Pratt.

Male poets are tougher. Men bring a lot of attitudes to writing, which I don't like. That side of literature isn't something I have anything to do with. But I read Mark Doty. I don't think he shares that—the self-preoccupation of the male point of view in general. It crops up in the oddest of places. I can read John Rechy, though, because that's what he does; that is his point of view. He's written so many different ways. You can always shop around with him and go for something that suits your mood.

I love Rechy. He's not somebody you'd think I'd like. His is such a strange point of view, and he's so wonderfully messy and extravagant. *City of Night* is seminal to me. One section of it—the "Miss Destiny" section in Los Angeles—is so extraordinary. I've never read anything that captured that life as well. That's one of the places in his work where he shakes off that male image for a while. His focus there is on the drag queen. He's never done that again in anything I've read. I think that's the best moment ever in his writing.

He's a curious political animal for gay literary people to deal with, I know. He didn't embrace the notion of being gay in those early books. He embraced the notion of sex with men, but that's a different politics.

RC   There are peculiar narrative leaps from one book to the next, which I guess you'd like.

JG   Yes. Some of them don't work. But some of Faulkner doesn't work. One thing that Faulkner said that I also believe is that if you're going to be very good, you have to take the risk of being very bad. I'm sure there's a lot of stuff in Rechy that I wouldn't put in my "Top Hundred Book List." But a couple of the books he wrote—*Numbers, The Sexual Outlaw*—are seminal.

RC   The drag queen section of *City of Night* you mentioned is rather similar in theme to your play *Mr. Universe*. Were you conscious of that work when writing it?

JG   The "Miss Destiny" section of that book is its finest hour, I think. I can't remember thinking of that book in specific when working on *Mr. Universe*, but I had read it a couple of times by then.

RC   I'm interested as we've strayed into gay literature at the idea of your books being labeled as written "from a gay viewpoint." How do you react to that?

JG   It means I was very open about declaring myself as gay in early interviews for *Winter Birds*. Gay critics picked up on that. In order to be able to write about the book, they had to mention the gay angle somehow. It was the only way they could get me space. Even with a book like *Winter Birds*. Craig Seligman reviewed it for the *New Yorker*. He slid the book into a review he was doing of three gay books because I was gay. I appreciate all that. It's good that it happened. But I don't think it means anything.

Someone once asked me—and I thought it was the dumbest question I ever got asked—whether I thought I was able to write successfully from a woman's point of view because I'm gay. I thought: "Isn't that stupid, given what 'gay' encompasses?" I imagine Dennis Cooper's approach to writing about a female character, for instance, would be very different from mine. But he's gay, and so am I. I don't think there's anything that makes gay men inherently sensitive towards women. I know a lot of gay men who are exactly the opposite.

Anyway, seriously, these people think too much.

RC   That's a leading comment.

JG   Well, I'm not so interested in engaging people's intellects as going a little deeper—into a dream place; a place where you become so engaged by the book and the story that you're in it. You're not really aware. Your intellect is bypassed. Writing about ideas doesn't interest me nearly as much as writing that evokes feeling—that doesn't go after it directly, but that gets it.

RC Where do you find that in others' work? One might identify elements akin to that in a lot of black writing.

JG Yes, and in Asian American writing. What they have in common is a rejection of intellectualism because it's Western and comes with a lot of cultural baggage attached. I think that's partly why I focus on that kind of thing when I write. I don't know what I think about "things." I don't have a philosophy, in the way Nietzsche had—though if I'm half-drunk, I could start talking that shit at a party.

RC Edmund White's a philosophical writer.

JG He is, and it's because people like him do it so well that I know it's not something I can do. For one thing, it's what an upper-class person can do that somebody from a class like mine would have trouble doing. In some ways I don't feel like I've got the education. A person that is around those ideas from the time they're two or three—exposed to art, exposed to music—they grow up in a different way, with a different kind of confidence about that kind of construct of the world. I can't gain that through studying those things now.

My stuff comes from a place that I understand instinctively, the same way Edmund White's does for him. It's just that his instincts work on a different set of lines. When he writes about those people, their summer cottages and nice apartments, their travel from continent to continent, it's very real. I know it is. When he tries to write about a poor or lower-class person, it doesn't strike me as genuine in the same way. I have the same problem in my writing. When I try to write about an upper-class person, I'm not confident. I don't have the same feeling for it than when I'm dealing with rural or lower-class people. There's nothing I can do about it. I can't change who I am, really, to that extent—not that I'm interested in doing that. I don't think literature needs that particularly.

RC I want to ask about the coherence of your linguistic world and use of metaphor on part of a given character. Take, for example, the idea of finding pity "like moistness in the air." Is that register—that ready use of simile and metaphor—easy to adopt? Is it ever difficult to arrive at? Or does it become immediate?

JG   I would say it's all of those things. Sometimes it's easy. Sometimes I get so carried off by it that it's just there. The scene where Nathan is killed in *Dream Boy*; where his head's bashed in: that fifteen-page section just came. I hardly had to change it at all. Other times, it's a matter of reading it over and over again, and writing it over and over again, with spaces of time between—enough to see that what you've done is bad; that something else would have worked better. Or of seeing, by the time you get to the end of a book, then that this element of it is important, but it wasn't there at the beginning. So then it's a question of going back and putting it in.

The metaphors are like that. I began to understand, working on *Dream Boy*, that this was a book about being underwater, in terms of the metaphors. There's a lot of "submerged" metaphors—a lot of moistness, a lot of water—in inappropriate places. It was throughout. So I started working with that—being aware of it; cutting it where it was too much.

Sometimes it's just a matter of having the right instinct for writing that way: knowing how to put a couple of words down on a page that, when you read it, will make you see something—something beyond those words or that image. To go for an image that registers in several ways, that has some element of change in it, maybe—but not to do that too much.

RC   We're returning to the idea of writing as exclusion and editing out. The stories you've written might have led to sentimentality in some writers. I wondered if that was something you've had to be scrupulous in editing out.

JG   No. I think I just don't have that as a point of view. I'm not sentimental about things, so I don't go there when I write. Although I do get sentimental if I have to write about lovers—that's when I have to worry. When I'm writing about people's hardships, I'm not at all sentimental because these are things I lived for the most part. I understand that sentimentality has nothing to do with it. It's deadly, in fact. You can't survive in these circumstances if you're sentimental.

RC   What of the dangers of overwriting more generally—of including too much, metaphoricizing too frequently? If you'd described one of the chase scenes in *Dream Boy* at twice the length, for example, you'd have explained the importance of that experience to the character so fully that you'd ruin it for the reader.

JG   Yes. You'd kill it. I work on the principle that if you reach for somebody's heartstrings, they're going to get too tough to pluck. What I try to do is lay it flat—keep those moments as flat on the page as possible. When I work with students, I tell them over and over again that when you are writing about violence, for instance, you have to do it quickly and cleanly and get out of it as quickly as possible, and not emote about it on the page. You can't, as a writer, want the reader to know that you don't condone this kind of thing. You're just there to see it, to report it—to be the vessel for transferring that information to somebody else.

I'm ruthless in cutting, and not just in terms of those kinds of scenes. I don't like "fat writing" at all. I don't like a paragraph where a character does nothing but think. This may change. I'm trying to free myself up just a little more in *Boulevard*—just to stop and observe. But in the first books, I've been very concerned that something had to happen in every paragraph. Something had to move the story forward. These are all delicate stories, especially *Winter Birds* and *Dream Boy*. You can't stop; you want the motion to go forward. If you let people out of there for a moment, they may not want to come back. The whole construct might fall apart.

RC   I can see why you bring those two books together and not *My Drowning*. In that book, there's a different approach to voice and to chronology. Perhaps that suggests the beginnings of a move away from this strict, material approach to events.

JG   Definitely. I thought of *Winter Birds* and *Dream Boy* as being shaped like freight trains running at you. You open the book and the freight train is on the tracks. You see it coming at you for the whole book.

RC   They have the suspense of a thriller.

JG   Yes. But I didn't want to do that again with *My Drowning*. I wanted a more complicated structure. I wanted to sustain a book without a plot that carried you so directly through it. I wanted to see if that could still be compelling. I hope it was. I've gotten responses that indicate that it was.

RC   So, are you now preoccupied with this tension between continuing to adhere to plot and something potentially at odds with that—using language, time, and the processes of memory more fluidly?

JG   Yes, especially time and memory. Looking back, I see that I've been writing about time in a lot of ways—especially in *My Drowning*. But the whole relationship that comes out of the point of view in *Winter Birds* is about time—the separation in years between the narrator and the "you."

I know I want things to be different. I don't want to write any more small, intense books—partly because I know I can, and don't want to repeat it. There's always at the back of your mind the concern that you're not being taken quite seriously by people because you write these kinds of books; that they're not quite literary enough. I'm talking about that male-writer point of view now: "You're just telling a story; but *I'm* working with language—experimenting; doing stream-of-consciousness." I run into that with my students all the time: "I'm experimenting, so that gives me license to do anything."

RC   A name I wanted to bring up was Cormac McCarthy. His work has materiality . . . is broadly sparse in its examination of psychology. But it is talked about intellectually. I felt there was something loosely comparable between his work and yours—in the narrative's surrender to plot at a very material level. In his case, I don't think people have suggested there was anything consequently unintellectual about his work.

JG   I don't know that people have suggested that about me either. It's more my defensiveness about what I do. Clearly it is intellectual work McCarthy is doing. I think his aims are much less toward feeling, though, than mine. His aims are much more at complex language structures that carry a plot forward—very directly like Faulkner, in his case, I think.

He's got that mantle, now, that blesses what he does. He didn't have it for his first five books. In fact, I like his early writing better than *All the Pretty Horses*. *Blood Meridian* and earlier I really liked. *All the Pretty Horses* and later I can't bear—partly because I don't believe it. I don't care how well written it is. I don't believe in a sixteen-year-old kid going off and having all of that—not quite that way. It seems almost like somebody's wet dream rendered really large, whereas McCarthy's earlier books are much more Gothic, more complicated in their language, in a way that resonates for me better.

I don't think there was any compromise for him. It's just that he'd done the other thing and wanted to move in this direction. There's no writer that I can think of where I like everything that they do. I certainly admire McCarthy.

RC   I was surprised to hear that *Dream Boy*, like *All the Pretty Horses*, has been snapped up by filmmakers.

JG   *Dream Boy* has been adapted as a play also. I didn't have anything to do with it, even though I'm a playwright. I liked it very much. I was surprised it could even be a play. But I didn't feel a need to protect it from the adapter, Eric Rosen. Also, I don't feel any great need to push it as a stage play. As good an adaptation as it is, I don't really like it being a play particularly.

RC   But you didn't block the idea?

JG   No. It didn't require any effort on my part. The same's true of the movie. I know it would help the book, in terms of getting people to know it's there. I trust Jimmy Black to make a credible film. Even if he doesn't, that's his problem, not mine. I'll help him in any way he wants help—though I don't think he will. The thing flies or doesn't fly on what he and his producer do.

People's perceptions of the book won't change because of the movie. I can't think of a movie that's ever hurt the reputation of the book that preceded it. They can help. They rarely hurt.

RC   I think only where a film seems to improve on a book—but that's usually where a book is rather skeletal. One thinks of Forster's *Maurice*, which is dead on the page.

JG   Yes—though people hate to say that. I think the film convinced some people that the book is better than it is.

RC   We're edging towards that maxim: "good film, bad book," and vice versa.

JG   But I don't think that's true. Günter Grass's *Tin Drum* was a good movie and a good book. It's probably the best adaptation I've seen. I know some writers who've had their books filmed and loved the results, even where they were different.

   Movies aren't important to me. I don't care about them. I go to see them when I'm too bored to do anything else, or when I'm with a friend that I don't really want to talk to. Movies aren't intimate to me. They're something other people work on and care about, so let them have it. I'm perfectly willing to collect a little bit of money to allow *Dream Boy* to be made. That's all there is to it. I don't feel excited about it.

RC   I wanted to ask about the danger of *Dream Boy* dominating your other works. Is it annoying the way in which critics or readers sometimes embrace a book by way of being attracted only to particular themes in it—in this case, the gay plot? What interests me is both the way *Dream Boy* might help find a readership for the other books, but also how it might hurt them—or frustrate you.

JG   It is frustrating. I've often answered this question in other ways. But being gay does make a difference. There's a tendency to shut all the gay writers in the room, and let the gay literary people deal with them and do their business all by themselves.

   My story is a little odd in that *Winter Birds* wasn't perceived as a "gay book" but was very well-received. It's almost like I've got two audiences—a women's audience and a gay audience. I've got some straight male readers too, but it's mostly women and gay men. The women, curiously, did read *Dream Boy*. I got a lot of responses from women to that book. So because I'd had this other book that had already reached that market—*Winter Birds*—I had less of a problem that way. But I know that if *Dream Boy* had been my first book, it wouldn't have been a contender for the Sue Kaufman Prize, which *Winter Birds* won.

RC   So you share the ambivalence of other writers concerning the idea of "gay fiction"?

JG   On one hand it's a guarantee of a good market. In my case, I'd say it has been. I can play both sides of the fence—and have done, fairly well, so far. It's not hurting me. It's frustrating in that there's something silly about the way people talk about it. But that's the whole of gay life—not just gay novels.

It's so parallel to being talked about as a Southern writer that it's uncanny. They have the same sorts of strange limitations that they impose on you. We had to work for three books to get the *New York Times* to review me because of the "Southern thing." The gay thing wasn't a problem.

After a point, I really don't think about that. All I have to do next is figure out what's happening in the book I'm working on.

RC   Obviously, writers can't allow themselves to be determined in this way in the execution of a work.

JG   No. But it's very hurtful if your point of view is dismissed as "subcultural"—if it's said that you can't really write something that's representative of the larger culture. I don't understand why my sexuality has to separate me from the mainstream at all. I don't think many gay people do—even those who tout the notion of ghetto literature as our highest achievement. The whole debate bores me silly, to tell you the truth.

RC   Probably the whole matter of gay identity and perspective will look ridiculous and baffling, fifty years hence.

JG   Yes. At some point we'll have to have our Andrew Holleran back-lash. People have to revise the extravagant things they said about *Dancer from the Dance* at some point. It's a wonderful book. But it's not the greatest gay novel ever written. It has nothing to do with the gay life I led during those same years.

I think what's been heaped on Holleran is unbearable. He's a very good writer, but he can't bear up under this sort of praise. Some people get praised to death. He's fast becoming one. Nobody's ever going to allow him to write a better book, because of the way they felt when they first read *Dancer from the Dance*. That's a magical thing to have happen, but it's also a curse. I love that book; I think it's gorgeous. But there are many books that gorgeous and valuable. He doesn't need to be singled out that way to be praised the way he deserves to be.

RC   Yet again, there's a ceiling on the praise in a sense.

JG   Yes—it's "just a gay book."

RC   The best it can be is . . .

JG   "The best gay book ever."

RC   It's the gay *Gatsby*. So one of us gays has written a book as good as Fitzgerald's . . .

JG   I do think it's as good as *Gatsby*. I'm not all that impressed with *Gatsby*, though—partly because the material doesn't reach me. Those people are interesting as ideas. But they're not people I know. I don't feel them. I have the same problem with all the writers who write about that New York scene. It's been done a lot, and was not something I knew or cared much about. They're fun books to read, but that's not the only place gay literature is. There are lots of gay experiences that don't have anything to do with the ghetto.

RC   Can you name some other writers you like who are at odds with this understanding of what "gay fiction" is?

JG   Scott Heim is a wonderful new voice coming out of Kansas, proving definitively that there were gay people in Kansas all along, surviving quite well. [*Laughs*] James Purdy's always been there. He's not part of the New York set. Brian Bouldrey, Fenton Johnson—people who write from outside New York.

RC   You said you had to keep up with contemporary fiction. Which other writers do you make a point of reading?

JG   Ha Jin; Ann Patchett; E. Annie Proulx; Dorothy Allison; Kaye Gibbons; Francisco Goldman; Margaret Atwood, pretty regularly; Alice Munro; Lydia Davis, a gorgeous writer people don't know much about. She's also a friend. We judged the Hemingway Prize here together.

RC   I wanted to ask about the writing process. Do you write longhand?

JG   I do sometimes when I get stuck and want a change. But usually I write directly into the computer now. I revise in longhand, and then enter it all into the computer.

RC   You're not superstitious about writing as against word-processing?

JG   Not at all.

RC   Some writers find the attractiveness of word-processed material means that the revision process gets curtailed; things look too good.

JG   Not for me. You can make this as precious as you want to. You can be as superstitious about this as you want to be.

RC   Is any time of the day better than any other for working?

JG   No. I won't let that be true. I've schooled myself to be able to write any time I get a minute. I have to work full time. I have huge commitments outside the time I can spend writing, so I can't get precious that way. If I'm going to keep writing, I've got to write whenever I can.

I don't put big burdens on myself. I try to write a sentence every day. Usually I can get more. But most of the time I can get at least that much. That gets me the feeling of still being there. I work on several things so that if I need to stop and think about the book I'm working on, I can work on a play or revise something. At noon, I'm meeting with somebody about a fantasy novel I've been working on for about ten years, *Kirith Kirin*. That's a project I've worked at between other things.

I find this keeps me from getting writer's block. If you're blocked, you're blocked on one thing. There are others.

RC   Some moments in a book cause problems, then?

JG   Yes. Especially if you write as I do, which is without knowing what's coming.

RC   What about the shape of a story? Do you know nothing about how it will be, or just a little?

JG   I have a strong feeling at the beginning, and I know more as I go on. By the time I get to the middle, I know most everything. Often there are still big surprises—like Nathan getting killed in *Dream Boy*. I never planned that. He just got killed that night. I stayed up to write the next chapter because I figured I'd be in a terrible panic if I woke up with a dead character.

I like that kind of surprise. I think if I surprise myself, I've got to be surprising the reader.

RC   That was Flannery O'Connor's maxim.

JG   Yes. Her essays are probably more helpful than almost anybody's on writing that I've read.

She's the perfect writer to revere. [*Laughs*] She's dead. She was glorious, truly. Those are stories that will hold up. She'll probably be the person that most folks think of as the Southern writer—even more so than Faulkner in the end.

RC   Was her *Wise Blood* any influence on your play *The Lizard of Tar-*

sus? I was thinking of your character "J.," or Jesus, who insists on a sort of Church Without God. Hazel Motes in *Wise Blood* founded the Church of Jesus Christ Without Christ.

JG *Lizard* had more origins in Dostoyevsky and the "Grand Inquisitor" section of *The Brothers Karamazov* than in O'Connor. I'm not a big fan of *Wise Blood*.

RC What about the length of the work, as opposed to its structure or plotline? Are there ideas you work on that you know are going to turn out as a short story, for instance?

JG Those usually come out as plays now, the shorter ideas. I don't have a good feel for short stories. I still try to write them. But I don't condense that way well. I did until I started writing plays. After that, when I get an idea of that kind of length, if that makes any sense, it usually fits as a play better than a story, the way I conceptualize things.

RC Of your plays, only *The Borderland* to my knowledge addresses the themes of regionality and class which so pervade your novels. Is this simply because you have felt freer to address other subjects in drama?

JG Yes. In drama I don't think my voice is particularly regional, and my interest in playwriting comes from the many intellectual ways in which one can construct a play. My plays come more from ideas than from feelings; I'd say the opposite about the fiction, most likely.

RC You once mentioned having written about twenty short stories while you sought publication for *Winter Birds*. Will they ever appear?

JG I'm hoping to put together a book of stories fairly soon. I do still occasionally publish short fiction, particularly in the science fiction and fantasy arenas.

RC You wrote a piece for the erotic fiction anthology *Flesh and the Word* which might be called a story.

JG   But I never thought of it as one. There's a story in it. I just didn't think about it that way at the time.

RC   Could you talk a little about sexual expressiveness in fiction? Thinking of *Dream Boy* specifically, I was interested in the clear sense of movement through that book in its sexual expressiveness. Your language in relation to sex is pointed and direct, or mystical and obtuse, depending on the psychology of your character.

JG   Yes. Sex between those two boys was in their state of mind. It was easy to write because they were innocent. They didn't have to construct themselves as gay. They were just boys who were in love with each other. It worked, so the book was sexy that way. But I didn't have to strain at it. And that's not ever been true for me before when I was trying to write about sex.

RC   Many writers say sexual writing is difficult.

JG   I know it is. It's hard as hell to make it sexy. Samuel Delany writes about sex well, but it's not always sexy when he writes it. It's very technical. My feeling is that when you get down to the level of the body parts, you've lost the war. It's not because it's pornographic. It's because when you're in sex you're aware. You're not thinking of any particular thing. You're just aware of the whole thing. If you can bring that feeling to it, it feels like sex. If you don't, it feels like a catalogue. I tend to think these days that as much as possible you've got to leave sex off the page—not for any particular reason except that mostly it makes for dull reading. I don't have any intellectual idea about it except that.

Boulevard, though, is about sex, so I can't leave it off the page. It's about a kid who moves from Alabama to New Orleans and gets a job in an adult bookstore. His life's about marketing sex and knowing what people want in terms of buying magazines. All of that is stuff that I've set myself up as trying to talk about. But when I get down to writing about sex, I try to stay in the mind of the person having it as much as possible, or between the two minds somehow, if that makes sense. When I was writing about Roy and Nathan in *Dream Boy*, a lot of times I felt they were so close to merging into one being that I could help them with that.

I could be between them when they were having sex, and not have to be anything but that. That space is erotic, so what I write about it doesn't have to be particularly detailed. It just has to be erotic. It can't shy away from saying they're having sex. You can't shy away from writing the word *cock* now and then. But if you use it in every sentence, the sexiness is gone.

The best example of that to me is Sade. He writes about nothing but the sex act, but it's never sexy. It's always mechanical; it's always domination—predator and prey. It's never anything you'd want to do yourself . . . I hope.

RC   What about D. H. Lawrence?

JG   Lawrence never really made a connection to me. I read *Women in Love* and *Sons and Lovers*. I admired them. But he's an example of what praise can do to you. I'd read about what a sexy writer he was, so when I read him, I thought: "This isn't much." Too much angst.

I think angst is the curse of the upper class. The people I know are too concerned with eating and paying the rent to have too much angst.

RC   We haven't talked about AIDS and writing at all so far.

JG   Well, I have to talk about that so much, I don't really want to. I've been HIV-positive for sixteen years. I get to talk about it enough. That's one reason I don't overtly write about it—I don't really care about it. It's in *Comfort and Joy*. Danny's HIV-positive at that point, and he and his lover are dealing with it.

★   ★   ★

RC   Congratulations on the appearance of *Boulevard*. You mentioned in an interview listening to different kinds of music while writing. Could you elaborate?

JG   Yes. When I was writing *Boulevard*, I was listening to a lot of the disco music we danced to in those days. It's odd to associate that music with

New Orleans, rather than jazz. But it worked. When I was writing *Dream Boy*, I was listening to a lot of Tori Amos, Toni Childs, the Indigo Girls, and old Joni Mitchell. With the play *Mr. Universe*, it was Simple Minds. For the play *In Berlin*, it was Emmylou Harris—especially her versions of "Wayfaring Stranger" and "Green Pastures." And if I want to write something melancholy, I listen to really sad love songs.

RC   The play *In Berlin* [2000] concerned the story of Walter, a disillusioned, middle-aged American gay man, and his experiences of S&M sex in Germany. That must have been both a further thematic and geographical departure for you. To what extent did you research the topic, and/or Berlin itself?

JG   I did a good deal of research for that play, including watching a dungeon session in Berlin that proved to be pivotal to the play. I don't want to go into more detail, other than to say that I don't see myself as a sadist or masochist. I'm interested in the notion that pleasure can be manipulated, though.

RC   You were working on a play entitled *Fascination* recently—about America's fascination with serial killers. I know you were reading about Jeffrey Dahmer a lot at one point. What particularly drew you to that topic, and has the play reached fruition?

JG   I completed *Fascination* over this past summer [2002] when I was invited for a residency at the O'Neill Playwriting Center. I'm working on it for About Face Theater, where I've been in residence since 1999. The two founding directors there—Eric Rosen and Kyle Hall—proposed the idea to me as something they wanted to use their theater to explore, and I agreed to take it on.

RC   Not many writers of so-called "literary fiction" also write fantasy novels, which you did with *Kirith Kirin*. What appeal does fantasy literature have? Are there things you can explore in it that wouldn't find an outlet elsewhere?

JG Speculative writing has always been one of my chief interests as a reader and a writer; I cut my teeth writing science fiction stories and trying to sell them to *Galaxy* magazine. Science fiction and fantasy offer a writer the chance to throw this world away and invent another one. I probably read more of this writing at the moment than anything else, though I read pretty widely. The speculation satisfies my need to wonder about the future. In particular for gay writing, it gives me a chance to frame a world in which homosexuality has always existed and always been accepted, as in *Kirith Kirin*.

Many of the writers I admire most write in this field, including Connie Willis, Nancy Kress, Joe Haldeman, Samuel Delany, and Michael Bishop.

RC For the last few years, you've been teaching creative writing too. Does that experience help in your own writing? What do you think can be taught?

JG I studied writing as an undergraduate under the tutelage of Doris Betts and Max Steele. Doris had no doubts about her ability to teach writing, as long as nobody presumed she could teach talent. I take the same idea in my own teaching. I should be able to make any student's writing improve if I know what I'm doing. So I guess the answer I'd give is, yes, writing can be taught and can be learned. Talent is not the whole picture, and talent is not ever enough, really.

RC In a recent discussion with Dorothy Allison, you mentioned wanting to write about Atlanta fictionally. Is that still the plan?

JG It is my plan to write more about Atlanta but not in the next couple of books!

RC Thanks very much for your time.

SIX

STEPHEN McCAULEY

STEPHEN MCCAULEY is the author of four novels: *The Object of My Affection* (filmed by Nicholas Hytner, 1998), *The Easy Way Out*, *The Man of the House*, and *True Enough*.

McCauley was born in 1955 in Woburn, Massachusetts. He studied English for a B.A. degree at the University of Vermont in Burlington, and went on to take the M.F.A at Columbia University. He then moved to Boston, taking a succession of jobs including teaching kindergarten and working in a travel agency. The publication of his first novel, *The Object of My Affection* (New York: Simon and Schuster, 1987), and its being optioned by Twentieth Century Fox soon afterwards, allowed McCauley to concentrate on his fiction writing.

A second novel, *The Easy Way Out* (New York: Simon and Schuster, 1992), was followed by *The Man of the House* (New York: Simon and Schuster, 1996). McCauley's fourth and most recent book is *True Enough* (New York: Simon and Schuster, 2001).

McCauley's short story "The Whole Truth" was published in *Harper's* magazine in 1993 and reprinted in Erica Kates, ed., *On the Couch: Stories About Psychotherapy* (New York: Grove Atlantic Press, 1997). His autobiographical essay, "Let's Say," was included in Patrick Merla, ed., *Boys Like Us: Gay Writers Tell Their Coming Out Stories* (New York: Avon, 1996). A second short story, "At the Threshold," appeared in the *Boston Globe Magazine* (January 3, 1999). McCauley's reviews, articles, commentary, and fiction have also been published in the *New York Times Book Review*, the *New York Times*, *Vogue*, *Sophisticated Traveller*, *Travel and Leisure*, and the *Boston Phoenix*, among other publications. In 1998 he was named Chevalier in the Order of Arts and Letters by the Ministry of Culture in France, where his books are bestsellers. He has taught Creative Writing at the University of Massachusetts, Wellesley College, Brandeis University, and Harvard University.

McCauley lives in Cambridge, Massachusetts, where this interview took place on Saturday, October 25, 1997. It was revised in August 2002, at which point the material following the asterisks was added.

RC   Reed Woodhouse's article, "Five Schools of Gay Fiction," bracketed you in a group of what he called "assimilative" novelists. What do you make of the term?

SM   A friend offered to send me the article but I declined. I find almost all literary criticism interesting in a theoretical way, but the more esoteric varieties—deconstruction, queer theory—don't have much to do with the way I read fiction. As a writer, I don't find that kind of intellectual analysis very useful. I don't have lofty intellectual goals in mind when I write—just the desire to tell a story, entertain the reader, and hopefully say something relevant about people's lives. I'm a self-conscious and insecure writer anyway, and to add the "Five Schools of Gay Fiction" and the question of which one I belonged to to my list of worries would probably stop me cold in my tracks. Especially since the assimilative school sounds like it's the most reactionary and dull. Oh well.

Writers can tell you what they wanted to accomplish or say in their books, but ultimately the work speaks for itself and is fair game for anyone's interpretation. I'm sure Woodhouse has a lot of great points. I'd lap it up if I thought it would be inspiring, but I'm afraid I'd find it stifling. I think writers are better off staying out those kinds of discussions.

RC   I agree that writers can get distracted by debates about their work. They can't ever master them—whereas they can master the process of writing the next book.

SM   Try to master, anyway. I do think I can learn from what critics have to say about my work. I have no illusions that my books are flawless. Far from it. But it sounded to me as if this was a criticism of the way I view the world, not my prose or my technical skills. And for better or worse, my world view is what it is. I work at improving my skills, but I'd rather let my view of life evolve on its own.

RC   Do you write with any conception of your readership generally?

SM   When I was writing my first book, I tried very hard not to fantasize about a readership at all. Of course I hoped it would get published, but mostly I just wanted to finish it. I was in my late twenties and I'd never finished anything. I kept entering and dropping out of graduate programs and taking jobs that weren't likely to lead anywhere. The desire to write was always in the back of my mind—but saying, or even admitting, to myself that I wanted to be a writer seemed too audacious. No one in my family read for pleasure, so reading was never encouraged, let alone writing.

When *The Object of My Affection* was published, I got a lot of mail. The novel's written in a very conversational style, and I think readers assumed the narrator was me. He's a pretty unintimidating, approachable person. A lot of women wrote telling me they were in a relationship with a gay man similar to the one in the book and asking for advice. Gay men wrote mostly to say they appreciated the fact that George, the main character, leads a very ordinary life they could relate to. I didn't end up feeling I knew who my readership was exactly, but I got a sense of what people were drawn to in my writing.

RC   Would you say this response from readers has shaped the books that followed?

SM   To some extent, I'm sure it did. Mostly I choose themes that have relevance for me at the time I'm writing—father-son relations, the difficulties of commitment, and so on. But I do want to please readers, especially the ones who keep returning to my books. I wanted *The Man of the House* to be a more melancholy book than my previous two, but still very much a comedy. Some readers told me they found it bleak and without hope, which wasn't my intention. They said the narrator's inertia was depressing. That's made me more careful and, hopefully, exact about creating mood and character in what I'm writing now. On the other hand, someone told me they were disappointed that *The Man of the House* wasn't as whimsical as my first book. But that really wasn't what I wanted to write, so I'm sorry, but too bad.

RC　You mentioned the letters that assumed the narrator *was* you. In *The Man of the House* there's a scene in the teaching class where the same mistake is made. How do you react to that kind of assumption? Is it simply a mistake?

SM　Not completely. All three of my books have narrators with voices that are basically variations on my own. They're getting older as I age. They have a lot of my observations of the world, and sometimes jobs I've done. But their lives are their own, and every scene in every novel is entirely invented. If a character doesn't take on a life of his own on the page, it's very hard—almost impossible—for me to write. Sometimes when I'm writing in the first person, I begin to filter my perceptions through the character and I become more like him. Like an actor, I suppose, playing a role. My narrators are more articulate than I am, so I don't mind if people assume I'm just like them.

RC　Compared to some writers, there isn't a lot else of you to read, apart from the novels. There's only the piece in *Boys Like Us*, which I notice suggests some vague parallels of experience with *The Object of My Affection*. Otherwise, there's little for a reader to draw on. Did you decide not to publish only autobiographical pieces?

SM　No, it's just that I don't get asked that often. When Patrick Merla asked me if I'd like to write something for *Boys Like Us*, I said I'd love to. I thought it would be easy, but it took me a long time and it's very short. I ended up writing it in the second person as a way of distancing myself from the material and pretending I was writing about someone else. That's kind of odd because when I write fiction in the first person, I try to get as close to the characters and material as I can.

I'm not that interested in memoirs in general. A lot seem to operate on the "this-happened-to-me-therefore-it's-interesting" theory, and end up formless. In fiction you have to earn the reader's interest a little more. That said, I think some of the most interesting literary writing about AIDS has been in memoir form.

RC   Perhaps that's because the form is conferred in that case; a structure is offered by the subject matter.

SM   I think you're right. And that might be a drawback of using AIDS in fiction—the limitations of having a form conferred.

RC   I didn't realize until I reread it that AIDS, or the fear of it, was quite so prominent in *The Object of My Affection*. It jumps out around page ten.

SM   Really? I don't remember the book very clearly. I have tried including AIDS more prominently in each of my books in assorted ways, but most often I end up taking it out.

I think of my books as comedies of manners, dealing mostly with relationships of various sorts. The tone is always fairly ironic, and I'm not real comfortable writing about AIDS in that tone. In *The Easy Way Out*, for instance, the characters obsess about their relationship problems and whether or not to buy a house. If you introduce AIDS, those problems just fade to insignificance. If they don't—if someone's still obsessing about real estate while a friend or lover is sick—the characters can easily become unsympathetic.

RC   Most AIDS fiction that has used comedy has done so in a way that involves a very strong identification of the author figure with what's in the book.

SM   Like David Feinberg.

RC   Yes. It's true in almost every case, except John Weir's *The Irreversible Decline of Eddie Socket*.

SM   Maybe so. He did it well—and with a good deal of irony, as I remember. I didn't mean to suggest one "shouldn't" write about AIDS in a comic or ironic tone, just that I don't feel comfortable doing it. I feel lucky in not having lost huge numbers of friends or, as happened to a lot of people in New York and San Francisco, an entire community and way of life, so maybe I've felt I've had slightly less right to write about it, especially in an ironic tone.

RC   What you said about structural balance interests me. I can see that once introduced, the subject of AIDS demands to become the emotional center of the book.

SM   Yes. It's a delicate balance. Likewise in *The Man of the House*, I originally wanted the narrator to discover—as he was having problems dealing with his own father—that he has a twelve-year-old son he never knew about. But as soon as that fact was revealed to him, it had to become the center of his life. Otherwise, he seemed like an uncaring shit, and his own problems with his father became less pressing and interesting.

RC   To return to AIDS briefly: who did you have in mind when you mentioned the memoir form?

SM   Of course Paul Monette's *Borrowed Time*, which is, I suppose, a classic of the genre at this point. I liked Fenton Johnson's book, too—*Geography of the Heart*. And I like Mark Doty's writing very much.

RC   What about Armistead Maupin's *Tales of the City*, as we've been discussing comic writing and AIDS?

SM   That really is a kind of ongoing social history of San Francisco over the course of a couple decades. The cast of characters is so huge and spread across the spectrum of sexual preference and gender and class, that there's a different approach to structure. It isn't about a small group of connected characters in the way that many novels are.

RC   Adam Mars-Jones found AIDS to be a real problem in the *Tales*: for once, it did threaten the kind of democracy of the series at the level of plot—what he called "the approximate interchangeability of crises." You didn't feel that?

SM   It's certainly true that the tone of the series changes when AIDS is introduced. But I think it was changing anyway, as Maupin began writing in the novel form rather than writing a newspaper serial. I think there was a natural drift toward deeper emotional crises and away from cannibal cult kind of crises, as in the second or third book, I can't remember which. I'd probably have to go back and read them straight through, as one long work, to have an informed opinion. I'm teaching now and can't read anything but student fiction for the rest of the semester.

RC   A lot of writers are ambivalent about their involvement in creative writing programs. Do you think the idea of teaching writing is sound?

SM   It is if you're being well paid. I don't teach on a graduate level, so there's no pressure about preparing students for careers as writers. Maybe I'd have problems with that. You can't teach talent, but you can teach structure and attention to detail. You can teach grammar. You can teach students to be better writers than they are, and to read with more appreciation of craft. And frankly, I try to get students thinking about their voices and their view of life. I hope there's some value in that, even if they finish the course and never write another word of fiction.

RC   Is there a wrong way for a gay author to write fiction? I was reading something by Gary Indiana which was dismissive of rounded, bourgeois, nineteenth-century, solidly constructed, middlebrow fictions.

SM   I'm so middlebrow—or lowbrow—in my approach to writing and structure, it's hard to relate to that idea. But I certainly hate the notion that there might be a "right" and a "wrong" way for gay writers to write. It seems to imply we're all the same, or that there's a right and wrong way to be gay.

RC   I was thinking of possible conflicts between typical gay life experiences and traditional narrative closures—as in *Jane Eyre*, say.

SM   You mean marriage?

RC For instance. One of the successes of your books is this sense of shape and form. A payoff. A closure is there—but it's identified at plot level with things which are quite subversive: a decision to break up, or even more awkwardly in *The Man of the House*, a mother's decision to listen to her son and move away from a relationship. The sense of moving away from relationships is often quite climactic.

SM That's true for all of them. You're right.

RC I wouldn't expect you were necessarily conscious of that.

SM I wasn't until you pointed it out. It probably has to do with my struggle to break from my family or something of that embarrassing ilk. I seem to write about characters who have misjudged their situations or misunderstood who they are and what they want out of life. I don't like ending a book with the suggestion that a solution has been found and everything is now going to fine. I'm not enough of an optimist to believe that's how life works. I prefer to get the characters to a point of self-awareness, where things have the possibility of working out. Getting out of a bad situation or an unsatisfying relationship opens up that possibility.

The Object of My Affection has a tidier ending than my other books, and if I were writing it today, I'd probably make it a little less neat. But even there, the real love story is between the gay man and straight woman, and the climax is his decision to move away from her and in with his boyfriend.

I know people like more unambiguous, plainly happy endings, especially in comedy. But I try to find what feels like the truth for the characters and stick with that, even if, as in *The Man of the House*, it displeases some readers. I have a pretty middlebrow sensibility, but I still can't imagine calculating an ending for the sake of sales.

RC I thought one of the best things about *The Man of the House* was the way you constructed a series of more or less parallel crises between gay and straight characters—but the parallel isn't pursued obsessively. The plot also allows for a moment that will deny that simple association of experiences. For instance, where Marcus says to Clyde: "You don't appreciate the perils of heterosexual sex." Clyde says: "Whatever they are, I'll take them over AIDS any day." A book that constructs parallels between gay and straight characters should not only do that, but keep a sense of the distinctness of experience.

SM It would be silly to pretend the experiences are the same. Something as small, even, as showing affection in public has completely different consequences for gay and straight people in most places in the world. And then there's the availability of anonymous sex for gay men, and the more relaxed rules of conduct in most gay relationships. But I think it's equally silly to pretend that a lot of the basic emotions underlying relationships aren't almost identical for gay and straight people, such as the desire for love, companionship, or acceptance—affection.

I like commenting on heterosexual behavior from a gay point of view. It challenges the assumption that straight is the standard against which all other behavior must be judged. I'm sure a lot of gay behavior looks funny to straight people, but a lot of heterosexual marriages look hilarious to me. Of course, my characters are most often outside of the dominant gay culture as well, so there's opportunity to comment from the outside on that as well.

RC In *The Object of My Affection*, at the end of one chapter, George decides to junk the situation as it is and go out to a club to be with the boys, "which is after all where he belonged," runs the phrase, I think. So although you write about exceptional gay figures, you use them analytically to focus on gay subculture too.

SM Like me, George feels out-of-sync no matter where he is; but after feeling pushed aside by his roommate and her boyfriend, he goes to a gay bar, hoping to feel more accepted and at home. I'm not sure how he felt when he got there. That chapter isn't in the book.

RC You spoke about the chance of using Clyde to comment satirically on dysfunctional relationships in straight characters.

SM Well, he has his own dysfunctional gay relationships.

RC   But they're not deeply identified with a particular, narrow notion of gay subculture—tricking and so on. Is that world less interesting?

SM   There are some things that are of great interest to me personally, but of less interest to me as a writer. Tricking is one of those. One of the pleasures of anonymous sex is the complete lack of emotional attachment. It's about bodies, not people, and sometimes, that's just what I want sex to be. But as a writer, I'm always interested in people, in relationships.

RC   Could it be to do with neatness and order? The subculture's behavioral codes are ways of classifying gay experience. I noticed when rereading your novels that there's an ongoing motif of neatness or cleanliness as slightly disreputable. Maybe, then, there's also a suggested attractiveness in the messiness or inexactness of relationships that are potentially more boundless.

SM   I can't imagine starting with something as general or organized as "behavioral codes" or even "gay experience." I have to start with some very specific characters in mind. Working out a plot is, in one sense, bringing some sense of order to chaos—out of tangled lives and psyches, and so on.

Gay relationships can be especially messy because we have so few sanctioned rules and rituals. You have to make everything up from scratch. It can be liberating—but confusing as well. A friend asked me if I thought his desire for a monogamous relationship with his lover was too imitative of heterosexual marriage. I was confused by the question. If that's what he wants, that's what he wants. Why not just go with it?

And there's the mess of ending gay relationships. A lot of gay male couples seem to segue into chaste roommates or companions who aren't exactly sure what their relationship is. One big advantage of having gay marriage would be in having gay divorce. You could say: "This is over. Let's split up the property, hate each other for a while, and then move on."

RC   Property is a part of it, and family as property is the other part, maybe. A homophobic commentator would probably say the problem we're describing is because there's so little at stake in gay relationships.

SM   Feelings are at stake, and those are ultimately more important than legal vows and public proclamations. Homophobes will always find a way to devalue and deride homosexual experience.

RC   As it features in the books so much, I have to ask you for a personal view on gay parenting. It features heavily in both *The Object of My Affection* and *The Man of the House.*

SM   I've never had any desire to have children, but parenting pops up in my books often enough to make me think the desire's there, subconsciously. Parenting is a good device for fiction, because it involves another life. High stakes, speaking of stakes.

RC   Do you think it is the right issue for gay rights campaigners to latch on to?

SM   A lot of gay people are raising kids now, so it's inevitable as a political issue. It's a reality of gay life. Gay Pride parades are beginning to look like recess at a day care center. Sometimes I have the feeling that gay people want to validate their relationships or themselves as people by having kids, but I suppose that's why a lot of straight people have kids too. Frankly, I think the world would be better if a lot more people, of every persuasion, decided not to have kids. The world is too crowded already.

RC   There's the character in *The Man of the House* who wants to donate a Y-chromosome, but not pursue any relationship beyond the immediate moment. Equally, there's the moment where Clyde reflects on having naively idealized Louise's situation. I suppose both of those moments suggest some scepticism about gay men's engagement with fatherhood?

SM   A friend of mine was recently talking to a woman who's looking for a sperm donor. He was very serious about it. He said: "The best thing is, she doesn't want any involvement from the father." I thought: "Well, what's the point?" It seemed to me he just had a narcissistic desire to replicate his genes. One of the great sorrows in my life was having a detached, emotionally uninvolved father. Maybe I took his comment too personally. But since gay people often have to go through great contortions to have children, you'd think the desire to raise them would be especially strong.

RC   Each of your narrators has a pressing relationship with his father remembered or shown. Do you object to readings of your book which would seek to identify that aspect with you?

SM   When a writer repeats certain themes in his books, you have to assume they're of great personal significance. There is one part of the narrator/author confusion that I do worry about. In order to write successfully about a character, an author has to know him better than he knows himself. You have to be able to see behind a character's defenses. If it seems that as the writer I'm too close to the characters to have that insight, then there's a problem.

RC   Something which reminded me of *Tales of the City* was a suspicion of traditional career structures. In *The Object of My Affection*, Howard's the only one who's fulfilled by work. Is there something general that could be said about the culture of work and its relationship to sexuality for you?

SM   I recently had a student, a straight guy, tell me that he wanted to be a writer but also wanted to get married to his girlfriend. He felt pressure to have a career soon after graduation, and he knew that if he wanted to be a writer, nothing would be guaranteed right away, possibly ever. A gay student would have the same needs to make money, pay off loans, support himself, but I think career expectations aren't as pressing. At least they weren't for me. I knew I wasn't going to have to support a family or impress a fiancée's parents with my career track, so I was freer. On the other hand, there were some professions that I felt categorically shut out of because I was openly gay.

RC   There are, though, now gay professionals—lawyers, doctors, bankers.

SM   True, but in the mid-seventies it was nearly impossible to be out and be, for example, a partner at a big law firm, or to be out and expect to advance at an investment firm. In some places in the country, it's still very difficult.

RC To become a writer takes a lot of commitment in material and financial terms. Are you suggesting that dedicating yourself to it wasn't difficult?

SM It was very difficult to dedicate myself to writing due to doubts about my abilities. But I don't think I was ever an especially career-oriented person. After coming out at nineteen, I spent my early twenties trying to settle into and establish a sense of identity as a gay person. For some people, those years are about establishing a career. I think my understanding of who I am as a gay man and, in a more general way, as a person came together for me when I found my voice as a writer, which was also finding my current career.

It's very hard to feel settled career-wise as a writer. I don't know when my ability to get published, or to write, will end. So I teach to keep career options open. I also do ghost-writing jobs, as another possible fallback position.

RC I want to move to a more general question about gay fiction. Did you have a sense when you started writing that there was much unexplored territory in gay life, or were there writers that had already captured certain truths about gay men's lives for you?

SM The gay fiction I was reading—the stories in *Christopher Street*, Andrew Holleran's *Dancer from the Dance*, Edmund White's *Nocturnes for the King of Naples*—dealt with a world that was very foreign to me. But I thought that was the only world you could write about if you were going to write "gay fiction." So I made embarrassing attempts at writing about things I knew nothing about. When that didn't work out for me, I tried writing in my own voice, about the kinds of experiences I'd had as a gay person. Suddenly, I felt I had something to say as a writer. Because, as I've said, it was all filtered through my view of the world, I didn't worry about whether or not it had been explored before. It was just my best shot at saying something that was genuinely mine.

RC   Does that lead you to the view that what are now often seen as foundational texts for gay fiction, in some respects offered an unhelpfully narrow account of gay lives?

SM   Not at all. Those books opened up the possibility of writing about gay lives in any way. They validated gay love and sexuality and desire as worthwhile subjects for serious fiction. And even if the worlds they described were unknown to me, there were certain universal emotional truths about desiring someone of your own gender that I could relate to.

RC   As a reader, then, you didn't feel what David Leavitt wrote about *Dancer from the Dance*—a kind of oppression as an adolescent at the prospect of entering a culture with a cult of beauty?

SM   I came out in the early seventies in Vermont. Being gay was part of the hippie culture and the political fringe. It wasn't about being beautiful; it was about being a vegetarian. It was about being earnest. By the time I read *Dancer from the Dance*, I knew I didn't fit into the culture of beauty, and to be honest, it didn't interest me that much. I'm as dazzled by beautiful men as the next person, but my sexual fantasies have never involved beauty or physical perfection. When I lived in New York, I had a fairly active social and sexual life without once going to Fire Island or a disco. Water has a way of finding its own level, if you see what I mean.

A good writer opens up a world for you. In the case of Holleran, it was a strange, almost surreal world, but the book brought it to life. It's a romantic book and very exotic. Dennis Cooper does the same thing. His sensibility is about as far from mine as you can get. I don't want to live in the world he describes, but he's enormously talented. He creates a whole world which he pulls you into with the strength of his prose.

RC   To what extent does sexual expressiveness matter in fiction? Some of the books you mentioned are pretty explicit and that was part of what was considered groundbreaking about them. By contrast, sex doesn't feature that explicitly in your novels.

SM   When *The Object of My Affection* appeared, some reviews in the gay press said: "This book is not sexually explicit." Like the flip side of those warning labels they slap on rap records. I found it odd, as if it might offend some readers that there was no graphic sex.

It's very hard to write good sex scenes, and if they seem forced or if you sense the writer jerking off as he's writing it, I find them excruciating. Alan Hollinghurst's *The Swimming-Pool Library* is one of my favorite gay novels. He writes brilliant sex scenes, and the book's full of them. They're erotic and titillating, but completely in character for the narrator and true to his life.

RC   It's integral to the work, you mean? Does that suggest that if a sex scene presented itself within your conception of a book's storyline—if there was a necessary truth to be told, and there was no other way—that you'd consider including it?

SM   Of course. It's not as if I have moral objections. I'm shy but not a prude. But mandatory sex scenes that reveal nothing about character— just lots of descriptions of genitals and bodily fluids—are boring and embarrassing. They remind me of those mandatory nude scenes in movies from the seventies. They no longer look shocking, risky, or politically interesting. They look silly.

RC   And this subject is a symptom of some not especially literary expectations being applied to gay literature. It's a narrow political view of literature which conflates sexuality and sexual expression, for instance.

SM   I think it equates being sexually explicit as a writer with being sexually liberated. I don't believe that's true. There's a British novel from 1950 called *Scenes from Provincial Life* by William Cooper. Two couples—one gay, one straight—share the use of a cottage in a provincial town in the 1930s, just before the Second World War. There's no explicit sex, but I found the casual attitude toward the gay couple—just another two people who argue a lot in a charming way, like the straight couple—extremely liberated.

RC   Who have you most enjoyed reading yourself? Who led you into writing in the first place? Or who are you reading when you think: "This is too good to write against"?

SM   Whenever I read Mann's *Death in Venice*, I think: "Why would any-one bother writing anything else?"

RC   Do you read widely in contemporary fiction? Some novelists prefer reading nonfiction.

SM   I don't read widely in contemporary fiction. I was badly educated in that I have a lot of literary catching up to do in the classics. I have some contemporary favorites, and I read everything by them: Richard Price; Alan Hollinghurst; Peter Cameron; Carol Anshaw. But I go through phases of reading nonfiction, sometimes to learn about a subject I want to use in a book.

Patrick White is one of my favorite writers. I reread *The Eye of the Storm* every once in a while. There's always more to discover in it.

RC   Are you looking at elements of style and structure preeminently?

SM   In the case of Patrick White, I'm not sure. Maybe it's just his love affair with language. His sentences have very odd rhythms. He's misan-thropic, even nasty at times, but very funny. You have a sense of a writer in complete control of his craft. It's exhilarating—like watching any ex-traordinarily gifted professional.

Christopher Isherwood is another writer I love. He's amazingly precise. He introduces a character, and within a few sentences you know him or her. They're in front of you. Unlike Patrick White, he doesn't draw at-tention to himself as a stylist. I especially love *The Berlin Stories* and *Down There on a Visit*.

RC   That's interesting. Most people name *A Single Man*, if they're choos-ing one of the postwar novels.

SM   That's a wonderful book. But there's something about it I don't warm to quite as much. I don't know why.

RC   It's the most accomplished book, but there's a certain lack of daring. What the book determines to show you isn't complicated or surprising.

SM Yes. It's a perfectly crafted and shaped book. I'm not necessarily drawn to books that feel perfect in that way. For instance, I love Theodore Dreiser, who's as sloppy, awkward, and wordy as they come. But when he's good—as in *An American Tragedy* or *Sister Carrie*—I love the "too-muchness" of it.

RC You mention writers whose reputations are potentially at turning points. None of them seems assured of "first league" status: Isherwood, White, Dreiser.

SM I'm not sure about their status, but people are still reading their work and that's about as much as any writer could ask for. White won the Nobel Prize. That's pretty good for one's stature.

RC The Isherwood diaries appeared recently. Do you pursue writers through letters and diaries? Is the biography of the writer interesting to you?

SM Not much—though I did just buy the Isherwood diaries. I won't sit down and read them cover-to-cover though.

RC The forthcoming biography by Peter Parker may reveal more.

SM I read his J. R. Ackerley biography. Ackerley's another wonderful writer. *Hindoo Holiday* is one of the more charming books you can read.

RC Is that another thing you look for—charm in a narrator?

SM It's an elusive quality and very hard to define. But you read the first paragraph of *Hindoo Holiday* and you're charmed, seduced. You think: "Okay, I'll listen to everything this person has to tell me." It's a quality that's easy to take for granted—to view as a trick the writer has pulled off and not as a genuine literary accomplishment. But in looking at that first paragraph, for example, you see that the appeal—the charm—comes from the exact structure of the sentences. In addition to being an elusive quality, it's fragile. If you change a few words, the beauty is gone. The meaning would be the same, but the charm would be lost. It's a real testament to Ackerley's control of language—his talent. It might not be a talent on the magnitude of Patrick White's, but it's very impressive in its own way.

RC Have James or Proust been important to you? They're almost totemic for so many gay writers.

SM Given the kinds of books I write, I'd feel silly saying I was influenced by Proust or James. But they give you a sense of how much you can accomplish in fiction, how much you can reveal about human nature. Proust in particular shows you the outer limits of what's possible, in terms of language, psychological accuracy, and beauty.

RC One of the great strengths of your books is this very exact sense of plotting—by which I don't mean correctness, so much as something to do with pace. The revelation of incidents is so measured and assured. Are these elements of craft developed simply through the practice of writing, or can you observe these things in other writers and learn that way?

SM I'm happy you feel that way. I'm very unsure about plotting, partly because I resist having too much happen in my books. Whenever I'm writing a chapter, I ask myself: "Why this scene on this day in the lives of these people?" There has to be some justification for choosing one moment over another. Something of interest has to happen, and it has to connect to events in the past and the future. That's how I think about plot. It doesn't have to be a big revelation or crisis, but it has to have roots in the past and consequences for the future.

RC Do you have any comment to make on the experience of the film adaptation of *The Object of My Affection*?

SM I just wrote someone about that. I said: "I wish I could say the book is better, but I haven't seen the movie, and I barely remember the book." What's interesting is that it took ten years to make *The Object of My Affection* into a movie. In that time the whole question of actors playing gay characters and the issues of AIDS and so on have gone through cycle after cycle. I read the final script and there were many characters I didn't recognize, and the whole social milieu was different from that of the book. But I like Wendy Wasserstein—the screenwriter—and Nicholas Hytner is an incredibly talented stage director. I suspect it will be a pretty good movie.

RC   Are you excited to see your work turned into film generally?

SM   It's a great thing for getting your name and the title of your book into the public eye. It's the kind of publicity a writer at my level can't afford to turn down. I feel lucky it's really happened. I'm not the sort of writer who's likely to win literary prizes. But in my mind, the movie is completely separate from my book. The book is what it is, flaws and all. I visited the set for two hours once and no one ever asked my opinion about casting or anything else. It's my book, but it's their movie.

RC   In Britain we still have debates about the relative cultural worthiness of films and books.

SM   I teach this literature course at Brandeis University now, and the subject is the comic novel. I was going to bring in a movie. A friend of mine said: "Don't bring in a movie. It's like showing them pictures of naked people. Show them pictures of naked people, and who wants to see anything else? Show them a movie, and who's going to want to talk about books any more?" But I've always loved movies.

RC   As a writer, the idea of films becoming dominant in culture at the expense of books doesn't concern you?

SM   All you can do as a writer is try your best to write whatever it is you have in you. People will always want to read books, and you just have to hope a few will want to read yours.

RC   Homosexuality as a theme divides films and books. Whatever happened in gay literature in the 1970s didn't happen in film. To an extent, it never has happened in film, for reasons of audience, marketing, and money.

SM   For financial reasons, movies have to appeal to vast audiences to turn a profit. They're much more cautious about offending people or turning them off. In many ways, television is doing a better job of presenting gay characters in a casual way, as just another piece of the whole social fabric.

RC   You don't think TV is still cowed by a conservative assessment of the audience? Take *Tales from the City*'s move from PBS to cable.

SM   PBS receives government funding, so it's a lightning rod for conservative politicians who want to appeal to their base of support. But the days when companies pull advertising from a TV show with positive gay characters seem to be long gone.

RC   Are you tempted to write something dramatic or cinematic yourself?

SM   I've dabbled with it off and on for a while, but never wholeheartedly.

RC   I notice the books tend to appear almost exactly every five years. Is there any reason for that?

SM   I'm trying to get the fourth one out quicker, but I'm not finished yet, so I don't know. It's definitely hurt my career that I write so slowly. People forget about you, and it's hard for the publisher to build momentum around your work. Your audience drifts away. It's kind of a painful subject.

RC   Some first-time novelists today appear so young and so prolific.

SM   Right. In my case, it felt like I didn't know myself that well until I got into my late twenties. Then I was able to figure out what it was that I had to say.

RC   Patrick in *The Easy Way Out* is a travel agent who's very resistant to traveling. As you worked as a travel agent yourself, I wanted to ask whether you thought travel broadened the mind.

SM   I guess it depends where you go. Some people are inquisitive by nature. For them, travel is broadening. But there's the other kind of person who looks at Notre Dame and says: "That looks like the church back home." They try to make everything familiar and resist the foreign. I'm probably somewhere in the middle. I'm very inquisitive about people. I love grilling people about their lives. But when I travel, I like to settle in a little and feel at home, establish a routine.

Like Patrick, I tend to think most people hate to travel but love to have traveled.

★   ★   ★

RC   Congratulations on the publication of *True Enough*. One obvious question concerns the fact that in this novel you've shifted from first- to third-person narration. Did the material seem to demand that? Was it particularly challenging or rewarding?

SM   I started writing it in the first person and then switched over to the third. The book isn't about one person's journey or transformation in the way my other novels are, so I felt it had to be in the third person. The point of view is still very much from inside the characters' heads, so it's not all that different from the first person, on a technical level. There was something very liberating about switching points of view. It was a lot less claustrophobic than working in the first person.

RC   Your 1999 story "At the Threshold" was written in the first person. Which voice do you expect to dominate in future material?

SM   I suppose it will depend upon the book or story. I love the immediacy of the first person and the intimacy of talking directly to the reader.

As a reader, I often find myself pulled in more quickly by a first-person narrator. But it does have limitations, and having written in the third person, I feel the limitations more acutely. Hopefully I'll continue to use both. It might be fun to try some sweeping omniscient narrator as well, but right now, that seems a little too artificial.

RC   In *True Enough*, you poked fun at the popularity of the memoir form with Rosemary Boyle's *Dead Husband*. Boyle is "prepared to provide an expert opinion on anything, as long as it helped promote the book." Your reading public, by contrast, would probably consider you pretty reclusive. Are you horrified at the idea of becoming a sort of public author figure?

SM   For better or worse, I don't see any imminent threat of that happening. A friend sent me a clipping from a gay paper in Chicago that said I had died. I guess I really am taking too much time between books.

RC   In *True Enough*, Desmond Sullivan observes that "there's a key to almost any life, a piece that holds the entire puzzle together and makes sense of the disparate fragments." That struck me as an apt summary of the biographer's need for clarification or rationalization of a life. By contrast, I suppose, a novelist can go a long way with irresolution or ambiguity in fictional characters. Could you comment?

SM   When I'm writing, I usually come across some aspect of a character's life that makes him or her come alive for me. I'd written many pages about Jane Cody, one of the main characters in *True Enough*, but still didn't feel I really knew who she was. And then I started writing a scene in which she was making a list of what she had to do that day. I realized she was writing everything in code, to deceive the people who might come across the list. Suddenly she made sense to me. I could see her and hear her voice. I made that scene the first one in the book, and I filtered all of her reactions and perceptions throughout the book through her impulse—or compulsion—to lie or alter the truth in some way. Those moments of recognition—when the pieces come together—are the most exhilarating for me when I'm writing. Unfortunately, they're also the arrest.

RC   Rosemary quips of Boston: "I can certainly understand coming here to die. It's coming here to live that I don't understand." You seem very settled. Have you ever considered living elsewhere?

SM   I've done a good deal more traveling since we last spoke, and every time I'm in another city, I wonder why I stay in Boston. As a writer, I could theoretically live anywhere. But I have family ties in Boston and lots of friends, and I suppose I'm a New Englander at heart. I make plans to move but never follow through on them. I don't suppose I ever will. But I do like spending brief spells—a couple weeks or a few months—in other places.

RC   Jane's rather horrifying experiences with her precocious son Gerald were very funny, I thought. I was trying to think of a literary source for his knowingness, and could only come up with Thomas Hardy's *Jude the Obscure*. Then again, perhaps you had a source from life? I remember you taught kindergarten.

SM   My impression is that kids are getting taller and smarter, or at least more verbal. Gerald is an exaggerated version of a couple of kids I've met. I wanted to write about a really difficult child, a little monster who isn't easy to love. I get tired of reading about wonderful, delightful children. They're not all so lovely. Some folks told me they found him implausible, but I had so much fun writing about him, I couldn't resist. I figure in comedy you have license to exaggerate for the sake of laughs.

RC   I noticed that film options had been taken out on both *The Easy Way Out* and *The Man of the House*. Is it likely that something will come of them?

SM   No.

RC   On that note, thanks very much for your time.

SEVEN

COLM TÓIBÍN

COLM TÓIBÍN is the author of a number of nonfiction books, and five novels: *The South, The Heather Blazing, The Story of the Night, The Blackwater Lightship.* and *The Master.*

Tóibín was born in 1955 in Enniscorthy, County Wexford, Ireland. His father Micheal was a secondary teacher in the Christian Brothers School in Enniscorthy and founded its Castle Museum. His writings on the town were later edited by Colm Tóibín and published as *Enniscorthy: History and Heritage* (Dublin: New Island Books, 1998). Tóibín, the second youngest of five children, went to school in Enniscorthy and Wexford. He left in 1972 to study History and English at University College, Dublin. When he graduated three years later, he immediately left for Barcelona, where he stayed for three years, teaching at the Dublin School of English and studying Catalan.

Tóibín returned to Dublin in 1978, beginning work on an M.A. on the American poet Anthony Hecht, which he never completed. He also wrote for *In Dublin, Hibernia,* and the *Sunday Tribune* (Dublin). In 1981 he became Features Editor of *In Dublin* and, a year later, the Editor of *Magill,* then Ireland's main current affairs magazine, where he stayed till 1985. In 1985 he edited *Seeing Is Believing: Moving Statues in Ireland* (Mountrath, County Laois: Pilgrim Press, 1985). He then began traveling—first throughout South America, and next in the Sudan and Egypt. A selection of Tóibín's journalism from the 1980s—including material on South America and Africa—was collected in *Trial of the Generals: Selected Journalism, 1980–1990* (Dublin: Raven Arts Press, 1990).

Tóibín's first novel, *The South* (London: Serpent's Tail, 1990; New York: Viking, 1991), set in Ireland and Catalonia, was finished in 1986 but not published for four years, having being turned down by most English publishers. It won the 1991 Irish Times–Aer Lingus First Novel Prize and was shortlisted for the Whitbread First Novel Prize. *Walking Along the Border* (London: Queen Anne Press, 1987), with photographs by Tony O'Shea, an account of travels between Northern Ireland and the Irish Republic, appeared in 1987. This was later reissued as *Bad Blood: A Walk Along the Irish Border* (London and New York: Vintage, 1994). Tóibín collaborated with O'Shea again on *Dubliners* (London: McDonald, 1990). In 1987 Tóibín's essay *Martyrs and Metaphors* (Dublin: Raven Arts Press) was issued as a pamphlet; it was later republished in Dermot Bolger, ed., *Letters from a New Island* (Dublin: Raven Arts Press, 1991).

In 1988, Tóibín spent a further year in Catalonia, writing *Homage to Barcelona* (London: Simon and Schuster, 1990; New York: Penguin, 1992; revised and updated edition, London: Picador, 2002). Tóibín's *The Heather Blazing* (London: Picador, 1992; New York: Viking, 1993) won the Encore Prize for Best Second Novel. In 1993, Tóibín edited *Soho Square 6: New Writing from Ireland* (London: Bloomsbury, 1993). His next book, *The Sign of the Cross: Travels in Catholic Europe* (London: Jonathan Cape, 1994; New York: Pantheon, 1995), was shortlisted for the Waterstones/Volvo/Esquire Prize for the Best Nonfiction Book of the Year (1994). In 1995, Tóibín edited both *The Kilfenora Schoolboy: A Study of Paul Durcan* (Dublin: New Island, 1995) and *The Guinness Book of Ireland* (Enfield: Guinness, 1995), and wrote a foreword to Francis Stuart's *Black List Section H* (Dublin: Lilliput Press, 1995; New York: Penguin, 1997).

Tóibín's third novel, *The Story of the Night* (London: Picador, 1996; New York: Henry Holt, 1997), set in Argentina, won the Publishing Triangle's Ferro-Grumley Award for Best Gay Male Fiction of 1997. An early version of a section of the novel had appeared in Marsha Rowe, ed., *Infidelity* (London: Chatto and Windus, 1993). Tóibín next edited Penguin's *Irish Short*

Stories audiobook (London: Penguin, 1997), and in 1999 was coauthor, with Carmen Callil, of *The Modern Library: The 200 Best Novels Since 1950* (London: Picador, 1999). He also wrote a chapter of the collaborative novel project, *Finbar's Hotel*, edited by Dermot Bolger (London: Picador, 1999; New York: Harvest, 1999), which appeared anonymously. Tóibín's article-essay, *The Irish Famine* (London: Profile Books, 1999), was later reissued in a volume containing related documents and coauthored by the historian Diamaid Ferriter: *The Irish Famine: A Documentary* (London: Profile Books, 2001; New York: Dunne Books, 2002).

The Blackwater Lightship (London: Picador, 1999; New York: Scribner, 2000) was shortlisted for the 1999 Booker Prize and the 2001 IMPAC Dublin Award. Tóibín has also provided introductions to *The Irish Times Book of Favourite Irish Poems* (Dublin: Irish Times Books, 2000), as well as for reissues of James Baldwin's *Another Country* (1960; rpt., London: Penguin, 2001), L. P. Hartley's *The Go-Between* (1953; rpt., New York: New York Review of Books, 2002), and Leo Tolstoy's *Hadji Murat* (1912; rpt., London: Hesperus, 2003). He also edited and wrote the introduction to *The Penguin Book of Irish Fiction* (London and New York: Penguin, 2001). His short story, "House for Sale," appeared in the *Dublin Review*, no. 2 (2001). His latest novel, which concerns Henry James, is *The Master* (London: Picador, 2004; New York: Scribner, 2004).

Tóibín has lately authored two further works of nonfiction. *Love in a Dark Time: Gay Lives from Wilde to Almodóvar* (London: Picador, 2002; New York: Scribner, 2002) collects pieces mostly published in the *London Review of Books*, for which he has written since 1994. In 2000, Tóibín was appointed a Fellow at the Center for Scholars and Writers at the New York Public Library, where he mainly worked on the Lady Gregory papers. A long article on Lady Gregory first appeared in the *New York Review of Books* in August 2001. Tóibín's subsequent book-length study is entitled *Lady Gregory's Toothbrush* (Dublin: Lilliput Press, 2002; Madison: University of Wisconsin Press, 2002).

During the 1990s, Tóibín regularly wrote for Dublin's newspaper, the *Sunday Independent*, on drama, television, and, later, politics. He has also written for the *Irish University Review*, the *New Statesman and Society*, the *New Yorker*, the *Observer*, the *Times Literary Supplement*, and the *Washington Post*. He has given workshops and master classes at Listowel Writers Week, the Arvon Foundation, and the American University (Washington, D.C.), and also taught in the M.F.A. program at the New School for Social Research (now New School University) in New York City. In 1995 he was given the E. M. Forster Award by the American Academy of Arts and Letters. His books have been translated into eighteen languages.

Tóibín lives in Dublin, where this interview took place on Wednesday, August 28, 2002. It was revised in October 2002.

RC You once commented that you started a novel with just a sound in your head, rather than an idea. By sound, did you mean the narrative voice?

CT I suppose a novel starts in two stages. First, something comes into your head. It could be something visual—the sight of something; a moment; a character. It stays there and grows. You've no inclination to write it down. If you did, it wouldn't work. You leave it until you get a sound for it—a single sentence. It could be the opening sentence, or the opening of a chapter. Nonetheless it has some sort of rhythm in it. It doesn't come if you force it, and it doesn't come quickly. But when it comes, you recognize instantly that you can now start work.

I can really only give examples. It's difficult to talk in general. *The South*, for instance, started when I used to go to Enniscorthy on the train from Dublin. That was always a fruitful journey out. Even when I was working as an editor, I'd think of things—articles for somebody to write or something. The way back would be useless.

Once, I saw somebody getting on the train who didn't look as though he should be. He was older—grander. Irish trains tend to have students on them, or old-aged pensioners, who get free travel. That thought was enough to start me off. With *The Story of the Night*, somebody was shot while I was in Argentina. It was suggested on TV day and night that it had been done by the government. All that occurred to me was—what if he were gay? That was enough to start the book. His true background— which was quite clear at the time—isn't used or even mentioned. It was just that business of: "What would that be like here?" With *The Heather Blazing*, I was in court a lot in 1984, as editor of the main current affairs magazine, *Magill*. One of the judges there reminded me of my father and my uncles. I was walking up the river one day and suddenly—"Fuck, Jesus!" That was enough. Then the beginning of the writing will start with a sound, and won't begin until that sound is in place.

RC   You started off writing poetry, didn't you?

CT   Yes. I only ever published a few poems. I was most interested in poetic form—sonnets, rhyme schemes, metrical systems. The poems took an awful lot of concentrated work, though, whereas novel writing is closer in certain ways to journalism. It's hard, dogged work over long periods of time to get something finished. With the poetry, you'd work and work on a single line until you'd got it right.

RC   You've spoken previously of learning to be a novelist through your journalism. At first I thought that your writing method had in some way been improved through journalism. But you went on to say that it had chiefly helped by mapping out the concerns of your fiction by contrast, or in opposition.

CT   I came back from Spain in 1978. Over the next two years I began to write for *In Dublin* and *Hibernia* magazines. I never worked in a newsroom or did daily journalism. I've never written a news story.

A group of us at *In Dublin* were deeply affected by the "New Journalism"—Tom Wolfe, Joan Didion, John Gregory Dunne—and also by people like V. S. Naipaul. All of us would have read their books. It was a listings magazine, but with a very alert editor who would commission 5,000-word pieces. He was interested in getting me to stop writing book reviews and start looking at things in the city. So I went to wrestling matches; I stayed up all night walking around Dublin. I developed a style I'd never used before—one I didn't know I had. It was done to please him and the others writing for the magazine. But I discovered you could get a response from other readers—from describing a girl puking into a shore, say, with the guy stood over her turning round, saying: "Fuck you."

Next, I moved into writing about politics. I learned to have a relationship with an audience. I learnt that this is for people to read—that I was involved in a process that will hit people. The journalism we were writing really worked on openings and endings. You didn't start until you had a proper opening, and your ending was always poetic, unlike, say, a news ending.

As I worked in more and more areas of journalism, I got a lot of my opinions out of myself. Then the novels became a return to the self. You'd go home from a day editing *Magill*. At that time *Magill* had a circulation of 30,000—in a country of 3.5 million people. It was read by all the Irish opinion makers, from the government down. At twenty-seven, I became its editor. That meant going home to write *The South* was like going home to a part of me that felt closer to me than this guy who was hanging around an office trying to get everyone else to work—trying to meet deadlines. The poetic style of *The South* took its bearings from what I was doing in my public life. With *The Heather Blazing*, similarly, it's unclear what I myself believe. I'd had enough of beliefs. The fiction involved reaching inwards.

So journalism had two effects. It was a way to give me an instinct towards hitting an audience, and an instinct to go inwards rather than outwards.

RC   Did you nevertheless have a certain idea of its readership?

CT   It was very much written with an audience in mind. That was never absent. When I was writing a chapter of *The South*, say, I was very alert to the fact that this must be clear. In fact, that was something so basic, it wouldn't even occur to me—the fact that this was for readers.

RC   But your idea of a readership wasn't specific in any way?

CT   No.

RC   You wrote some of *The South* at least in Portugal, didn't you? Could you comment on the importance of writing away from the terrain that is in your fictions?

CT   That was just two weeks' holiday from *Magill*. I'd be bursting with the book sometimes. The magazine would take you over, take up all your time. Sometimes it just wouldn't be possible to write; at others, you'd not be able to. Times were snatched. In August 1984, I thought of going to Faro, getting a taxi to a hotel, putting my manual typewriter on a desk, and simply writing for two weeks. That novel has it written all over it—the manic, frantic way it was written.

RC   Was there a sense in which the novel was still accumulating inside you when you couldn't work on it?

CT   All the time, yes. I'd be staring out of the window in the middle of a meeting—straight back in there.

RC   Regarding narrative voice, there's a peculiar aspect to *The South*. At various moments, you leave the third person for a first-person section, using diaries, letters, and so on. But there's also a first chapter which doesn't announce why it's in the first person. Then the shift to the third person isn't announced either. How conscious were you of your reasons for moving between voices?

CT   Not conscious at all. The first time I read from that book in public was when it came out in London. I read out one of those first-person chapters—a letter—without announcing anything about it. When it came to the end, I said: "Katherine." My publisher said: "When you're reading that out in future, you should try to introduce it. People thought it was a bloke." Sure enough, immediately afterwards, a girl came up and said: "My girlfriend and I were so glad that this gay man was writing about all this stuff. But then you said 'Katherine.' Why did you do that?"

Well, because it was central to me. I inhabited Katherine very fundamentally. It wasn't a simple matter of a gay man creating a female character. There were several more complex elements involved. For one thing, it's perfectly normal for an Irish male writer's first novel to have a woman protagonist. Take John McGahern's *The Barracks* or Brian Moore's *The Lonely Passion of Judith Hearne*. These novels were mentioned everywhere and read by everyone when I went to college. There's also Joyce's Molly Bloom. She's not a governing presence, but she's another example of the way Irish male writers have used the female voice. In Ireland that voice is so vulnerable, nervous, uncertain of itself; so ready to be wounded, so in control of its own modulations. That's because it's in control of almost nothing else.

So it wouldn't have been difficult for somebody like me to imagine such a voice and feel absolutely confident in writing a novel in it. The other element in this, though, was of course that I was a gay man in the public eye—as editor of a prominent magazine. Only my friends knew I was gay. A lot of people didn't. I realize now what I didn't then—that you can only keep this particular genie in the bottle for a certain number of years. It will make its way out somehow or other. The way I worked with Katherine, the way I wanted to inhabit her, was part of that genie making its way out in the best way it knew—which was to find a literary tradition in which you could inhabit her without anybody knowing why. At the time I wouldn't have been conscious of that. I would have been too happy dressing up as her.

So I allowed these two reasons to meet—rather wonderfully, from my point of view—in Katherine. But if I'd known I was doing that, I probably wouldn't have done it.

RC   Why did you go to Portugal to write it?

CT   Cheapness.

RC   It doesn't signify at all?

CT   No.

RC   *The Heather Blazing* was written entirely in the third-person voice. But there's lots of free indirect discourse—allowing yourself to move freely in and out of the consciousness of the characters. Again, was the narrative mode entirely unconscious?

CT I suppose first of all that was the way it came to me. But I did consciously want to write a much calmer, more Irish book. I wanted to enter into the things I knew. I never knew when I started how closely I was going to follow that idea. I was originally going to make Eamon Redmond, the judge, much more hypocritical. As I worked, I softened him a great deal. I was surprised with how *The Heather Blazing* turned out. What I'd really wanted to do was write the dullest book I could think of—one with no colors; no Spanish life; no sex; nothing other than the dullness of his sort of life.

RC Was that a reaction to *The South*?

CT Initially it was just how it came to me. But I was pleased with it. The problem you immediately have with having a single male character in a book set in Ireland is this: the men around me when I was growing up were mostly silent. There's a cliché about Irish men being drunk and loud. But honestly it wasn't like that. The man worked; he had that sort of power. But in the house, he was almost dead. Women did all the talking, moving, arranging, answering the door, expecting visitors. The man just sat being polite. He'd have no color at all. Once you start trying to build an Irish male, you really don't have any color.

Also, I'd really been deeply affected by Camus's *The Outsider*, by the Sartre trilogy *Roads to Freedom*, and by Hemingway's *The Sun Also Rises*. At a crucial age I'd soaked in those books. I think that makes a very big difference to what you end up writing—the books that hit you at that impressionable age.

One thing you learn to do in this respect is develop versions of how things occurred which may or may not be true. You end up telling a story about how books occurred which may be a mask for how they genuinely occurred. The problem is that you always can't remember how they started because you're not conscious when they start that it's them starting.

RC So you've just got to give in to the process—the book almost starts leading you?

CT Yes. Also, there was something crucial about the publishing context with *The Heather Blazing*. First, nobody in London would publish *The*

South. By the time it was accepted by Serpent's Tail, twenty publishers had turned it down.

Then, various publishers wanted the paperback rights to *The South*. But I wanted whoever did that also to commission *The Heather Blazing* blind. I realized that if that book was sent around publishing houses, nobody would even finish it. I'd go through a two-year process of being turned down by everybody. I didn't want much money for it, but if they'd commission it blind, I knew I could hand it to an individual who was waiting for it and would at least finish reading it.

RC   How much of *The Heather Blazing* had you written?

CT   Half, or maybe less. But I knew it was a problem.

RC   That it was unsellable?

CT   In terms of London publishing at that time. I sensed nobody would finish it—that it would be held for two months by somebody who'd eventually look at it and say: "Jesus—we can't publish this." But if a publisher could read the book in the light of having commissioned it, he might end up thinking that maybe it was OK. Meanwhile, I'd then feel more confident when writing the rest of it about keeping the mood of it down—keeping nothing happening.

RC   Was that the specific problem?

CT   I didn't think I had the problem. It was a London problem. This was the same year Patrick McCabe's *The Butcher Boy* was going to appear. It was the beginning of Roddy Doyle's career. So Irish novels would have a certain color in them—some heightened dialogue; some fun; maybe a murder. This was what one wanted from Ireland. While I knew that Faber had published John McGahern—who wasn't like that—nonetheless his was by then a very long career. This was all about young editors, who were out every night, and who wanted only a certain thing from books. People then were talking about "fucking and shopping" novels. Whatever *The Heather Blazing* was, there was no fucking or shopping in it. I realized it was the least trendy book and that editors wouldn't buy it.

RC   When you start these books with this one idea, do you have anything else, or does the book reveal itself as you write?

CT   By the time I start writing, I have the whole book.

RC   Are there notes?

CT   Never. It's all in your head. You'd lose the notes. But the whole thing will be worked out—even the structure, to a large extent. Sometimes when you're working, a new detail or incident will come in. But the character itself is fixed. *The Heather Blazing* first occurred to me in 1984. I wrote the first chapter in 1987. Between those times—over three years—I went to South America with only that in my head—thinking about the judge over and over. It wasn't deliberate. But that was my one daydream.

RC   So when you talked of being surprised by the book itself . . .

CT   Well, as the thing gets made flesh and you start looking at it afresh, you get some idea of what impact it might have on a reader, outside what it's having on you—some objective idea of what the book's like.

RC   What is the process of revision like? You mentioned, for instance, a piece in *The South* in which Katherine went to Lourdes, which was later removed.

CT   *The South* was really worked on. A lot was added at a late stage, and a lot left out. I had a very good editor at Serpent's Tail called Marsha Rowe, who'd been an editor at *Spare Rib* magazine. I learnt a lot from her. No matter what you're doing when you start out, you can always be improved by having somebody pointing things out.

RC   So whole sections were removed?

CT   Two—a first chapter, and another towards the end. One chapter was added. I think they were surprised too at how much I was ready to play with the book. But *The South* had that sort of form. You could do anything with it, whereas you couldn't have touched *The Heather Blazing*. That was created in its form, in the way the chapters hit against each other. You couldn't add a chapter for no reason. *The South* was like a pack of cards. You could juggle it all sorts of ways.

RC   Does that have anything to do with its being your first novel?

CT   Yes. I think I wanted to play with the form and see what I could do. I didn't want to write a traditional novel.

RC   The other novels are all rather seamless.

CT   Yes. Often one is a reaction to the previous one. You could read each of them usefully as being a response—usually negative—to the one before. In other words, whatever is conscious in the way the imagination works includes the fact that you say to yourself: "I won't do that again." You feel somehow that you've been up to tricks—forms of deception; getting things wrong in the previous books. So you'd better see if you can really write what you want to in the next. Then there's the whole business of being gay and of being Irish—of exploring these two things and finding you've either done so too much or too little in the previous book. So you need to do it in a different way.

RC   Eamon in *The Heather Blazing* was originally writing an Irish account of the Irish rebellion. That detail was removed, wasn't it?

CT   Yes. It was bearing down on the book too much. It wouldn't have been an unusual thing in Ireland—for a judge to spend his summer holidays every year doing more research on some topic, building all this material up. But it added an area of significance I thought he didn't need. Also, at an early stage, he had an affair with a local girl, whom he drove back to Dublin a few times. I don't think I even wrote that down. But it had to go. It was weighing down the book too.

RC   Were both books written on a typewriter?

CT   Yes. *The South* was then redone on a manual typewriter. With *The Heather Blazing*, surprisingly, most of it just came out like that. I think I did write another version on a manual machine. But the changes were not great.

RC   Do you still use a typewriter?

CT   No. *The Blackwater Lightship* was written in longhand, *The Story of the Night* on a word processor.

RC   Is there anything significant about that?

CT   No. Once you start with the tone, the sense, the rhythm of a book, no machinery's going to make you break that. I worry about the word processor, in that you can make changes too easily. But when you're in the primary stages of composition, nothing can fuck you around.

RC   Why did you move to longhand?

CT   I just started to love the physical aspect of it. Also, I was in Barcelona. I didn't know when I was going to start writing *The Blackwater Lightship*. But I hadn't got any machinery with me. So I had to go and buy a notebook. I'm writing the new book in longhand.

RC   On the subject of your reacting to previous works, *The Story of the Night* is the first novel written entirely in the first-person voice. That's a clean break. There's also a dominant gay theme. It's very tempting to make a direct link between these two facts, since the book effectively announced the theme of homosexuality in your work.

CT   I think there is a link. I was toying with another book at that time, one concerning the fact that I was in Spain when Franco died and for three years afterwards. That was an extraordinary period in history, with a great deal of drama surrounding it. I still have something going on in the back of my head about it. I was talking about it to Marsha Rowe. Some of the scenes I would have written for that book took place in that very liberated London of the late sixties that I knew nothing about. Marsha was describing these scenes to me into which my Spanish character would have arrived.

That book hasn't been written. But I told her this other story too—about the Argentinian guy; about what I'd seen and imagined. Marsha said: "You must write that book." So *The Story of the Night* began as a sort of Borgesian story about a writer who had died and whose apartment had been sealed up. I'd met somebody who'd inherited an apartment in Barcelona, which had literally been sealed while there were difficulties over the will. Nobody could get in. I loved the idea that a Hispanicist scholar, from somewhere like Manchester University—somebody like Ian Gibson, say—arrived in Buenos Aires because this apartment of a colleague of Borges was going to be unsealed. There were clearly a lot of papers relating to everything about his life in there. I remember taking particular pleasure that there were a great number of thirteen-line sonnets. I wrote it all up; it's around here somewhere.

The next version I wrote for an anthology Marsha was then editing called *Infidelity*. The bit she published was changed later. In the *Infidelity* version, Richard's mother was a writer. In *The Story of the Night*, finally, she isn't.

Writing down and publishing *The Story of the Night* was a great personal liberation for me. There was the genie making another appearance from the bottle. Putting it all in the first person felt almost like a confession. If I could have thought of a proper way of doing it, I probably would have called the book "The Confession of Somebody."

So there is a connection between its being my first time dealing with all those issues—what I suppose one could call the drama of being gay in a fragile society—and finding a first-person voice for it, so that there was no separation between you the writer and the material. As for setting it in Argentina, that was another way to keep the bottle slightly corked still.

I was playing all those games right up to that time. I'm still playing them, really, but not as much. I think you lose a certain sort of power when you let the genie out of the bottle completely—when you become fully conscious of everything; when you don't have your own dark, unexplored territory. I think you lose a great deal.

RC   That brings us to *Love in a Dark Time* generally, and also to the claim you made in the introduction to the *Penguin Book of Irish Fiction*—that *The Picture of Dorian Gray* was the greatest gay novel.

CT   Well, chapter two is the most marvelous account of two older men and a younger one engaging with each other across the room. There's nothing as good.

RC   But if it can be described as an account of a set of gay relations, it's certainly indirect or obscure. And it's haunted by darkness and foreboding, isn't it?

CT   Well, I can't think of a better one.

RC   I feel we're skirting around the edge of what would in narrow political terms be considered unacceptable—the idea that repression or self-repression might bring forth creative fruit.

CT   Yes, yes exactly—that it brings forth *A Passage to India*, say, rather than *Maurice*.

RC   You're happy with that?

CT   I am. But it doesn't really mean anything. You can write any amount of novels from any set of personal circumstances. It's just that in a repressive society, every single gay man's story is fascinating—how you deal with daddy, mammy, brothers, sisters, friends at school, your job; how you deal with Saturday night, how you move in the world. That in itself is dramatic, in a way that if you're French, out to everyone, have a nice boyfriend and a house in the country and two dogs, it's not intrinsically as interesting. It's as basic as that. That doesn't mean the other situation is precluded from being interesting in a novel. You can do anything as a novelist. But the repressed life is a ready-made tale. And a repressed writer is like a dog in a locked kennel who has sniffed meat.

RC In *Love in a Dark Time*, you asked why there weren't any Jane Austen-like happy endings in gay fiction. Now it sounds like you wouldn't want happy endings for gay lives—in literature anyway.

CT Well, gay liberation is very like Northern Ireland. Once the troubles are over, the novelists have a different story to tell—one which isn't intrinsically as dramatic. This doesn't mean for a single moment that any of the suffering caused was worth any of the fucking novels. It wasn't. Nonetheless, since I was brought up in Ireland and still live here, and although things have changed tremendously here, I'm still locked into a certain narrative of "here." I'd better try and live a little more in terms of what's happening now, or in the future. Nonetheless, the business of what happened in the past here haunts me. I find it immensely dramatic. But as a citizen, I want everyone to be happy; and as a novelist, I'd love to make Jane Austen endings—but storytelling where I come from has not had the luxury of Jane Austen's society.

RC The essay in *Love in a Dark Time* on Henry James indicates how fascinating you found him. Now you're writing a whole novel about him. If there were a gallery of authors whose sexual self-searching intrigued you, who else would be there?

CT Proust. Thomas Mann.

RC You described finding Mann's works compelling before knowing anything about his sexuality. There's a common sense of secrecy or indirection, still, isn't there?

CT Yes. I must say that the writing comes first for me. I don't really mind that Conrad was straight, for instance. It doesn't make *Nostromo* less or more interesting. When I read *Nostromo*, I was in a state of delight. If I'd discovered later on that Conrad was gay, I would have been really interested. The mystery of how that might have mattered for *Nostromo* would have intrigued me. It would have been the same for Thomas Wyatt, or George Herbert, and so on. Anything about them would have been fascinating—but especially this idea that there was something that they couldn't disclose, and that the writing may have become a code for that, or equally might not have done so.

Take James's *Washington Square*—how could one read in his homosexuality? It's fascinating, because one can't. That's as interesting as the thought that one might be able to. Or finding out that Elizabeth Bishop was lesbian, or that Thom Gunn was gay. I know it's clear from some poems in his case. But it wasn't clear to me initially what the importance of it was to him personally. It's just a lovely thing if you like a writer to know more about them personally. If they're gay, you realize that something happened to them which also happened to you, and that didn't happen to everybody else. There were moments of disclosure; there was the art of concealment, the danger of being found out—for Casement, for Wilde, and for Mann, who left his diaries behind in Munich when the Nazis were busy making writers public enemies. When he got back, writing more diaries—and making *Death in Venice* utterly autobiographical so his wife and brother would have known everything. Elizabeth Bishop left these poems that are only now beginning to appear. She didn't want to publish them in her lifetime.

But James is even more interesting because he left so little in this respect—the letters, and a number of short stories that one could read in several ways.

RC   In the essay, you object to the cruder "reading in" strategies. You say it's astonishing how successfully James managed to exclude his sexuality from his work.

CT   Yes. Unless you wanted to claim that James's homosexuality is so all-pervasive that it's either there in every sentence or in none . . . Otherwise, you can read "The Beast in the Jungle," say, three other ways. You can read all the letters as just late-Edwardian flourishes. James had been living in London too long for an American. So he got the tone slightly wrong. But then there's that imagination of his—the sheer delicacy of it; the level of understanding of the plight of certain figures, mainly women . . . That's who he was. You can read the works like that much more usefully than in terms only of his sexuality. And it won't destroy the books or make you understand them more.

In other words, James had what is called supreme artistry—what we're all striving for, in a way: that entire loss of self, forgetting the self, annihilating it, while you're in the primacy stages of composition. You simply do not exist.

RC   To a certain degree, then, James's greatness lay in his sympathy with women. The analogy with Forster and *A Passage to India* is a good one.

CT   Yes, but think also of what James could do with men. It's the level of his sympathy for anyone he described. Also, he was very interested in voices that are dark, controlling, and repressive. James hit against the sort of people who are Emersonian; these figures are defeated by a cruel darkness.

I'm terribly interested in James as a man, but I'd be afraid to start reading his work as code for his homosexuality, rather than being utterly and completely informed by the person he was: an American; the son of Henry James, senior; the second son; a homosexual; someone very interested in privacy and solitude.

RC   You wrote an essay about his Irish ancestry for the *Dublin Review*, didn't you?

CT   Yes. His Irishness is very like his homosexuality. He's constantly hiding it, reinventing parts of it. He invents an English ancestry he doesn't have too. He rails against the Irish.

RC   Where?

CT   Mainly in letters. But it's peppered through the books. In *Washington Square* there's a line something like: "We won't go there because it's been infested by the Irish." In the essay on Hawthorne, James refers to the "Hibernian tide" ruining certain villages.

When I first read his novels, I thought James's life would be of no interest. Then I slowly discovered that his life was enormously dramatic.

RC   Do you take on James's voice in the novel?

CT   No. It's written in the third person. But it's all seen through James's eyes. It's called *The Master*. I hope everyone realizes that's slightly ironic. All my titles have been, except *The Story of the Night*. *The Blackwater Lightship*—the lightship isn't there. *The Heather Blazing*—there's no heather blazing. *The South*—no one's actually in "the South." They're in the north, even when they're in Spain.

One thing I love about James is his extraordinary reserve and reticence. What one knows about the London of his time—1895, say—was that you could hide yourself in the pursuit of pleasure. Most people did. He didn't. I love that as a dramatic subject—though not as an actual life. In my book, Edmund Gosse turns to him on the night following the Wilde trials—when all these Englishmen are crossing the Channel—and says: "Is there something . . . ?" James turns from the bookcase which he's been studying and says: "No; nothing."

James subsumed everything to his work, but retained something of that Puritanism which was his mother's as much as his father's, and also an enormous personal reticence and a great interest in dignity—even with his servants. There's a marvelous letter he writes to Burgess Noakes, his valet. Poor Burgess finally goes to fight in France in 1914. James writes: "Do pay attention to the French. They're marvellous people. You'll get great rewards . . . " James in this case was being considerate—treating Burgess as if he was from James's own mold.

RC   You talk about what James didn't do. Didn't he woo these younger men though—like Hendrik Andersen. If not, the letters are extraordinary things to have written. There's so much love in them—until the two of them actually meet. Then something clearly went wrong.

CT   It's like one of those modern e-mail relationships. It works wonderfully until the two poor people have to meet. You immediately realize the flesh is what the problem is.

RC   When James and Andersen meet, there's a sense afterwards that there was a fundamental misunderstanding—something which hadn't been imaginable beforehand. Or perhaps it was that James had a fundamental revelation—that the addressed person in the letters wasn't the actual person.

CT   I think James did inhabit two universes in his life. Up to a certain age, homosexuality wasn't illegal, named, or spoken of. That doesn't mean it didn't exist. But after a certain year, it certainly did exist—let's say, after the indecency law was passed in 1886. By the late nineties, James starts grasping for this other world, the one that didn't exist before. In his lifetime, then, he straddled two worlds. But I think mostly he withheld himself or withdrew. For a novelist, oddly enough, that's much more interesting.

RC   In your essay on him, you compared the imperfect aspects of James's late stories to the great final novels. Again, I thought of Forster. The express homosexual sentiment is in these late, suppressed, and particularly unsatisfying stories. Likewise, you describe the James stories as fey, allusive, and oddly incomplete.

CT   But I think a lot of novelists' short stories are like that. Short stories often read like fragments—underimagined, half-imagined. James seems quite happy though with certain stories which aren't anywhere like the novels, in terms of complexity or depth. They're a sort of sidetrack—a waste of time, almost. Forster's read more like sketches.

RC   You haven't written much shorter fiction.

CT   I've had one story published—"House for Sale."

RC   Yes. What is the relationship between that and *The Blackwater Lightship*? There are superficially rather similar descriptions of a day trip to Dublin by train. It's shared by a brother and sister in the novel, by two sons in "House for Sale." Both feature a meal in Woolworths.

CT   It's the same emotional landscape—one associated with loss, and with time moving. It's more or less autobiographical, and is something I'll go back to.

I've written a second story in longhand. They're both 15,000 words. I have a third in my head, for which I've written the first sentence. Unfortunately, the fourth one that I wanted to write is slowly getting longer. I haven't started to write that, but I had it firmly in my head as going from here to there. Now, unfortunately, it's not.

"House for Sale" was written in April 2000, at the same desk, in the same house, in the same month as the first chapter of the Henry James book. It was a nice antidote to it, in that it was such a completely different world.

RC Do you have any idea why a number of short stories have occurred to you lately?

CT When I started writing and the poetry wouldn't work, I wrote a few short stories. They were very bad. The minute the idea of the novel occurred to me—seeing a figure in history, over twenty years; seeing that you could have descriptions of things; moments that didn't have to add up to anything—I began to feel free. It's funny the way certain DNA hits upon certain literary forms. It's very much bound up with the quality of a sensibility, I think. It's mysterious the way one sensibility could produce a play, for example. I couldn't! I could make a chair rather than write a play.

RC You've tried?

CT Yes. It wouldn't get beyond a few pages. It wouldn't be interesting.

RC The difference with James was that he got his play produced, bad as it was thought to be. Obviously, there's something very dramatic about his spectacular failure in the theater.

CT My novel opens with the opening night of his play *Guy Domville*. That's the great dramatic night for James—when he's booed offstage.

RC Some writers have different periods in a career. They start with one form and feel led to another. It's rather sudden that the story ideas are coming to you.

CT It's a funny business. You don't know what's going to attack you next, or at which moment. That's like *The Blackwater Lightship*. It came to me while I was driving around a roundabout.

RC Did it lodge in your memory immediately? Did you know you wouldn't lose it?

CT If I'd lost it, it wouldn't have been any good. With that novel, I can tell you I wished I hadn't gone around that roundabout. I wished: "Please Lord—do not let this idea go any further! Keep it away. I don't want to write this book."

RC Why?

CT Because one of its subjects I'd covered in *The Story of the Night*. Another I'd covered to some extent in *The Heather Blazing*—that landscape; aspects of that family. In *The Story of the Night* I'd dealt with the consequences of being gay in a fragile society, and also with the tragedy of AIDS. I didn't want to go back to that.

RC As AIDS narratives, they both predate the new drug therapies.

CT Of course. I can't work to the moment. If I could, I'd already have written my novel about the Irish boom. It's vaguely hinted at in *The Blackwater Lightship*, which was set in 1993 but didn't appear until 1999.

RC There's the computer industry; the Mary Robinson[1] cameo.

CT Exactly—to show it was that year. With Ireland today, you're dealing with something that over the last twenty years has really moved and changed.

RC Do you want to be so contemporary?

---

1. Mary Robinson (1944–): former President of the Irish Republic (1990–1997); later, United Nations High Commissioner for Human Rights (1997–2002).

CT   Not at all. But I have to be aware of the fact that other people want you to be.

RC   So when Mary Robinson walks into your fictional landscape, it's just an accident?

CT   She's there as a kind of anchor for the book—to anchor it to those specific years.

RC   Still, having had that sense of not wanting to go there again, with *The Blackwater Lightship*, there was still no question that you could let it go.

CT   No. I remember when the first sentence came to me. I went to see a Catalan film at the Irish film center. I remember I drank a double espresso, and then went to see this film, in Catalan with subtitles. I found it very moving, though I think it was probably a very bad film. I get very nostalgic for all sorts of things if I hear Catalan in Ireland—if I put on Catalan music, say. Then I came home and wrote the first page of *The Blackwater Lightship* on the computer. During the film, I'd got the first sentence in my head. It wasn't much of a sentence: "Helen woke in the night to the sound of Manus whimpering." That's in a way the point. I promise you— deep inside it, it had a rhythm you can follow. It was very different to the start of *The Heather Blazing* or *The Story of the Night*. When I was going to Spain, I had the first two pages printed out in my bag. That's what I started to work from in longhand.

RC   On the familiarity of a certain landscape to you—in the Irish fiction anthology, you wrote of William Trevor having no such locus . . .

CT   Yes—no place that he's from, that he can describe in any detail: where the ditch was; which tree; where the shadows fell. It's deeply disabling not to have that.

RC   Which part of Ireland feels yours this way precisely? The southeast coast? Enniscorthy specifically?

CT Not even that. It's the inside of about three houses; the stretch of a cliff; two lanes, and another that connects them. Nothing else. It's a tiny stretch of childhood territory very clearly fixed in the memory. And any time you try and describe anything else, you tend to use that anyway.

RC   Do you go back?

CT   Yes. The house in Enniscorthy's exactly the same.

RC   But does it resonate for you in the same way?

CT   Even more now. Because you've lost it all. It's gone.

RC   If it continues to recur in your work, will you be happy?

CT   It seems unlikely to go away. But I also love getting out of it.

RC   The James book takes you out of it.

CT   It sure does. Also, remember that I myself ran away from that place. I got out—like Katherine Proctor. So—the idea of being there, of being immersed in the feeling surrounding those rooms and lanes also has its exact opposite: the sheer pleasure of being thousands of miles from it, geographically and psychically.

RC   In *The Blackwater Lightship*, both Helen and Declan are happy to have got away. Quite a lot of the book, in fact, is acidic towards the older generation. But it's mostly through Helen that you describe that urgent need to move away from what you describe as the dark force of History. But History comes to have a tangible human form too—the figure of the mother.

CT   Yes. The feeling of unbelonging is as important as that of belonging. It isn't like dislocation exactly. The original place is still there. You're still from it. But the life you've invented for yourself takes on a whole beautiful golden resonance sometimes. Helen talks about that. It's in *The South* too.

RC   This seems to be about departing, not arriving. It has nothing to do with getting to Dublin, for instance, where you now live.

CT   I'm not aware that I'm in Dublin. I'm in a few rooms.

I've never written about Dublin. I couldn't. It has no life for me—no resonance; no interest. I don't know why. It would be lovely to be able to write a book set in Dublin. But I wouldn't know how. Maybe one day I could. I've been living here so long. But it doesn't really mean anything to me.

I wish you could explain that to me. I can't understand it. It's not the case with Barcelona or Buenos Aires.

RC   But you're based here. You must call Dublin home?

CT   I call these rooms home.

RC   Did you write about Barcelona when you were living there or afterwards?

CT   I'd left. Perhaps if all this went—so I could never come back to it—it would start to interest me enormously. Maybe that's what it is.

RC   You also went back to the third person with *The Blackwater Lightship*.

CT   Yes. It was a much calmer book. I was trying—as in that first sentence—to attempt no style at all. There's hardly a single sentence where you could say: "That's a good sentence" or "That's good style." There's a little bit when Helen looks at the sea from a cliff for about two or three paragraphs. Other than that, any color in the book occurs in moments of dialogue. The rest is just: "She sat down. She got up." If the book hits you emotionally, you can never really tell where that was—in what sentence the emotion was.

RC   *The Story of the Night* and *The Blackwater Lightship* do feel very different. Both, though, introduce this AIDS-related death sentence upon one character; in both cases, you suspend it. There's a sense of wholeness or roundness—something positive—at the end.

CT   Yes—that that particular day anyway will be OK, and that the truth has been told. There they are, with each other, in whatever fragile way. You've got to take that as something important.

RC   It's as positive an outcome as an AIDS narrative could have wished for at that time. To have an open ending is quite rare. Had you read other AIDS-themed literature when you began *The Story of the Night*?

CT   Well, that book was quite quick to write, and was published almost immediately. I must have started it in 1994, and finished it in the spring of 1996. I'd certainly read Michael Cunningham's *A Home at the End of the World* by then. But the AIDS stuff only really comes in at the very end of that, and it was the beginning—the mother-son relationship—that I loved more than anything else. I'd certainly have seen Thom Gunn's *The Man with Night Sweats* the day it came out. I saw *Savage Nights*—the film by Cyril Collard—and took a great interest in it.

RC   I'm touching on the extent to which such reading might inform your writing, however indirectly.

CT   It doesn't really. Things are really very different once you put them into Ireland. Once you add AIDS to the Ireland I know, you're talking about dynamite, for instance. With France or America, it might be so different.

RC   You're talking about society; politics?

CT   The politics of families. Politics generally.

RC   I was fascinated to find some quite overt references to homosexuality as a political question in the eighties journalism you collected in *Trial of the Generals*. They predate your coming out by many years. In particular, there was a long travel piece on Eastern Europe. Suddenly you asked a group of Romanians about gay rights.

CT   Remember that those were also the years leading up to the changing of the law in Ireland. I probably would have had a number of pieces on the topic in the *Sunday Independent* at around that time. Someone did once say: "You came very close last Sunday to actually saying it." In the political column, I was arguing in the strongest possible terms for the change in the law against homosexuality. It was crucial that the new age of consent wasn't made twenty-one. That would have been a disaster. Changing it at all would be better than nothing, but since they were do-ing it, it was better at seventeen.

RC   Was that equality?

CT   No. Sixteen would have been. So I wrote about it, but never joined the movement. There were people who did who were much more vul-nerable than I was in career terms. Everyone's vulnerable in family terms.

When I wrote about Richard's politics in *The Story of the Night*, and his response to any attempt to invite him towards making a statement, I cer-tainly knew what I was writing about. My interest in this wasn't made up. Also, in *The Heather Blazing*, the judge has never made a statement or a stand about anything. All of that aspect of that novel can be read in this light—as something that interested me for personal reasons.

RC   You mentioned people being vulnerable in family terms. That very much suggests that sense in *The Blackwater Lightship* of the son's life hav-ing become unknown to his family. In your own move to Dublin, was there that sense of distance?

CT   Yes. All of us in those years learnt these ways, strategies, systems—some people to tell; some not to tell; some to half tell with hints, clues, bits and pieces. But the American declaration of "coming out" didn't catch on in Ireland. As the time I am charting moved, very few people I came across had ever told *no one*. But in Argentina there *were* people who had told no one. That was still very common. Here it would always be: "My grand-mother's very old, and I really wouldn't like to." People would deal with it in a gentle way, so as not to offend people more than was necessary.

RC   In Latin cultures, it's *pudor*, isn't it—"shame"?

CT   That's correct. Here it's just a way of trying to make things easy for everybody. That's a very southern Irish way of dealing with politics in anything. You compromise, evade; you constantly create double-sided structures that everyone's comfortable with, ones that have hypocrisy built into them. That's how society functions. Obviously, there were great exceptions—people who made a lot of personal noise or came out on television. I certainly wasn't one.

RC   It makes me think of *The Master*—the changes in social attitude and circumstance experienced by James in his lifetime; your concentration upon his reticence. It's not a million miles away.

CT   It fits in rather gloriously with what I'm describing. James got away from his family quite early on. He kept away, having been immensely close to them emotionally—obsessively involved. His homosexuality was something he never fully dealt with, something he'd always be able to keep back, should anybody come too close. Also, he used his homosexuality as a reason to remain distant and solitary from people.

RC   Some might say you're risking confusing cause and effect.

CT   It's strange with James. One feels that at his very core was a desperate desire not for intimacy but for solitude. Being a bachelor suited him. Had he been straight, it would have been harder. Because he was gay, it was very easy. I don't know which is the chicken and which the egg.

RC   You've written about real-life figures before—even living ones. Charles Haughey[2] has a small walk-on role in *The Heather Blazing*.

CT   Well, Haughey would have been a great hate figure for most of my Irish readers. They'd have presumed somebody like me felt the same. Indeed, I'd written vehemently against Haughey in a lot in articles.

But I brought him in as somebody the judge likes in *The Heather Blazing*. There was almost an element of mischief in that—to do the opposite to

---

2. Charles Haughey (1925–): Irish prime minister (1979–1981, 1982, 1987–1992).

whatever's expected. That's often the thing to do—the opposite of what occurs to you first. In the case of Haughey, everyone would have known that I hated him. But what if the judge liked him? What if, instead of him doing something outrageous, it's just a strange, almost poetic moment—one that leaves Eamon puzzled and slightly uneasy, but nothing more.

What this was really about was me annihilating myself. There's no "me" there. Also, taking something political and making it just poetic. That's fun if you've been working on a political magazine—to dull something, to make it mean nothing.

RC When you spoke of making the language of your fiction neutral, it reminded me of comments in your introduction to the *Irish Fiction* anthology. You argue strongly that if you want barely noticeable language, you've got to look at English fiction, not Irish fiction. You wrote of not finding that transparent prose style in Ireland.

CT One thing as a novelist you try to have—and this is one of the important things a novelist can have—is an ability to disguise and undermine your own intelligence, so that no reader could ever know how smart you are at the end of a book. So I hate describing anything I do consciously. I love the mystery of the unconscious and working blind. But I'm sorry—I have the other thing too: intelligence; cunning; an interest in structure. And sometimes I quite knowingly do something within a certain tradition.

In that introduction, I made two main points—first, that Irish novelists are full of style. The other was that there are no happy families in Irish fiction. I mention Oliver Goldsmith's *The Vicar of Wakefield*; Roddy Doyle's *The Snapper*, a book I really like. But look at the opening of *The Blackwater Lightship*. There it is—a family having a party. That wasn't a broken home. The children are being cared for, thought about, looked after, worried about. The novel opens with a mother taking a child into her arms while it's asleep. The man isn't a big, shouting Irishman.

This opening scene was almost a conscious way of setting up something in the Irish suburbs where nothing strange is going on. These people are quite happily married. The children are quite secure. There's nothing that belongs to the Irish tradition in it.

No style can ever be fully deliberate, but inasmuch as it was deliberate, that book's style is saying: "Now I'm going to do what's not being done here normally, in images that are not used normally." The only point in recognizing and trying to describe a tradition is then to fuck it up—to take it and throttle it.

RC Is there a connection between the stylistic embellishment and even caricature you identified in the Irish tradition, and Irish history, which you've repeatedly described as more like fiction than fiction itself? In a way, your sense of doing the opposite to the fictional tradition is a sort of literary equivalent of the historical revisionism you've been associated with, isn't it?

CT There's a literary politics involved, say, in *The Heather Blazing*. But my own opinions are all turned upside down by that character. All the things you'd expect of an Irish character don't happen either. The style's really nonexistent. I take pleasure in that.

With *The Blackwater Lightship*, too, I'd have been conscious of that—of trying to make the women, especially the granny, complex, oddly powerful, and intelligent. There's no long-suffering Irishwoman in any of my books; no oppressed woman. That would come from instinct, and experience, but also from trying to make things different—just to be more interesting. Brian Moore said of the mother in his *An Answer from Limbo* that he could have written her with his eyes shut. He probably did—she's such a cliché.

The same goes for Catholicism. In *The Heather Blazing*, the judge isn't especially Catholic. In *The Blackwater Lightship*, the mother and grandmother don't believe.

In Ireland, whatever you write, you have to be so alert as to what the stereotypes are, and exercise your intelligence enormously in combating them or at least giving into them in a new way.

There was a conference on Irish writing in Brazil. Someone went to the lecture on me given by my Japanese translator. What pleased me most was that it wasn't on sex, nation, or dissent, but on silence in my work.

Being a sad boy comes before anything in my case. Any ideology or intelligence in my work comes from being sad, generally—especially on my own, when I'm working. I'm all sad. That affects things much more than anything else.

RC Do you think that's genetic?

CT No.

RC But it is pervasive?

CT Yes.

RC Is it productive?

CT Sure. When you try to explain yourself, it's quite an important three-letter word. That's not to suggest "gay" isn't. But you should consider doing an anthology of interviews with sad writers; sad bastards. [*Laughs*]

RC In *Love in a Dark Time*, you wrote of having never directly written autobiographically in your novels. Some of your journalism has been astonishingly autobiographical though—like the central essay in *The Sign of the Cross*.

CT I never intended to write that essay. It wasn't done for the purposes of writing as such. But I couldn't stop talking about that story. So I wrote it down.

In the novels, there are moments—familiar landscapes and so on. You tend almost to grin to yourself, saying as you come upon one: "Look what I'm going to do now—make a big raid on the real. I'm going to fit it in here; describe exactly what something was truly like. I'm even going to tell a story that's so out of life, it'll be embarrassing when it appears. Anyone who knows me will know I've used it from life." In the next chapter, you'd make something up entirely. There's a lovely guilty feeling in that—that you're doing something quite inappropriate. You're going right in there—into the most private things that happened—and tacking them onto what is essentially a form of entertainment.

It's not a way to become a good citizen. It's quite dishonest. You're taking things that belong to other people, taking things that should be private, and putting them into things that are invented. If you look at a novelist's face very carefully, there's often—how would one put it?—quite a lot of malevolence. He or she is somebody not to be trusted in any way. What's odd is that you get proud of it.

RC Wilde was obsessed with forgeries and forgerers.

CT It's like the Parnell trial and the question of whether he wrote the letters, or whether they were forged. Lady Gregory; Henry James: Wilde—they all went to look at Parnell in the dock in 1889. The letters were forgeries in the end.

RC You don't regularly write political journalism now. But you maintain a public profile. The letter you wrote to the *London Review of Books* concerning September 11th was quite provocative. You seemed to be arguing for the innateness of evil, drawing an analogy to Irish terrorists.

CT It was something much more basic than the innateness of evil. I don't know what evil is. The letter arose from the view that somehow terrorism is necessary in certain political conditions. All I know is that the political conditions in Northern Ireland in 1970 did not include the necessity for terrorism. Regarding the people that got most involved in the violence, if you saw them playing football or anything, there was that sense of them being that little fucker beside you in class who was always waiting to hit somebody—to hurt or bully somebody. It was somebody who had that natural disposition.

I thought that should be pointed out to the sociologists, anthropologists, and philosophers who, from their studies, knew nothing about the actual ground on which terrorism takes place. Still, they felt free to believe that you should listen to these people. I got into a rage.

In the columns I wrote over the years in the *Sunday Independent*, those were the two things I would consistently have been against—the Church and the IRA. We won on both. On the IRA, it's now proven that the violence and cruelty were never necessary.

RC What were the consequences of that journalism?

CT Well, over a number of years, public opinion shifted. It had a drop-in-the-bucket effect. Nonetheless, if everybody goes on arguing the case over a number of years, you might in the end have some influence. Also, there was my *Walking Along the Border*, where I showed the effects of all that bloody stuff.

RC   You must have had people tell you not to say certain things.

CT   It was never like that. The IRA did not kill journalists.

RC   I was thinking of irreverence to the Church.

CT   There was never a problem.

RC   You've often referred to 1973 as a pivotal year for Ireland's development. John Banville's novel *Birchwood* appeared; Ireland joined the European Community. Consequently, frankly, European money changed Ireland, didn't it? The cosmopolitan Ireland; the secularized state—it's a Europeanized Ireland, isn't it? Yet you've spoken of how culturally Ireland could never be part of Europe, as "no symphonies were written here."

CT   If people asked me: "What do you want?" I'd say: "Sweden; Denmark—a Scandinavian society." They'd say: "But what about the tradition of the Irish novel? It won't survive." I'd say: "Great. We've already had that." What I'm saying is that the darkness which produced the valuable products of Irish culture wasn't worth it. No one should think it was.

RC   And what is the place of Ireland culturally in Europe?

CT   No place.

RC   But you made the case for Joyce's significance in that introduction. In his reading, his travels, his sense of culture, Joyce was internationalist. So was Beckett.

CT   Joyce wrote from a deeply political perspective. Setting a novel in Dublin and having as its main character Leopold Bloom, a wandering Jew—a man with enormous wit, power of noticing, and this great private life. That was a political act in 1922, when Ireland was ready to become the most insular place in Europe—to talk about and praise this variety at a time when monoculturalism was going to become the order of the day. As a presence in Ireland, Joyce is immensely liberating. Politically, there isn't anyone in the twentieth century who offers the same possibilities in terms of the images he created for Ireland.

RC   Beckett you mention more briefly.

CT   He said some great things—like that Irish people don't give a fart in their trousers for culture. The plays seem more and more like games being played—games I'm not that interested in. But I love all of his fiction—most marvelous.

RC   Is there anything you'd like to add?

CT   Only to return to this question of the genie in the bottle that won't always stay there. There's a point where you find people who came before you who faced the same difficulties—two gay writers in Ireland in the 1940s and '50s, John Broderick and Kate O'Brien. They played at living in England, coming back here irregularly. They didn't quite put it into their novels. Both were from rich families. They were odd—posh, patrician Catholics. They stood out, since people in those years tended to be poor. Looking at the whole body of their work, it's not as though this particular drama hasn't been enacted here so many times—the question of how one should deal in public with matters which are anathema in private.

It's all changing now. In Keith Ridgway's *The Long Falling*, the gay characters have a wonderfully easy time in Dublin. They try to liberate the older generation. I thought that was all interesting. Emma Donogue, similarly, has a much more open universe. I'm just slightly too old to have experienced that liberation so that it fundamentally entered my spirit.

RC   Because it happened later here than elsewhere?

CT   Yes.

RC   That sounds like a suitably sad note on which to close. Thanks very much for your time.

EIGHT

PAUL RUSSELL

PAUL RUSSELL is author of five novels: *The Salt Point, Boys of Life, Sea of Tranquillity, The Coming Storm,* and *War Against the Animals.*

Born in 1956 in Memphis, Tennessee, Russell studied English at Oberlin College in Ohio, and was then admitted to the graduate program in English and Creative Writing at Cornell University, where he was awarded an M.A. in English, as well as an M.F.A. in Creative Writing for a collection of stories and a novella entitled "The Longing in Darkness," which remains unpublished—deservedly so, according to Russell. Russell received his doctorate in 1983 for a dissertation on Vladimir Nabokov. A number of Russell's short stories appeared in journals during the 1980s: "The Witch and the Goatboy," in *Black Warrior Review* 7.2 (Spring 1981); "Leiza," in *Akros Review,* no. 6 (Fall 1982); "After Mariah," in *Swallow's Tale* 1.1 (Spring 1983); "Ricky," in *Carolina Quarterly* 37.1 (Fall 1984); "Emma," in *Souwester* 11.3 (Winter 1984); "Brushes," in *Epoch* 34.2 (Summer 1985); and "A Hospital Room, a Tesseract, a Box Canyon," in the *Crescent Review* 5.2 (Fall 1987). Russell also wrote an unpublished novel entitled "A Child's History of the Rain."

Russell left Ithaca when hired to teach English at Vassar College. He initially moved to Poughkeepsie, New York, where his first published novel, *The Salt Point* (New York: Dutton, 1990), was set. This was followed by *Boys of Life* (New York: Dutton, 1991), in which Russell wrote about Memphis, his birthplace, for the first time. Russell's third novel, *Sea of Tranquillity* (New York: Dutton, 1994), spans a twenty-year period, shifts between four narrative points of view, and is set in America, Turkey, and on the moon. *The Coming Storm* (New York: St. Martin's Press, 1999), set in a claustrophobic school in upstate New York, concerns the relationship between a pupil and his gay teacher, and won the 2000 Ferro-Grumley Award for Gay Male Fiction. Russell's latest novel is *War Against the Animals* (New York: St. Martin's, 2003).

Russell is also the author of *The Gay 100: A Ranking of the Most Influential Gay Men and Lesbians, Past and Present* (New York: Carol Publishing Group, 1994). Recent short stories and essays include "Underwater," in Clifford Chase, ed., *Queer Thirteen: Lesbian and Gay Writers Recall Seventh Grade* (New York: Morrow, 1998), "The Golden Book of the Civil War," in Matthew Rottnek, ed., *Sissies and Tomboys: Gender Nonconformity and Homosexual Childhood* (New York: New York University Press, 1999), "White Lily," in the *James White Review* 16.2 (Spring 1999), and "Delicacy," in *Gastronomica* 1.1 (February 2001). His work also appeared in George Stambolian, ed., *Men on Men 4* (New York: Plume, 1992).

Russell now lives in Rosendale, New York, and continues to teach English at nearby Vassar. The interview took place in Paul Russell's work office on November 1, 1997, and was updated in June 2002, at which point the material following the asterisks was added.

RC Could you talk a little about your experience of teaching gay literature at Vassar?

PR In 1987, I initiated a multidisciplinary course called "Minority Culture in America: The Gay Experience." Then I started a course for freshmen-only called "Queer Alphabets," which consisted of readings in gay and lesbian literature. I did so with some trepidation. These are eighteen-year-old students, and this is their first class. I thought: "I'd never in a million years have walked through that door when I was eighteen. Maybe I'll get three students." I had no idea what the demographics of the class would be.

I was astonished. The class limit was nineteen; it was full. Ten people were on the waiting list. Now I teach it every year, and students are knocking down the doors to get in. The class is usually a third "out" gay and lesbian, a third straight—and I believe them—and a final third who . . . Well, the first paper I have them write, I ask them why they are taking the course, and what they expect to get out of it. I say I'm not expecting them to out themselves. With some students, the first sentence runs: "I've known I was gay since I was twelve years old." Others start: "You must understand that I have a purely intellectual interest in this subject matter. It does not in any way relate to my personal life." I read these and think: "Oh yeah. This can be hard or it can be easy. You can come out in two or three weeks, in three or four years, or it can take a lifetime." Often with those students, six months later we have a good laugh about that paper. They're always amazed I completely saw through this elaborate structure of denial.

RC It could make for a difficult class atmosphere.

PR Managing the volatility of the class takes a lot of energy. But most years the mix is very congenial. The class develops a kind of solidarity. The last time I taught it, it was difficult though. There was a deeply conservative Christian black woman in the class. The other students were shy about confronting her directly because of the state of race in America. They had to negotiate several fronts simultaneously, and weren't sure how to do it. There were some awkward moments. She remains a deeply conservative Christian. But she rose to the challenge of the course admirably, and was both thoughtful and thought-provoking. After the first two weeks, I thought: "This is going to be a nightmare." By the end of the semester, I thought it had been good for everybody concerned. I don't think we changed her mind, but she thought about a lot of things she hadn't thought about before.

RC To what extent do you pursue personal enthusiasms in the selection of books?

PR I frequently find that some books just teach well and others don't. All that says about a book is that it either teaches well or doesn't. It says nothing larger about its literary merit. Certain novels which I absolutely love I have tried teaching once and have said: "Never again." Some things you don't want to expose to the light and air of the freshman mind.

RC   In my undergraduate course, I was always disappointed in responses to Andrew Holleran's *Dancer from the Dance.*

PR   It's one of the great novels—a masterpiece. Because I think it's so important, I insist on teaching it year after year. But I get the same response as you. I'm astonished how many students hate that novel. They find it depressing beyond belief, without being able to see its celebratory aspects. You almost don't know where to start in trying to refute this notion of theirs that it's no good. I don't think it's generational. And in fact some students do love it.

I've ended up teaching it as a religious text, finally. Malone I read as a martyr in the religion of love. Like all martyrs, he and a number of the characters are extremists. Once you decide to believe that the pursuit of love contains the profound meaning of existence itself, you don't undertake it halfheartedly. You do it excessively, in the same way that Christ was excessive—turning over the tables of the moneychangers and so on. That extremism makes people nervous.

RC   Is there a school of gay devotional literature? One thinks of Genet, whose Catholic iconography your first novel *The Salt Point* played upon.

PR   One reason I like *Dancer from the Dance* is that I understand that emotional territory. It's my own preoccupation to a certain extent, although it manifests itself in different ways to Genet or Holleran. I do think the pursuit of love and beauty are quasi-religious quests. All my books are about that, one way or another—the way those pursuits get mangled or thwarted.

RC   Holleran also deploys religion alongside other elements of the characters' backgrounds, often as a counterpoint to the romantic or sexual quest.

PR   Yes. He sees homosexuality as a complete antithesis to all of these "normal" values—like home and the nine-to-five job. It's almost as if homosexuality is weightless, as opposed to all these other "anchored" modes of being. His characters have to negotiate an absolute leap from one mode to the other. When Malone enters homosexual life, perversely it's almost like entering a monastic life. Naturally, it's the very opposite of monastic. But it requires the shedding of everything that went before. His characters inhabit an almost Manichaean universe: you cannot have one and the other. You have to jettison and sacrifice all that stabilizing stuff in order to enter the beautiful, rarefied, and tragic—because unanchored—world of homosexuality.

The easy thing would be to say that Holleran was just another self-hating, homophobic writer. But it's a lot more complicated and richer than that. That's one thing that makes *The Beauty of Men* problematic for me. In some way it presents Holleran's nightmare: that you escape into that other world of religious life, where true meaning for the homosexual is found. Then your mother gets sick and you have to recross that absolute divide. You find yourself in Florida. There's the boat ramp. But since it's such an "either-or" proposition for Lark, the boat ramp's an entirely unsatisfactory compromise. There is no real compromise possible. Lark has chosen the swamp of his mother and is left with a desolate longing for that other world, absolutely and breathtakingly disconnected from this one.

RC   There's something consoling in the significance of ritual in gay life in Holleran's books. By comparison, family matters are always messy.

PR   Several things always happen at once with him. That's one thing that makes *Dancer from the Dance* so rich. Much of its symbolism is so deeply ambivalent that it's constantly shifting. On the one hand, it's a way of saving and preserving something from home. But it's also the desecration of that. Sutherland sits at home, reading the nativity narrative from the Bible, and then hops into a cab to go to the baths. Holleran and his characters take a guilty pleasure from that profane juxtaposition. The sacred and the profane keep changing places. In the energy of that interchange I think he and his characters find something vital, if also desperate. There's an energy of meaning-making that happens precisely in that continual transposition and retransposition of sacred and obscene iconography.

RC One of the borrowings from religion which is easiest for the gay culture in his novels to replicate seems to be hierarchy. Lark's cruising in *The Beauty of Men* is subject to hierarchy. It's just that his position has slipped, compared to that of characters in *Dancer from the Dance*.

PR Yes, but what distinguishes the two novels finally is that *Dancer from the Dance* is about hope, whereas *The Beauty of Men* is about hopelessness. I wish Holleran had kept its original title—"The Boat Ramp." But that novel upset me as few novels have. It carried me as a reader into territory that may not finally be sustainable in a novel. That hopelessness represents a kind of cessation of motion. Novels in fact depend on a trajectory. The only one in *The Beauty of Men* concerns not whether Mom's going to die, but when. Everything else has settled into a deathlike state. That's profoundly disturbing as an ontological experience, but it presents very difficult territory for a novel to traverse.

RC Your novels strike the reader as very carefully plotted.

PR That's nice to hear. I don't start with plot. In fact, I seldom know the plot more than a few pages ahead of where I am at any given moment. That's a dangerous way to live, but as a writer it's the only way I can live. When you look at Dickens's outlines for *Bleak House*, it takes your breath away to see him conceptualizing this thing more or less completely, with just the details to be worked out.

RC Perhaps for him the necessary imaginative anarchy lay in the characterization and caricature, rather than the plot.

PR Although there is a kind of anarchy of plot in the late, great Dickens novels. I find *Little Dorrit*'s plot very confusing—not because it is badly plotted but because it develops a fiendish complexity that is expressive of the increasing darkness of Dickens's own imagination. And with the unfinished *Edwin Drood*, all attempts to complete the story by other writers are baffled. Either the mystery that Dickens has established at the beginning has such an obvious solution that it's impossible to imagine him settling for it, or it has a solution that's so twisted, so complicated, that it's not even suggested in the pages we have. I suspect that if Dickens had finished it, we'd be very surprised by what ends up happening.

I can't write that way. Every time I try, I end up with this lifeless thing which has mechanical movement but is way too neat. Clearly one difference between myself and Dickens is that he's able to inject into that planning stage a kind of liveliness that I simply can't achieve. I set an ensemble of characters in motion, and then continually ask myself: "Given who this character is, and what she/he has just done, what has to happen next?" You're continually improvising within the fairly contained parameters you've established through your characters. There's not an infinite set of possibilities to confront on every page. In some ways I think of my plots as like a series of last-minute "saves." The accumulation of these, I hope, gives the plot a kind of contingency, and therefore a liveliness, that I can't achieve if I plot it all out in advance.

RC   Is the process of revision for you essentially minor in consequence?

PR   Yes—at least so far. I hope that remains the case. Writers work differently. I tell my students all the time to figure out how their own brain works. If it works in a weird, messy way, there's nothing they can do about it, as much as they might like to transform themselves into a different kind of writer.

RC   Does the writing flow easily for you, or do you get stuck because of this constant need to resolve questions of plot?

PR   I take Thomas Mann as my writing model. He wrote seven sentences a day seven days a week, 365 days a year. He said anyone who did that for fifty years would in fact produce a substantial intellectual legacy.

Mann's a great example of a writer who wasn't necessarily blessed with an inordinate amount of natural talent. Through enormous will and Germanic discipline, he managed to take that talent and make something stupendous out of it—incrementally: seven sentences a day. For me—someone for whom things don't come particularly easily—Mann provided a very valuable model of a way of working that allows you to take your meager talent and sustain it over the long haul. So when I'm writing—

which doesn't happen when I'm teaching, but only during the summers, during leave, and during the month-long winter break—I try to produce a fairly finished page a day. That also usually means tidying up the pages of the previous few days.

RC   One could argue that Thomas Mann's sense of what a novel was expanded throughout his career. Is this true in your case too? On the most basic level, your novels are getting bigger.

PR   I've noticed the disturbing tendency that each of my novels is almost exactly a hundred pages longer than the one before. When I finished *Sea of Tranquillity*—which came in at around 400 pages—I thought that was long enough, especially since that book had a more epic scope temporally and thematically. I told myself: "I'm going to reverse this trend. The next one's going to be a nice, 250-page novel." I'm now closing in on 500 pages with *The Coming Storm*. There's nothing I can do about it. A novel demands its own size. I hope that doesn't mean *The Coming Storm* is bloated, because its scope is more intimate than *Sea of Tranquillity*. It only takes place over nine months. Again there's a quartet of characters—this time all in the third person—and the book alternates between their points of view in 35-page-long chapters. There's not the quick flitting around between points of view that there is in *The Salt Point* or *Sea of Tranquillity*. It aims to be a more magisterial novel than those more fleet-footed projects.

One reason why the novels keep getting longer is because they keep getting more ambitious. Although *The Coming Storm* is ostensibly more intimate in scope than its immediate predecessor, it explores the past that haunts its present much more fully than in my other work. So in that way I think it's got the most "depth" of any of my fiction. Thomas Mann himself makes a personal appearance, so he's very much been on my mind recently. The novel takes place in a fictional town located in the Hudson Valley, a little south of Poughkeepsie. It turns out that Mann and his family vacationed at the Mohonk Mountain House, a resort a little way from here on the other side of the river. When a colleague of mine here at Vassar was fifteen, he worked as an elevator boy at the hotel, and remembers Mann vividly. So I stole this detail from real life to weave into the novel's fabric: Louis the headmaster remembers being aware as a fifteen-year-old elevator boy of the famous writer's gaze.

RC   On some level, then, this "knitting-in" of detail can happen before you start writing.

PR   Yes. I exaggerate in almost everything I say. I had fifty pages of notes, thoughts, sentences, and observations for *The Coming Storm* before I wrote the first sentence, just as I'm already accumulating random pages for the next.

I keep a running notebook. I've sometimes wondered whether my novels aren't in part produced by the random process of what's caught my attention over the two-year period preceding them—the things that have ended up in my notebook. Given that I have certain obsessions from novel to novel, part of the project of each one is to figure out how to include as many of them as possible coherently. The danger is that there may be a centrifugal tendency. At times in *Sea of Tranquillity*, there ended up being too many distracting elements, perhaps. The main narratives are surrounded by this shimmer of other objects. On the one hand, I wanted to create that rich shimmer; on the other, I wonder now whether a bit more discipline might not have banished some of them and made for a cleaner texture.

RC   Are there always two years of note-taking?

PR   Roughly. Usually I'll start collecting stuff for the new novel when I'm in the final year of writing the previous one. I wish I were like Anthony Trollope and could draw a line at the bottom of the page and start the next novel. But I have about a year of mental exhaustion before the next book starts to coalesce.

RC   The first two novels came out close together.

PR   That's because *The Salt Point*, which is my first published novel but in fact my second, took a while to find an agent. It made me look awfully prolific at the beginning of my career. I'd written an earlier novel, "A

Child's History of the Rain"—how's that for an awful title?—which I'd shipped around. It got lots of nice rejections—all of which at the time infuriated me. Now I agree with those editors who thought it a very promising first novel that didn't entirely succeed. In retrospect I'm glad it wasn't my first publication. It served its purpose. It taught me which mistakes not to make again.

RC   Some writers feel the cord has been broken once they have seen a book into publication.

PR   I break the cord consciously. I can't bear to look at my previous books. I know that if I did, they'd bring bottomless pits of regret. I did the best I could at the time. I don't think anybody's well-served by the writer who spends his whole life writing one perfect book. That book isn't there to be written. And if you try that, you end up on your deathbed with one unfinished novel.

In some way I think of my novels as journals. They're not autobiographical in any sense. But they're a kind of psychic or metaphorical autobiography. They record my emotional and intellectual state during the time they were composed. For that reason they're very much documents of their time. You wouldn't go back and revise your journal from ten years ago based on who you are now, and in some way I see my novels as mileposts in my psychic life. I'm content to let them remain, flaws and all.

RC   Where does short fiction fit in?

PR   I have a terrible time with that. I hate writing it, and I don't think I'm any good at it. I don't particularly enjoy reading it either. I'm really a novelist and a novel reader. What I love about the novel as a reader is what I love as a writer—the generosity of scope. In some ways, I'm a real nineteenth-century romantic. I'm enamored of those big forms that promise to create their own world. I love the symphonies of Mahler. I feel a great affinity with the way a Mahler symphony creates its own world. A satisfying novel does exactly the same.

I do write short stories from time to time. But it's almost as difficult to write one short story as it is to write a novel. The really agonizing, unpleasant part of the process is the beginning—when I don't know the characters or the feel of the fictional world. I'm totally at sea. I hate that state of being in a perpetual muddle. With the novel there's a pleasure in living inside a world you think you know your way around, finally. With a short story, as soon as that fun part begins, the damned thing's finished. It's the same amount of effort for me to get them up and running. One runs for three hundred miles, the other for fifteen. I admire short-story writers tremendously because of the economy they have to practice.

RC   Do you have ideas for fiction that you reject?

PR   My head's always full of ideas that—basically, for lack of time—I don't write up.

RC   Some writers claim an immediate engagement with their feelings when they write. You seem to be speaking of a time delay, of ideas or feelings being distilled through the note-taking process. Have you ever had an experience or feeling that insisted on being accommodated more urgently in your writing?

PR   I don't think I'd particularly trust that if I found it happening—which isn't to say that every day's writing isn't influenced by every day's living. Constantly I seem to find exactly the thing I need right when I need it. That's not magic. It's just that one is hyper-alert and notices those things at the right time. I'll be stuck on some detail, and I'll go to the grocery store and happen to see something that is exactly what I need to solve that little problem—an image; a face; a tone of voice. In that way life certainly feeds it. But those are microscopic things. With larger things, I couldn't work them in even if I wanted to.

RC   Some writers draw on dreams.

PR   I get much more from the grocery store than from dreams! [*Laughs*] I don't think I've ever gotten anything from a dream that I could use fictionally.

RC   You've previously cited D. H. Lawrence, Joyce Carol Oates, and Patrick White as big influences. Lawrence in particular very much divides gay writers. There's perhaps a more obvious trajectory in gay-themed writing from Henry James, say.

PR   Well, I immensely prefer James to Lawrence as a novelist, just as I immensely prefer Faulkner to Hemingway. Privately I think of *The Coming Storm* as my Jamesian novel—though James himself would have been horrified by it. About Lawrence I feel deeply divided. I'm very resistant to him. He wrote an awful lot of awful stuff. But I also think that when he's "on"—as in the first half of *The Rainbow*—he's really onto something quite revolutionary.

What I was able to learn from Lawrence stemmed from his intense interest in the rhythmic back-and-forth between people. That can be absolutely maddening. His interest in it wearies even me—and I'm interested myself. He doesn't know when to stop. But I respect the intensity of his focus on his characters as these bundles of cosmic, electrical, sexual energy. In some ways, it's almost as if they don't have bodies. They're sort of incandescent, disembodied appetites that aren't neatly containable in the nineteenth-century mold of character-making. That's what I find compelling—Lawrence's ability to render human beings as complicated, contradictory, electrical constellations. I was able to take a little of that away with me to work into the mix of my characters. Lawrence rendered a certain spark that I too wanted to render.

RC   They're invariably incredibly sexually driven.

PR   He sees their sexuality as inextricably interwoven with the fabric of everything else. It's not as if his characters are purely sexual. Their sex, intellect, emotion, spirit, soul, whatever else—it's all seen as a single matrix. I believe in that too. I don't think these things can be disentangled.

RC   Which stage of James's career has been important?

PR   The latter stage. *The Wings of the Dove*, as a friend of mine said, has only a single flaw—it's unreadable. Otherwise it's perfect! [*Laughs*] I remember my first experience of reading it in graduate school. I'd never read a book I didn't understand before. I thought: "I'm not stupid. So why have I just read ten pages, yet I couldn't tell you what on earth's going on; what these characters are talking about?" Late James is weird like no other writer. But it has its own, inner coherence. Once you get acclimated to the clouded language, you can move around it with some ease—though *The Golden Bowl* has always eluded me.

One reason I like *The Wings of the Dove* is because it has my favorite plot. Forget everything else. It's that story of Merton Densher and Kate Croy collaborating to take advantage of Milly Theale. It's Merton Densher at some point realizing he's fallen in love with the woman he's going to dupe. He knows, first, that he's going to achieve exactly what he intended, but, second, that, in the process, he can no longer take the reward. That's such a poignant emotional scenario.

RC   Has the impact of James been more at this plot level—the theme of innocence despoiled, for instance?

PR   Well, that's been my plot, again and again. In a weird way what interests me in James is what interests me in Lawrence, though they come at it in completely different ways. James is utterly fascinated by human psychology. That incredibly intricate, nuanced language, which grows ever more so, is really in the service of an almost scientific scrutiny of our states of being, which we know shade into one another with enormous subtlety. James is continually trying to refine his language so that he can take account of these minute, unconscious shifts in our psyches which, nonetheless, often have enormous consequences. The psyche James conceptualizes exists on another planet than Lawrence's. Given that difference, their projects, though, aren't as alien to one another as they first might seem. One describes the geography of Venus; the other, that of Mars. But they're both describing the psyche.

RC   Both writers have been accused of extreme narrative digression.

PR   Yes. I think my own narrative trajectory is more reined in than either of theirs—though the Jamesian digression for me feels essential to the project. The Lawrentian digression often feels like lack of control. That mars the last half of *The Rainbow* quite seriously.

RC   Who else is important to you stylistically? You studied Nabokov at length.

PR   If we're looking for the Oedipal struggle, it's with him. I spent many years of my life deeply invested in his work. As a young writer I set out to emulate him. I made the prolonged, painful discovery that—surprise!— Nabokov was inimitable. It was the death of me as a writer to try to write those glittering, bejeweled sentences. The failure of my attempts to imitate him is what sent me to trying to figure out who I was as a writer. Disappointingly, I wasn't another Nabokov. I couldn't be. It took an embarrassingly long time to discover that.

RC   You once referred to having had to work through a misguidedly aesthetic approach to narrative.

PR   In my Nabokovian phase, I'd have been horrified if you'd shown me the books I'd eventually write. They're so antithetical to what I then thought novels were about. I started out—and thank God there's no published record—wanting to be a kind of rarefied aesthete. I wanted to write books like Edmund White's *Forgetting Elena*—obviously a Nabokov-influenced project. In retrospect, I realized my flight into aesthetics had everything to do with my own closetedness. I was going to use those gorgeous sentences as a weapon or shield. I was going to enfold myself in aesthetic preoccupations to the point where I'd become invisible.

Though I have this guilty sense of abandoning the high, noble project of Nabokov, one review of my work stated: "Russell's real subject is art." Of course that was Nabokov's real subject. Maybe the surface of my books has changed but their preoccupations haven't so much. This critic said they were about how the imagination shapes the Other to conform with the imagination's needs, desires, and hungers. And that's really about the morally clouded process of making art—and making art out of human beings, particularly. Nothing ever disappears. It just gets buried. So my Nabokovian preoccupations still fester under the surface.

RC How was Patrick White influential?

PR What I liked about Lawrence, Oates, and White was that each is wacky in his or her own way. I've spent a lot of my life being intimidated by my sense of what was appropriate. To me, these three, for whatever reasons, were unafraid to do what they wanted as writers. My own breakthrough point as a writer came when I realized that if I wasn't writing about gay identity, I wouldn't be any good. The only way I could be good was by exploring my obsessions and preoccupations—all the things about my psyche that made me nervous—without thought for the consequences.

These three had discovered how to write about all the things that made them queasy or squeamish. That was what made them good. They're all hugely different to one another—and hugely different from my writing. It was my sense of their courage in simply forgetting what they were supposed to write about; in discovering their subjects, however weird and perverse these might be.

RC Has wit got anything to do with it? I find your books quite witty.

PR Thanks. Nobody ever says that, but I agree. I try to put wit in. Joyce Carol Oates doesn't have much of it. Nor Lawrence. But Patrick White's a hoot. He's a campy old queen masquerading as a stern modernist. I like the twinkle in his eye.

RC Perhaps your rather dark subject matter blinds people to the wit.

PR A lot of people find my work depressing. They're certainly free to. When a friend said she found *The Salt Point* depressing, I asked if she hadn't found some parts witty as well. She replied: "Yes. That just made it even more depressing."

RC You've referred now both to lay readers and critics of your novels. Do you ever resist reading reviews?

PR I can't really read them. I skim them with a sick feeling in the pit of my stomach, and then put them away. But reviewers aren't writing for me. And they shouldn't be.

RC On the need to write about gay identity: does this suggest you're comfortable with the idea that there is a coherent gay identity or literary tradition?

PR I don't see any reason why either should be coherent exactly. I don't think there's any coherence to gay identity. Like any other identity, "gay" represents a continuum. All possible shades of anything and everything are to be found there, and that's fine.

The question of the coherence of the gay novel is more interesting. There's at least the possibility that certain forms have evolved since 1945. I taught a seminar course once called "The Gay Male Novel in America, post-1945." I came up with a series of texts as a way of interrogating the proposition that there was in fact something called the "Gay American Novel." We started with Gore Vidal's *The City and the Pillar*; James Baldwin's *Giovanni's Room*; excerpts from John Rechy's *City of Night*; Christopher Isherwood's *A Single Man*—in some ways the best portrait of an ordinary gay man I've read.

In all my other courses I've integrated gay and lesbian material, with varying degrees of comfort. It's not entirely clear to me that they belong together. I understand absolutely the political reasons for putting them together. I also think that sociologically, aesthetically, and on any number of other levels, they really do represent two discrete bodies of work. I wondered whether it would be politically incorrect to announce a course on gay male fiction only. Fortunately, a colleague decided in the same semester to run a course on lesbian literature.

RC Does Isherwood interest you mostly thematically, or also stylistically?

PR If my style seemed anything like Isherwood's, I'd be greatly flattered. His style in some ways is the absolute opposite of Nabokov's. Isherwood wanted to develop a clean, almost transparent style. For the fictional projects he was engaged in, that style's absolutely workable.

We also read William Burroughs's *The Wild Boys*, which in some ways seems completely out of the orbit of the course—or suggests some parallel possibilities which we returned to when we looked at Dennis Cooper's *Frisk*. Cooper's another writer who seems not to be in any tradition described by Vidal, Baldwin, and Isherwood. Of Edmund White, we read both *Nocturnes for the King of Naples* and *A Boy's Own Story*. Rereading them back-to-back, I found *Nocturnes* more interesting. Most surprisingly, it seemed much gayer now than in 1978. Clearly that must be me. The novel's the same. At the time, I remember being disappointed that it wasn't a "gay novel," whatever I thought that was. When I reread it, every sentence seemed gay.

The whole question of whether there's such a thing as gay culture is fascinating and vexed. I felt, in the intervening years, I'd somehow become more educated, or my ear had become better trained at picking up on a kind of innuendo which, in 1978, I couldn't hear.

The question is to what extent books like *Nocturnes for the King of Naples* in fact created that kind of music. There's a reciprocity there. Literature isn't journalism. It doesn't simply mimic reality. It creates reality. One of the powerful things gay literature can do is to act as a sort of self-fulfilling prophecy. The world of possibilities gay people live in now has been enriched and enhanced by the possibilities literature first articulated. It's exactly the nightmare of cultural conservatives. These books do change reality. Wilde was right—life does imitate art. By telling stories that never happened but should have, we in fact enable them to happen in ways that they wouldn't have, had these stories never been imagined. We tell stories to make them possible for others, if not for ourselves.

The book we ended the semester with was Louis Begley's *As Max Saw It*. I put it there because Begley—as far as I know—isn't gay. Yet here's a really good novel whose subject is two gay men and the course of their lives. Is that a gay novel? I don't know. Can a gay novel only be written by a gay man, or is it simply one that deals with gay people as subjects? Does its form and structure inherently differ from the straight novel—so that *Nocturnes for the King of Naples* may be a gay novel without ever using the "g"-word?

RC Vidal, Baldwin, Rechy—these early "out" gay texts adopted an essentially realist mode. From the later books you mentioned, one could infer that this mode has rather withered away.

PR I think there was a certain historical need for what I'd call the gay tourism novel, which Vidal's, Rechy's, and Larry Kramer's *Faggots* all were: "Come, reader, I'm taking you on this fascinating, perhaps lurid, tour of the gay underworld. This is what gay life is like. Get your cameras out—you won't want to miss this!" Both for gay readers and for the straight world these novels served several important functions. For a fledgling gay community, they coalesced certain things. By describing a community, they in part created it. Then the community evolves . . .

Writers are in a different position now. It's hard to imagine anyone writing *Faggots* or *The City and the Pillar* today. In some ways there'd be no point. Could you imagine a novel in which a character goes to visit different kinds of gay people? That's really the plot of *The City and the Pillar*: "Here are the Hollywood queens; here are the New York gays; here are the effeminate ones; here are the masculine ones." It articulates a taxonomy of gay life, so it's rather external to gay life, whereas more recent novels seem to come from the inside out.

Baldwin holds up best, I think, because of the ferocity of his imagination. *Giovanni's Room* is the one book among these in which I see something new every time I teach it. David's psychology is so unyieldingly complicated and contradictory. Baldwin does such an unstinting job—rendering that without apologizing; without tidying it up any—that I never know exactly what I think. That's the mark of a great novel, as opposed to a good one—there's a kind of openness to its meanings that keeps one coming back.

RC Why is Holleran's *Dancer from the Dance* not a tourism novel? The opening letters explicitly conjure up an "outsider" readership.

PR It may mark the end of the tourism novel by self-consciously mocking it. It adopted the rhetoric of the tourism novel but then subverts it. *Dancer from the Dance* couldn't have been written in the 1950s or '60s. It allows itself to become a real novel, not a sociological tract. One function of the letters is similar to that of the "psychiatrist's" introduction to *Lolita*. He gives you the nice, moral reading which the book proceeds to subvert.

RC   What's the significance of Edmund White's *A Boy's Own Story?* In a sense that marked White's retreat from highly aestheticized prose to a more Isherwood-like, realist style.

PR   It's important as a phenomenon—maybe because it marks the moment for White not terribly unlike my own discovery that I shouldn't veil my interests. *A Boy's Own Story* is in some ways the first nonpathological coming out story. Even its title is finally in a cultural position to assert with some confidence that what we're reading isn't a psychiatric case study. It's not: "Let's see how a freak becomes a freak." Rather, it says: "This is about a boy who is completely ordinary. His gayness is just part of his ordinariness." Isherwood did it in *A Single Man*, but George is an adult. Still, it's probably no accident that White wrote the novel in an Isherwood-type style.

Maybe prose style and the closet have something to do with one another. My students talked about how White's gorgeous sentences closeted their sexuality. That's what those sentences are about—the act of closeting. The transparent sentence of Isherwood outs itself with each speaking. With *A Boy's Own Story*, a certain kind of coming-of-age story comes out in a way which, culturally, it hadn't been able to do previously. And its popularity is testament to its occurring at exactly the right moment.

RC   George in *A Single Man* strikes me now as a little too perfect. The ending of White's *A Boy's Own Story* doesn't quite foreshadow the boy's maturation, though. It leaves open the possibility that his liberation may remain an illusion. The boy's still very crushed and damaged—and behaves so.

PR   I agree completely. George is too good to be true. It's interesting to think about the titles. With Isherwood, George is "A Single Man." But he also carries the burden of a kind of positive portrayal of the gay Everyman. The "Own" in *A Boy's Own Story* becomes more and more salient. It becomes a kind of reclaiming of the character, with his flaws and damaged-ness, from the various burdens of story: the story as tourist account; the story as psychopathology; the story as positive, affirming, coming out story with a progressive political bent. It does become the boy's own story, with all its somewhat unsettling compromise.

RC   Did your class come to any conclusions concerning the possible aesthetic of the gay novel?

PR   In the end, the results were entirely inconclusive. I'm slated to teach the course again. I'm interested to see if anything different comes of it.

RC   Returning to the centrality of gay themes in your writing—does this impact upon any sense you may have of your readership, either actual or intended?

PR   Writers are always fascinated by the question of who their readership is. You get tantalizing glimpses, but there's so much you can't possibly know. My sense is that the readership for gay novels has probably changed since the seventies. The Violet Quill writers, I think, were very much a group of elite gay men writing for a fairly elite audience of similarly inclined urban gay men. That's not to denigrate them. That probably was the initial gay readership. From there, a ripple effect has spread. My sense is that I've got readers all across the country, and from such diverse situations that it's difficult to generalize.

RC   Do you feel that our literature and culture still cling to the idea that gay experience is at its most heightened or consequential in urban environments?

PR   I'd agree that both writers and readers cling to that. I don't think anybody's well served by the creation of that kind of myth. In some ways, *Dancer from the Dance* is the prime example of the creation of a certain definitive gay lifestyle. A reader of my novels once told me: "I don't find your novels very gay." The subtext clearly was that they weren't recognizably gay because the characters didn't tend to do the things by which—in literature—we've come to recognize gay people. They don't go to Fire Island or Key West, or go to dance wherever gay men are dancing in the city these days.

RC It's interesting how many pre-liberation gay narratives had nothing to do with the city. Take Southern Gothic authors like Tennessee Williams or Truman Capote.

PR There may be reasons for that. In some way it's because of the urban centers that a nonpathological gay identity was created. Williams's homosexuals are always pathological, so of course they're in small towns. That's the source of their pathology.

RC You spoke of not knowing where your plots were headed. With *Boys of Life*, though, you set up a narrative that is in a way closed—the guy's in prison; the murder's happened. With *Sea of Tranquillity*, Jonathan's moment of closure—when he tests HIV-positive—occurs relatively late in the story. I'm fascinated as to when these examples of "closing down" a story occurred to you.

PR With *Boys of Life*, my initial impetus was reading a biography of Pasolini. I was fascinated by his being killed by one of the hustlers he'd picked up—though I was also intrigued by the possibility that it was a political assassination. Originally, that was what the book was about. I decided to make Carlos a film director. Still, I couldn't set it in Italy. It had to be America. As soon as I translated Pasolini into America, I realized that a figure like him—someone who was both a political and an artistic figure of great stature—simply wasn't possible here. You couldn't imagine Robert Altman or Martin Scorsese also being novelists, critics, and poets, and intensely controversial politically. So the possible ambiguity about the murder dropped out of the book. But you're right otherwise. I knew at the beginning that my narrator would be in prison and there was no doubt that he'd killed Carlos.

Then I showed a friend the first half of the manuscript. She wrote back: "I started to get the horrible feeling that Carlos was going to make something like a snuff movie." That had never occurred to me, but I thought: "She's reading carefully. I think she's right." Till then I'd known I wanted the title to be *Boys of Life*, but not why. I thought: "What if the film he made is called *Boys of Life* too?" Now the title made sense. Also, Tony has a brother who had been left way behind in Kentucky. Tony has these complicated feelings about him. I thought: "What if I bring the brother into the film? This'll give Tony a reason to kill Carlos." I was halfway through the novel before I'd any idea that Carlos made this kind of film, or that Tony was going to be part of it, or that their film was called *Boys of Life*. Those decisions came late, but weren't arbitrary. They were the result of my trying to be as alert as I could to the internal logic that the situation had already set in motion.

RC   Some reviewers thought the novel was about either Robert Mapplethorpe or Andy Warhol.

PR   As I was writing, I was thinking consciously of Pasolini and Fellini. But then my agent said: "Oh, it's about Andy Warhol and the Factory. That's how we'll pitch it to the editor." Later, a review argued that Carlos Reichert was obviously based on filmmaker Paul Morrissey. I knew the work of Morrissey but—consciously at least—he hadn't entered my mind before.

One important change was that, in the original manuscript, Tony Blair had AIDS. My editor made me take that out. He didn't think it added anything to the power of the book, and in some ways distracted from what else was there. AIDS was a supernumerary burden on an already powerful story.

RC   It pervades the novel nevertheless.

PR   Yes, and it seems to me, given how he'd loved, that Tony almost certainly would have had AIDS. I even think I know where he got it. There's a Ugandan businessman he mentions sleeping with. But I guess he used a condom at the last moment, so he escaped!

Part of the reason for featuring AIDS as part of the texture of *Sea of Tranquillity* was because I felt a degree of frustration by then. I thought: "I can't be writing now without thinking about and writing about AIDS. If I couldn't do it in *Boys of Life*, I'm going to make sure I introduce it in a fundamental way in *Sea of Tranquillity*." I knew all along with that book that Jonathan would get sick.

RC   Were you concerned, though, at the possible narrative consequences?

PR   That's one reason why Jonathan's voice is only one of a quartet. AIDS becomes an aspect of that novel's world, but it doesn't entirely dominate it. In purely narrative terms, the devastating thing about AIDS in the eighties and the early nineties was its absolute finality. There was the sense that once it was introduced into a fiction, there was only one possible plot. And once you took away from your characters what Grace Paley has called the "open destiny of life," in some sense there's no more story. Every AIDS story's the same. But by surrounding the finality of that AIDS story with others more open-ended, I hoped I could put AIDS in its place in some way.

There can be this horrible bleak consolation in surrendering to a sense of inevitability. In some ways it's even more difficult to preserve a sense that, for all of its tragedy and finality, AIDS is not in fact the end of everything. Someone has to survive—and survive intact enough psychologically to be able to go on. This is what storytelling's all about—commemorating the dead but enabling the survivors to continue.

RC   What led you to render only the father—Allen—in the third person in *Sea of Tranquillity*?

PR   When I tried to render Allen in the first person, all I was getting was this flat, clipped, inflectionless astronaut-speak. That's how he talks. It was only through the third-person voice that I could get through that disciplined, repressed surface and suggest the stuff going on in the depths.

RC   One result is that the novel seems to refuse to authenticate Allen's experience. At the level of plot, that ultimately feels justified. On the other hand, the more "redeemed" figures are still dysfunctional—heavy drinkers, or whatever. What was it like rendering Joan's drunken voice?

PR   I think—and this is just one reader's opinion—that Allen's the most lost—frighteningly so. He travels the farthest in miles, but goes nowhere.

The other characters all travel much farther. Joan I think of as triumphant. She starts at the lowest depths. By the end, she has completely transformed herself. She knows exactly who she is, and it's not anybody she was taught to be. It's a heroic and strange destiny, but it's her own destiny. Joan's drunkenness in the first half is so bleak that it may overshadow her transformation in the second half. But I think all the characters except Allen find that their quests end triumphantly. Even Jonathan, who, by the novel's end, is on the verge of being reborn as another avatar of Krishna—though some readers may have missed that in the somewhat surreal prose of the penultimate chapter.

RC   In terms of social authority, Allen stands undiminished.

PR   Yes. Allen finally has the weight of authority behind him. If the third-person voice contributes to that, I think that's good. It seemed important not to give in to the temptation to give Allen a satisfying comeuppance at the end. I wanted to leave the reader unsatisfied there. That reflects my view of how things are.

I have to tell you something about *Sea of Tranquillity*. A few weeks ago I got a letter. It said: "I'm the son of a famous astronaut who walked on the moon. I'm gay. I just read your novel. I feel like you must know me. Do I know you?" He wrote of how uncannily accurate he found my portraits of both Allen and Jonathan Cloud. It thrilled him. But he wondered—how could I have possibly known him so well?

It was one of those great moments. Sometimes as a writer you think: "What am I doing with my life? I'm just sitting at my desk, making all this stuff up. It doesn't mean anything." But you're not just making it up. Life and the imagination really are connected at some level way below the conscious. I was able to get it right. I didn't know this real-life gay son of an astronaut, but my imagination was able to get to some place that was awfully close to knowing him.

And the really strange thing is, when I was fourteen or so, I'd seen a photo of the three astronauts for this particular Apollo mission, and their families. I remember I had this kind of crush on the oldest son of one of the astronauts. Then years later, one of the impulses as I was thinking about writing *Sea of Tranquillity* was to write about a boy who knows—

and has a crush on—the son of an astronaut who walked on the moon. Somewhere in the back of my head was that photograph. It never consciously occurred to me that the boy in the photo might have been gay. But I guess in some way I knew all along.

RC   Now, a jump. Have you noticed how much sex there is in your novels?

PR   I have a couple of reasons for putting explicit sex into my books. One's personal; the other's political. The personal one is that I think it's fun both to read and to write about sex. There's pleasure in it. The political reason is that it seems to me there's no point writing about gay characters if you don't write about sex. There's no point drawing aside the veil so far and then leaving some of the territory just as murky as it was before.

I like to make people nervous when I write about sex, just as I like to make them nervous when I write about other emotional states. I guess I like to make myself nervous too. If I'm not moving into territory that makes me a little squeamish, then I'm not moving close enough to the edge. When I'm writing, I constantly ask myself: "Are you talking about things that give you a moment's pause? If not, you've got to push it a little further, because you're not doing your work."

I also think sex enables us to see the workings of power within relationships at both its most naked and most devious. That's straight out of Foucault. But what I think is most interesting about sex in a novel is that it can create a second level of narrative, where social relations between characters are retold at the level of the body or desire. Sometimes the two stories are congruent with one another; at other times, they're interestingly divergent. It's like doing sonar soundings. It gives you a second echo location.

That's true in *Boys of Life*, I hope, which was very influenced by a really underrated gay novel from the early eighties by Paul Rogers: *Saul's Book*. Our sense of what's really going on between Tony and Carlos is made clearer by their sexual encounters. These tell us things that Tony intellectually doesn't understand—or doesn't want to. If we just listen to Tony's patter, we get one version of things. We get a much more unsettling version if we watch what they do.

RC   That's technically hard with just one narrator.

PR   That's one reason I shifted to four voices with *Sea of Tranquillity*.

RC   It's fortuitous that you brought up Foucault. I was jokingly going to ask if *Discipline and Punish* was your model in writing fiction.

PR   [*Laughs*] It really is. I'm an unreconstructed Foucauldian. Reading the first volume of *The History of Sexuality* was a very important intellectual moment for me. There was a point early on in *Boys of Life* where I imagined the novel ending with the prose metamorphosing into the final paragraphs of *The History of Sexuality*. That would have been a much more experimental novel than anything I'll ever write. But that's the extent to which I was under the ideological sway of Foucault when writing that novel.

RC   On this point, your characters generally don't seem to engage with questions of identity until these are suggested to them.

PR   With Tony in particular I was very interested in investigating somebody who was innocent of a stable identity, and who is taught in various implicit and explicit ways the rules of sexual identity, but never quite learns them, because, in fact, he's too liquid. I guess I admired that about him—despite everything, he retains a kind of integrity in his incoherence. He refuses finally to tame his unruly self into the fixed identity that some readers would have been more comfortable with. It really bothers them that he goes off to get married.

RC   The most compelling aspect for me lies in your repeated, Foucauldian insistence on desire and pleasure as taught phenomena. This premise—that desire is very malleable—appears rarely in fiction.

PR   I'm glad you say that. *The Coming Storm*'s about this too. Aristotle said the purpose of education was to educate us to think and feel the appropriate things in a given situation. Once you think of education that way, it becomes 100 percent ideological. No act of education's innocent.

Each is necessarily coercive. That's a deeply disturbing but also fascinating possibility. As a teacher, I always ask myself: "What is it I'm actually teaching my students?" There are disturbing moments when I think I'm basically a propagandist for the state. I'm preparing them to move as smoothly as possible into the larger structures of society. The state has a lot of vested interests in my doing that, and all too often I seem happily complicit in the state's agenda. I often wonder whether even my riskiest subversions may not in fact serve a larger purpose which isn't subversive at all.

RC   To return to the idea of desire as footloose—I'd suspect many fiction readers today would rather not think of it in that way.

PR   My experience has been that many don't. There's the interesting question of reader expectation. Obviously, if there's this thing called the "gay novel," it must produce certain formal expectations. We all know that audiences—ourselves included—often demand a kind of conformity. We've all had that moment of dissatisfaction when a book we thought we were reading because it was this kind of book betrays us. It turns out a different kind of book. We throw it against the wall. On the other hand, I hope we feel guilty once it's broken the lamp, so we pick it up again. If it's an important book, it has to challenge those expectations.

In a sense, only mediocre gay novels can be gay novels. Truly great gay novels cease to be gay at the point where they become great. It's only by thwarting expectations that they do unconventional work.

RC   The ideal of expansiveness seems one unconventional element in your work. *Sea of Tranquillity* crazily stretched the conventions of the realist literary novel by shifting between America, Turkey, and the moon.

PR   In some ways I find myself in Allen Cloud's position. Where do you go after you've been to the moon? Chris Bram and I have talked about this. His *Sea of Tranquillity*-type book was *Almost History*. *Father of Frankenstein* was a graceful way of showing how you can pull back. I was thinking about that transition when I was trying to move on to *The Coming Storm*.

RC   What gay literature have you found rewarding of late?

PR   I read a very good first novel recently—Gary Reed's *Pryor Rendering*. It's a beautifully written coming-of-age story set in Oklahoma. I also read Mark Doty's *Heaven's Coast*—actually with some reluctance. I've a very low threshold for contemplative books that find consolation in nature or literature. By the end of the first chapter, I had tears in my eyes. I thought: "I can't believe he's pulling this off." And he kept on pulling it off.

Consolation's the most difficult thing to believe. Often it's talking bravely in the face of the abyss. By the end, I believed in the consolations Doty had found. They seemed hard won; I'd witnessed the battle, and could attest in some way to his winning it.

I really liked Mark Merlis's *American Studies*. I like Chris Bram's work a lot. *Gossip*'s very tight. Murder mystery as a genre doesn't interest me. But he did a great job of making the solution to the murder become a startling political statement. As I got close to the end, I'd no idea who the murderer was. I'd gone through all the possibilities. None worked. When it turned out to be the father, I thought: "Of course; he was sitting there in full view!" But I'm culturally trained not to suspect him. I examined everybody and skipped over him. I thought: "I've been caught in my own cultural presumptions." It's precisely those presumptions that let this sort of thing happen. That was dazzlingly pulled off.

One novel that's really driven is Carole Maso's *The Art Lover*. She went to Vassar. All its formal experimentation seems deeply rooted in what the book's about. It doesn't feel forced or frivolous. It's one of the great AIDS novels.

I have fairly catholic tastes. I could never be part of a school because I don't think there's ever one way of doing things. I hope each of my books confounds the people who'd like to attach me to a school.

★   ★   ★

RC   I noticed that your third and fourth novels both had different working titles. *The Coming Storm* you'd been referring to as "The Pederast"; *Sea of Tranquillity* as "Shehzade." Could you comment?

PR   That's what you get for talking about works in progress. They change. *Sea of Tranquillity* went through a number of lame titles before returning to its original. "The Pederast," however, will always be the real title of my fourth novel—it captures the book far better than *The Coming Storm*, but was nixed for depressingly obvious reasons by my agent and editor alike. What I liked about "The Pederast," besides its starkness, was the way the term hovered over the book as it unfolded, leading one to ask, along the way, who exactly is the pederast in all this? Because it's not clear to whom that term should refer. There are various overlapping pederasties at work in the novel.

RC   In *The Coming Storm* you described a teacher-student relationship in a very nonstereotypical way. It's a rather brave thing for someone working in education to write about. How concerned or cautious were you with this material? Have there been any difficult consequences?

PR   I didn't give it a second thought. If I worried about giving offense, or being inappropriate, I'd never write a word. I think it's essential to shut yourself off from all those censoring voices in your head. Anyway, Vassar has always been splendidly supportive of me. The book did stir up a certain amount of controversy in the larger world, stemming mostly from a very favorable review the book received in the *Washington Post*. The outrage seemed to come not so much from the book itself, but from the fact that a newspaper like the *Washington Post* would praise such a book. The conservative *Weekly Standard* picked up on the controversy and ran with it, featuring me in an article called "Pedophile Chic Revisited." It was clear that the article's author, a columnist for the *Wall Street Journal*, hadn't bothered to read the novel, only the review of it in the *Washington Post*. Very disheartening, really, but typical.

RC   What are you working on now?

PR   My latest novel, "War Against the Animals," takes place in a little town in upstate New York, where tensions are rife between the locals, who've been there for six generations, and the newcomers—often gay—who have been moving in. It involves the points of view of two characters.

One's a middle-aged gay man, a landscape architect who's recently been brought back from death's door by the miracle drugs, only to find that his boyfriend takes his return to some degree of health as a chance to bolt from the beleaguered relationship. The other's a nineteen-year-old local boy who, under the somewhat sinister influence of his adored older brother, gets involved in a scheme to take advantage, emotionally and financially, of the gay man's vulnerabilities. The challenge of the project was to get inside the head of this straight—or perhaps not so straight—"redneck," and render him as convincingly and sympathetically as I do the gay man, his not unwilling "victim."

Astute readers will detect in all this the wingbeat of a certain gentle Jamesian bird.

RC   Indeed. Thanks very much for your time.

NINE

PETER CAMERON

PETER CAMERON is the author of a number of short-story collections and four novels: *Leap Year, The Weekend, Andorra,* and *The City of Your Final Destination.*

Born in 1959 in Pompton Plains, New Jersey, Cameron grew up there and—for two years—in London, where he attended the progressive American School. He graduated from Hamilton College, in Clinton, New York, in 1982 with a B.A. in English Literature, and moved to New York. He worked for a year in the subsidiary rights department of St. Martin's Press before starting administrative work for nonprofit organizations. From 1983 to 1988 he worked for the Trust for Public Land, and from 1990 to 1998 for the Lambda Legal Defense and Education Fund. In 1987, Cameron first taught Creative Writing at Oberlin College in Ohio. From 1990 to 1996 he taught in the M.F.A. program at Columbia University. Since 1988 he has taught in Sarah Lawrence College's M.F.A. program.

Cameron sold his first short story to the *New Yorker* in 1983 and published ten further stories there over the next few years. This led to the publication of his first volume of stories, *One Way or Another* (New York: Harper and Row, 1986), which was awarded a special citation by the PEN/Hemingway Award for First Book of Fiction. A second collection, *Far-Flung* (New York: Harper and Row, 1991), appeared five years later. Cameron's short stories have also been published in *Grand Street,* the *Kenyon Review,* the *Paris Review, Rolling Stone* magazine, and the *Yale Review.*

In 1988, Cameron was asked to write a serial novel for the just-launched magazine *7 Days.* This serial, which was written and published a chapter a week, became *Leap Year* (New York: Harper and Row, 1990). From then, Cameron effectively stopped writing shorter fiction. *The Weekend* (New York: Farrar Straus and Giroux, 1994), his second novel, was subsequently made into a film (directed by Brian Skeet, 2000).

The Half You Don't Know: Selected Stories (New York: Plume, 1997) contained material from Cameron's first two shorter fiction collections alongside two new stories. *Andorra* (New York: Farrar, Straus, and Giroux, 1997) was Cameron's third novel, and the most recent is *The City of Your Final Destination* (New York: Farrar, Straus, Giroux, 2002). He wrote the "Afterword" to Jocelyn Brooke's novel *The Scapegoat* (1948; rpt., New York: Turtle Point Press, 1998).

Peter Cameron's work has been translated into a dozen languages. This interview took place at his home in New York City's Greenwich Village on Wednesday, October 29, 1997. It was revised in July 2002, at which point the material following the asterisks was added.

RC   I want to start by asking about something that may seem very specific, but actually leads to a general question. There's a comical exchange between Marianne, Lyle, and others about the state of the novel in *The Weekend*. Marianne reads novels in secret and with some embarrassment, saying that the problems novels can solve have gone. Presumably as a novelist you have a different view.

PC   I knew that dialogue was risky. Some people told me it shouldn't be there. But I liked the idea that within a novel there's discussion of the state of the novel. I also liked it because some reviewers picked up on it and asked what right I had to write this novel if that's the way I felt about it. That irritated me—the idea that I couldn't have ideas separate from my characters; the notion that I approved of any ideas my characters have. I can have them say whatever I want. It doesn't mean I agree with them. I don't necessarily agree with Marianne, but what she's talking about is something I'm interested in.

This is also about the kinds of novels I have found interesting myself—novels that come from a time when there was more personal repression. I've concluded that repression is good for fiction and bad for people. Now, however, people are living their lives in a number of ways much more freely and openly. That poses the question of what gets written about, and how it gets written about.

RC The inference that the author is behind every idea in a book seems common in communications from readers to writers. Maybe you wouldn't expect it from reviewers or critics, however.

PC I don't know if it's natural, but people seem to read fiction and assume certain things about you based on what they've read. I've always written fiction that is not about myself in an autobiographical way. It gives me great freedom because I don't feel I'm revealing myself at all in my fiction. To a certain extent I am, of course, but it's an extent nobody can be sure of.

RC Novels are increasingly bracketed according to social types and groups, I'd say. The idea of "gay fiction" is something every writer is likely to have problems with. In your case, though, the diversity of characters and experiences in your works especially thwarts the kind of reading some will want to bring—not identifying you with specific positions or experiences so much as thinking of the book in terms of a particular social identity. one that characterizes its author. Do you resist this?

PC To say I'm strongly resisting it would say that I'm doing something deliberately, and I'm not. However, I feel like I have very little control over what I write. My books are all things that have come to me more than I've come to them. In none do I consciously set out to do anything, or to write about any sort of person. In that way, I have no agenda at all. I'm simply writing the books that have come to me, that intrigued me on some level.

But then again I realize that those books go out in the world and are perceived in any number of ways. It's perfectly fine with me for people to perceive the books in certain ways, or to see whatever they want in a work once I let it go. I can disagree, but it's certainly their right to draw whatever concerns from it they want as readers or critics.

RC   When you write, does this feeling that the books determine themselves give you some necessary sense of release?

PC   Sometimes I've tried to interfere with the world of the book in a deliberate way. For instance with *Andorra*, I started thinking: "Maybe he should be gay, the main character." I kept thinking: "I'm a gay man." I kept going back and thinking about it: "Maybe he is gay, or should be gay. Or there should be more homosexuals in the book." Then I just thought: "No. It's like having children. I don't think you should try to dictate the sexuality of your children, and I don't think you should try and dictate the sexuality of your characters." He wasn't gay. There was nothing I could do about it.

RC   There's a literal analogy to that in *The Weekend*: the exchange between Tony and Marianne about the sexuality of her child.

PC   Right.

RC   I wondered about the relationship between *The Weekend* and *Leap Year* and the short stories that seem to be excerpted from them. With *Leap Year*, there's the story "Departing." In the case of *The Weekend*, there's a key difference from the story. Robert and Lyle meet at [the AIDS activist group] ACT UP in the latter; in *The Weekend* it's at an artist's colony.

PC   Yes. I've had what seems an odd career as a writer. When I started out, I wrote a lot of short stories and first became known as a story writer. For a long time I despaired of ever becoming a novelist. I don't understand why, but all the ideas I got early on seemed to be ideas for short stories. Or every idea I got I was able to reduce in some way to a story. Once I was able to do that, I thought: "If you can tell this as a short story, there's no point in telling it as a novel. You're just telling something long that should be short." I kept thinking that if you're going to write a novel, you have to wait for an idea that's inherently complicated enough to be a novel. At the same time, I got a lot of ideas for writing stories, so I wrote a lot of stories.

In the last five years, it's been just the opposite. I've gotten fewer and fewer ideas, and they're harder to come by. I never get ideas for stories anymore, and I've kind of stopped writing them. I really regret that because I admire writers that do both simultaneously. That seems to be something I can't do. Around writing *The Weekend*, this change happened. I got the idea, and wrote it first as a story. It wasn't that I wasn't happy with it. I liked it. But it was the first time I'd written a story, finished it, and still felt there was a lot there that intrigued me. That's when I decided to go back and tell the same story again, but fill in all the ellipses, or the ones that seemed compelling. That was an interesting process—to go back and tell the same story, then have it change as I was telling it, and have things like the circumstances of how the two men met change.

RC   Did that change dictate itself to you when you returned to it?

PC   That could have been about how, when I was writing the story— probably a year or two before I started developing it as a novel—ACT UP was something very much in the forefront of people's consciousness here in New York. It was very vibrant. Two years later it wasn't. It didn't feel dated in any way, but I was less wedded to it. I felt like I'd forced that on the characters. As I got to know them better, I couldn't believe that's how they'd met. I couldn't picture either of them there.

From time to time I have felt that my work should be more political. But whenever I've tried to accommodate that, it hasn't been a good idea.

RC   Does your work with the Lambda Legal Defense and Education Fund reassure you, then, by making it possible for you to be engaged politically outside of writing?

PC   I wrote *The Weekend* when I was wrestling with that whole question. Early in the nineties, there were a lot of important books—novels and nonfiction—coming out about AIDS. I felt, directly from some people and obliquely from others, some pressure to be writing more politically, and to include AIDS more in my fiction.

I realized at some point that I wanted to write the kinds of books that I've liked most and felt like I've learned the most from and been most moved by: very personal works. Their being personal works doesn't necessarily equal being decadent. The more personal the novel, the more effective I think it is in the long run. That freed me to go back and write *The Weekend* the way I wanted it to be, which is as a very personal book. It's about the really trivial aspects of people's lives in certain ways, which I find very important and compelling. To me that's the very interesting stuff of fiction.

RC   Does the suggestion that you should be writing "more" about gay sexuality and/or about AIDS remain annoying? Do you hear that often?

PC   No. I don't have a very public discourse about my writing. It's not like I have some dialogue where I get feedback on what I should or shouldn't be doing. I guess it's me listening to public discourse, and then imposing those sorts of ideals on myself. It's not as if people have come up directly and told me certain things. But as I write more, I realize that the more personal my work is, the better it is for me—and for the reader. I think the wonderful thing about any art is people expressing their own individuality. The idea that there should be these things that people are doing uniformly at certain points in time: I don't understand that. Why shouldn't we all be, to the best of our ability, expressing our own experience?

RC   One parallel debate to this is the question of sexual representation in fiction—sexual explicitness.

PC   Yes. It's not that I don't respect or value that in other people's works. I think there are a lot of ways to reveal character. Writing frankly about sex is certainly one way. But there are other ways I'm better at, that I'm more interested in and skilled at. If my characters felt to me like they weren't alive on the page to the extent that I want them to be, I'd feel maybe I owe them a fuller sexual life. But I feel it shouldn't be there unless I feel the need for it to be, and I don't. There are certain things about a character's life you assume readers can figure out for themselves.

RC   You spoke of the complexity of an idea dictating the form of the novel, as opposed to the kind of ideas that went into short stories. Now that you've experienced that transition, do you still hold to that idea? Do you think it is a question of complexity versus simplicity?

PC   No, I don't now. In the 1980s, when I got an idea, I'd try to reduce it to some very small sort of thing. Now I do just the opposite. I start looking right away for the ways in which this idea is complicated, or the ways in which it unfolds, rather than folds in on itself. So now I don't really believe that ideas are inherently for stories or novels. I think it's really what you're interested in writing. Now I'm more interested in writing novels.

It could also be a very self-protective thing. The fact is I get fewer and fewer ideas, so it's in my best interest when I get an idea to turn it into a novel. At least then I have something to write about for three years. If I decided to make it a story, I'd be spending a lot of time not writing—which I already do, and it's frustrating. Then you look at someone like William Trevor. That just amazes me—that there are all these ideas for story after story.

RC   Part of the craft involved, presumably, is that the reader can't sense the kinds of turns and resolves in the work, which might have led it to go another way.

PC   Right. I think ideally when you read things you should feel: "Of course this is a novel; of course this is a story." That shouldn't be a question in the mind of the reader.

RC   With *The Weekend*, there's the question of how the subject matter of AIDS might affect its structure.

PC   Well, when I was writing it, I didn't consciously think of *The Weekend* as a book about AIDS. It was a narrative element, the fact that one character dies of complications of AIDS. But the book was about so many other things simultaneously that I think I'd have frightened myself if it had occurred to me I was writing a book that turned out to be "about AIDS." It's like saying: "*Anna Karenina* is a book about suicide." Books are about a lot of different things. They can be about different things to different people. Some people can read *The Weekend* and not be very cognizant of the fact that Tony has AIDS.

RC   I wasn't suggesting that this particular subject matter, unlike anything else, proves hard to handle, though some writers have felt that. It was more that within a text, for some writers, AIDS has introduced a sort of emotional imbalance. But you move easily between the various elements of the story in *The Weekend*. Comic social exchanges survive, perhaps because the figure of Tony is both there and not there. That's due to this very liberating narrative structure. Did that come easily?

PC   Structurally, *The Weekend* was interesting because when I'd written the story and felt interested in rewriting it as a novel, there was all the stuff in the present that I wanted to go back and fill in. But I became aware that there was all this stuff from the past too; that that weekend was also its present in some way, as well as what happened in the present, because the book was all about remembering somebody who isn't there, and about how viscerally present people's memories are.

Again, it's not something I deliberately wrestled with or had a hard time with. I just wanted those flashbacks to be as present as any other scene. I was moving from the past into the present seamlessly. I wanted it not to be jarring to the reader. I wanted readers to be in the past before they realized they were—to be able to move back and forth between those two places as easily as the characters did.

RC   So it's by instinct that you find your structures?

PC   Yes. I think my instinct as a writer is better than anything I try to do deliberately. A lot of fumbling is involved, and a lot of writing stuff that doesn't end up in the book. But that needs to get written. In some ways I'm a very cerebral writer, in that a lot of my process of writing happens in my head before I start to write. I'm not somebody who can sit down without having a lot in my head. I can't start writing until I'm sure of quite a lot, even to the extent of a certain language that gets formulated. Then I start. Of course, a lot happens when I'm writing too.

RC   Do you rework plot in your head at that stage?

PC   Yes, though I feel determined to be a certain extent ahead of where I'm writing. It's like shining a flashlight in the dark; you see a little bit further and a little further. Hopefully at some point you see to the end.

RC   By contrast with *The Weekend*, *Andorra* has a relatively straightforward structure chronologically. There's a withheld secret, and various incidents lead to its revelation. Was there the same need for revisions and the writing of surplus material in this case?

PC   For *The Weekend*, in the original version of the novel, there was a lot that preceded *The Weekend* itself: Robert and Lyle back in New York, getting to know each other, for example. It was stuff I had to fumble through. Then I realized the reader didn't necessarily have to fumble through it too. Then I realized the book was really just about "the weekend."
   Basically the form was there. It was about shifting the focus from one part of the book to another. With *Andorra* it was very different. I started out wanting to write a more complicated book—a novel within a novel. It was going to be about a prisoner in a writing program who was corresponding with a writer. It was chapters of this novel he was writing that were being sent back and forth between him and the writer, along with letters from the prisoner to the writer and from the writer back to the prisoner. Then there were scenes from the prisoner's life and from the writer's life.
   I went a long way with that idea; I was really wedded to it. Then I realized, the further I went, that as a writer I was more and more interested in the novel the prisoner was writing, less and less interested in the frame around it.

RC   So you took all that scaffolding away at a late stage, having written a lot of it?

PC   Yes.

RC   There's a small residue—the circularity of the book's story.

PC   Yes. That was hard to get right, because I knew even after I took them away what the circumstances were of the story being written. The problem was how to reveal that to the reader, once you've taken away the apparatus that does that. Again it was just about being selfish, finally; about trusting that what interested me as a writer would eventually interest the reader.

RC   How do these various drafts exist? In longhand?

PC   No. I work on a computer. *Andorra* was the first book where I kept a notebook and wrote things down in longhand, because I've come to the point where I realize that I forget a lot of what seem to be good ideas at midnight when I'm drifting off to sleep. In the past I was so sure I'd remember them in the morning. Often I didn't. So I started keeping notes.
  Basically, though, I work very well on a computer, writing and rewriting. When I was writing stories, there was a very different procedure. I was using a typewriter and was very lazy. That's why I got into a habit of writing a lot in my head. It was much easier to revise there than it was to retype something fifteen times. I'd actually not type the story until it was pretty much all in my head. Now I feel much freer to get it on the page, and then fix it.

RC   You're not superstitious about the process of writing longhand, then?

PC   No. I started out with notebooks for all my stories. Sentimentally I like the idea very much. I like seeing the work there. But, practically, it works for me to depend on electronics.

RC   Critics have commended the precision of both the stories and novels. Thinking of what you were saying about taking so much out, have you ever doubted yourself and thought you'd taken out too much or too little?

PC   That's something I don't think too much about. Happily for me at least, when I'm finished with something, it feels finished in a way that doesn't beg me to reconsider it. Abstractly I think it's interesting though. I could go back to my work and there could be all these things that bug me about it. But practically I'm not interested.

There are some books I know of where somebody has gone back after fifteen years and revised them so that there are two versions. There's something creepy about that to me. If it makes the writer happy, that's fine. But I think you have to trust your initial impulse.

RC   I am interested in whom you feel may have been a literary influence on you. I know the name of Barbara Pym has come up in the past.

PC   The writing I most admire and am most interested in emulating is done by British women in the middle part of the century: Rose Mac-Caulay; Rosamond Lehmann; Elizabeth Taylor; Barbara Pym; Elisabeth Bowen. Penelope Mortimer's wonderful too. For me, the domestic novel—this form I'm very interested in—reached a peak then. These women had a wonderful command of language; they were able to use it incredibly elegantly and eloquently. They also had this very wise understanding of human nature and a very perceptive view of the world. All these things come together in their novels, which I think are wonderful examples of what the novel can be.

Reading and writing are really intertwined for me. I think what I'm reading and enjoying as a reader definitely affects what I'm doing as a writer. Starting out, the person who had the most influence on me was Ann Beattie. Her short stories for the *New Yorker* seemed so beautiful and contemporary. She seemed to be writing about a world that was familiar to me in a way that the world of literature seemed removed from. She got me very excited about what you could do in a short story. Margaret Drabble's another person whose earlier novels were influential to me.

RC   The type of fiction written by those interwar British women novelists has a curious reputation, currently. I wonder whether that's to do with their lack of interest in the formal rule-breaking aspect of modernism. There's a certain romantic idea of writers as revolutionaries that may have nixed their reputations, rather.

PC I'd hope their reputations haven't been nixed, but rather subdued. It's not to say all those writers are great. But they certainly succeeded in doing what they set out to do. Their books have in that sense a sort of perfection that's quite an accomplishment. After a while, I think technical bravura gets tiresome. I'd much rather read something that moves me on a personal, human level than something that excites me on a linguistic, technical level. I feel in their work there's a lot of compassion for the small moments in people's lives.

RC The compassion in your own works is notable. I have to throw a spanner in here, though—the early stories in particular strike me as quite cruel. There's something waspish and unsentimental about them.

PC That might be because I think humor is really important. If you want a reader to come on this journey with you, I think you're obliged to a certain extent to keep them entertained. Humor is one way. Also, I'm very interested in people who are miserable and unhappy. Happy people aren't very interesting in a novelistic way. So I've tended to write about people who are depressed or having problems. That's not to say there's not something humorous about their lives.

RC But they might not be privy to that.

PC Right. But you, as a reader, can find them amusing without feeling guilty.

RC Would you mind if somebody thought your world view, as expressed through your fiction, suggested that people were predominantly unhappy, insecure, or dissatisfied? Notions of attainment, success, or achievement seem jeopardized. Romantic ideas in particular are jeopardized or undone.

PC No, as long as they don't then try to understand my life based on that. It's fair game. What you put out there, you cannot then interfere with, or with how people perceive it.

RC   On the one hand you say that happy people are not narratively interesting, which I understand; on the other, ultimately, given the fact that other books do achieve optimistic endings and closures, a reader might want to say: "This person is happiest analyzing dysfunctionalism of various kinds." Would you be comfortable with that analysis—that you were happiest constructing a world in which things tended to go wrong, to prove dysfunctional; in which relationships atrophied, or were founded on lies?

PC   I'd argue that although there might not be happy endings in my books, I think my characters haven't wasted their time. They learnt something about themselves that brings them closer to being happier people. Those are small steps on the road to happiness, but . . .

RC   I'm not bringing charges of neglect or cruelty concerning your fictional "children"! It was more a question of what strikes a reader over the range of material. Casual lying is certainly common in the stories, particularly as against the nineteenth-century books Marianne refers to in *The Weekend*, which have hypocrisy of certain endemic social kinds in them—the hypocrisy of adultery, of homosexuality. But you have just as much material which is acted out in similar circumstances: the easy lie, the "my wife is pregnant" lie, or the "I love you" lie. I'm trying to push you, I know, towards something you're entitled to resist: the idea that this element of social observation is something a reader might ascribe to you . . .

PC   I think this is just something very practical I've found out. If there's a relationship where people aren't lying to one another, where things are fine and happy, there's not narratively very much to be said. It's when people deceive one another that there's tension. That's why I think Marianne's totally wrong to say that because people can get divorced and so on, there's no tension anymore. I think she's running around creating a lot of tension in her own household, for instance.

It's an interesting thought, though. If you write about people this way, are you giving a lopsided view of the world? It's not like I feel people are duplicitous at heart, or that the world is full of evil, lying people.

RC   But there are worthy lies too. In "Fast Forward," Alison lies to her dying mother.

PC   I think most people lie with good intentions, or out of laziness. But as a writer I'm interested in what happens after people start lying to one another.

RC   Now, a leap. Are there writers from within the "gay canon"—however fabricated the idea—that appeal to you, even if they're not literary models?

PC   The work of Tennessee Williams affected me over a long period of my life. It continues to affect me and resonate with me. It has a roundness and an intrigue that seem inherent. At some level it does have to do with homosexuality, in very tangential or veiled ways.

That's why that discussion comes up in *The Weekend* about homosexuality. I'm interested a lot in the fact that gay men have been writing novels for a long time, and for a long time it wasn't explicitly about gay themes. There's something really interesting happening when people can't write about their lives explicitly. With a lot of the writing I find interesting, you do feel the repression. This summer I wrote an "Afterword" to a novel by Jocelyn Brooke called *The Scapegoat*. It's a fascinating, really creepy, homoerotic book about an uncle and his nephew. It could only have been written at that certain place in time. A lot of work like that is more intriguing to me than gay stuff that was written in the seventies or eighties.

RC   Is it the prose of Williams that engaged you or the drama?

PC   I think it's the poetry of his prose, his rendering of the human condition, and the characters he invents that I find so heartbreakingly moving. The other writers I'm really excited about happen not to be gay.

I don't know what a gay aesthetic is. To me the distinction is more to do with masculine and feminine. There are writers who seem more interested in the external or physical world, and writers who are more interested in the interior or domestic world. A writer like James Salter, for instance—I think his prose is so beautiful. I love the way he writes about a sensual appreciation of life. William Maxwell is another writer whose work I love. His novel *The Folded Leaf* is very homoerotic. It's about growing up and friendship. It's such a beautiful book. There's something about it that really moved me in some way, as a gay man. It's weird and spooky. That's something I think is neat about literature—you don't have to be a thing to write about it. Your influences can come from all different directions.

RC   Speaking of repression, nineteenth-century names spring to mind, like James or Melville, for instance. There are homoerotic elements in the works of both. You could say, though, that each is interested in the social or external world, according to your distinction.

PC   There's a whole question when you're writing a novel about action and whether things have to happen. There's a very Woolf-like debate about what constitutes an action. I'm working on a book now, for example, in which it seems like, on some level, nothing's happening. I'm conscious that I'd better make something happen. But for me, in a lot of people's lives nothing does happen. That doesn't preclude them from being interesting.

Some writers are very good at making things happen. A lot of readers appreciate that and are drawn to it. I'm not as interested in that as I am in the reasons why they're not happening.

Regarding James and Wharton and so on, there used to be this kind of book, which was about the individual versus society. That made for great novels. Then, all of a sudden, society wasn't as rigid as it used to be. It's not that I wish society were more rigid. But it does preclude a certain sort of narrative that I think was very satisfying.

RC   There's a preoccupation with appearance on the part of many of your characters. It's played out finally with rather oppressive or despairing consequences. The idea that a guy should have to shave off his beard to get a job is one; your character Freddy toys with having one earring or two, then worries about which ear it is in. He feels confident he's got the right ear. The problem is the wider social world, in which the code is confused. Some people don't get it right; they "read" it wrongly. On one level this is meaty social satire; on another, one could read a slight horror at the pre-occupation with the external and the physical in light of what you were saying about literary distinctions between internality and externality.

PC   Well, to a certain extent how you appear physically impacts your existence and your circumstances in a way that narratively can be interesting. I do take advantage of that in my stories. But I think it's actually the tension between who you are internally and how you present yourself externally that's interesting too.

RC   For me there was a kind of horror that the same weight was given to apparently trivial or inconsequential aspects of appearance as to matters of deep feeling; or, rather, a horror that characters themselves didn't distinguish between one and the other.

PC   Of the examples you gave—the guy shaving off his beard to get a job—that's just that he's moving between one job and the next. He was an academic trying to get a job in corporate life. The facts of life are such that he's not getting far with a beard, so decides to shave it off. When you're working on the small canvas of the short story, it also becomes very symbolic. During that story he's changing himself, so altering his physical appearance like that is just a correlative of what's going on internally. It's the kind of thing where, when I was writing that story, I wasn't aware of that. It's just narratively what I saw him doing. I thought it would make a good scene. I like the idea too—that by changing your appearance, you think you're changing who you are in some substantial way. Yet of course you're not.

RC   In *Leap Year*, you make a good comic case for the way the smallest of materials can bring a tremendous emotional inference. Take the great coincidence of the sperm donation. There's a playfulness about the idea that what the sperm bank insists is the issuing of incidental material collides with the tremendous emotional baggage of the subsequent pregnancy—and doubly collides, because of the coincidence you introduce. Then there's fission! That's very dramatic, and contrasts with this idea of little happening in your work.

PC   *Leap Year* got written the way it did because some years before it, I'd written a very "quiet," literary novel, which never got published, where absolutely nothing happened. It didn't get sold. People liked the writing and characters, but there wasn't enough going on to sustain the narrative. That's when I really panicked. I thought I'd never be able to write a novel because I couldn't make things happen. Then I got this opportunity to write a serial novel for a magazine, *7 Days*. I wrote a chapter a week. The whole assignment was predicated on the fact that every week something had to happen. I thought it a great opportunity to challenge myself to do something that I didn't feel able to do until that point.

RC   Did you find serial publication forced you into ways of writing you hadn't considered?

PC   Yes. It freed me to let stupid coincidental things happen, and to push the narrative more towards events and away from introspection. At the same time, I very consciously wanted to have a book that was very comic in some respects, but where the characters also had an emotional life that seemed believable, so that at some moments they seemed like cartoons but at others like real characters, talking about things like love and loneliness in this comic context. It was helpful for me as a writer to experiment with imposing an event on the narrative, then seeing how you can use it down the road.

RC   Were there aspects to the experience that didn't appeal? The serial's demand for closure, for example?

PC   I think what was not interesting was that every chapter had to be a certain length. Now I like writing one scene and letting it dictate its length; respecting that; moving at a less regulated pace.

RC   Did you strike up a relationship with your readership that felt significant as you still wrote the serial?

PC   The only times people responded by letter to the editor were when something really bugged them in terms of probability. I was interested what got people fired up enough to write. It was the kind of stuff that wasn't very interesting to me as a writer though.

RC   Did you know where you were going with that book?

PC   That was the wonderful thing. I never knew where I was going beyond the next week. Basically I knew how long the book was going to be. You realized, though, that if you made things happen without knowing why, you had to trust yourself. It was an amazing experience. I had the chance to revise *Leap Year* before its publication as a book. At first I thought: "Good, I can take out all this stuff." But it was amazing how little there was to do, how much it fell into place. That felt like it wasn't about me at all, but about the narrative taking care of itself. It was a big relief because it could have turned into a big mess.

RC   I was thinking of Solange after her "death." It turned out not to be a trick at all. Was that something only serialization allowed?

PC   Yes. There were things in that book I'd never try in another. This tone got established that I don't think I could do somewhere else. I don't think I'd do another book like it in fact. But it was fun to do a book where I could indulge sillier aspects of narrative.

RC   You spoke of the time spent not writing fiction. Did the process of writing for serial publication encourage a routine to your writing which has stayed with you? Does writing come easily anyway?

PC   No. And that was interesting. Being forced to write each and every week was in some ways good. It certainly wasn't my natural process, but the narrative had a certain momentum, which allowed itself to be written in that way, however.

RC   The three novels seem so different to one another.

PC   That's part of the process I have no control over, and feel very much at the mercy of. When I finished *Andorra*, it was over a year before I started writing another book. During that year, I felt I'd never write again. That part of my brain just goes dead. It's frustrating because I like writing a lot. It's not painful to me. I don't understand writers who say they hate writing, that it's all torture. I'm always depressed when I'm not writing. It's a part of my life I value.

At the same time, I can't force it. I have to be very patient. Looking back, I feel I've published consistently. It seems that ideas do come. But it's not something I can convince myself of when I'm not writing. Incidentally, the year I was writing *Leap Year*, at a chapter a week, was wonderful financially. It was really nice to get paid for the book as you were writing it, then get paid again when it was published. That was the one year of my adult life where I didn't work at another job. But I realized that was a big mistake. I got very depressed and lonely. I realized I'm not a full-time writer. I couldn't occupy myself in a productive way as a writer full-time. I need to have something else going on in my life. I was very happy at the end of the year to go back to working.

RC   There is a tradition of writers who feel that—but it's probably outweighed by those who beg to be released from other commitments. But you find the integrating of writing in a life with other work beneficial?

PC   For me it's a comfortable balance of things. This all turns on who you are and what you're able to do with your time. But the year of *Leap Year*, I was going to bed at eight o'clock because I'd been alone all day. I write for a couple of hours only. That's a lot for me, and I can get a lot done. It's not something I can do all day. So there was a lot of time where I was forced to entertain myself, and I wasn't good at it. So I was just miserable. With my job now, I go to work at noon every day, so I have the mornings—for me, the most creatively productive time. I can work for a while writing new stuff in the morning, go to work, then come home in the evening, and, if I have the time, look at what I've written and revise it. That has worked out as a good pattern, though I don't have any strict schedule. There are times, even now, when I start something new and weeks go by where I don't write. I wait to feel ready. I'm very selfish as a writer. I write when I want to, when I feel there's something I should be writing. I don't try to force it when there isn't something there.

RC   Does nonfiction writing appeal at all?

PC   It doesn't. I wish it did, because I like people who have those two things going on in their life. Also, as a career move it's smart. It increases your chances of making money from your writing. That said, another thing I love about my job is that it frees me from having to depend on my writing to make money. It's not like I make a lot of money at my job, but I make a certain amount of very dependable income, so I don't have to write stuff I don't want to. I like writing too much to end up in the situation where I end up doing journalism. That's why I feel writing's a very selfish thing, because I do it to make myself happy.

RC   If writing other things doesn't interfere with fiction, does reading? Do you ever experience difficulty when you read something whose narrative voice overshadows your own writing style?

PC   No. If I did, I'd stop reading whatever that was. I know myself well as a reader, so I'm drawn to stuff I like. When I was writing *Andorra*, I can remember this period where I was rereading *Emma* and reading Proust. It was lovely. There was a flow between what I was reading and what I was writing. Things were getting channeled from one part of my mind to the other.

RC   Is fiction what you choose to read?

PC   Yes. I've read very little nonfiction. I wasn't a very good student, so the idea of reading nonfiction reminds me too much of being in school and doing research. I resist it. I'd much rather be very lazy and use my imagination to make the world up in my head than go out and research it and get it right. I'm very comfortable making mistakes.

In some ways, I wrote *Andorra* so I could indulge myself in making up a world. The whole premise of *Andorra* is about that. But I've always set stories in places I've never been. It's funny because the *New Yorker* is a big stickler for getting things right. They'd have these fact-checkers who would always be exasperated at me. I'd a story set in Arizona. I had palm trees, because I thought it must be warm enough in Arizona for that. But there are no palm trees in northern Arizona.

RC Did you insist on them?

PC No. When they told me there are no palm trees in Flagstaff, Arizona, I said: "Fine, change them to pine trees." As a detail it didn't bother me.

RC In *Andorra* the imaginativeness of the setting has been remarked on. Equally, critics have wondered why you chose to invent things—a coast-line, for instance.

PC Yes. I got a voice-mail message at work the other day. Some reader was giving me a really hard time because Andorra is land-locked. There was this indignity: "I read your stupid book, and you don't even know enough about the country to know that it is land-locked." [*Laughs*]

I feel if you get the emotional life of a book right, you can get away with getting the physical world of the book wrong. I know editors have a hard time with that, and find it distracting. That's why readers have responded to *Andorra* in a certain way. Some people who know Andorra buy the book because they think it's about the country. They get indignant when that's not the case.

RC Part of me still wants to ask: "Why Andorra?" Did it literally come out of the air?

PC When the readers I show stuff to started to realize what I was doing, some of them thought it was a mistake to use the name of a real country. They said I should make up a name, and then do what I wanted. I didn't want that. I think I picked Andorra because I wanted the reader to start out thinking they were reading about a real place, though a lot of people apparently had never heard of the real Andorra! But it does exist, as a name and a concept. But it's a tiny country. When you say "France," all these images come to mind. When you say "Andorra," a lot doesn't leap to mind for most people. So it's this theoretical country in a way, not an actual country. Then it became very funny, because when the book came out here, I got this call from the Andorran ambassador.

RC   Did he object to the fact that his brother was the policeman?

PC   Almost. He wanted to take me out to lunch because he'd heard I'd written this book called *Andorra*. I called him back and said I'd love to meet him. Then I thought: "God, this could get really ugly." I called back and said: "I just want to make sure that he knows this is a novel; that my Andorra is not necessarily his." His secretary said: "Yes, he knows it's a novel."

So I went to this lunch at the UN. I was a little anxious, because he'd promised to read the book. I was thinking he might say: "What the hell are you doing here? What did you do to my country?" But he was perfectly charming. He loved the book, and understood exactly what I was doing and why. He wasn't at all insulted by the liberties I'd taken. The one thing he did say was really funny. During lunch he pointed out that the police in Andorra are very civil, and that there is in fact a good judicial process.

RC   Are the readers you show work to writers themselves or friends?

PC   They include my brother, who's not a writer. He's just familiar enough with my work and a smart reader. He's comfortable enough with me to be critical. Then my editor at Farrar, Straus, and Giroux is wonderful. I feel really lucky about that. I know it's a very rare thing.

RC   Has anyone ever approached you about film possibilities?

PC   Actually, *The Weekend* has been optioned by these two guys from England. One is a producer called Ian Benson. The other is a writer and director called Brian Skeet. They've done some small films for the BBC. I was really pleased because, with *The Weekend*, I thought it would just take somebody who'd read it and fallen in love with it and could see it as a movie. That's exactly what happened. They read it when it first came out in the States, inquired about the film rights, and were misinformed. Then, when it came out in England, they read it again and called again, thinking the option maybe was over. When they were told it was available, we worked up a deal.

RC   But it's not something you would have anything to do with yourself?

PC   No, I'd rather spend my time doing something else. With *Andorra*, some people have been interested, but nobody has put their money where their mouth is, as my agent says.[1]

PC   Are films themselves important for you? Some writers have this insecure feeling about fiction in relation to visual culture.

PC   I'm really interested in that whole question. In some ways my work is so informed by literature. One thing that was fun about *Andorra* was writing a book about a world that was very much informed by other books, one that was imagined through other works of literature. I also wanted to write a book that was about the experience of reading and the world that gets evoked in books and nowhere else. At the same time, the whole time I'm writing a book, I think very cinematically. I'm writing in terms of scenes and so on.

I'd love to do a study about how novels have changed in response to films—how they're told differently and perceived in the writer's mind differently. I think it would be hard to write a book now and not imagine it going on at some cinematographic level. Maybe that's just something I do to help me see it in my mind so I can get it on paper. But it's definitely something I do, which I don't think you could have done before movies, or not in the same way.

---

1. "The same team that made *The Weekend* subsequently optioned *Andorra*. Their three-year option expires in March 2003" (Peter Cameron, July 2002).

RC The conception of a scene must have been different for Austen, say: it must have been influenced by drama but equally by life. Do you go to the cinema?

PC I actually go to the theater a lot more than I see movies. I rent a lot of movies to watch at home. I have a problem with other people in movie audiences. I get annoyed.

RC Does the audience "participate" in films in New York?

PC Yes. You have to go with that. I resist it, so end up getting very annoyed.

RC Do you travel much?

PC I wish I traveled more. The one thing I hate about my job is that you're stuck here in New York. I get four weeks' vacation a year, which for a job in the United States is pretty good.

I've had very good experiences going to artists' colonies when I'm working on a book. It makes traveling hard to do, because I have to use my vacation to do that. That's one thing I'm frustrated with in my life at this point. If I did make a change to my life, I'd like to take a year or two off from being committed to a job, to lead a life where I could travel and live somewhere.

RC In Britain half the country thinks travel broadens the mind; the other half, that it narrows you.

PC I lived in England for two years. It was a great experience that happened early on in my life. As a family we traveled a lot in Europe. I got this exposure to the world when I was very young, then that stopped. We moved back here and things became very insular. I think it's wonderful to have experiences of other places and cultures.

RC Where did you live in England?

PC   In London for a while, and then out in Walton-on-Thames in Surrey. I was reading all of Enid Blyton, who was a big influence on my work. [*Laughs*]

RC   What's her status in America?

PC   I don't know if she's even been published here. I don't think she is widely read. It's too strange a world. That's what made it so intriguing. There's another English children's book writer who I think really has been an influence on me: Ruby Ferguson. She wrote a whole series of books about Jill and her ponies. They were so well-written. It was the first time I'd read a book as a kid where there was an authorial voice that was witty and charming. It made me start thinking about who was writing the book. I got seduced by the voice, whereas with Enid Blyton, it was only by the story.

★   ★   ★

RC   Your most recent novel, *The City of Your Final Destination*, is once again set outside the States. Is your fictional Uruguay once again effectively unresearched?

PC   I did a little research. I looked at maps and encyclopedias. But again, I didn't want to be too influenced by reality. I see things more vividly through my imagination than through my intellect. And I thought that as the novel is set in the middle-of-nowhere, I could get away with it.

RC   It's very much concerned with the relationship between writers' works and their biographies, and seems to side with your character Arden's mistrust of artistic biography in it. She comments: "I think their work should speak for itself." Are you essentially sympathetic to this view?

PC   Yes, I suppose I am. Although if that's the case, I shouldn't be answering these questions . . . But because my work comes almost completely from my subconscious and my imagination, it's really only biographical in an emotional sense.

RC   Some readers might assume that Omar's somewhat naive, even farcical, approach to his proposed life of the writer Jules Gund reflects either circumspection or mistrust of the academy's treatment of literature on your part. Would that be a fair assumption, given that even Omar comes to realize his own folly and abandons his academic career aspirations?

PC   No. Again, I don't have an agenda when I write. The ideas I propose are not necessarily mine. Omar is ill-suited to academia; it's not what he should be doing, so of course that world seems absurd and tiresome to him. But that's not to say it is an absurd or tiresome world.

RC   I noticed that the novel closes with Deirdre and her date's conversation being interrupted by the resumption of music at an opera performance. Did you mean for classical music to stand for a form of art to which biographical concerns regarding the composer are most evidently irrelevant?

PC   The idea you propose about classical music is interesting, but not something I was thinking about. I don't think about ideas at all when I write. They're at the opera because I wanted a place where Deirdre could encounter Caroline. The opera seemed a logical place. I think like that—practically; narratively. Of course I hope the narrative then has ideas and associations lurking in it that I'm not aware of. But I don't feel I can take credit for them—at least not conscious credit.

RC   Thanks very much for your time.

TEN

MATTHEW STADLER

MATTHEW STADLER is the author of four novels: *Landscape: memory*, *The Dissolution of Nicholas Dee: His Researches*, *The Sex Offender*, and *Allan Stein*.

Stadler was born in 1959. He grew up in what he has called "a liberal academic family" in Seattle, though for a short while the family moved to England. Stadler describes his mind as "dormant" through high school. At seventeen he moved to Washington, D.C., to work for a Quaker lobbying group. He then decided to study for a B.A. in political theory at Oberlin College in Ohio. As part of this, in 1979 Stadler studied for a year at the London School of Economics, where he was able to pursue a developing enthusiasm for punk rock. He next moved impulsively to Cannes, France. Returning to Seattle, he took a job monitoring the volcano Mount Saint Helens for the University of Washington before reenrolling at Oberlin, where he learned to play guitar but failed to complete his degree.

Stadler next returned to Washington, D.C., to work for a Democratic congressman, but instead became a bicycle courier, playing in rock groups until he chose again to return to Seattle in 1981. He worked demolishing buildings and played in a band called Food. Moving to New York a year later, Stadler worked in a bookstore and later tended bar, while continuing to perform. He spent seven years in the city, during which time he was befriended by Patrick Merla, then editor of the *New York Native*. Merla encouraged Stadler to write, and his first fiction—"23 July 1981"—appeared in *Christopher Street* magazine in 1984.

Stadler was appointed National News Editor of the *Native*. He studied in the M.F.A. program at Columbia University while also teaching philosophy—and later also English and history—at a private high school. Stadler began writing for various magazines and worked at a number of publishers while still teaching full time. In 1988 he completed *Landscape: memory* (New York: Scribner's, 1990), then on an impulse moved to live in Groningen in the Netherlands, where he researched and wrote his second novel, *The Dissolution of Nicholas Dee: His Researches* (New York: Scribner's, 1993; reissued by Grove Press in 2000 with an introduction by Michael Cunningham). This novel later featured in Robert Drake, *The Gay Canon: Great Books Every Gay Man Should Read* (New York: Doubleday, 1998).

At the time, no publisher would buy *Landscape: memory*. Stadler left Groningen for Seattle, where he then settled for twelve years, becoming a senior writer for the Seattle paper *The Stranger*, and writing two further novels, *The Sex Offender* (New York: HarperCollins, 1994) and *Allan Stein* (New York: Grove, 1999), which won the 2000 Lambda Literary Award for Gay Men's Fiction. He was also on the board of directors of the Richard Hugo House Literary Arts Center and was part of the core Writing Faculty at Bard College.

Stadler has recently moved to Portland, Oregon, where he and a friend are raising their son. He is the literary editor of the design magazine *Nest*, and wrote the introduction to Joseph Holtzman, ed., *Every Room Tells a Story: Tales from the Pages of Nest Magazine* (New York: Distributed Art Publishers, 2001). Stadler was also guest editor of *Arcade—the Journal of Architecture and Design in the Northwest* 20.3 (Spring 2002), for which he wrote an introduction, "Hello My Delicate." His article on the Dutch architect Rem Koolhaas, "I Think I'm Dumb," appeared in *Wiederhall* (the Netherlands) in 1994 and was republished in *The Raven Chronicles* (United States) in April 1998.

Stadler is also the author of "The Power Lines," in *Grand Street* 40 (1990), "Homo Sex Story," in Patrick Merla, ed., *Boys Like Us: Gay Writers Tell Their Coming Out Stories* (New York: Avon, 1996), and "Love Problem," in Robert Drake and Terry Wolverton, eds., *His 3: Brilliant New Fiction by Gay Writers*

(Boston: Faber and Faber, 1999). His writing has also appeared in George Stambolian, ed., *Men on Men 4* (New York: Plume, 1992); Nayland Blake, Lawrence Rinder, and Amy Scholder, eds., *In a Different Light: Visual Culture, Sexual Identity, Queer Practice* (San Francisco: City Lights, 1995); Brian Bouldrey, ed., *The Best American Gay Fiction 1996* (New York: Little, Brown, 1996); and Robert Drake and Terry Wolverton, eds., *His: Brilliant New Fiction by Gay Writers* (Boston: Faber and Faber, 1996). Stadler has cowritten a number of stories with other authors, most of which remain unpublished.

He was awarded a Guggenheim Fellowship in 1992, an Ingram-Merrill Foundation Award for Fiction Writing in 1994, a Whiting Foundation Writers Award in 1995, and the Richard and Hinda Rosenthal Award for Fiction by the American Academy of Arts and Letters in 2000. Stadler has also written for *Spin* magazine, *Frieze*, *Artforum*, *New York Times Book Review*, and on design in particular for *Wiederhall*, *Guardian*, and the *Seattle Times*. He is the editor of Clear Cut Press, a publishing and distribution company based in Astoria, Oregon.

This interview took place on Friday, November 28, 1997, in a restaurant in Seattle. It was revised in July 2002, at which point the material following the asterisks was also added.

RC   In both "Homo Sex Story," the autobiographical essay you wrote for Patrick Merla's anthology *Boys Like Us*, and the story "Love Problem," you challenged many assumptions we make concerning gay identity, about coming out: the idea that gay identity is gradually revealed, that this leads to a sense of liberation when you tell others, and so on. In fact, none of your work seems to follow common tropes of gay literature, like the coming out narrative. Does that stem from a conscious refusal to tell expected stories?

MS   I've never experienced my work as a refusal. Its failure to participate in other patterns or conventions comes more out of my affinity for conventions that perhaps aren't widely shared. For example, I write out of doubt. I think declarations of knowing or belief are only possible in a constructed form. You need to create an artificial world, a construction within which you can experience belief or knowing. Maybe it's knowing you're gay, or who you are, or knowing you love someone. Those things happen within intellectual constructions, ones that often become evident only viscerally.

For me, writing is the material and the ground for these constructions. Pretty consistently, when I write my way into a fiction, primarily what I'm concerned with are the mechanics and structural dynamics of the act of writing, and the way those limitations define and make possible moments of knowing. Sexuality is so central and visceral an experience of knowing that it's been my subject a lot. But I think my subject is just as often other visceral states of knowing—whether memories that are fleeting enough only to be grasped at a visceral level, or feelings of fear about loss which are not technically sexual but feel sexual because they're hard to grasp except through the body.

RC One dominant theme in both *The Dissolution of Nicholas Dee* and *The Sex Offender* is the appropriation of knowledge on the part of institutions. In both, you cover a great range of social institutions. I was less sure this theme was present in *Landscape: memory*.

MS I think you're basically right. The impact of social institutions on the private experience of knowing interests me. In *Landscape: memory*, it's there in the family, in Max Kosegarten's mom and dad, but it becomes more broadly institutional in *Nicholas Dee* and *The Sex Offender*. One thing I circle back to in *Allan Stein* is the mother—I mean the institution of the mother. A lot of institutional relationships are sort of elaborations on the mom-and-child thing.

RC Do you mean that the mother-child relationship is replayed in institutional contexts?

MS Yes. It becomes a matrix on which other institutional relationships are patterned. This is total speculative bullshit on my part, but I want to connect mom and son to these other institutional relations. I didn't think about any of this when writing the first three novels, but part of why *Allan Stein* interested me was how obviously primary and formative this relationship was for him. In any case, this private and perverse experience of knowing happens inside a social context, and it's always impinged on and made possible by that social context. So for me, the move from Max Kosegarten's family in *Landscape: memory*, to *Nicholas Dee*'s university, or to the police or the doctor in *The Sex Offender*, simply involved shuttling between almost interchangeable discourses.

RC   I first noticed this preoccupation with the organization of institutions in the treatment of the police in *The Sex Offender*. Once it had occurred to me, though, it seemed everywhere in your work. You've reacted as if it were something you were aware of all along, or are you speaking with the benefit of hindsight?

MS   It's mostly hindsight. When I start work on something, I have a sense of the question I'd like to ask. The pursuit of that question dictates the book and the direction in which the fiction develops. It's rarely a question that's sociological. In fact, the question itself is usually expressed in the book explicitly: "What is the precise nature of your desire?" is the first line of *The Sex Offender*. That's the question I was curious about in relation to that protagonist. If he were asked that question, where would that lead? In *The Dissolution of Nicholas Dee*, the question is: "Is it possible to insure against personal loss?"—a question I ask on page two. In *Landscape: memory*, Max's mother tells him very early on that the mind is a template made of gold—brilliant and malleable—but that the written word is fixed. The relationship between these two ideas forms the question in that novel.

Usually it's that simplified and naive a question when I start. The fact that I'm really interested in it keeps me going—that, and the fact that I usually know some other things besides. For instance, I usually know how the protagonist or narrator speaks. I can't write it unless I know how he talks.

RC   The idea of a governing question explains a lot. But where do you think the concerns that lie behind these starting points originate?

MS   I think it's probably very personal.

RC   You're assuming there's a special relevance to the question for you, aren't you? That behind it there's some contemporary or personal worry?

MS   Yes, they're obviously rooted in my life. For these to be productive questions, they need firstly to compel me—so they need to be as relevant to my own circumstance as possible—but they also need to have not found any answers in my real life. If my life could answer these questions, I wouldn't write the novel.

RC   Does this explain why you don't write more evidently autobiographical material?

MS   Probably. My life, per se, is boring. I'm not capable of doing really interesting things. So autobiography just isn't a very fruitful ground for discovery. And to try to make my life more fruitful could be an extremely pig-headed thing to do. But writing has a great range and flexibility that my life does not allow. So I don't feel so much that I've chosen to forsake the exploration of questions relating to my life; rather, I've chosen writing as the practice through which to live.
  Fiction is a very productive habit of inquiry. It's one I only tried after failing at other solitary habits of inquiry, such as philosophy, playing music, and trying to live my personal life fully in the world—all those dead ends. I enacted those kinds of impulses in my life with my friends—trying to make a public discourse out of my private life. It was so unrewarding and uninteresting—for me and my friends. My experiments with that happened not as a writer but as a good child of American liberals. I was brought up to believe that that's how you achieve mental health.

RC   What led you to fiction?

MS   I had quit playing music but still wanted to spend my time deliberately making something, some kind of refined thing. Writing was cheap, I could do it by myself, and I liked reading. At that point—1984 or so—I was mostly excited by some out-of-date novels about repressed homosexuality: Fritz Peters's *Finistère* and James Purdy's books. For a number of reasons, including what I was reading, when I decided to write it seemed clear to me that the virtues of writing lay not in autobiographical exploration but in the chance to find formulations or possibilities that did not exist in my life. That doesn't mean they're divorced from my life. But the potential and allure of writing is to transcend or transform that starting point into something more permanent and valuable.

RC   Still, there is a large body of autobiographical or semiautobiographical gay fiction—what Edmund White termed "autofiction."

MS   I think Edmund White does not practice what most understand by "autofiction," despite the fact that he's been the primary explicator of the term. His work goes so far beyond that. The degree to which he allows art to transform life, and allows the act of writing to supersede what has been lived is much more thorough-going than what we might imagine from the term "autofiction." It's much more like Nabokov to me.

RC   White has spoken of the tension between the influences of Nabokov and Isherwood in his writing. I agree with you that invoking Isherwood, though thematically handy, is a kind of dead end. In the title *A Boy's Own Story*, there's this self-evident quality, like Isherwood's *A Single Man*. But with White, it's a cover for what lies within, which is incredibly inventive, formally attentive, rich, aesthetic—and difficult.

MS   Yes. I think he's a double agent.

RC   He talks of having had the realist and the fantasy life in his writing, the fantasy life ending with *Caracole*. His response was to pursue the more accessible work. But the more you look at it, the less this distinction holds.

MS   I agree. A lot of the criticism surrounding *The Farewell Symphony*, for example, has involved this petty counting of the autobiographical "coins"—what he said about whom. There's a complete failure to engage with what seems to me to be going on: a much more interesting fantastic play with the material of autobiography—but that's all it is: material. In this regard, I've always felt an affinity with Edmund's work. I find my own interests reflected in his; also in Dennis Cooper's, Kevin Killian's, and, in a more general way, James Purdy's.

RC Could you elaborate a little on the thinking behind this particular selection of names?

MS Well, I give a great deal of thought to Purdy. He's so important in every way. One is just as a model of what it means to work—to be committed to one's own work, and to recognize what one's work is. A great difficulty for anyone who writes is that you end up with so many voices describing back to you what you do—all inviting you to start doing their work. A critic might write about your beautiful depiction of the West, because they care about the West and would love you to describe it. A publisher might praise your depictions of sex, because they want more sex. At whatever level, Purdy stands as a pinnacle to me, an example: he remembers what his work is, and never wavers from it—to his economic detriment, often.

Another thing I find appealing about this group of writers is that they're disparate. They deal with quite different material, and yet one quality unites them: a disinterest in psychology. They've all pursued inquiries that are not aimed at explicating the psychology of a character. Alas, the books I think are great sometimes get trashed for not having "believable" characters, or not having enough insight about motivations.

With Purdy, his interest in a kind of Greek notion of fate suggests a pre-psychological idea of predestination. The mind has a structure which determines its conclusion. Purdy explores that quality by seeing how people talk, and letting the way they talk lead them to their fate. Ed White I think explicates social manners, not psychology. The whole nuance of social positioning; his reflections on navigating the social world, as opposed to the psychological—these seem to constitute the richness of his books. Dennis Cooper has stripped his characters of psychology completely. That's one reason a lot of readers are so hostile to his work. They don't see what qualities are allowed to rise to the fore when the markers of Freudian psychology are displaced. This is an interesting point to try to make in the wake of *Guide*, a remarkable book which I really admire. But here's why it complicates my point. Dennis seems willing to turn the engine of psychoanalysis back upon himself. He allows his narrator to be introspective, in a pattern psychoanalysis might lead to: an inspection of the uncanny; imagery which otherwise might float unconnected. But I don't feel the payoff of this is that we come to understand the psychology of the narrator. In fact, the payoff is that you can basically just forget us; that whatever insight is generated by that dismantling is disposable; that if this is the place to which this inquiry delivers us, we're done; we're moving on to something else. Did I forget Kevin Killian?

RC Lyricism is a quality you could ascribe to each of your four writers. That may or may not be incidental.

MS Right. A devotion to voice or sound can displace the need to make psychological sense—to make things add up. That's obvious in Purdy. In a way, these are all writers who are so interested in the mind that they have no time for psychology.

RC There's a connection between "psychological" writing and realist prose, isn't there, which this attention to language distinguishes you and these other authors from? The exploration of motive in fiction suggests a narrative need for realism—to display things in accessible or simple ways. The paradox is that if you start naming works that fit into this realist school—say, Gore Vidal's *The City and the Pillar*, though apparently nuanced in describing something eternal . . . psychology—in fact they date quickly. The very mode of writing—essentially realist prose—is so much of its time. One inference from what you've been saying is that in writing, you have to learn what not to write; how to show things without explaining them.

MS My job as a writer is to construct language. The places that this role leads to often don't have resolutions. It leaves you in places of ambiguity and doubt, rather than certainty. Also, it focuses your attention on structural issues. The ideal readers of my books will appreciate their structure or shape and their music. I think the rest is just gravy. But this might not satisfy a reader who needs the "backstory" or resolution or answers of some sort. Here's another reason I admire Dennis Cooper's work—his attention to structure is so rigorous. Maybe it's the same part of my brain that loves geometry or angles. Purdy will always deny he has thought like that. He talks instead about having visionary episodes, during which he is spoken to by his grandmother.

RC   Coleridge claimed *Kubla Khan* sprang complete from a vision in sleep, but notebooks suggest the poem was carefully drafted.

MS   But I believe Purdy. I believe it means he's read so thoroughly in literature which is patterned that those patterns are embedded in him.

RC   Did the attention to the sound of language and the importance of the voice ever lead you to verse?

MS   Do you mean line breaks and stuff? Line breaks never occurred to me, just because I think the music I'm interested in creating can still be read with an interchangeable line break.

RC   In publishing terms, people understand a distinction between poets and prose writers.

MS   Yes, though Dennis Cooper is both. How do we know which piece of his is a poem and which is prose? The distinction is made mostly because of line breaks, I think.

RC   Has poetry been important in your own reading?

MS   Sure, since I started writing—not so much before. I never studied English in school. I majored in political theory, studied philosophy, and was really into music. I hadn't read enough literature at first to have found poets who are meaningful to me. When I did, I found them in odd places. Richard Hugo, who grew up in Seattle and died in the 1980s, is a poet I read a lot, and whose sense of music informs mine. I am writing about Seattle now, so I have the task of writing about an unwritten place, a place that has not been turned into literature; it's essentially a raw wound. So Hugo has been very important there.

RC Obviously you reflect on Seattle a lot, and have to for your journalism. Apart from the new book, how does the city inform your previous books?

MS It informed *The Dissolution of Nicholas Dee, The Sex Offender,* and *Allan Stein* a great deal. The cities of *Nicholas Dee* and *The Sex Offender* are the same city, essentially a drag version of Seattle. Like a drag queen, it goes by a different name—"The City"—and is both inverted and exaggerated. Also, Seattle informs my fiction in that I'm interested in narratives that self-destruct or undo themselves—books where the end-point of the narrative is its own dissolution and disappearance. I have a predilection for moments of inarticulateness where what is really meaningful can only be indicated by an inability to speak. I think most of these habits—a tendency towards the dissolution of pattern, the undermining of heroic narratives, and an inclination toward being inarticulate—are rooted in the culture of this city. Look at Nirvana: "(I think I'm) Dumb." Take it as an answer to Descartes. Maybe only the dumb think, or we only think in our dumbness. I don't mean stupidity. I mean speechlessness. You can be smart and still be dumb. To go further with Nirvana, they showed a radical, horrible commitment to self-destruct in the face of the heroic narrative of pop success.

RC In this case, the traditional rock career. It sounds as if Seattle might pose a challenge to a writer, though. It sounds like a city whose relationship to literature is tangential.

MS People buy lots of books here and read all the time. But reading is a private, perverse thing. The public culture around writing and reading here is a lot less articulate than New York, where I lived for seven years. That's got its blessings and its problems. It means you can do your work and not be afflicted by others' opinions. It also means that when you do something which you feel is significant, it's a crapshoot as to whether anyone here notices. But being noticed is such a temporary thrill. I think the benefits of being free of other people's agendas far outweigh the disappointments of not being applauded. There are lots of writers' groups here, but there isn't a rigorous critical discourse around writing. Most of the culture around writing here is support groups: "what you do is good."

RC   This seems typical of the West Coast.

MS   Well, in Seattle we have a lot of heartache and insecurity, so we devote our public discourse to praise and support. Doubt and discernment can be carried out in private. It's certainly different from New York. One reason people from New York might hate it here is that no one argues with them; no one talks back. Polite praise, which of course masks real feeling, can never substitute for the energy of being critical. But where do you end up when the public discourse is critical?

RC   It can certainly become addictive, and the culture of literary gossip is often a substitute for reading.

MS   Yes. It's the opposite of reading. It can also be prescriptive. When a critical public discourse becomes fuelled by money and power, it can be a very important conversation to listen to. It can pay your bills. It's difficult then to sustain the kind of focus James Purdy has. I'm weaker than James Purdy, so I needed to live someplace like Seattle where that conversation, first, is hardly present, and, second, isn't backed up by anything. It promises nothing.

RC   Purdy looks out onto Brooklyn Bridge, but Manhattan must seem a million miles away.

MS   Still, he constantly talks about his antagonism towards Manhattan and New York publishing, like worrying a wound.

RC   You previously told me the title of your current project, "The Voluptuary." Do titles always come early?

MS   Too early in this case; that's not the title anymore. Now it has no title. I've been working on this book two years now. Typically I've started

books about three years into whatever previous book I'm working on—
and, typically, I haven't finished a book until five years later. So I often
have this period of overlap.

RC   Is it productive creatively to have two books in progress?

MS   I guess so. I think having another project claim my attention helps
me finally give up and finish the earlier book. I feel best about my work
when I'm nimble—when I feel the realm of possibility is pretty broad.
That feeling is enhanced by having a few things going on at once. Without question, though, there's a long stretch of time in any of these projects when I can't think about anything except that. I need to be single-
minded. That has happened with all four books so far, so it must also be
a part of how I work.

RC   Have you ever aborted a project?

MS   No. I have projects I've started and still not completed. *The Dissolution of Nicholas Dee* started when I lived in Holland. In the middle of
working on what was then a fiction set in the seventeenth century, I wanted to write about a man arriving at a train station. Since there were no
trains in the seventeenth century, I couldn't possibly put it in the book,
but I was fairly compelled by it, so I started writing a scene which eventually became the first thing in *The Sex Offender*. In quite a short time for
me, I wrote a full draft of *The Sex Offender*, and then set it aside, liking
what I'd done. I had a contract with Scribner's then for whatever my next
book was. I gave them *The Sex Offender* and said: "I know I told you I was
working on this Dutch seventeenth-century thing, but I wrote this, and
really believe it's a substantial piece of work. It's what I want as my next
book." My editor didn't agree. He told me that publishing it at that point
was a bad idea. He wanted me to finish the other book. So I went back
and finished *The Dissolution of Nicholas Dee*. During the same stretch of
time, I started a nonfictional project on the history of sleep. With *The
Dissolution of Nicholas Dee*, I was learning a lot about the anthropology of
sleep—how people set up bedrooms; whether they go to bed together, or
have their own private chamber. It's a project I continue to work on. I

haven't come near to finishing it, but I may well do before I finish my next novel. I've delayed it for seven years now, but I don't feel I've ended it. I have a lot of shorter fiction that went nowhere. That I just keep in a pile.

RC To my knowledge, with one or two exceptions you haven't published short fiction except as excerpts from novels.

MS I've written three pieces that I thought were viable as short stories: "Love Problem," "Homo Sex Story," and a story I published in *Grand Street* in 1990 called "The Power Lines." It came from reading Flaubert's *The Temptation of Saint Anthony*. I'd also seen a performance by the Wooster Group and Ron Vawter—a remarkable actor—of their version of *The Temptation of Saint Anthony*, and I wrote "The Power Lines" to try to get a little closer to what Ron Vawter did to me—to have a stronger relation to the effect he'd had on me.

RC When you say that otherwise the short fiction you've written "went nowhere," are you suspicious about your execution of that form?

MS Yes. What I did was not satisfying, and looked like it wasn't worth other people's time. They were stylistic exercises; they seemed mechanical. An inquiry has its own trajectory, and you'll discover what its shape is if you manage to focus your attention well enough. I've pretty consistently gotten engaged in inquiries whose shape was long—novel length.

RC So you do have ideas which dictate a shorter length, but you haven't executed them in a way that does them justice?

MS I haven't had them at all really, except with "The Power Lines." *The Sex Offender* was a fairly intense and unusually unplanned engagement for me. Right in the wake of writing what was a very wet book—in *The Sex Offender* it's constantly snowing; there are fluids in it; it's very messy—I had a tremendous need to write an extremely arid, dry thing. It felt almost visceral. I had a dream one night which left this residue in my head—a man whose bones are turning into dust inside of him. He's an engineer who lays the power lines. I took that idea and pursued it for what amounted to two months. This man is in a small desert town, planning the geometry of the power lines. But he has to deal with the fact that his bones are turning into dust. He goes to an osteopath, who tries to help.

Its longest drafts were around fifty pages, and its finished draft was about twenty-nine. It seemed very telegraphed to me. It was quite clear where he began and where he would end. I had no intention that it would be a short story. It just was. With "Homo Sex Story," though, it was more an act of deliberation.

RC Wasn't that shaped by its commissioning?

MS It was. In a lot of ways, I'm disappointed in that story. I rarely give it to people as an example of my own work, partly because its contingencies are so mixed up. Some of them are mine; some are other people's. I was thinking about a lot of people, and it's hard for me to work when I think about other people.

RC Do you feel you could write shorter fiction if the circumstances were right?

MS There are lots of different ways to write short fiction. I could be mercenary about it and try to write a story that would appeal to other people. On that level, I'd be better informed now than I was ten years ago—maybe more successful at it. A lot of my attempts were written about ten years ago when I was in an M.F.A. program that required short fiction for its workshops. To submit a longer piece was such a burden to everybody else. And at that point I didn't know a lot about the different ways I could write. I was more ignorant technically, and I also didn't know so clearly what was valuable to me. So I stumbled round in the dark. I tried to write stories that looked like what I thought short stories were, and where the subject matter was close enough to my own concerns to be meaningful to me. But I hadn't yet realized that the structural and epistemological levels of engagement were the most rewarding to me, as opposed to the psychological.

I had previously written a story that was published in *Christopher Street* in 1983 or 1984—called "23 July 1981." It was the first fiction I ever published.

RC   So your first M.F.A. projects didn't become your first published fiction?

MS   One did: the last one. The end of my second year at Columbia, I took an anthropology course from a woman named Elaine Combs-Schilling—a graduate seminar in symbolism. She recommended Burton Benedict's book about the San Francisco World's Fair of 1915, *The Anthropology of World's Fairs*. I was interested in a building at the fair, the Palace of Fine Arts. It was built in the manner of a ruin because the architect, Bernard Mayback, felt that any ancient building would, at that point, be a ruin: to have twentieth-century buildings mimic Greco-Roman architecture would logically oblige you to design a ruin. I made this building a starting point for my fiction.

I was teaching high school full time so wasn't writing much during the school year. I was scrambling just to get stories into the workshops. Then, in the summer, I'd write a lot. One summer I managed to get a job house-sitting in Berkeley and wrote the first draft of what became a novel called *Landscape: memory*—alone in the house with a dog, just sitting there working.

RC   So *Landscape: memory* both came and didn't come out of the workshops?

MS   It came out of Elaine Combs-Schilling's class, and out of Maureen Howard's reading of my work. She was my workshop leader then.

RC   It's an important distinction, surely? There's that moment in *Landscape: memory* where the mother is given the line: "We mustn't become slaves to our teachers."

MS   I take potshots at teachers in every novel.

RC   But your own experience doesn't sound that unrewarding.

MS   Anywhere you can enter into conversation with intelligent readers, you'll find something of value for your work. A writing program formalizes that relation. It requires people to be readers, and some of them will be intelligent. They may be your teachers or your fellow students. But I think the practice of making a lucrative industry out of that is morally corrupt; it's just despicable.

RC   *The Dissolution of Nicholas Dee* attacks universities pursuing education in marketing terms.

MS   As you pointed out, I'm pretty interested in social institutions and the patterns that circumscribe individual behavior and choice, particularly the way we think.

RC   Is it fair to characterize your work as hostile to institutions?

MS   There seems to be a consistent momentum in my work toward unconstrained, inarticulate moments of dissolution that, in a sort of classically or Germanic romantic way, are occasions for the sublime, if not for truth or beauty.

RC   Are you thinking of painting?

MS   Or Goethe. In *The Sorrows of Young Werther,* part of the allure of Werther's frustration is that what's most valuable lies in complete dissolution—in death.

RC   You're the only gay writer to mention Goethe . . .

MS   [*Laughs*] My favorite gay writer! I've been outed as a romantic. How embarrassing.

RC   In terms of your own life, you've hardly avoided institutions. You've been a teacher.

MS   Yes, I've loved teaching. I just don't want big real estate concerns—

like, say, Columbia University or the University of Washington—to skim profits off it by charging my students tens of thousands of dollars or exploiting them for cheap classroom labor.

RC   Some aspects of journalism are institutional.

MS   I think I take pleasure in operating within a conventional forum in ways that are disruptive.

RC   In both cases, exceptional teaching and journalism break the very rigors of form imposed by the institution. With great teachers there's invariably something dangerous and anarchic in what they're doing.

MS   Yes. They're all sex offenders! In this state we have a history, at least in the last ten years: the Teachers of the Year, and other prize-winners, are regularly unmasked the next year as having had sex with one or another of their students. Fascinating!

RC   I'd like to return to the specter of romanticism. Against or within these institutional forms, your novels tend to feature figures of a certain naïveté. Many of these are young men. Some are attracted to youth in a way that ultimately becomes sexual. When you spoke of reproaching yourself for romanticism, you may not have meant this exactly. But you have described very directly the attractiveness of people who are, in our present culture, very young sexual beings. In *Landscape: memory*, the observer is the same age; elsewhere, he's older. Whether you seek controversy or not, that's difficult and questionable to many today.

MS   People get nervous if you show them how sexy kids are. But that element in my fiction is the most historically circumscribed, narrow one. Those images wouldn't have the power they do in another time or place. I lean on this in my fictions—sometimes to my detriment, because the way I do is often upsetting to readers. Kids contain a lot of things, or adults make them do. Robert Glück wrote a really smart review of *The Dissolution of Nicholas Dee*. It talked about this odd equivalence of nostalgia and boys, how in my books they became equivalent.

Allan Stein, the subject of my fourth novel, was the nephew of Gertrude Stein. He died after a fairly miserable adulthood. But he was a cherished and blessed child, doted on by his aunt and parents. Yet his adulthood was terrible. Part of the reason he became so fascinating was because I had an opportunity to look at this confluence of nostalgia and youth, all in one character.

When I began *Allan Stein*, one of the notes taped up on my desk was: "Dismantle nostalgia." I wrote it to myself in the wake of Bob Glück's reading of the earlier book. Nostalgia was probably an immanent quality in all the boys I'd written. I needed to parse it out and unpack it, so the naturalness of my placement of that quality—of any quality—in the figure of the boy could get disrupted. That was partly why I was so affected by and so admire Dennis Cooper's *Guide*. I've never witnessed a more successful unpacking of anyone's own shtick than there.

RC   Cooper took risks in *Guide* by engaging with the things that, in retrospect, are clearly absences in his earlier novels—things he was frightened of including.

MS   Yes. That clears the ground and allows him to go on. It's hard to empathize fully with this condition—that of becoming trapped within your own fecundity; your own ability to create this world—unless you're building elaborate things for yourself—novels, or pop-song careers. Dennis has always been tremendously conscious of what he's creating. He also has a contrarian's instinct for devaluing it.

RC   The catalyst for that act, according to Cooper, came from the shallowest of responses to his work. He had to confront the public image of himself as a monster, rather than a writer.

MS   Sure. Isn't it interesting that we could be having this discussion about that book, yet that discussion wasn't reflected in any public discourse? I think it'll be a long time before the trajectory of Dennis's work is evident.

RC   This doesn't imply a lack of faith in readers?

MS   No. It implies an ultimate faith in readers as the only location of meaning.

RC   Have you ever written with particular readers in mind?

MS   Yes. I often think of a specific person in my life, who I want to have read this. It's been a different person with each book. It's very important to me, firstly, that it's a specific person. For instance when you write a letter: putting "Dear Larry" at the top allows you to speak in a wholly different way than if you put "Dear Dad."

RC   When you look at the finished books, does the figure of that person haunt their significance to you?

MS   Yes.

RC   What's the relationship between that specific reader and any wider sense you have of readership?

MS   None. Zero. It's hard for me to imagine a general reader. I can function when there's an editor I'm sending this to, or when so-and-so asked me to write about X. In my fiction, I function very well remembering the person I want to have read this, but I don't succeed ever in imagining a general reader, or a gay reader, or an educated reader.

RC   They're fictions.

MS   Yes, and not very good fictions. In some ways it's the saving grace of writing that you know this effort is going to end up in a private space. It's going to find its realization in an extremely intimate and sheltered moment with one peculiar, weird person entering into a matrix of language. That interaction is deeply meaningful, and quite different from, say, playing music to an audience. I played guitar and saxophone in some tossed-together punk bands. But I was petrified by standing on stage and playing to people. I hated it. Writing is one of the few arts that is completely private. It's written in private and it's read in private. The good feeling I have about books is that they will survive any public discourse. It doesn't matter what's made of them by critics or in public forums as long as the book lives in the world and continues to find its way into private intimate interactions.

RC   The paradox is that you only get your book into this private space through publicity, through journalism.

MS   If so, then a writer has a second job—being a public person. It can be fun, if you turn it into a fiction that pleases you, and live that as your public persona.

RC   Do you suspend writing when you're doing publicity?

MS   No.

RC   I want to return to the question of your resistance to what we might call "master narratives." In the first two novels, the reader experiences an interruption to the dominant narrative or plot strand quite literally—in the interpolation of various different kinds of competing narratives. That's less true of *The Sex Offender*. Though two distinct plots develop in it, they remain coherent, and coherently alternated. Did this mark a conscious moving away from the hybrid narrative of *Landscape: memory* and *The Dissolution of Nicholas Dee*?

MS   Kind of, though the real chronology isn't so neat. I certainly wanted to find the right structure for *The Sex Offender*, and I knew it wasn't going to be collage. It had to be something more theatrical. Ethel Eichelberger, the drag queen whose stage performances guided a lot of my choices in *The Sex Offender*, led me to a kind of burlesque grand opera. She exaggerated the conventions of opera so completely and embodied them so thoroughly that the artifice became obvious—even comical— while remaining, paradoxically, dead serious. I wondered whether it was possible to do this in a novel. I tried. Going to press, at my editor's behest I removed the headings which had said "Overture," "Acts One, Two, Three, Four, and Five," and "Epilogue"—but you can find in *The Sex Offender* the structural pattern of a grand opera.

RC   Tell me about the structural sources for *Allan Stein*.

MS   What happened in *Allan Stein* is that I read Proust, finally. I also, for the first time, read a lot of Nabokov. Proust's style invited me to wonder whether I could adopt a relatively seamless fabric of narrative which did not rely on overt disruption or parody, yet deliver the reader to both an awareness of the narrative and its dissolution. If you think of Proust's work as all of geology, I'm maybe, by comparison, in a sandbox shaping a little mound of dirt. But having finally looked at geology for the first time, I'm a little more informed about how to push the dirt around. *Allan Stein* is one man speaking—trying to relate his narrative. It doesn't have the residue of any other imported structure.

Regarding narrative technique, I really admire Guy Davenport. In *Landscape: memory* I wanted to make something he would admire. He wrote a story called "O Gadjo Niglo" which appeared in *Conjunctions* in the early 1980s. It wasn't included among his collected work until *A Table of Green Fields*. I spent several fruitless summers poring over this story, trying to find in it the voice of *Landscape: memory*'s protagonist Max Kosegarten. When I finally gave up on that, I found Max's voice. The collage structure that I use in *Landscape: memory* and *The Dissolution of Nicholas Dee* really began for me with reading his work. Since reading Proust however, it's hard to imagine the rewards of that exercise. The allure of a single voice seems so complicated and rich to me, in a way I wasn't aware of before. I said that my tiny evolution as a writer was marked by people reading my work. I guess it's also marked by my reading of other people's.

RC   Do you worry about other writers' voices and techniques overshadowing your work as you write?

MS   Yes. I'm reluctant to read certain things when I'm working. For instance, while I was writing *Landscape: memory*, I didn't read any Guy Davenport. I read Forster, who was just perfect. He was so anally retentive in getting every detail right. Yet he was removed from what I was doing. If I'd been reading Davenport, it would really have screwed me up.

RC   Thematically, Forster shares one scene with that work: *Maurice* has a scene with a shrink, as does Max.

MS   That's interesting. I wasn't reading *Maurice*, actually, but *A Passage to India*. So that wasn't one of the stolen scenes in the book. The stolen ones came from films. But I'm more mature now. In *Allan Stein* I put all the stolen material in quotes.

RC   Have you ever been tempted by third-person narration?

MS   I tried it with *The Dissolution of Nicholas Dee*, *The Sex Offender*, and *Allan Stein*. I started out very deliberately wanting to write in the third person. You may remember there's a line in *The Dissolution of Nicholas Dee*: "Beware the third person. It is a cold and impersonal deceit." This must be my attempt at self-criticism, because in fact I've read a lot of third-person fictions that are completely effective and meaningful to me. But I haven't yet written in the third person in a way that did not feel like a deceit. And I must say I've read a lot of books where the crippling defect is the use of the third person.

RC   You spoke of *Allan Stein* as being written after reading Proust. With *The Sex Offender*, I felt the shadow of Nabokov. The subject matter reminds one of *Lolita*; you have Nicholas Nicholas, rather than Humbert Humbert.

MS   Yes. It's ridiculous, and probably completely unbelievable, but I hadn't read any Nabokov when I wrote *The Sex Offender*! I'm very poorly educated—a real indictment of the American colleges. But there are a number of ways these influences can get to us, besides through reading them. Writers like Nabokov or Proust are obviously enough aligned with a kind of zeitgeist to have currency and therefore they echo throughout the culture. Their styles bleed so completely into the culture that you don't need to read them to be affected by them. That's certainly true for me. For instance, now that I've read Nabokov, I see my sense of humor is rooted in the same things that delighted him, especially the odd sounds of words—the way a wrong word can sound right, and thereby make the wrong thing right. I probably learned this from Firesign Theatre or my dad, but now that I write novels, it's "Nabokovian." Then there's the "double rumble" of Humbert Humbert, which I'd never heard when I named my protagonist Nicholas Nicholas. Reviews of *The Sex Offender* kept mentioning Nabokov, so I decided I should read him. He's intoxicating. There's a whole draft of *Allan Stein* which was much more affected by Nabokov than by Proust. But I dumped that one.

RC   What else in Nabokov did you ultimately come to revere?

MS   His unrelenting duplicity—that he never gives a key to his fictions; his insistence on their autonomy. That's really inspiring. In some ways, too, his hostility toward Freudian psychology is as heroic to me as Purdy's toward publishing.

RC   Are you happy for your novels to be described as anti-psychological?

MS   I enjoy fiction because it's a location of mystery, and in many ways mystical traditions are more relevant to my work than analytical traditions.

RC   Where else does that lead us? Be a promiscuous consumer—in literature or elsewhere.

MS   It leads me to punk rock, which is a location of inarticulateness, or the pose of it, and an ecstatic experience of the dissolution of the self, with a refusal to explain. I'd never presume to make the subject matter of my fiction the world of punk rock. That would be a crippling debilitation. I nevertheless feel like most of my fictions are aimed toward the same place; the same moment I've experienced and enjoyed—a deafeningly loud kind of dumb music.

RC   Name names.

MS   Minor Threat.

RC   "Punk" can be taken as so many things, which is why I asked you to be specific. And there's a problem with talking about punk intellectually.

Many Europeans, at least, remain skeptical about talking about popular culture intellectually. You have to detach the fashion element—remove the "drag" or surface to discover the essential in it.

MS   Yes, and you need a new vocabulary for what is intellectual. The vocabulary that gets imported is hostile to the qualities I'd want to highlight. That's why this position of inarticulateness and this insistence on being dumb is so interesting. In some ways it's the insistence on clearing room for a different vocabulary. It's saying: "I'm not going to talk about it the way you want to talk about it." Anyhow, to broaden the list, you could add Jonathan Richman, the Black Outs, Pere Ubu, the Replacements, the Descendants, and, for accessibility to everybody, Nirvana, who are a grand example of what I'm talking about.

RC   You're not speaking of the "art school" end of punk.

MS   Absolutely not. The opposite. Clever bands, or even, say, the literally art-school bands like Talking Heads, aren't what thrill me. I'm interested in the inarticulate, where the inarticulate asserts itself. That's never a very pretty place, and it's usually simple. It's power—life—manifested without being articulate. What are the mechanisms; what is the physicality through which it is manifested?

You could search for answers to that question everywhere. You could look at architecture and ask whether Rem Koolhaas's contrarian insistence on using degraded materials to build monumental structures is an articulation of the same mentality. In literature, you could ask if Dennis Cooper's masterful use of ellipses and words like "uh" is in fact creating space for the manifestation of what is normally thought to be inarticulate. Or you could look at music, and try to observe the difference between Nirvana and Guns 'n' Roses. To find the difference, you not only have to be an astute listener. You also have to look at the nuance of their relationship to their work.

RC   If punk rock introduced such a significant cultural moment, could you say a bit more about why that could not become the subject of your fiction writing?

MS   First of all, yes—this is a significant cultural moment for my work—

more significant, really, than my reading. When I first formed any sense of participating in social culture, it was through music. My exit from being a performer into the world of writing came because the immediacy and absence of reflection that attended performance was crippling. I write because it means I can reflect a lot, can fashion my presentation and say exactly what I mean, and not be crippled by the fact of my own being.

RC   But isn't there something about the polishing of writing—about rewriting—that is antithetical to the spontaneity of punk?

MS   I don't think so, though I agree that there is a tension. But you never mitigate the possibility of getting it wrong by polishing. The moment of realization of a fiction is the moment of reading. To me, any fussing over my end of the bargain—getting the materials ready; preparing the stage—is really so that the real performer—the reader—can step into the right circumstances for reading. This notion of getting it wrong, of the spontaneity and multivalence of the moment, is guaranteed by the act of reading. The fact that writing itself is a reflective, fussed over, and polished act doesn't compromise that moment of performance. When the reader gets there, God knows what will happen.

RC   Does this mean it's easy for you to distance yourself from completed works?

MS   I don't know if that's why I feel at ease about the finished project, but I do. I don't have a lot of the anxieties some of my friends have about the thing being in the world. It's a thing, and its existence at any moment is someone else's business.

RC   Could a misreading—if you'd even allow the term—annoy you?

MS   Sure. There are always misreadings that drive me nuts. The same thing happens when I'm at a show with friends, and the band is fucking up and screwing around with the purity of a song in order to ease their own insecurity about being original. I really get angry, and if the person I'm with doesn't notice it, I get angry with him.

The same thing happens with readers. Certain readings of my work make me angry. But it's very similar to that dynamic of being at a show with friends and wanting them to see what I see, which isn't so singular, though it is specific. Equally, when a reviewer, especially one with a lot of influence, misses the program I think is embedded in my fiction, I get fed up by the inability of my fictions to survive in other contexts.

To return to the question of the particular cultural moment of punk, I suppose I let it inform my sense of formal and structural choices, rather than subject matter. The subject matter—you know, the clothes and lifestyles and the music and no money and all—isn't what's really profound about punk. Those things are just all the same old manly hero romance we've been stuck in forever. Just read [music critic] Greil Marcus and saddle up your horses one more time. I'm tired of cowboys, so the subject matter, per se, isn't very interesting to me. But punk, for me, is a structural pattern—a way of making choices. This sort of internal wiring of the phenomenon is what I brought from punk to my writing.

The world of punk as subject matter can drag a writer into naïveté. It's a world that has its own momentum. You'd have to be really focused and bright to be able to deal with that subject matter and still make a piece of lasting art. That's why I'm in awe of what Kurt Cobain did. I think it's a miracle that somebody could live in that world and make something lasting. I'm not just thinking of his music, but of how he conducted himself in that world. I couldn't do that. It's insane and impossible.

Punk has always been an undercurrent of connection to Dennis Cooper. He knows that aesthetic, that way of making choices, and draws on it. He's even located his subject matter close to it—and successfully. I couldn't get that close and still keep my head on my shoulders. I think that's a real achievement. Punk music of all things is the most seductive and terminal music form. To survive that and discover yourself in its wake is so rare and difficult. I think something of the position Dennis faced in his own work was similar. Having perfected a form that was so nuanced it offered no way out, he wrote *Guide*—and he's out.

RC   How old were you when you first heard punk?

MS   Eighteen. Jonathan Richman. He's punk, yes? I mean he's also very sweet, cloying even. He was my first hero, displaced only by James Purdy. This is the trajectory you must navigate to have a clue what I'm doing.

RC I want to connect your experience as audience member then with your writing now, and the reception of that writing. Is there a simple way of describing your work as an attempt to regain some particular moment?

MS I'd like the reader to be delivered to an experience of disruption and dissolution. If I can create the circumstances in which they enact that, I'm very happy. For me the switch from playing music to writing books was through the recognition that I couldn't enact that state for others, but I could create the circumstances in which it happened.

In a more quotidian way, my shift was also the result of feeling frustrated by collaboration. I couldn't work with other people. I had to be by myself to make these things, to create that situation. Another aspect was wanting this potential for moments of the dissolution of the self and the disruption of received patterns of thought—wanting the occasion of that to persist in the world, not just be one moment in a performance. That desire guided me toward fiction also. A book just keeps on going; a performance doesn't. Given that desire for autonomy, collaboration in writing might not seem very attractive to me, but in fact when I like people a lot, I enjoy writing stuff with them. I write with other people lots.

RC Tell me about your "Mother and Son," your story collaboration with Kevin Killian.

MS Well, I've probably written five or six hundred pages of work with other people, just at parties. I mean pass-the-typewriter parties. We all have typewriters and pass them around. It's fun and leads to some unplanned gems. I've got files and files of these stories. But I never experienced collaborations as a formalized, public act until Kevin entered my life.

RC But how does it work? Let's examine one obvious contradiction. When you're writing, you choose one word as opposed to others: this is the word you'd like. With collaboration comes compromise. Which word survives when there's a difference of opinion?

MS   There's no arguing about words. Just write more. Write the ones you like. Collaborating in writing is a lot more like playing in a punk band than it is like writing a novel. You're all just having fun together, and whatever comes out of it—great. The idea that it would be of value to a reader is the last thing in the world I think about. Essentially, you're having a social relation with the other people at the table. Whether it's a guitar in your hands or a typewriter, you're still engaged with those people in the room. The moment of composition is a social moment. That's why it wouldn't have occurred to me to publish the stories, or give them to anybody except the people I've written them with. I xerox the stories and give them to whoever was at the party, whereas Kevin often offers them to others and has faith that they will be of value to readers. I'm sometimes horrified. I was shocked he'd shown this thing we did together to a magazine, which then printed it. But I'm flattered too, because I really admire Kevin and he's a million times smarter than me.

RC   The only other example I can come up with is Robert Glück, soliciting manuscripts from other writers to draw on in *Margery Kempe*, though that is a different form of collaboration.

MS   Another West Coast superfreak! A few years ago I was asked to comment on a Dutch architect's "Manifesto of Bigness"—Rem Koolhaas. He speculated, among other things, that gratuitous size in architecture might ultimately give rise to a reinvention of the collective. By coincidence, I grew up twenty miles from the largest building on earth, Boeing's airplane factory in Everett, Washington. The short version is I think the grotesque scale of urban space and built space on the U.S. West Coast is literally "spaced out" and gives rise to a cultural pattern that is also spaced out—a purposefully dumb, inarticulate pattern that is unpredictable, difficult to organize, and forgetful. I think this pattern has the virtue of catalyzing new forms of collectivity.

RC   I'm asking people to comment on working method. Do you write longhand?

MS   No. I write at a keyboard.

RC   You don't have superstitions about that?

MS   No. I think it's physiological. When my hands are in this position at a keyboard, my brain feels nimble. When my hand is in the cramped position of grasping a pen, my brain feels pressured. I don't know why that is. I write when I wake up in the morning. It helps me a lot to be groggy and still unhurried. What stops my writing is that, by one or two o'clock, my head gets so clogged with duties and responsibilities that I can't navigate the fiction anymore.

RC   Do you write every day?

MS   Yes. I like writing. If I don't write, it's only because somebody's preventing me. Usually that's because I've agreed to some assignment for money that keeps me from fiction, or I'm teaching, or there's some other responsibility I value but which interferes with my morning.

RC   Is the work produced at a constant rate?

MS   I have very different stages of work. There's a long period when I'm reading a lot and writing a little. That's when I know what my fascinations are—in the case of the current book, that is early twentieth-century music—Arnold Schönberg in particular; logging on the Olympia peninsula; guitar feedback; and divorce, I guess. Oh, and a climate that will not kill you. One interesting thing about the climate here is that you could crawl out of here into the bush, trying to die, and it won't kill you. It refuses to kill you. It's too mild. That's interesting.

  You can see how amorphous this collection of concerns seems. I'm reading a lot about all of these things, and writing some speculative, tentative moves towards a narrative that might gather around the characters I know who are involved in these issues. This may persist for a year or two, then give way to a more demanding narrative, which I know I've got to write. Then I don't want to do anything but write it. I'll leave town to do it; this typically occupies about a year of my time.

RC   Are there parts of narrative which hold you up? Are there kinds of scenes you know will come slowly?

MS   I never know ahead of time. If I try to guess, I'm usually wrong. I always presume I'll be better at the stuff I've done before. So far, that's not been the case. I'm truly surprised by what seems easy and what hard each day. You'd think I could write a description of a belly button by now, but it's still difficult.

RC   Are there other figures we should mention as influences; people whose work you look out for?

MS   Sherwood Anderson was my first favorite to read. I liked his regionalism and the possibility of finding what's meaningful in a very restricted locale. Then, of course, there's his interest in voice and the Gothic. The little prelude to *Winesburg, Ohio*—"The Book of the Grotesque"—is pretty weird, pretty great.

I'd read Anderson and loved him before reading Purdy, but he blossomed into this meaningful thing in the wake of reading Purdy. Equally, Gertrude Stein became a real obsession in the wake of the peculiarity of Purdy's language. Purdy became a bridge to some of the more autonomous work of Stein, which is what led me to write *Allan Stein*. I felt like an idiot trying to comment critically on Gertrude Stein's work, yet I wanted to write near her work; to explore why her sentences are meaningful to me—especially in the interminable *Making of Americans*. When I look at that, given the context and world it comes out of, it blows me away: that she could have the focus to have remembered what she was doing throughout that whole book, then to have done it.

RC   The writers you've spoken of have rather uncertain literary reputations.

MS   Oh? I guess these are sometime thought of as "minor": always "Sherwood Anderson below Hemingway," or "Stein below Joyce," or "Purdy below everybody." Those judgments are just indicative of a fairly temporary historical predilection for one kind of inquiry over another.

RC   I'm interested that Joyce came up. I thought of him when you talked of the relevance of musical structures to your writing.

MS   I liked reading *Ulysses*, though I've hardly ever gone back to it. And the way in which Stein has been denigrated in relation to Joyce interests me. Primarily it's in her refusal to indulge the mechanisms of heroic narrative. Joyce manages to dismantle or achieve a critical perspective on those mechanisms, yet he's quite willing to use them. Stein doesn't. She never lets you get it up.

RC   But aren't all the "big" names in modernism hybrid? Take Virginia Woolf. She was wildly experimental in her less successful work. But everybody teaches *To the Lighthouse*.

MS   Yeah, I guess. It's available for use. I really admire the way Stein made herself unavailable. In some ways, that created the same autonomous space I'm so fascinated with in marginalized cultures— whether that be Seattle or repressed, pre-Stonewall gay writing: a culture which parlays its marginalization into a perversity that is really rich and lasting.

RC   Who besides Purdy are you drawing on?

MS   Proust, I guess. So much of the power of his writing is repressed sexuality. There's such a rich blossoming of sensuality that it in some ways erases the question of sex. Everything becomes a kind of sex. Otherwise, besides Purdy, it would be Fritz Peters and Denton Welch. To follow up what I said about Stein's refusal to exercise the tools of heroic narrative, I should add that heroic narrative is such a powerful public manifestation of climax that to be constantly involved in undermining and perverting it is very gratifying in a way that may be tied to sexuality.

RC   To accept the fantasy of a "gay canon" for a moment, are there other important gay texts from the last thirty years that you'd want to mention, apart from James Purdy?

MS   First, one last mention of Purdy: the most candid thing he ever said about my work was when he read *Landscape: memory* and called it "a nice collection of pretty lies." I was very chastened by that. What I do in my work is quite different from what he does.

In terms of the last thirty years, the two writers I'd mention are actually straight. Guy Davenport's work is essential to any understanding of the public discourse of sexuality. Steve Weiner's *The Museum of Love* is a remarkable book. He makes homosexuality into a universal condition—a historical force rather than a token of the individual personality. And he's so funny. It's hard when someone's written one book to have any sense of what they're up to, but Weiner's *The Museum of Love* announces such a broad-ranging intelligence that I feel confident this is a writer of enduring value.

★   ★   ★

MS   I should mention that it is now 2002, five years after the drunken dinner that gave rise to the above conversation. Richard has allowed me the troubling luxury of editing this interview. The trouble is how full of shit and misleading I can sometimes be, but that's the hazard of ever opening my mouth. I've struck the worst of it, and what's left I'm willing to live with. On the bright side, Steve Weiner's second novel, *The Yellow Sailor*, has come out and confirmed that he's a total genius who will teach us all a great deal about sexuality and writing.

RC   Thanks very much for your time.

ELEVEN

PHILIP HENSHER

THE ENGLISH writer Philip Hensher is the author of four novels—*Other Lulus*, *Kitchen Venom*, *Pleasured*, and *The Mulberry Empire*—and a collection of short stories, *The Bedroom of the Mister's Wife*.

Hensher was born in London in 1965. He went to school in Yorkshire and studied English literature as an undergraduate at Oxford University before taking a doctorate at Cambridge. He then began work as a Clerk in the House of Commons, while also writing fiction and journalism.

His first published novel was *Other Lulus* (London: Hamish Hamilton, 1994). Hensher left Parliament on the eve of the publication of *Kitchen Venom* (London: Hamish Hamilton, 1996), which won the Somerset Maugham Award. A third novel, *Pleasured* (London: Chatto and Windus, 1998), appeared in 1998. Hensher's shorter fiction, collected in *The Bedroom of the Mister's Wife* (London: Chatto and Windus, 1999), had previously appeared in *Critical Quarterly*, the *Erotic Review*, *Granta*, the *London Magazine*, various editions of *Vintage New Writing*, and A. S. Byatt, ed., *The Oxford Book of English Short Stories* (Oxford: Oxford University Press, 1999), among others.

Hensher's latest novel, *The Mulberry Empire* (London: Flamingo, 2002; New York: Knopf, 2002)—the first to be published in America—concerns the British military campaigns in nineteenth-century Afghanistan. He writes a weekly column for the *Independent* newspaper, reviews art exhibitions for the *Mail on Sunday*, and is chief book reviewer of the *Spectator* magazine. Hensher has written introductions to reprint editions of books by John Buchan, Ivy Compton-Burnett, Henry James, Nancy

Mitford, and Geoffrey Willans and Ronald Searle. He was one of the Booker Prize judges in 2001, and is among the youngest members of the Council of the Royal Society of Literature. He is also the author of the libretto for Thomas Adès's acclaimed opera *Powder Her Face* (1995).

Hensher lives in a flat in South London, where this interview first took place on August 3, 1998. It was revised in March 2002, when the material following the asterisks was also added.

RC   What is the significance of the various city settings in your novels?

PH   When I started *Other Lulus*, I wanted to write a novel about a city that was only in my head. I'd never been to Vienna. But all my life I'd been obsessed with the whole Viennese "thing"—this incredible, cream-cakey city, in the middle of which was a small, hard nut of people doing the most extraordinary things, but surrounded by a lot of fluff and bubble. Afterwards people said: "I loved all those descriptions of Vienna." I said: "Which ones?" They'd go through the book, trying to find a single descriptive passage. But the only thing I ever wrote about what the city looks like is something about "looking at the big white buildings."

Cities in books are always imaginary. For Dickens's readership, it wasn't about him conjuring up a real city. It was about erecting a phantom city which might stand in the same place as the real one. It had the same streets, but basically it was just there—in their heads and Dickens's.

With *Kitchen Venom*, the city—London—is again fantastical. I write about it in almost metaphysical terms. Right at the beginning, the book talks about the west, east, north, and south of the city. That's very interesting—the way we carve up cities to get hold of their character; to transform the world into a reasonably graspable shape. I wanted to write a fantasy novel about London—one with the same tone as the stories in Italo Calvino's *Invisible Cities*. In the middle, however, there'd be a quite realistic sort of action.

Kitchen Venom is almost written in the magic realist mode—oddly, because it's one which, as reader and critic, I rather despise: all those novels about people growing pigs' ears, or whatever. I wanted to write a realist novel by the back door—to write about a real city—one I knew very well—but to write as if I'd seen it for the first time the day before.

The choice of the city was more obvious in *Pleasured* than *Kitchen Venom* because it's foreign. Berlin I know very well and have always loved a lot—before the Wall fell as well as afterwards. There are elements of that *Kitchen Venom* fantasy about the way the city is viewed, though. It's very geometrical; it's quartered in the same way. One had to write about Berlin like that when writing about the fall of the Wall. But it's much more of a solid, real city overall.

I love cities. Whenever I go away, it's to a city. It's not that I don't like the countryside. But it's a bit difficult because I don't drive. And I like people, cafés, streets. I get freaked out if I can't hear other people talking.

I'm writing a novel set in an Islamic city currently—Kabul. What tempts me about that is that one can write absolutely anything one likes because you can't get into Afghanistan now. It only exists for one's readers as a series of magical descriptions. The nineteenth-century descriptions of Kabul are just wonderful—great cherry trees over the street, and so on. What tempted me is an exercise in something one's supposed to deplore very strongly—Orientalism. I'm attracted to those things one isn't supposed to do generally. Orientalism's a fantastic literary mode. I've always wanted to write about London or Berlin in an Orientalist spirit.

RC How does the amount of research you've undertaken for the Afghan novel compare to that for previous ones?

PH I seem to be doing rather a lot—more because the literature's incredibly interesting and entertaining than out of duty. The other novels haven't involved hardcore research. *Kitchen Venom* didn't need it; it's so autobiographical. If I hadn't known so much about parliamentary procedures, there'd have been things I'd have had to check. But it was my job. The only thing I remember consciously researching was a cabinet meeting, something I didn't know anything about. I remember finding out only very late in the day that the cabinet assembles beforehand in an anteroom, not the cabinet room. No doubt there are blunders there.

Pleasured I did research, but not hugely. I made sure I got a few things right. Then I started coming up with odd little facts. I vaguely remembered that the Wall came down on the anniversary of the first Kristallnacht. The research brought that back to my attention. The only blunder Berliners pointed out is that no bar in East Berlin would ever have had matchboxes with its name on them. I can live with that.

I used to be very much against researching novels. I always thought it rather deadening. It does bring dangers. You tend to write in order to get things in. That can be fun. For instance, I like Lawrence Norfolk's books very much. I like the fact that he puts absolutely everything he ever finds out in his research into his books. The results are hilarious—huge, wandering ragbags of odd historical facts. But only a particular sort of writer can do that. I like books which know all about the romance of scholarship. I know about that, but my books don't.

The other great danger—which I'm paranoid about, because I think there's a blot upon *Kitchen Venom* in this respect—is that you make your characters know what's going to happen in the future. Historians always talk as though people must have known at the time that something was going to happen. Take *Pleasured*. I remember 1989. Days before the Berlin Wall came down, everyone was saying it would never happen. The very idea only got on the agenda three or four weeks beforehand. In the summer, all these Hungarians were going shopping in Vienna; Czechs were going to the German embassy in Prague. But people still didn't draw this particular conclusion.

So hindsight is always the great temptation. Few historical novelists resist it. One who does is Penelope Fitzgerald, whose books are wonderful. She could never make her characters say, as Dickens does in *A Tale of Two Cities*: "But out in the forests, trees are growing which will make up the planks of the guillotine."

As time goes on, you have to do a bit of research or you'd end up writing the same novel over and over. It's surprising, in fact, how much I've started thinking of myself with *Pleasured* as a historical novelist. As a *jeu d'esprit*, when *Kitchen Venom* came out I said it was a historical novel—a paradoxical thing to say about something set five years in the past. But *Pleasured* feels very much like a straight historical novel. The Afghan book's going to be a proper historical novel too.

RC Friedrich prominently displays free will in *Pleasured*. When you speak of other novelists' failings here, it sounds as if what you're actually talking about is free will—one of the essentials for the novel.

PH That's very true. People living through great historic moments have no insight that people who aren't living through them don't have. When Mrs. Thatcher fell or when the Wall came down, it was because a certain group of people—people in the right place at the right time—made a decision that this was going to happen. When the Wall came down, you could probably put it down to the collective decision of no more than thirty to forty people—perhaps not so many. The boy in charge of the crossing at the Brandenburg Gate on November 9th, 1989, had absolutely no instructions. All he knew was what the whole of East Germany knew—that a minister had given a press conference and said: "Crossings may be applied for without precondition." The boy at the Wall made the decision to say: "Show your passports and you can go through." Then it was a fait accompli.

So it's always a few people. And they aren't at the mercy of great historical forces. I was arguing precisely against that whole notion in *Pleasured*. At the end, Mario—who has thought all his life in Marxist terms of inexorable, irresistible historical forces—is presented with something he can only interpret as a great historical movement. Yet he can't accept it. The logic of Marxism both insists that's what the fall of the Wall is, and also that this sort of thing can't possibly happen.

RC A historian might argue that, though you naturally have the fiction writer's inclination to focus on individuals, the story *Pleasured* narrates has its origins outside Germany—in the Soviet Union and its satellite states. In part the narrative starts from Gorbachev.

PH Yes. But I don't think you're arguing against what I'm saying. It's still a succession of individual decisions. If the Russians hadn't put Gorbachev there in 1986, who would they have put in? It was an individual decision. The force of Gorbachev's personality too made him see, finally, that the future of the Eastern bloc was more important than his personal survival. He took that decision in a tragic and extraordinary way. But these aren't great historical forces. The way Marxists talk, or the way old-fashioned Whig historians used to talk when they discussed, say, the causes of the French Revolution—before you knew it, they were talking about employment rates in sixteenth-century Estonia. I don't say such things aren't contributory. But personal free will is always at the end of it.

Maybe I just believe this because I'm a novelist. One couldn't write a novel in any other terms. Well, one could write about how employment rates in sixteenth-century Estonia led to—whatever. But it wouldn't be readable.

RC   The rise of Hitler is a celebrated example of what we are discussing.

PH   The thing about that certainly is that it always comes back to the individual responses of those who supported him. Everybody who voted for Hitler made a moral decision. That's why you don't let the Germans off the hook. That's why we shouldn't. Those people voted for Hitler. They kept him in power. They carried on supporting him. They weren't at the mercy of great historical forces they couldn't do anything about. Sure, they were in a miserable state. They saw how things had gone wrong with Germany. They thought Hitler was the one to put it right. But it was their moral decision.

RC   You don't spell it out in *Kitchen Venom*, but one could describe the exigencies concerning the downfall of Mrs. Thatcher in the same way.

PH   Yes. *Kitchen Venom* didn't turn out the book I meant it to be. *Pleasured* is much more the sort of book I meant to write when working on *Kitchen Venom*. The book I had in mind had layers of personal drama happening in bedrooms and sitting rooms in west London, while this equally personal drama unfolded in the House of Commons—the downfall of Thatcher. It looked to the outside world like a great public issue. Actually, it was just a matter of people sulking and having a go at each other out of pique.

Then I wanted a third layer, which is sort of there but partly got squeezed out: the implications of all this. I'd very much wanted to write a book about the state of the debate about Europe with *Kitchen Venom*. When I started writing, I thought the whole Thatcher downfall had got hold of the European debate and knotted it into the tiny period of a few days. The more I thought about it, the more I couldn't quite see what the implications of the sacking of Mrs. Thatcher before the big debate over Europe were. I was trying to say two incompatible things—one, that sacking Mrs. Thatcher had been a great issue of principle; the other, that it had been a personal matter. Having two incompatible arguments in a book isn't necessarily a problem. *Pleasured* is full of absolutely contradictory things. But with *Kitchen Venom* I wasn't ready to incorporate the great European debate.

Whenever I start writing a novel, a weird demon takes over. My books end up saying the opposite of what I myself think. Take the whole, postwar European project—the European Community. It's an absolute disgrace and ought all to be shut down. We ought to close our borders and never have anything to do with each other again, except buying each other's books and listening to each other's music. I'm a European by cultural instinct. But I'm not like one of these awful people running the Community. Still, my books seem to be arguing terribly in favor of the brotherhood of nations. I don't know what they're like! It's one of those strange things that come over one.

The so-called themes of a book are only useful pegs to hang other things on. Some themes one finds intrinsically interesting. I know I could write a book that talked and talked about money, for instance, or about music. Other things, even if I'm interested in them, I couldn't write about: the visual arts, say. They're not quite right for a novel. Some themes come into your head and are useful to hang a whole swathe of rhetoric upon—like Europe. They offer an opportunity to say a variety of other things you've always wanted to say.

Ultimately, I think of novels as closed linguistic worlds. The reason people write them is to create a closed linguistic world, with the cunning illusion that it's actually the real world.

RC   So you want to strip us of the illusion that the theme of a novel is all-determining in the writing of it?

PH   That's exactly how to put it. It's present; it's substantial. But it's not determining.

RC   Concerning shifts in narrative, on rereading *Kitchen Venom* I was astonished at the bravura playing with the narrative voice. You obviously had a lot of fun with that—with daring to use both "I" and "she" for the Mrs. Thatcher figure, and then pushing the two together.

PH   That was the tiny nut that book started from. There's always a strange kernel from which things start. Most startling was with the libretto I wrote for Thomas Adès's opera *Powder Her Face*. The starting point was the idea of having an aria for the soprano in which she seduced a man and then gave him a blow job. It sounded ridiculous, but the more I thought about it, the more it resonated with other ideas—with the idea of the historic silencing of women's voices, for instance.

With *Kitchen Venom*, the starting point was very much the idea of having a novel narrated by Mrs. Thatcher herself. I remember one very defining moment near the end of her administration. She used to get these strange bees in her bonnet. At one point the obsession was with litter. So there was a walkabout photo-opportunity in St. James's Park. Charles Powell, her private secretary, or some underling was deputed to walk in front of her, scattering litter—like bread in front of a duck. She dashed about, stabbing away at it. I was mesmerized. It was as if there was nothing too trivial for Mrs. Thatcher to take an interest in. In the whole United Kingdom, there was no doubt that at some point "Mrs. T." was watching over you in a benevolent, interested spirit. I used to have a little card in my wallet that said: "In the event of my being involved in a major accident, I in no way wish to be visited in hospital by Mrs. T."!

Then I made a ridiculous connection between this idea and the old-fashioned omniscient narrator. It was a kind of complicated joke.

RC   You sustained this split first-person/third-person narration until the very end.

PH   Yes. She renounces the omniscient voice.

Other Lulus was a ridiculous technical exercise in a different way. I wanted to see how far I could get with just one narrative voice. It was hilarious when the reviews came out. They said: "This is amazing. He's managed to put on this extraordinary voice." All my friends said: "It sounds just like Philip leading forth after dinner."

RC Was the use of the first person constricting with *Other Lulus*?

PH No. But it becomes more constricting. Henry James thought it very constricting. Actually, using the first-person voice is quite a good way to begin as a novelist. One knows how to do it. I've had to wean myself off it. I kept thinking of having a first-person narrator for *Pleasured*. It was going to be Mario. But in one way he knew too much; in another, not enough. It didn't work.

RC *Kitchen Venom* and *Pleasured* share the third-person narrative mode. In *Pleasured*, though, there are moments when you destabilize or undermine this—sometimes brutally, sometimes subtly. I don't mean simply with free indirect discourse. There are odd moments where the narration takes on a specific narrator's mantle. It has a very rhetorical, assertive, subjective feeling, and then moves back out of it. Did this happen instinctively?

PH No. And on the whole it's quite a bad tendency. There's a particular temptation I have as a novelist which I always regret afterwards—putting in a small, bravura chapter of a strangely formal nature. People always enjoy them. But I want to fight against them.

RC It's a modernist itch.

PH It is—which is odd. I don't think of myself as a modernist writer. It's one of those urges one feels are bad. But one also wants occasionally to let them win the argument. I'm thinking of the chapter in *Kitchen Venom* where they all get dressed. I argued with myself a lot about that. Actually, it was quite a good thing to do at that point in the book. Some things in *Other Lulus* I'd definitely take out. With *Pleasured*, there's a chapter at the end of the first section called "Things Worth Seeing," where Martin's niece comes to stay. I was terribly tempted there to give her school project in full, to give a nine-year-old's history of Germany. I could see it was the sort of temptation I ought to fight, though—and I fought against it and won.

RC   Did you write it?

PH   Yes—about twenty pages. Fortunately nobody saw it.

The formal matters one wants to work with concern things like narrative voice. Point of view is terribly interesting too. It's surprising the number of writers who don't grasp it. And I'm absolutely obsessed with pace—pace and timing: how you make an incredible number of things happen; how you can have people chasing round and round until the reader's head explodes. To achieve that and an underlying kind of stasis simultaneously—I love playing with that sort of thing. That's why I like the clothes chapter of *Kitchen Venom*. It's a sort of energetic fermata over the action. And it tells you quite a lot about what's going on.

RC   It makes me think of Woolf's *To the Lighthouse*, with the middle section in brackets.

PH   Never heard of it. Is it any good? [*Laughs*] She's shit, isn't she, Virginia Woolf? Can't write at all. She's been responsible for putting more people off fiction than anybody. Whenever people ask a schoolmaster what the great English novel is, they're always told: "*The Waves*." My God! What's that about?

RC   We're back to modernism.

PH   I'm not a modernist, but I respond to aspects of it. I have a slightly dodgy tactic in this regard which you're very free to argue with. If I ever start to love an author, I always start to think he isn't modernist. I don't think Proust's modernist, for example, though I can see why people say he is. Nor Henry Green. He was just drunk. People always talk about Green's "clipped modernist sentences." Actually, they're the sentences of the English upper class.

There has to be an iron center of old-fashioned nineteenth-century realism running through anything that's any good. Once you get rid of that, you've thrown away the book. For the life of me, I can't see realism as just another literary mode. I know that's unfashionable.

RC   Insofar as we should have models of realism to learn from, who do you mean?

PH   Everyone has their own models. The novelists that are important to me are quite odd ones for anyone writing within a gay sensibility. Joseph Conrad; Thomas Mann: they're not gay role models. Proust used to be important. I'm between readings of Proust. I loved him ten years ago and will probably love him again in ten years' time.

RC   You prefaced an edition of Ivy Compton-Burnett's novels.

PH   Yes. I'm on a pretty sticky wicket, claiming her as a realist novelist. I have a strange fascination with Compton-Burnett's work. I respond to it in a complex way. When people aren't keen on her, I feel they're watching their own reactions as much as reading her books. There's an outrageous silliness to them—what I'd think of as a very English quality: not caring what anybody thinks. There's something extraordinary too about a novelist who goes through all the motions of plot and hardly gives you anything else. That's all her novels are—sheer plot.

I'm fascinated by fictional universes like hers—ones which are completely linguistic. There's no pretence that there's anything else in the world other than the words these people produce. Every so often there's a description of what someone looks like. Then she goes on.

I wouldn't want to read only her for the rest of my life. Sometimes the novels seem like the bones from which one might make a vicious soup. But everyone could learn something from her, even if in the end her novels aren't quite great. They're like a brilliant master-class in how to handle blocks of material.

Compton-Burnett is also the absolute queen of pace. She has a brilliant sense of when to grind on the reader's nerves for fifteen pages with an element of plot that's not going anywhere. Learning when to bore the reader is important for novelists to learn.

Boredom for me is a really interesting possibility. I associate it with embarrassment. The one thing you know about both things is that they're absolutely sincere responses, and so quite powerful ones. But boredom's useful for any work of art that exists in time, that uses up a bit of one's life. I first started thinking about this as a teenager. I couldn't work out why I liked Wagner so much. A lot of the time I'd be sitting there thinking: "If this goes on one minute more, I think I might scream." The wrong response is to think you're waiting for the highlights. As you know, if you ever hear a concert which is just the exciting bits, they're nowhere near as powerful as they are in context.

Wagner wears you down with boredom. Then, when everything escalates, you're putty in his hands. A lot of the novels I like best do something similar—Pynchon's *Gravity's Rainbow*; Mann's *The Magic Mountain*. They wear you down until you're almost crying with tears of boredom. Then, say, Joachim's ghost turns up at the séance, and you're still crying. I liked it when reviewers said the first chapter of *Pleasured* was extremely boring, and that there were bits of *Powder Her Face* that were almost embarrassing. It seemed a bit naïve of them to think I hadn't meant that. I wouldn't want to write anything that was boring from beginning to end. But it's a useful tool in the armory when you're planning a real assault on a reader's emotions.

Weirdly, I actually like boring things for their own sake now. My favorite films are all very boring ones. I remember once going to watch Jacques Rivette's *Céline and Julie Go Boating*, a wonderfully dull and repetitive film. Suddenly someone shouted: "Christ, not again." I liked that. I thought it was high praise, really—that a film could get under your skin to the degree that you'd shout at it.

RC To return to Compton-Burnett, there are moments in your prose that reminded me of her pristineness or tautness.

PH They're probably homages as much as anything.

RC I was thinking of the beautifully concise murder of Giacomo in *Kitchen Venom*.

PH That's not stolen from anything exactly. But I know who I was thinking of there: Leonardo Sciascia, the best Italian author in my opinion. He has a wonderful trick of winding up a short story with a sentence that seems to open up a whole universe. That's fun to do. It's one of the things in that novel that I kept wondering whether it was right to do, that sentence. In the end I gave way to temptation. I was so cheerful the day I killed Giacomo.

RC Does the tautness emerge through revision, or is it the consequence of slow writing?

PH Neither. There's a process of revision, but probably not the way you're imagining. People always think I write slowly, but I don't. Or that I've cut a lot out, which isn't true either.

I'll explain my working method. Basically, I write something—ten or twenty pages—and then put it in a drawer and forget about it for between three and six months. When I go back to it, I go away somewhere for four weeks—somewhere I'm not going to be disturbed, and where people are going to cook for me. It's very important not to be worried about domestic chores and so on. I live on room service and do nothing but write. I come back, and then leave whatever I've got for another six months. All the time the thing's going 'round in my head constantly. Then I go back to it again and do whatever else needs to be done for a first draft. I'll leave that a bit longer, and then work right through the manuscript. This last process is much less about crossing things out than about moving great blocks of material around.

At this stage I always have to reduce the number of characters. I'll turn two characters into one, or three into two. I'll always have to add things. It looks like Compton-Burnett: just the bones. You have to send your characters for a walk down the street. You have to put in descriptions of the weather. You pump air in. The novels still might look terribly laconic at the end. But I'm getting much less so. The direction I want to go in is to become a very relaxed writer. I'm always shocked when people say my novels are very cold. I think: "My God—what could I possibly do to make them less cold?" If there was any more fucking and murder and illicit passion in them, there wouldn't be much room for anything else. I suppose they mean they're quite formal—that if they express passion, they do so grammatically. And the people in them aren't always very open. People seem to confuse the demeanor of characters with the nature of the book. The characters in *Kitchen Venom* aren't upfront with their feelings, but the novel itself could hardly be franker.

The other thing I wonder—which I hesitate to bring up, because it sounds like boasting—is whether readers are accustomed to particular formulaic ways of writing. When a writer does something unfamiliar or novel, initially it seems remote and chilly. I never set out to be original. I only ever wanted to write a novel which would be exactly the same in all respects as the novel Conrad would have written if he'd lived to 150 and got more interested in hot gay sex. Fortunately, no one judges novels against their perpetrator's intentions, as none of mine quite manage to be that. Instead they seem endowed with a literary virtue I don't believe in: originality. That's something people only started to like in the nineteenth century. No one should set out wanting to be original. But the three words I seem to be saddled with in reviews are "eccentric," "elegant," and "original." I hate to say it, but if I was original in the way I wrote about emotions, I suppose at first it would seem unfamiliar and perhaps cold. You can only hope you've done something good, and that readers will get used to it.

RC It seems an uncommon working method—adding rather than throwing away, finally.

PH But you mustn't ever talk of a right or wrong way of writing a novel! You mustn't even start thinking which working methods people have in common, or which are unusual. That way lies madness for a writer.

RC Is there anything that distinguishes a novel idea from a short-story idea?

PH Yes, though you don't know it until afterwards. I thought *Pleasured* was a short story until I was sixty pages in. I told myself: "This is opening up in a horrible way." I didn't want to write a novel at that point. I was convinced the thing I wanted to do was to write a really good book of short stories, and, in five years, come back to novels.

Ideas and feelings have their own scale. You can play with it to a certain extent. You get quite striking effects by writing something that naturally feels quite big in only twenty pages. But on the whole things are as long as they are. I think I write at roughly the right length. Some things I've written are too short, but not many are too long. Maybe *Pleasured* is a bit short. The sentences seem bigger than the book.

Everything comes when it comes, finally. I have periods when I can write short stories and periods when I'm writing short stories which are rubbish, so I throw them away. I'd like to do nothing but write short stories for five years, but publishers won't let you do that.

RC   Do you write stories to commission?

PH   No. The trick is to have something in your bottom drawer. I've never managed to write a short story to order. I'm a slow worker on stories. With one story—"The Geographer"—I realized I'd been working on it for years. I started off typing it, and then left it. Next I added other bits on pieces of paper. That's how I always work. Finally I finished the bloody thing, sent it off, and got it accepted by someone. And it was only sixteen pages! Why one does it I don't know. You could write a novel in the same time. But stories are good to do. They improve your technique. They make you think. They exploit a part of you which you can't access in a novel. If you wrote a whole novel in the style of a well-put-together short story, it would be unbearable—too planned; too conscious; too jointed. That last 20 percent of the unplanned lunacy you always have to leave in a novel—the part where you don't really think about whether what you're doing looks right. You can't do that with a story.

RC   Do you discriminate between writing on a computer and writing longhand?

PH   Yes. Things have a different quality according to what you write them on. *Other Lulus* I wrote on a word processor from beginning to end.

Kitchen Venom I wrote partly at the office, partly at home. So with that I was writing odd things on a typewriter. Then I started to play with writing other things for it by hand, which turned out to be quite useful. *Pleasured* I wrote from beginning to end with a pen on a piece of paper. I thought: "My God—suddenly I'm a proper writer!" Prose written by hand is more intricate.

RC   Two of your first three novels—*Other Lulus* and *Pleasured*—pretend to have been written in German, which is unusual.

PH   Yes. I don't know why I did that. *Other Lulus* isn't really about Germany. It's set in a German-speaking country where nothing bad ever happened. *Pleasured* is about Germany. It has a German inflection from time to time, and a taste for those compound nouns German likes so much— "muscle-memory" or "moon-lovely." It was quite unconscious, though, and was probably because I was living in Germany when I was writing it and wasn't speaking English much from day to day.

I remember both times feeling it was something I absolutely mustn't think about. After all, when Germans talk, they don't think: "I'm speaking German." They open their mouths and out comes the Muttersprache.[1]

RC   You use slippages of language in your plots too.

PH   I like writing foreigners. I'm interested by the way they speak English. I love International English—you know, when you listen to a conversation between a Dutchman and an Italian and it's in English, but not exactly English English: "I maybe should now go to start work." Some of my favorite novels are written by foreigners about England. I love Michel Butor's novel about Manchester—which he calls Bleston: *L'emploi du temps* (*Passing Time*). Butor gets things wrong, but that's an important part of the novel's appeal. Another is the Spanish novelist Javier Marias's book about Oxford, *All Souls*.

---

1. "Edmund White said in a review of *Pleasured* that he thought it was weird that you forgot the characters were talking in German, which I thought was a bit bonkers. I suppose he was expecting the usual thing—to have a conversation in English between two characters, and at the end, one will suddenly say: 'Auf Wiedersehen' " (Philip Hensher, March 2002).

In my case, both times I wanted to write a book that would seem alienating, or rather alienated from its location, to anyone who read it. If a German read it, he'd be alienated by it just as an English person would be.

In the end, you don't really care what your contemporaries think. If you worried what people thought, you wouldn't become a novelist in the first place. There's a particular sort of not-very-good novelist who does second guess what reviewers are going to think. It's not the recipe for writing a good book.

Some American literature now appears so market-driven. You can tell some things were written more or less to commission. Nothing's coming out of the left field completely, apart from grand old men like Pynchon. There's a particular kind of novelist you can tell isn't saying what he wants because of what his friends will think. I've never been one of those. Maybe I should be. But I'm always writing things that I know are going to make my parents hang their heads in shame. Actually, my mother did make me take one sentence about a dildo out of *Kitchen Venom*.

RC   At what stage did you let her read it?

PH   In manuscript. It's the only thing I've ever changed in that way.

RC   Have your parents always read your novels?

PH   Yes. They're very interested. They're the sort of people who'd be proud of me if I were a lavatory cleaner, so they certainly take an interest. It must be a bit odd—I mean, my novels are much more open than I am.

RC   Are there friends you might consult?

PH   Not on the whole. Friends will read a book when it goes into proof. That's not because I wouldn't like them to read it sooner. Apart from the fact that I wouldn't be very likely to pay attention to any criticism, I have a sense of what an incredible imposition it is to ask anybody to read a manuscript. I wouldn't readily do it. I don't know why reading manuscripts of typed A4 is such hard work, but it is. I've done it a few times. Every time I've found it difficult to come to a view as to the quality of the thing. Once it's bound up, you do have a sense of how good something is.

RC   It's something to do with typesetting.

PH   That's right. Typefaces can influence your reading. I'm obsessive about typefaces. I've always got a clear sense of the right typeface for a particular novel. The *Kitchen Venom* typeface was wrong. It gave everybody a headache. For *Pleasured*, it looks like a children's book.

RC   I noticed in *Kitchen Venom* that you appeared to be rendering "Trafalgar square" with a small "s" deliberately.

PH   That was a tiny joke to tease the clerks in the House of Commons. It's Hansard style. Whenever they refer to a street or square, they use the lower case in Hansard. It's consistent through the book.

RC   Now to a rather formidable question: why do people become novelists? You proposed one answer through the hapless Henry in *Kitchen Venom*. He panics about posterity—about his children dying and so on. This seems as near as he gets to a motive for writing the book, which he doesn't finally finish anyway. Gore Vidal once referred to the hopelessly antiquated, nineteenth-century idea of writing for posterity. Is that what you were suggesting when you said that one doesn't write for one's peers?

PH   Partly. You can't write for posterity, of course, because you don't know what people's interests will be. But I try not to write anything which will be meaningless in fifty years' time—pop-tarts and Prada bags and J-cloths. You hope you've done something which will last. But it pretty well has to please your contemporaries first. A few writers were unknown in their lifetimes—Emily Dickinson, Gerard Manley Hopkins—but most of the canon is made up of writers who were great successes in their day: Dickens, Shakespeare, Byron. Of course, most writers who are successful in their lifetimes are quickly forgotten afterwards. But Dickens is more typical than Hopkins.

My convictions concerning this have waned a bit. When writing *Kitchen Venom* and *Powder Her Face*, I had a conviction that the primary motive for a great deal of human behavior was the impulse to leave something behind. Alongside the sex instinct and the death drive in Freud, there should be a child instinct. I think it doesn't really matter whether you have children, or paint a huge portrait, or commission a great big tombstone over your head, or write.

RC   It sounds rather like Richard Dawkins's "selfish gene."

PH   Well, that's quite convincing. It's certainly true that homosexuals often have drives towards creativity which could be explained quite naïvely through the whole issue of childlessness. I think people are fulfilled by the existence of children in a way which is similar to the attempts by artists to find fulfillment by creating things.

My thoughts are a bit broader now on this. I'd say there's some kind of psychic wound in artists which is much more general than that rather pat initial explanation. In some ways it's beyond either examination or cure. And even if you could cure it, you probably wouldn't want to.

RC   As an artist, presumably, you wouldn't.

PH   As an artist, yes. Maybe the human being would.

RC   Does one read Freud as an artist, or as a human being?

PH   I read Freud in a complicated way. I'm fascinated by what he got wrong. He was wrong pretty well all the way through. But as a narrative and as a world view, and in terms of understanding why people often do what they say they least want, I think Freud's works are absolutely masterful. Incidentally, Kazuo Ishiguro's last novel, *The Unconsoled*, really found out something about the motivations of artists—that they can't be consoled.

RC   Do you use the term "artist" readily to include writers, artists, and composers?

PH Well, they have some things in common. Psychologically, something unites creative figures. But they have such different methods of composition that in the end they don't have a great deal to talk to each other about.

RC The composer-writer is a rare figure: Anthony Burgess; Paul Bowles; Lord Berners.

PH That's the category I'd put myself in. When I was a boy I wrote music a great deal. I got as far as having my orchestral music played. I still understand how composers work in a way that's probably quite unusual. I think of my books in terms which suggest they were musically constructed—in terms of harmonic movement, the development of sections, and so on. These probably aren't useful for critics or readers to explore.

I gave up writing music when I was eighteen or nineteen. It wasn't very good. I had a revelation—that if I carried on with it, I'd be all right. I wouldn't starve. But I could see the very end of what I'd ever be able to do. That was very different from writing. I think writing music might be therapeutic, though—rather like doing crossword puzzles, and in a way that writing poetry wouldn't be—for me, anyway. I might go back to it at some point.

RC How did this sense of how composers work inform your opera collaboration with Adès?

PH The realization I came to once I'd written *Other Lulus* was that you need a sense of form in any work of art. Composers have it easy. Form in music is so codified that any piece always has some kind of discussion with the idea of sonata form, fugue, or whatever. Novelistic form is much more nebulous and improvisatory.

I felt I could wing it once, but that it would be better to start thinking about form systematically. The libretto was a really good exercise. I consciously constructed scenes like classical musical forms. The first scene is the double exposition of a concerto, for instance. There was a personal reason for this, too. I was going through quite a messy "divorce," and probably wanted to feel in control when I started to write. Anyway, those musical forms spilled over into *Kitchen Venom*. I don't want anyone to look for them, but they're there, and in a more diffused, relaxed way in *Pleasured* too. I learnt a lot from the way I wrote the libretto.

There's a connection between composing and novel-writing which is literal and real to me, in a way that the connection between an artist and a novelist would always only be metaphorical. When you talk about the rhythms of prose and of music, it suggests a literal connection, whereas the "color" of prose is a metaphorical idea. Many people do think there's a connection between art and prose. But I consider the novel as a line moving through time, not as static. The great effects of all the classic novels involve playing with questions of timing and of delay; with making the reader wait for a resolution; with recapitulation. Proust's use of recapitulation was amazing. When he describes the same party he had fifteen hundred pages earlier, it's beautiful.

RC   You worked as a clerk in the House of Commons while writing *Kitchen Venom*. How would you compare balancing the demands of that job and writing with your current "beast at the door," journalism? Many writers have found it difficult to juggle writing journalism and fiction.

PH   You're absolutely right to suggest it was easier to write when I worked in the House of Commons. One had the summer recesses—three months when you weren't disturbed. I was doing bits of journalism at the same time too. But certainly it's more difficult now. The solution is that I get away from my regular commitments when I need to. I can juggle it so that I get as much as four weeks off. It would be difficult to get much more. But you do need time off. You can't write journalism on Monday and Tuesday and fiction the rest of the week. You need long stretches—weeks and weeks—for fiction.

RC   Is there anything in journalism which helps in writing fiction?

PH   It teaches you not to hang about—a useful lesson, at least in some respects. In others it could be disastrous. Novels ought to have an element of hanging about pointlessly. Journalism teaches you to keep your ears open too. For the opinion column in the *Independent* I have to have some sense of what's going on around me, of ideas in the air. That gets you out to talk to people.

And it's money. You just need so much money in London.

RC   You've written in the past about the "homosexual aesthetic"—not a notion everybody would agree exists. Do you still believe in it?

PH   I stick by it. I can see why people have problems with it. I share those doubts. But one's objections lie in the idea that it's something confining. I think of it more as a great big jumble sale to which we all bring something new. There are still some things one can recognize in a homosexual aesthetic which aren't necessarily shared by everybody but nevertheless constitute part of a whole which is bigger than all of us.

RC   You wrote about it originally in relation to dealing with the idea of an inner sickness.

PH   Physical sickness, yes. I was saying that, for obvious reasons, there are themes that loom larger in homosexual writing than in straight writing, or that strike us as appropriate, for whatever reason. I don't say it's good that homosexuality has always been associated by various writers with physical sickness. And to me there's a clear line drawn between the two in Mann's *Death in Venice.* Equally, just as many writers have played against it.

There are other common queer themes. Secrecy's a great one, for obvious reasons. That cuts into works which are part of the homosexual aesthetic but not necessarily by homosexual writers. The great homosexual fiction is Conrad's "The Secret Sharer." Why isn't every schoolchild made to bow down before that story? It's so fantastic.

Then there are things you'd expect to be part of a homosexual canon which don't surface. It's surprising how seldom sex comes up, if one thinks about it. The amount of sex in Ronald Firbank is minimal. The camp aesthetic and the erotic are quite diametrically opposed. You couldn't have a buggery scene in the middle of his *Prancing Nigger.*

In my short stories, I've written some things about sex which were designed to insult people—to shame them with their own embarrassment.

That's why we put a blow job in the opera. I wanted to say to people: "What's the big deal?" I wish I could write more about sex generally. With *Pleasured*, I began with the firm conviction that I was going to have a heterosexual sex scene. That diminished as it went on. Instead the whole thing was going to revolve around this huge sexy game. Finally that got reduced to a single sentence with a rude word in it—"snatch." Then they said: "You can't use that word. It's offensive." So it had to go.

It's quite hard to find ways of writing about sex because it exists in a sort of pre- or post-linguistic state. There's no limit to the ways you can treat it in other arts. Last week I was looking at some Matisse drawings. I thought: "My God—the absolute luck of being able to do something as erotic as that. One can't do anything obscene in literature." There's that urge to do something shocking. But, actually, it's all been done.

RC Conrad's "The Secret Sharer": not such a familiar work, perhaps. Could you elaborate on its appeal—and on how explicit it is?

PH It's fantastically smutty. A young captain on his first voyage one night comes across a naked swimmer, who is pretty well his double. He's escaping after having killed someone. There's no one else about. The captain conceals him in his cabin, and at the end he swims off. Nothing happens, but the whole thing's wonderfully overheated—faces pressed against each other in the tropical night. I don't think Conrad saw how much it stinks of sex. But if you try and read it as an adventure story, it doesn't work. I mean, why would he conceal the swimmer in the first place? The great thing about it is that Conrad doesn't actually say anything about sex from beginning to end. The reader does all the work. It's terribly powerful.

RC I'm interested that you've been using the term "homosexual" frequently, and "queer" too. What do these terms signify, as compared with "gay"?

PH "Homosexual" is a nineteenth-century medical term; "gay" and "queer" are political ones of different vintages. One wouldn't say "the homosexual community." I don't much care for any of them, though of course you use them. I have a slightly prissy sense that they're all to do with identity, and, though I like being a poof, it's not the overriding fact of my existence. It gets you out of the house. It gives you an interest. You get to meet all sorts of people you wouldn't otherwise—burglars, dukes, whatever. But it's boring when you're never allowed to write about Afghanistan, but always "Gay Philip Hensher Gaily Discusses What Afghanistan Means to a Gay Like Him." I think identity labels like *gay*, *queer*, and *homosexual* are part of the problem. Lesbians are lucky. Theirs is at least partly cultural in origin, rather than stinking of the mental hospital or playground. I suppose the root of my feeling is the idea that all this—girl-boy sex, boy-boy sex, boy-sheep sex—is just acts, not who you are. I'm not saying every sexual act is a conscious choice; just that there are other things about you which are more interesting and maybe more fundamental.

Personally, I find being English a more fundamental component of my identity than being gay. I could imagine someone like me who wasn't in London carrying out different sexual acts and not developing the same sexual identity. But in no circumstances could I imagine altering my Englishness. It would be like trying to turn yourself into a dog. So I resist those identity labels.[2]

RC   There's no sense of a ghettoized gay life in your work. Explicitly, familial relationships—filial ones in particular—feature prominently. And key questions of loyalty and commitment are addressed through parent-child relationships.

PH   Yes. I think we'd all be much better off if we got on with our families. I love mine very much.

One journalist told me: "You obviously have a really dysfunctional relationship with your parents," which was a bit shocking because I always thought that I had a very sunny relationship with them. Certainly it's fraught—or rather, freighted. The relationship one has with one's father

---

2. "That was one of the appealing things about writing *The Mulberry Empire*, set in the 1830s: homosexuals didn't exist. It was just acts. Maybe 'sodomite' would be a good label: 'I'm not married—I'm a sodomite.' I might try that" (Philip Hensher, March 2002).

is always interesting. The odd thing is that, though I wouldn't say I ever had a difficult relationship with him, I feel very close to him now I've reached the age where I can remember what he was like at my age. My mother and I have always got on very well. But there's an edge to it, which comes from the fact that if you have a gay son, at some point you're going to have to discuss that. There's a bit of a double whammy here, because artists are monsters, and novelists are the worst monsters. Imagine: "Congratulations, Mrs. Hensher: you've got a fine, healthy, novelist." It can't be easy.

I think these family relationships are fundamental to all human relations. They're the one kind of relationship one can't do without—even now we don't all live in nuclear families. We still all mentally live in a family. Try writing a novel where none of the characters is related to each other and no one ever thinks about his or her family. You could just about do it. But it would be very disorientating. You only have to listen to how often people refer to their mums, brothers, and sisters in casual conversation to see how fundamental these things are.

RC   Now a leap. Do you have any sense of your readership in mind with any of your writing?

PH   No. Once or twice I've said to the *Spectator* when they have suggested a book for review: "Actually, do you know what I think about this subject?" They'll say: "Er, yes. We should probably give it to someone else."

Even with the libretto, I shut out the idea of the audience. When *Powder Her Face* opened and an audience responded by being shocked, I was surprised. I never think about who will read something, only about the sort of sentence I'd like to read.

One mustn't think about such things when writing. It would be catastrophic. You'd think: "What's my mother or boyfriend going to think about this?" The thing is to have no shame. The only time you have no shame at all is when you're on your own and in bed, really.

That's why I can't write a word if there's anybody else in the flat. I've got to have a locked door. The other weird thing is that when I'm writing fiction, I always turn the desk around so I can see the entrances to the room. Nobody could possibly sneak up and lean over my shoulder. That's an aspect of the whole shamelessness idea. You mustn't be embarrassed by what you're writing. You must put yourself in a position where you can imagine you're unembarrassable. Remember that when *Kitchen Venom* came out, I was sacked. Once you've been through that, nothing can embarrass you again.

RC   You wrote a doctorate on the eighteenth century. Why did the period appeal especially?

PH   I did a whole paper at university on Alexander Pope. If you go through Pope inch by inch—if you read nothing else for eight weeks, as I did—you start to see how literature's written. He's one of the three or four greats. I can't tell you how sexy Pope is.

RC   The doctorate was on painting, however, wasn't it? What drew you to that context particularly, and have you ever been able or keen to place what you studied then into another form?

PH   It ended up being about painting because you could only tell half the story through literature. Basically it was about the moment around 1760 or so when satire, which had been a formal classical genre, started becoming a sort of mood you could drop into or out of at will. Sterne went from sentiment to satire in about three sentences. The style of the time wasn't that concerned with originality. It liked to demonstrate its credentials by allusion, so you can identify all this quite clearly and see how incompatible some of the sources were.

The painting took all this a lot further. It mixed low and high styles up fairly indiscriminately. The interesting thing is that it all happens fairly democratically. The styles are next to each other for a change of mood, rather than to influence each other. It's quite different from the mock-heroic.

It's stuck with me to the extent that people often say that my novels don't stick to a particular genre, which is right. I have quite an austere view of genre. It's basically that the real ones were set out in Ancient Greece—romance, tragedy, lyric, and so on—and that the realist novel came so late in literary history that we don't know what it is. It's more a medium than a genre—like film. I like it to be able to draw on genres when it wants to, but not be defined or confined by one particular genre.

The thesis is unreadable, though. Apart from being called "Dr. Hensher" by airline stewardesses, the only thing it's contributed to my life is a bizarre party trick of being able to identify the authorship of crap eighteenth-century English paintings at fifty paces. I startle my friends by saying: "Fine John Hamilton Mortimer on the far wall there" in galleries.

★ ★ ★

RC I want to discuss a couple of autobiographical pieces you've written for *Granta*. "Brandy," a piece about losing interest in music, only appeared in 2002 (*Granta 76*). The older piece, "Work," is included in your story collection *The Bedroom of the Mister's Wife*, but seems autobiographical.

PH Yes. Including it wasn't a profound gesture. One doesn't have much opportunity to put something like that within covers. If you don't think you'll ever collect your journalism—as I certainly don't—then that was certainly the place to put it. I did so slightly reluctantly, knowing that people read short stories differently to the way they read things they take to be memoirs. I couldn't see any other way to do it though. I wasn't going to put in a note stating: "This is autobiography."

RC What's wrong with collecting journalism?

PH It seems a bit pompous. There might come a point where I'd want to collect the stuff I've written about Afghanistan over the last couple of years. A couple of those articles proved quite prophetic. One weird one, which I wrote just after they blew up the Buddhist statues at Bamiyan, said: "If we don't start talking to the Taliban soon, this is going to lead to acts of destruction next to which we'll forget about stuff like this."

RC In "Work" there's a comment towards the end about the "dream of the Enlightenment"—"that one could understand the world by seeing it." Your experience of the foreign trip undertaken by the British politicians led you to write that—in fact—one traveled "to fail to understand strangers." That was interesting, given your subsequent decision to write a fiction about Afghanistan, an impenetrable state.

PH   Yes. The reviews all zoomed in on that comment. I started to think it had just slipped out and that I rather regretted it. It seemed that a rather pompous moral had been drawn—one I'd not known how to suppress.

I prefer the stories that don't have a one-line moral at the end—"Forbidden Etudes"; "Dead Languages"; the one I named the book after. "To Feed the Night" made me laugh a lot. That's about an estate agent who turns out to be the devil. It's stolen from a brilliant story by Tolstoy, "How Much Land Does a Man Need?" I thought that was the most famous short story in the world. I read it when I was eight. But no one's noticed. It turns out I'm the only person in the world to have read it. In the Tolstoy, a peasant discovers he can acquire all the land he can walk around in a day. He walks around all this land, but it kills him. It ends: "His servant picked up the spade and dug a grave long enough for Pachom to lie in, and buried him in it. Six foot, from his head to his heels, was all he needed." Mine finishes: "And for him that was space enough."

RC   People will expressly be looking for moral conclusions in *The Mulberry Empire*'s treatment of the nineteenth-century British campaigns in Afghanistan.

PH   Yes. There's one part-chapter of crashing moralizing in chapter twelve. I put it in because I didn't finally think it was absolutely clear what I was saying. Burnes, the English traveler, and Mohan Lal, an Afghan guide, sit down after the emperors have gone and talk about the meaning of empire. Again, the novel has a final sentence which isn't exactly my own.

RC   "[T]he street was as it always was, and it swallowed them; the noisy and the eager, and the arrogant and the lonely, and the wise, frightened and good, all at once, making their usual uproar."

PH   Yes. Compare: "As they passed along in sunshine and shade, the noisy and the eager, the arrogant and the forward and the vain, fretted and chafed, made their usual uproar." That's the last sentence of Dickens's *Little Dorrit*, which I adore. There's another bit reminiscent of Dickens's *Our Mutual Friend*—when Burnes and Bella go down to the river.

RC   What led you to the anachronistic appearance of the jet plane at the end of chapter twenty?

PH   I can't explain that rationally. It's one of the most instinctive things I've done. I could see it coming a long way off—probably from six months before I got to write it. Increasingly I felt the necessity for it, without quite understanding why it had to be there.

RC   Did you know it would lead into the "Anthropological Interlude" which breaks up the narrative?

PH   Not exactly. Rather, the interlude sprang from the jet plane. Then I knew that what I'd wanted to do was break the historical illusion. You can't immediately start putting that illusion back together, so something else had to follow. I'd compare this to the murder of Giacomo in *Kitchen Venom*. That comes at pretty well the same point of the novel, and it does the same trick. It comes completely outside the moral scale you've established up to that point. Similarly, it had to be followed by a sort of cadenza.

RC   I'm interested in the account of colonialism in *The Mulberry Empire*. Your final chapter talks of the "vainglory" of the British Empire. There are ironic references to the English thinking they would "give them civilisation." At more or less the same time, however, you wrote an "Introduction" to John Buchan's *Greenmantle*, in which you touch on Buchan's assumptions of English superiority. He writes: "we are the only race on earth that can produce men that are capable of getting inside the skin of remote peoples." You add: "There is something in that," citing approvingly the "curiosity" of English colonialists.

PH   I said before that my books often end up proposing what isn't exactly my view. I don't think there's a singular, coherent view of imperialism or of the British Empire in *The Mulberry Empire*. The prevailing one—which is one of vainglory—is probably not one I share. I think the Empire was an absolutely brilliant thing for the British to have established—both for themselves and for its subject peoples. There's only one point where my own view comes out violently—where I suddenly had to step out in propria persona and say what I thought. That was where the narrator says, of the invention of photography, that Akhbar is going to start a rebellion to make his people poor again for no reason. That's the paradox of this whole episode. The Afghans would've been much better off in the long term if they'd lost this war. They'd have infrastructure and all sorts of things. But they valued freedom and self-determination higher from the start.

I was very determined to make it absolutely plain that imperialism in my view isn't solely a Western or European phenomenon. People talk as if it were. In fact, in nineteenth-century Afghanistan, the imperialist urge was driving Dost Mohammed as much as it was driving the British. The Mughals were imperialists too. I felt one couldn't issue a blanket condemnation of imperialism per se.

One wouldn't expect to find a particular view proposed in the novel. In the end, it comes down to my powerfully contradictory conclusions, I think.

RC   The more belittling rhetoric of colonialism you give to Burnes. He calls the Afghans "children."

PH   That's an original sentence of Burnes's—from his book *Travels in Bokhara and Cabool*, which I acknowledge in the bibliography. There are only two or three direct quotes. That was him being frightened—seeing something he couldn't understand; pretending he understood it and persuading himself he had. There's a terrible irony when you come across that moment in the first of Burnes's books. He says: "You can see through their stratagems immediately." In the end, he didn't see through them, and they killed him.

RC   What about Stapleton, who never travels, but writes books from research?

PH He's a construction. But there were quite a lot of people around who fit the bill—all those followers of Edward Bulwer Lytton. I have an urge I don't quite understand which first appeared with *Kitchen Venom*. I find myself exorcising the demon of self-doubt by constructing a completely crap version of what I'm trying to do, and then bunging it into the book. I was imagining what bad historical novels about exotic places were like. It's slightly indulgent.

RC You chose Kabul knowing you couldn't go there.

PH Exactly—I followed my own instructions. I stayed at home and failed to understand the people from here. The difference is that I've deliberately failed to understand them. I don't believe it's possible fully to understand a culture that's so removed from us in time and place and which left very few written records. We don't know anything about the rituals at Dost Mohammed's court—apart from what Western observers noticed, and they're famously unreliable. They probably made a lot of it up. So I wrote the Orientalist fantasy I said I would. I thought if I'd tried to give the most scholarly, hard-nosed view of the East, it would end up an Orientalist fantasy anyway.

RC Did you study Persian?

PH No. I've read quite a lot of Persian poetry over the years. But I didn't bother looking at any of it specifically. There's a national Afghan epic, but it's never been translated out of Persian. It seemed like more trouble than it was worth.

I picked up a bit of Persian—enough to have an elementary conversation, but not enough to read it. I've had a couple of conversations with Afghan refugees driving minicabs here. They're always terribly startled.

RC You write of Masson inheriting a new personality when speaking Persian.

PH Yes. I got enough Persian to understand what Masson says of it— that it's the most beautiful, ravishing language on earth. There's little grammatical structure and no gendered inflection. Most of it is done through various vivid idioms and fairly casual chopping and changing. The result is a poetic, improvisatory language. It's not at all like Arabic, which is dense, difficult, and highly structured. Persian is like a conversation with children. It doesn't sound like much else . . . perhaps the language the Orks speak in *Lord of the Rings*.

RC   You spoke before of the importance of Englishness to you. In "Brandy," you wrote of discovering your French ancestry . . .

PH   Yes. That discovery's come so late that it doesn't stand much chance of sinking in. The odd thing is that if you speak more than one foreign language reasonably well, you develop alternative personalities. I have an Italian identity, a German identity, and a French one. If my Persian was better, I'd have a Persian one too. I'm chillier in French—more formal; less mumbling. In German I seem more flirtatious. I think German is quite flirtatious—all that deferring the verb till the end of the sentence. If you're asking somebody to go for a drink, or go to bed with you, or see a film, in German the crucial word wouldn't arrive till the end. I have a strange view of German. I think of it as deeply romantic. My Italian self is irresponsibly childish.

You can see how this could become a kind of escape. Every so often I wonder what it would be like to live in a foreign country and sit down to write in a foreign language. But I'm too lazy. Beckett managed it by removing one of the things that's very important to me as a novelist—those very small nuances between register. That's extremely difficult to catch in foreign languages. One should never swear in a foreign language, because one simply doesn't know the exact register of these things: merde, Scheisse, shit. They're at subtly different social levels. Those distinctions are extremely difficult to catch, and you deal with them in every word you write. Beckett's style means he doesn't really work with those refined shifts. Having said that, I think *Endgame* a subtle, refined work. As far as I can tell, there's no false note in it, in either language.

RC   Publishers say the British have less interest in reading translated novels than other Europeans.

PH   Yes, but if you're English, you've got the best literature in the world. Imagine if you're Swedish. With the best will in the world, there's not that much to read. Strindberg—perfectly good. There are a few. But you don't have the sheer volume of English literature. How many novels were published in this country in the nineteenth century? God knows—hundreds of thousands. There wasn't anywhere near that number in any other language.

RC   People are bound to pursue the coincidence of the recent military campaigns in Afghanistan and the nineteenth-century British involvement in *The Mulberry Empire* to ask what the fruitful parallels are.

PH   Yes. Two great rules of how to be a successful imperialist: One: Don't invade Russia. Two: Don't invade Afghanistan.

RC   Some say the West has triumphed.

PH   Of course they're wrong. We're only at the end of part two of my novel. We haven't achieved what we went in to achieve. No one has any serious proposal as to what's to be done there. No one has any idea what to do with the hundreds of thousands of people who, until a few months ago, were supporting the Taliban regime. The Taliban are being treated like war criminals—held up and chained. Their foreign minister, Wakil Ahmad Muttawakil, was somebody we could plausibly have started to do business with, if our attitudes had been slightly different. He was arrested the other day.

   We went in saying we wanted a government of Afghan unity, but we've supported one faction. It's following exactly the course of the war in *The Mulberry Empire*. It won't necessarily go on like that. But it's too early to start talking in a triumphalist way. The thing that would stop it going any further is serious investment in Afghanistan. My God, it needs it. But we're talking about going there for three months, sending sandwiches and then leaving again, which is a recipe for disaster.

   I still haven't worked out what I think about the coincidence. I don't claim any great prophetic powers for myself, in that anyone who looked at Afghanistan since the Taliban took Kabul in 1996 could see that something was going to happen there.

RC The allies have gone quiet about the original aims of the war. It's Orwellian.

PH Yes. What's happened to Al-Qaeda? Where are they? I don't think bin Laden is still in Afghanistan. He's probably in Yemen by now. At the beginning of the war, it was: "We're going to go in, and if the Taliban are prepared to hand over bin Laden, then we're not going to mess with them. Suddenly, overthrowing the Taliban was supposedly their purpose from the start. You're right—it's very much like *Nineteen Eighty-Four*.

RC What will you write next?

PH I feel written out for the moment. I don't have a novel on the go. In the last year, I've finished two short stories. But I won't publish them yet.

I feel the next novel will probably be contemporary, but more than that I don't know. If my reading's anything to go by—and certainly that was how this one started—I seem to be reading one political memoir after another. So it might have a political aspect.

I've suddenly become fascinated by Clement Attlee's personality. He couldn't have been a politician fifty years later. He was so uninterested in image. He was also probably the last prime minister who wrote poetry that was any good. That period—1945 to 1951—was a very rich one for the English novel: late Evelyn Waugh; Henry Green; Elizabeth Bowen; Nancy Mitford. They were all coming to terms with the postwar settlement in antagonistic ways. I'm not the person to write it, but there might be a book to be written about the novel under Attlee.

RC Thanks very much for your time.

TWELVE

DALE PECK

DALE PECK is the author of three novels: *Martin and John* (published in Britain as *Fucking Martin*), *The Law of Enclosures*, and *Now It's Time to Say Goodbye*. His most recent publication, "a work of creative nonfiction," is *What We Lost*.

Peck was born in 1967 on Long Island (New York) but brought up in Kansas. He went to Drew University in New Jersey, where he submitted his first (unpublished) novel, "All the World," as his senior honors thesis. Peck then moved to New York City although, in 1994, he based himself in London for a year. His first published book was *Martin and John* (New York: Farrar, Straus, and Giroux, 1993), published as *Fucking Martin* in Britain [London: Chatto and Windus, 1993]). An excerpt from *Martin and John* appeared in George Stambolian, ed., *Men on Men 4* (New York: Plume, 1992).

Peck's next novel, *The Law of Enclosures* (New York: Farrar, Straus, and Giroux, 1996; London: Chatto and Windus, 1996), was later adapted into a film by John Greyson (2000), for which Peck cowrote the screenplay. His third novel was *Now It's Time to Say Goodbye* (New York: Farrar, Straus, and Giroux, 1998; London: Chatto and Windus, 1998), and his most recent book is *What We Lost* (New York: Houghton Mifflin, 2003).

Peck's article, "Making History," appeared in David Deitcher, ed., *Over the Rainbow: Lesbian and Gay Politics in America Since Stonewall* (London: Boxtree, 1995). The story "S/M, or Sunday Night, Monday Morning" was published on the Web site www.Nerve.com in 1997. Peck's "The Law of Diminishing Returns" appeared in *Granta*, no. 65 (Spring 1999). He has had a number of pieces published in *Conjunctions*: his tribute to

Shirley Jackson (no. 29, Fall 1997); the stories "Thirteen Ecsta-
cies of the Soul" (no. 30, Spring 1998), "Fever Dreams: A Geography of the Mind" (no. 34, Spring 2000), and "Fruit Salad"
(no. 36, Spring 2001). He wrote the "Foreword" to Clifford
Chase, ed., *Queer 13: Lesbian and Gay Writers Recall Seventh
Grade* (New York: Morrow, 1998). The stories "Making Book"
and "Bliss" were published in *Zoetrope* 3.1 (Spring 1999) and 4.2
(Summer 2000), respectively. "Bliss" won an O. Henry Award
and was reprinted in Larry Dark, ed., *Prize Stories 2001: The O.
Henry Awards* (New York: Knopf, 2001).

Further writings by Peck have appeared in *Artforum, Bomb,
Bookforum,* the *London Review of Books,* the *Nation,* the *New
Republic,* the *New York Times, Out, QW,* and the *Village Voice.*
Peck was awarded a Guggenheim Fellowship in 1994. He teaches Creative Writing at the New School University in New York
City and lives in an apartment on the Lower East Side, where
this interview took place on Tuesday, November 4, 1997. It was
revised in October 2002, at which point the material following
the asterisks was added.

RC   In the article "Making History," you wrote about language being
"like a sense, a way of capturing something and bringing it inside yourself, and this capturing is only a beginning. Words, like food, have to be
digested." Your novels are deeply concerned with the relationship between language and the material world, aren't they?

DP   Yes. I've always felt that fiction—maybe all writing—is about the act
of writing itself to some degree. It might be conscious or unconscious,
or—more likely—some kind of seesawing between the two. When I
write, I'm acutely conscious of just how much isn't showing up; how
much I'm not getting; the incredible gap between this completely non-
corporeal thing—writing—and the real world. The relationship, for instance, between this table and the word "table" is tenuous and purely
mystical to me.

Language is like money. It exists only as belief. You believe in it; there-fore it has power. Ninety-nine percent of the time, that serves you well enough. When it doesn't, that's fairly amazing. That's when language is most interesting—when it causes problems; creates solutions. That's the interesting part to write about. You could write all day as a linguist or semiotician about how language works. But it's much more interesting when it doesn't.

For me, something that characterizes a weak fictional text is an uncon-scious relationship to language—when an author assumes he's telling the entire story, simply because he is telling the story. I never believe that. A fictional text in this post-postmodern age has to acknowledge the gap be-tween language and reality.

This may all be a product of my education. I started writing immediate-ly after I got my English degree. I'd learned about reader-response theory, deconstruction, and New Criticism. But for me this awareness marks the real division between a good and a bad book. A lot of times I'll find that, once I like a book, I'll start looking out for this. A case in point is Michael Lowenthal's novel *The Same Embrace*. Many people said it was just a Vic-torian novel—sweet, old-fashioned, by turns schmaltzy and emotional. I liked the book, so had to prove to myself that it wasn't just that. And I do think it's self-conscious, that it deals with its own construction.

RC   A number of contemporary novelists happily inherit the tradition-al—let's say nineteenth-century—novel form. Alan Hollinghurst would be one. Is the form always inappropriate today?

DP   I love nineteenth-century novels, and I can take great pleasure in reading contemporary books written in that mode, which is how 95 per-cent of fiction today is written. But I don't consider the new ones inter-esting aesthetically. For me, that has to be one criterion in judging a nov-el. There's what it's about—how it's written and the form it takes. If I had a simple gripe with Hollinghurst, whose books I actually quite love, it's simply that they are nineteenth-century novels. I'd like to see him push against that.

Ultimately, why literary forms are always evolving—why the Victorians lost out to the modernists; the modernists to the postmodernists; the postmodernists to something we aren't quite sure of yet—is because the old forms aren't useful anymore. They're too familiar. Someone said one of art's duties was to make the familiar strange. When those forms become as familiar as what they describe, they can't do that.

RC   That sounds distinctly modernist—making the familiar strange.

DP   I suspect it is. Ezra Pound said: "Make it new." On a fairly instinctive level I agree. People like to be surprised—or certain people; those with excitable minds. There's something to be said for slipping into a certain kind of book like you slip into a comfortable pair of old jeans. But there's more to be said for breaking in the book yourself, figuring out how it works. I've always been more drawn to the latter. I don't quite go for the idea of mimesis today—the idea that contemporary, fragmented fiction, say, represents our fragmented world. One's experience of life has always been fragmented. We just happen to have a vocabulary for it now that we're infatuated with. Fragmentation was the darling of both the modernists and the postmodernists. They turned the novel into a jigsaw puzzle. What you, the reader, essentially put back together was a Victorian novel. Hence many people went back to writing Victorian novels once they'd figured out how to do the puzzle. Why blame them?

Martin and John was another jigsaw puzzle—a high postmodernist novel. I realize much more now that it was a departure point for me. My education left off with the postmodernists, so that's where I started as a writer. Now I'm trying to move into something else. Some people think *The Law of Enclosures* involves the same sort of puzzle. To me, it's much more involved with questions of belief in the invented story; with why people choose to believe in such stories; and with the usefulness of fiction, the relationship of fiction to real stories; the authority of the author.

One problem I personally have is that I'm almost constitutionally incapable of reading something and believing it's untrue. I believe in novels as I believe in nonfiction. For me there's no difference between the very first *Godzilla* movie and what filmmakers come out with today, in terms of special effects. I see the plastic crease. It doesn't matter. I believe in created stories because they satisfy a need. All people do. They believe in them even as they say they don't, even as they poke fun and criticize them. And they believe in them even more today—in a world where we no longer believe in God—because they need that substitute. That's the most dangerous temptation of all—to use your belief in stories as a substitute for God; to use it as a cushion against the encroaching darkness, or your fear of death; to do that unconsciously. I think that's what fiction is for. But it can't be done unconsciously. That's dangerous. It's as bad as organized religion. Hence I'm constantly drawing people out of the reading experience—reminding them this is a book; that I created these characters for certain reasons; that you choose to identify with certain characters for certain reasons. "Make these characters useful to you," I'm saying. "Don't let me make them useful to you."

RC   How do these concerns relate to the common identification of fictional stories with authors' own experiences?

DP   Interestingly, *Martin and John* is often lumped into the category of "autofiction." It's not at all. The situations are almost entirely made up. I'm very hesitant about transforming sizable chunks of my own life into pieces of narrative.

RC   Do you mind the misreading?

DP   Terribly. That's the point. With *Martin and John*, that fairly traditional reader strategy of conflating character and author becomes silly. Characters—buffoons, heroes, whatever—are still somehow lionized. Simply because they're characters, they're deemed worth reading about. I don't think authors necessarily are. It depends what sort of life they've led, how interesting they are personally. I was more interested in someone looking at the reasons why I'd choose to invent a character this way.

Many people opted for the easy answer—because he was like me. It simply wasn't true. I borrowed certain details from my own life—the violent father, the dead mother, the geography. There were prudent reasons. At twenty I knew very little about the world. These were some things I did know. There were obsessive reasons for borrowing too. No matter what I started writing, it tended to feature violent fathers, dead mothers, the landscape of Kansas. But I specifically didn't want people to assume my character was like me. So I put a clearly demarcated, italicized biography of the main character into *Martin and John*, then had the stories printed in roman type.

RC You warned people not to equate you with anything in it.

DP Yes. They did so anyway.

RC How does a writer respond to not getting the reception he wants?

DP My response was to write *The Law of Enclosures*. It was fairly clear from the reviews of *Martin and John* that people were conflating me and my narrator far too closely. So in *The Law of Enclosures* I wrote fifty pages of nonfiction about my parents—the real-life originals for the characters I'd created, but nothing like them either, except for certain key details of class and gender.

RC You included certain dates.

DP Yes. A lot of people thought that was when I wrote it. But it's when the fictional part of the book takes place. There's a trick there which you could call postmodern. The two parts of the characters' lives that I write about are separated by forty years, yet it all takes place at exactly the same moment. Some people speculated that these were two different sets of characters with vast similarities in background.

RC Do you have an answer to the confusion you created with that?

DP Sure. First, I sat down knowing that I wanted to write about these characters both before their children were born and after their children had left home. I opted for the number forty because it was biblical. So— forty years. Then I thought: "Now I'm faced with the prospect of making these characters old in the present and having them young in the Eisenhower years." The Eisenhower years came with such an enormous freight load of baggage—especially where families are concerned—that I simply didn't want to go there. I thought I'd make them young in the present

day, and have them old forty years in the future, when, assuming techno-
logical innovations continue, the world would be practically unrecogniz-
able. It'll have twice as many people in it. The whole agrarian dream
won't stand—even as a dream.

The second justification was that time seemed purely incidental, vis-à-
vis this love and this relationship. If I'd felt society was going to make a
difference to how the relationship was carried out, I'd have been forced
to write differently. One problem in the 1990s, however, is that we're still
in the process of dismantling the Eisenhower fiction of how the family
works. I saw no reason to take the book back to its source and populate
it with historical details. That doesn't interest me.

The ultimate answer to all this is: "Because that's the great freedom of fiction—you can do what the hell you want." And you ought to. The sad thing
is most people don't. They find themselves stuck with all these rules.

RC   In your first two novels, you hand the rules over to a "you" figure,
the reader. You speculate over whether the reader wants a description of
sex in *The Law of Enclosures*. In *Martin and John*, you give instructions on
how to read the novel at the end.

DP   I wrestled a lot over including that. From surveying the state of fiction—though I don't think there's anything formally that original in
Martin and John—my sense was that it was going to seem unfamiliar to
most readers. I made the politest nod to that fact by putting a sort of key
in at the end, in case people who'd read that far wanted to apply it to what
they'd read. I received a lot of flak from sophisticated readers. This was
considered, as one reviewer put it, my "Rosebud." It's true. It simplifies
the book. It's almost a flaw.

My American editor was the only one really working with me on *Martin and John*. I insisted that the small, italicized chapters be dispersed
throughout the book in alternation. But he wanted to publish them as a
single story opening the book, which would then essentially become a
collection of stories. He thought people would be confused the whole way
through otherwise. But I said: "No. They won't be if you explain it. Write
in the jacket copy that the italicized sections relate to the 'real' character,
and the roman parts are what he made up." That's what happened. My

own feeling then—maybe because I was fresh out of college—was that, since lots of people have written books telling you how to read, it didn't seem too presumptuous to put this paragraph in, and another as jacket copy, especially since they seemed to be needed.

RC That bothered you less than the prospect of reconstructing the book?

DP The book needed to be the way it was. It would become an entirely different book if you didn't have the stories set up that way.

RC But if the essence of the closing paragraph is also divulged on the book jacket, it is given to the reader at the outset.

DP When it came to it, I was probably a little coy in my explanation at the end. I didn't say it straight out—in language as plain as that on the jacket. In fact, even the language on the jacket wasn't terribly plain. Both American and British editors didn't want to explain just what the book was. So it says John "keeps a journal and then begins to write stories. Each of John's stories features a couple named Martin and John." Well, there is no journal, and it never simply tells you: "In this book, the italicized sections are what really happened, and the roman type imagined." It was as if that would be embarrassing or demeaning. I never understood why. I tend to think only the reader who needs that sort of assistance tends to look at jacket copy anyway. I'm not congratulating myself, but I never do. I look at who's blurbing the book, and then read the first page.

On the American jacket of *The Law of Enclosures*, there's a line about the fact that the action takes place at the same time: "Time is incidental to the psychodynamics of love." My editor threw this in at the last minute without me seeing it. It's fabulously pretentious. I couldn't tell you what it means. I thought: "This is going to confuse things even more." Bully to him for doing it, but nobody's going to know what he means. It comes across as rather philosophical.

RC The British version reads: "Informing this narrative is a searingly powerful memoir which lies at the heart of the book. This section, Dale

Peck's account of his own parents, is written in language of almost unbearable intensity, and its presence opens the novel wide." There are interesting consequences in the decision to describe that section as pure
memoir.

DP   That's what it is. I wanted to call the book "a novel and a memoir."

RC   Was the middle section always integral to *The Law of Enclosures*?

DP   Yes. The evolution of *The Law of Enclosures* is like the evolution of
the first twenty years of my writing career. I wrote *Martin and John* because I wanted to be a writer. As much as anything else, it pays homage
to the writers I'd loved. With *The Law of Enclosures* I had to decide who I
was, what I was interested in, what I was going to write. I spent a lot of
time reading the good and bad press about *Martin and John*. I was troubled by the conflation of author and narrator. I knew the second book
would be about heterosexuals. I decided that in advance. I didn't want to
be stereotyped as nothing but a gay author—a futile effort, I have to say
now. Also, I genuinely wanted to write about a heterosexual relationship.
I wanted to say certain things about my parents' relationship. I knew people were going to make inferences—because again I was writing about
lower-middle-class people and so on.

Two things fell into place. First, I decided to make the book a sort of sequel to *Martin and John* by reusing the parental characters. I also knew that,
as well as the fictive novel about John's parents, I was going to write the
truth about my own parents. God knows I'd long written about them without publishing anything. I was going to put these together so people could
see both relationships, see how ephemeral and essential the similarities
were. In essence, they were emotional and psychological correspondences.

The great burden with *The Law of Enclosures* was that I'd decided that,
if the characters were going to have any sort of triumph or epiphany, it
could only come at the very end. For me, the great tragedy of my parents'
lives—and of huge numbers of people—is that there is no triumph or
epiphany. Poverty's something most people don't get out of. Even if you
get money, you've learned an impoverished mindset. Most people are
stuck with it.

After *Martin and John*, I found myself with the freedom to invent any story I wanted, to tell it any way I wanted—fantastical; surreal; postmodern; gritty; romantic; whatever. Yet with *The Law of Enclosures* I bound myself tightly into one mode, into a very tight set of characters. I wrote about people who didn't do other things, didn't think about them. All they tended to imagine were slightly different versions of the lives they led. It made for an extremely claustrophobic reading experience. It also made for a terrifying writing experience—especially for me. I like to go off on flights of fancy. I had to curtail that.

The insertion of the memoir keeps the book from being almost unbearable. It suddenly explains why the book is as it is, why these characters' lives are deadeningly, maddeningly dull. It opens up this vast emotional mire that I think people have to cover over so as not to fall into—all that chaos and sadness; the sadness of things not done, not seen; possibilities that exist but aren't acknowledged.

The particular jacket line you quote I actually wrote. I think the memoir does "open the novel wide." And it makes the end of the book. They do get their release: Henry gets his triumphant vision; they have their vast wealth, their pastoral paradise. You realize, of course, that it's simply a fairytale. In real life, they'd have gone to bed miserable their entire lives. They wouldn't have been reconciled, or gone to their deaths happily. The book becomes a fairytale which—for reasons made clear in the memoir—I needed to believe in, and that readers would want to believe in. I offer it, but they can choose to disbelieve it. The final scenes are written as though they could either represent Henry's delirium, or they could actually have happened within the narrative scheme.

I should tell you something. I had a vision in my senior year in college. I came up with the ideas for the first seven novels I was going to write. I came up with them all in three or four months. "Vision" makes it sound like it was a single flash. It wasn't exactly that. For some reason, though, when I was twenty-one, I came up with all these ideas for novels, one after another. Obviously, hundreds of ideas come to you over time. You throw most away. For some reason, I knew these books were the ones I was going to write. Maybe I chose to believe it. But with *The Law of Enclosures*, it clearly became a series. I consciously decided not to try and write all seven at the same time, nor completely to plan the entire series, but to let it evolve, to let each new book answer questions raised by the last—both in the book itself and in its reception. I didn't want it to be stagnant. I didn't want something Proustian. But now they've become seven integrated books describing John's story. There's a seven-word title too—*Seven Days and Nights of My Soul.*

My dream—virtually untenable in the contemporary publishing climate—is to do as Henry James did: to rewrite the novels after I've published them. I want to write the first seven books, then rewrite and reissue them all. Clearly there'll be things I'll want to fix, so that some themes carry all the way through, as well as to make certain things that are incongruous remain incongruous.

I hate Proust, incidentally. I don't want mine to be a straightforward series. It won't be parsed out or make rational sense. It's an irrational progression. Time is completely thrown away; it's illogical. Characters, situations will change. People are continually changing ages, dying, being reborn, reinvented, and recast. But there's a very clear, singular narrative—John's story. He seems absent in *The Law of Enclosures.* That's deliberate. But anyone familiar with *Martin and John* will be aware who these people are, who John is in it.

In *Now It's Time to Say Goodbye* John goes under a pseudonym, though there are several hints to readers familiar with the earlier books. Those who aren't don't have to know. In the fourth novel, it's revealed who John was in the third. The fourth book, which I'm writing now, really brings it together. It's the one with which I've finally allowed myself to decide to do this project. My career seems solid enough now that I can safely announce this completely pretentious project to the world! In the fifth book, John dies, finally, of AIDS. In the sixth, somebody assumes his identity and becomes him. The seventh book, at this point, is planned as a recapitulation of the first six. I'm going to rewrite them all from the perspective of whatever age I am when I get there. The first six chapters will comprise the six books retold according to my opinions of them. The seventh chapter will be something new.

RC   Many writers talk of letting older projects go, letting readers interpret them as they like. This series, by contrast, suggests a lot of dangers—in keeping the same characters, for instance.

DP   Yes. But there are good reasons for doing that too. One's the fact that writers aren't able to write free from financial worry. I have to produce books for a paycheck. This means I have to let them go—perhaps before all the polish is put on them. There's nothing wrong with that per se. But there's nothing right about it either. There's no reason why a book should be finished at any one time. Why shouldn't I say "I had to hurry this. I have more ideas. I can make it better"?

For me there's also a big fear too of running out of things to write about. In essence, though I may finish a book now, I haven't finished the big project yet. So I always know I'm working on something. The end of this project is a big wall I can't see beyond, however. I wonder if I'll have anything to write about then. I have a dream that I may have become independently wealthy by then. I won't actually have to write. Also, there's nothing wrong with writing just seven books as the sum of a career. I may be vain, but I'm very proud of my books. So far, I think they stand as perfectly fine products of a literary life. After they've been revised, they'll be irreproachable.

The real fear is turning into a writer who no longer has anything to say but still writes. That's why I admire Kurt Vonnegut. He realized he'd run out of things he needed to say and stopped. Most writers continue to write books because they're alive and bored, and because they think they need to. I desperately don't want to do that. I don't want to dilute the good things I've said with bad, unnecessary, or extraneous things. If seven books sum up everything I have to say, that's fine. I hope I'm in a financial position to rest.

RC   What seems odd is that you've determined the desire to rewrite the books in advance. A lay view might be that a writer's commitment to the project in hand needs to be fueled by the necessary fiction that the work can be completed, achieved. It's a conceit, but a vital one.

DP   For me the only thing that makes a work of art finished is the death of the artist—especially with a book that can be changed again and again. What you speak of is artificial. I've no need for it. Whitman revised *Leaves of Grass* for fifty years. He added to it, took things away, changed the existing poems. For people who were following his career, there was something great in watching the new editions come out, in seeing how they changed. Today the amount of words in the different editions is too monumental to take in, unless you're a scholar. We have a sense, however, that the only reason we have the *Leaves of Grass* we have now is because Whitman died and couldn't write anymore. Were Whitman two centuries old today, he'd still be changing *Leaves of Grass*. What's wrong with that?

When I talk of revising my books, remember that I've written three already. I'm thirty. I suspect I'll be finished by the time I'm forty. Then I'll revise them. It's not something I expect still to be working on when I'm a doddering old man. I'm sure too that there'll be a choice between revisiting old material and going on to new things. Who knows—maybe I won't do the revisions. Maybe I'll wait for years because there are other books I want to write. At the time, the question will be: "Which is more valuable: revisiting old material and making it better, or writing something new?"

As much as anything, this idea fits in with my wider literary aim—to emphasize the inventiveness of each book; to say: "OK, however many readers there have been—who have read these seven books and liked or disliked them this way—now I'm going to change them, a little or a lot, because that's what I can do." I'm going to say: "These books are more useful to me now in this new form. Maybe they'll be more useful to you; maybe not."

RC   Is this also a stratagem which liberates you when you write?

DP   That's something I think about all the time. The key thing is not to use it as a crutch. There are a few things I've got to make really sure I don't do. One is to write gratuitously—to write things now that won't have any meaning until later books are published. I'm not going to say to my audience: "You have to wait five, ten, fifteen years until you find out why the hell I wrote this paragraph." I also don't want to say: "I know this isn't right, but I'm just going to leave it, knowing I can come back to it in fifteen years."

But it helps me to know, for example, that in *Now It's Time to Say Goodbye*, one character with a small but crucial role will become the narrator and main character of my fifth book. There are certain mysterious elements to her that don't have to be elucidated in *Now It's Time to Say Goodbye*. All the characters' backgrounds are somewhat mysterious in that book. But hers will be cleared up. Another character in it is the antagonist of my sixth book. Again, he has a small role here. There's no reason to think that anything else about him is of importance. In his case, I didn't know this until well into writing the book.

RC You raise a compelling question concerning the series: what is left for you, in terms of imaginative freedom?

DP The structure of the books isn't predetermined—only what they're about. For example, when writing *Martin and John*, all I knew about *The Law of Enclosures* was that the characters would start out happy, spend most of their time unhappily, and end up happy again.

RC I'm especially interested in the novels' different structures and forms. Perhaps determining these aesthetic questions preoccupies you especially, since the plotting is somewhat known.

DP You're right. Many people would say that as a critique—the idea that a writer is more concerned with how he's writing than what he's writing about. For me this is crucial; it's my subject, underneath the more obvious one of what we choose to believe in and why. I'm concerned with the stories people choose to believe in and why. My whole project involves finding a new way to tell a story—one that will, I'm sure, come to seem archaic in twenty-five years, or fifty. That's how long literary movements tend to last.

Martin and John is 99.9 percent a work of high postmodernism, with a deconstructive edge. More and more, deconstructionism has come to inform the way I write a story. But I don't want to write criticism disguised as fiction, like Kathy Acker or Lynne Tillman. I want to look for what most people are looking for now. People seem especially to want the classic "narrative" books, as they always have. For a while it looked like we were going to be able to get rid of that. The moment passed. Still, people want the stories, but not told the same way. They want to have their cake and eat it—to have the story but to have freedom from it too. They want to believe, but to have power over what they believe. I'm trying to find a way to answer that.

Among the biggest influences on my writing right now are Hollywood movies. The well-made ones, if nothing else, deliver stories people crave and go to see in huge numbers. In movies, the stories are completely irrelevant, especially for sophisticated viewers. The stories are presented in their barest bones, in the most clichéd, familiar ways. They never once approach believability. It's not the point. It's simply that people want classical narratives as ways of shaping the discussion of other issues. The insidious thing about Hollywood is that the discussions end up being conservative, anti-intellectual, or shallow.

I'm not saying the stories are good. But directors and producers have found a way of using them without becoming enslaved by them. Even though you give people what they want—the special effects, or Arnold Schwarzenegger, or quote-unquote "risqué" scenes—nevertheless, no matter how clichéd or unbelievable, there's a real story there. There has to be. I'm interested in using the same techniques to frame more sophisticated discussions.

Naturally, I'm attributing too much to filmmakers here. I'm interested in the reception of the films, the audience response. This is all very much in my own head; people don't poll movie audiences and present the results to the public. Yet, as I look at these mind-numbingly awful movies, I think: "Why do people go to see them, aside from the fact that there are no alternatives?"

RC Filmmaking is an odd analogy to writing. I'm thinking especially of how much can be changed through editing.

DP With *Now It's Time to Say Goodbye*, something similarly drastic happened. I cut out a 160-page chunk which was a freestanding novel, and then a further hundred pages. The book was incredibly long when it was typeset—partly because it has about three hundred chapters, many only a paragraph long. Originally, I wanted them all to begin on a fresh page. Financial concerns made the publishers run the chapters together. I'd meant to offset some people's fears of long books, though. You'd have turned the pages very quickly. I'm a little concerned now that that book is still long.

Now you turn the pages at a conventional speed because the chapters have been run together. I'm concerned people will feel bogged down.

I get weird notions about how big a book should be. I knew *Now It's Time to Say Goodbye* should be big. I didn't know it would be this big. I felt in my gut that *The Law of Enclosures* was running too long. Originally it was twice as long. With both works I cut half the text out. It's sat in a drawer.

RC   What about the "freestanding novel" you mentioned?

DP   One of the main characters in *Now It's Time to Say Goodbye*, Colin, is a writer. He wrote his first book when he was twenty, and has been attempting to write his second for twenty-something years. He hasn't finished it for many reasons—everything from writer's block to sabotage on the part of his lover, who destroyed one of the manuscripts.

Colin's the Martin doppelgänger. Immediately after moving to this town in Kansas with his lover, a girl is raped and kidnapped. Colin is framed, but no one believes he did it. He stays in town for a while until blood tests clear his name. Then he stays because he wants to know what's going on, why someone would try to frame him. Deeply inspired by the events, he suddenly writes his book. Later you discover that in fact he's written lots of books, but thrown them away because they're no good. You're to decide whether this one is or not. It's loosely inspired by the parent story of *Now It's Time to Say Goodbye*—the kidnapping. But Colin writes a different kidnapping story—a surreal one, with a male protagonist. In the parent story, the kidnapped girl clearly suffers. In the story Colin writes, the kidnap victim falls in love with his kidnapper. So there are parallels and differences.

It's the same game I played with *The Law of Enclosures*, essentially. In that novel, the stakes were much more serious. Here it was a game. That's finally why I took Colin's novel out. It was fun but unnecessary. In fact, it was much more exciting to talk about it without having it in. So I had someone steal the book the minute Colin finishes writing it. You never find out who that is.

RC   Would you like it to appear—as, say, novel 3(a) in the series?

DP Yes. It's called "The Land of Make Believe." It deserves to be published. I thought it would be fun to publish it under Colin's name simultaneously with *Now It's Time to Say Goodbye*. But the only way people wanted to put it out—many publishers did like it—was if I'd leave my publisher and go with them, which I had no intention of doing.

RC Your publisher wasn't drawn to the idea of publishing both?

DP They were afraid it would seem like overkill, two books simultaneously—or else too much of a gimmick. Also, I got my current publisher to give me a lot of money for *Now It's Time to Say Goodbye*, far more than I've demonstrated I can earn. I did a bit of a diva act, selling it. They're most concerned with recouping the investment. I could have published it through a tiny press. I just didn't want to. If nothing else, it'll show up in a book of collected ephemera eventually.

RC You seem prolific. Does writing come easily?

DP It always feels hard. But I seem to be writing an awful lot. I'm always terrified I'm not writing anything. With *Now It's Time to Say Goodbye* I wrote eleven hundred pages in eleven months. I thought I wasn't writing a damn thing. Every minute I didn't spend with my pen pressed to the paper would magnify in my mind to weeks, months, years. I thought I was wasting my life, my youth, my productive years. That's a great trick to keep you writing. Unfortunately, I have a more rational perspective now. I realize I write a lot more than most.

RC Do you work regularly, at specific times of day? And do you write or type?

DP I write fiction longhand; nonfiction on the computer, for some reason. I do all my revisions on the computer, except when something's a real mess. Then I copy it by hand and start afresh. Laziness is a great asset in writing longhand. You think of a few words, but don't want to write them because your hand's sore. Then you realize they weren't necessary anyway, so you skip them. For me, "overwriting" has always been my un-conscious strategy. It could also be my downfall if I'm not careful.

I do most original composition in the morning and most revision in the afternoons. I tend to work every day. The weekend's no different.

RC   Is it important to start immediately?

DP   No. It's important to have coffee in the morning and be fully awake, and to read while drinking coffee. The most important part of the day—almost the most valuable—is getting straight out of bed, picking up a book, and beginning to read. That's when your mind is least guarded and you're most open to entering a fictional world. Some writers can't read fiction when they're deep in composition. I read more. My answer to un-certainty is always to read somebody else's book. I take great comfort knowing someone's created a good book. If they can do it, so can I. I've nothing whatsoever against imitation either, conscious or unconscious. So there's an enormous amount of nineteenth-century British fiction in *The Law of Enclosures*: George Eliot, Henry James. That's almost all I was reading then. Mostly it appeared unconsciously.

RC   Have you ever noticed an echo and regretted it?

DP   I've noticed them but never been unhappy. I wrote an entire chap-ter for *Now It's Time to Say Goodbye* which I later cut, which parodies Joan Didion's writing style. I adore it, but it didn't need to be in the book.

I did something with *Now It's Time to Say Goodbye* that I don't really believe in. I wrote in voices. Generally the idea's a charade. I don't think the written word approximates spoken language at all. I don't like writers who write solely in dialect, as though it were natural—Maya Angelou, for example. I hate "tough guy writing," too—people who leave the *g*'s off the end of the —*ing*'s to imitate Italian accents. Nevertheless, that's hugely popular right now, for sentimental or romantic reasons. So in *Now It's Time to Say Goodbye* I wrote the characters completely in their dialects, but in a deconstructive way—to emphasize its artificiality. Each character becomes obsessed with the way he speaks. The narrative's revolving first person. So every single character is—unconsciously on their parts, very self-consciously on mine—obsessed with claiming ownership of the text they appear in. They address a "you" figure, but never tell "you" they're writing anything. It veers on the irrational, and the dialect's fake. The book's concerned with the enormous conflict between blacks and whites. I think one of the huge bases for that conflict lies in the question of whose language is better, or what the proper way of using language is.

For me these dialects weren't meant to be taken literally. Many were based on parodies of a number of writers, including myself. The two main characters—Colin and Justin—parody my own writing from different directions. Justin's overly romantic; Colin overly critical. Both positions are false; both represent flaws and virtues in my writing. Other characters are based on other writing styles. The black speech is based on Toni Morrison, James Baldwin, or Maya Angelou. Others are based on other writers or types of writing. One character's a failed academic. Her writing's inflected by the sort of artful academic prose which I think is the most atrocious thing in the whole world. I can't stand it—that tendency to mix arid, precise language with florid metaphor.

Another character is the biggest cipher in the book. He's there to create structural unity, as there are two gay couples in there. The second pair are Wade Painter, a painter, and his lover Divine, a young, black, semi-drag queen. Divine's an actor, essentially—someone who's been so influenced by media images of other people like him—black males between the ages of eighteen and thirty—that he imitates them all. Sometimes he's a snap queen; sometimes an effeminate homeboy; sometimes a gangster rapper; sometimes a Southern black.

I found myself drawn to Divine. I enjoyed writing him. Wade I was much less interested in. I decided to turn the disinterest into a virtue. So I made him a cipher, a fictional creation who exists solely to provide structural unity. At one point I considered making him more substantial. I invented his past and looked for a voice. Didion—besides the fact that she's my favorite living writer—also specializes in obliqueness, in characters whose distance from their emotional lives is chasmlike. So I reread four Didion novels and wrote Wade's past. But ultimately the book worked better without it.

RC   Earlier you mentioned *Martin and John* coming out of writers you admired at college. Name names.

DP   *Martin and John* pays homage to certain modernist writers—especially Virginia Woolf and Ernest Hemingway—whose works I revered in some ways, and also to the postmodernists whose ideas I adored but whose books I hated: Donald Barthelme, Thomas Pynchon, William Gaddis, William Gass. Reading their books I found almost impossible. They lacked an interesting story. The modernists took interesting stories apart and made jigsaw puzzles you could reassemble. The postmodernists just threw them out completely. If you were lucky, they subverted the idea of the story in funny ways. Those were the ones I liked, like Pynchon's *The Crying of Lot 49*. Generally, though, I had an infatuation with the various ideas such books stood for without liking them. I wanted to write a postmodern novel that I myself liked.

RC   Does Didion survive this kind of analysis, or transcend it?

DP   I don't think Didion's postmodernist. She's part of whatever comes afterwards. But the stories are strongly inflected by postmodernism. Didion has always told very coherent, coercive, taut, suspenseful stories. She and Kurt Vonnegut are practically siblings in how they tell a story. One reason I love both authors is because I think they and I are about the only people who walk into our own books. We do so in two different ways— as ourselves and as fictional versions of ourselves. Vonnegut, who's more prolific than Didion, has done it in different ways in each book. The most useful is in the form of a prologue or autobiographical preface. These work like the memoir at the center of *The Law of Enclosures*. Didion's way is simply to introduce herself—"Joan Didion." In one novel, she writes: "For the record, let the reader be introduced to me, Joan Didion, sitting in my house at such-and-such an address." In *The Last Thing He Wanted*, it's simply: "By now you know me."

RC   I remember thinking with Didion's *The Book of Common Prayer* that every sentence contained some lyrical truth which is simultaneously also called into question. You could feel both moves in each sentence. That might be said of *The Law of Enclosures.*

DP   Like Didion, I'm obsessed with language intellectually and musically or lyrically. With *The Law of Enclosures* I was trying to cotton on to what I thought was a very American, Whitmanesque rhythm. The sentences are much longer than in *Martin and John.* The cadences are always just slightly longer than a human breath. So it's a hard book to read out loud. I did that even more in *Now It's Time to Say Goodbye,* where the language really pushes into prosody.

There's almost an aesthetic of shortness today. But certain things you can't do with shortness. You asked earlier if I conceived of my books as a particular length. I do—but in the series, as a kind of arc. *Martin and John* is tiny. *The Law of Enclosures* is more than half as big again. *Now It's Time to Say Goodbye* is twice as big as that. I see the next book being as big as *The Law of Enclosures;* the one after as the size of *Martin and John.* It's the two after that I'm deeply confused by.

RC   Let's talk about the range of your subject matter. You write about much more than "gay lives."

DP   Yes. This relates to our current cultural moment and the politics of identity. I feel the real upshot of the "age of identity" wasn't to say that you can understand no one but yourself and people exactly like you, but to remember that your understanding of others is invariably inflected by who you are—by your cultural experiences. So when I write about a fifty-year-old black lesbian in a small town in Kansas, I write it from the point of view of "Dale Peck," a thirty-year-old gay urban New Yorker. This inflection is built into the text. It informs how I write about the character. No sophisticated reader ought then to mistake her for a purely naturalistic invention, someone to be taken at face value. Instead, she's based on my understanding of things.

That's where the freedom and great benefit of identity politics and identity-based writing lies: not to say that all gay writers ought to be writing about gay men, but that people should look at books as reflecting a certain identity experience. That experience will partly be a rather stereo-typical one, and partly an idiosyncratic, individual one. It's the writer's duty to tell you in essence what that inflection is. So I introduce readers to my characters and myself. Then I let them make the conjunction—put the two together.

RC   Is there anything you wouldn't write about?

DP   Something I knew absolutely nothing about. I don't feel I have to know a lot about something, though, as long as the reader is aware that I know very little. Clearly, there's an enormous conservative strain in con-temporary thought that says one cannot see out of one's own identity-based category. I just think it's wrong. I like the word "inflection" better, or "colored by."

RC   What's interesting is that you actually see a point to identities, even as your fiction projects don't refer to them.

DP   They refer to them, but aren't bound by them. It moves through them in ways that aren't always analytical. I leave a lot to the reader; I ex-pect a lot. In many instances my analysis is open to interpretation as much as to exegesis. That's the difference between fiction and criticism.

Identity writing I think of as very much a reaction against the former tradition in fiction. That essentially consisted of the straight, white, male author as paradigmatic figure, writing about all kinds of groups that weren't within his purview—writing from a hierarchical position, one in which his authority and ability to make judgments went unquestioned. That was bad, and was reacted against very strongly. The movement against it went too far in the other direction, though—in the idea that people should only write about themselves. I don't think people write about themselves any more objectively than they do about other peo-ple—perhaps less objectively, in all honesty.

RC   Now, a leap: could forthcoming plots in the novel series adapt to fundamental circumstantial changes? What about developments in the treatment of HIV/AIDS, a major theme to date?

DP They can. I can make the available therapy whatever I want, and kill John whenever I want. In fact, this fourth book takes as its subject the state of the HIV-positive person in the age of protease inhibitors, in an age where AIDS has passed from the national consciousness as something of paradigmatic proportions. One of the main characters becomes HIV-positive in 1997. To the vast majority of heterosexuals, AIDS is in essence cured now; protease inhibitors work. It's a fiction, of course—but one that works for them. The book's about what it's like to have AIDS now, in the midst of a cultural backlash—a reaction against ACT UP–style politics, and against the enormous amounts of money spent on AIDS, to the perceived detriment of other diseases that affect numerically far more people. I think it would be sociologically terrifying right now to become someone with AIDS. After over a decade of people working very hard to make AIDS one of the major national subjects of discussion, it no longer is—in America, at least. It's something we like little updates on. We assume everything's on track. Essentially, we've got the treatment and we're just perfecting it.

RC The context of protease inhibitors obviously couldn't have occurred to you when sketching out the series.

DP Not at all. The books to come—the farther you get into the future—are increasingly skeletal. Even as I've come up with various scenarios, plots, and characters, it's still subject to change. They react strongly to what's happened in the world—in my life and my writing. Equally, I tackle certain aesthetic questions in one book, and then react to them with the next.

It's been nine years now that this book—the fourth, called "The Garden of the Lost and Found"—has been percolating in my head. Only last year it suddenly hit me that it's about an orphan—a gay boy called James, who doesn't know his mother or father. When he's twenty-one, his mother dies and leaves him a store in New York. A slightly older woman named Claudia becomes his best friend. As the novel progresses, James is trying to figure out who she was, because she's no longer present in his life. He begins inventing a story for her—writing in her voice. It's an investigation into the politics and morality of storytelling and speaking for other people. It's primarily in a single voice, a lyrical exploration of this one character's psyche. The narrator's very unstable.

And now I've decided also to reclaim the oldest narrative—the Oedipus story. So the boy kills his father and sleeps with his mother. That's the essence of the story here, though it's told differently. Among other things, he doesn't kill his father and he doesn't sleep with his mother. [*Laughs*] There are hints of Antigone as well. And it's also a kind of bildungsroman.

RC You examine the working process so closely. Does this mean you also keep returning to the stories you tell, trying to find the reasons why they interested you?

DP Yes. Originally, *Now It's Time to Say Goodbye* was simply going to be about a rape. I was pretty sure it was going to be of a woman by a man. It's simply an obsession of mine. But why? What did that mean? In essence the answer came in the second book, *The Law of Enclosures*, not the third. It was because my father used to rape his wives. As a child I was aware of this. I probably even heard it. It inhabits my subconscious. But there were many other reasons for writing about it. I've come to believe that rape and the incest taboo are huge societal preoccupations. Those, and black-white sex—especially black man–white woman sex—which is yet another preoccupation in *Now It's Time to Say Goodbye*. That book's really about America, the American imagination and fascinations, particularly the "unhealthy" or dirty ones.

RC You lived in London for a while. Did that suggest the potential theme of cultural exchange?

DP Not especially. From the British perspective, I suppose I'd think of America as in some sense starting out as England's grander dream of itself, then turning gradually into some version of its own thing. America's this weird runaway from Britain. The interaction between British and Continental culture and America is strange.

I think American literature's closer to British literature than America itself is close to Britain. America the nation is a huge melting pot—a loaded term, that—of cultures from all over the world. Its democratic experiment's probably based more on French ideas than British ones. But American literature, simply because of the language, struggles with the anxiety of British influences. One reason I eventually opted for the title *The Law of Enclosures* was because it's British. "Enclosure laws" come from thirteenth-century laws of agrarian reform. These culminated roughly in 1776, under George III—the same time as the birth of America. A reaction against enclosure law led to the first major waves of British pastoral fiction because the enclosures act essentially took land away from the common people. Before, you owned the land by living on it. After, you had a piece of paper that said you owned it. It's a sea change I don't think we can fathom anymore—the idea that you could step on something and it's yours.

There was a strong pastoral theme in the book already. It was essentially written before I determined the title; then I revised it in certain ways. The pastoral myth is central to America. But it originates in Britain. British people first came here because it was wide open country. America was perceived of as empty. You came because your place was old and used and crowded, and you wanted the freedom of space and autonomy.

RC Now a leap. How important has the topic of AIDS been to the reception of your work?

DP Immensely. On a very real level, my career was made when someone decided there was going to be such a thing as "AIDS fiction"—the bastard offspring of "gay fiction"—and that *Martin and John* was going to be its cornerstone. There had been plenty of books beforehand. But *Martin and John* was published at the right moment. For a year it became an "AIDS book" and made my career, no doubt about it. Mainstream critics were looking around for an AIDS book they could embrace, as much as anything else to point up their lack of bigotedness, their sensitivity.

I've since come to believe that *Martin and John* isn't anything to do with AIDS. It's a metaphor for my mother's death. AIDS isn't there in the documentary fashion that it exists, say, in Allen Barnett's *The Body and Its Dangers* or John Weir's *The Irreversible Decline of Eddie Socket*. Ultimately, the emotional impact of those scenes for me relate to my mother's death. I have written some little pieces about AIDS. The best, "Thirteen Ecstasies of the Soul," is a series of prose poems.

RC   Who has written well about AIDS?

DP   Well, there are interesting things going on in Christopher Coe's novel *Such Times* and in Michael Cunningham's *A Home at the End of the World*. I loved Tony Kushner's *Angels in America* too. It's overlong, but among the best works of art about AIDS.

My favorite single work is Barnett's *The Body and Its Dangers*. It's a deeply self-reflective book of stories. Barnett does some funny things. One story's dedicated to his doctor, but the dedication doesn't appear till the end. There's a strange formal leap between the wonderful first story, "Snapshot"—which has nothing to do with AIDS—and the rest. It's like a graft, an extra arm. The book isn't cohesive and isn't meant to be. That's highly reflective of Barnett's abbreviated life as a writer. Yet there's a way that he's also totally in control. In two hundred pages, this book trumpets all its limitations and makes them strengths. The dozens of things it cannot do it makes you aware of, in ways that are numbing and amazing.

RC   Where else in gay fiction do you find this level of formal complexity and knowingness?

DP   First, I must say that I think "gay fiction" will cease to be an interesting category for most writers. It may remain interesting to critics. Writers will play with it. I did, with *The Law of Enclosures*, which I myself consider a deeply queer book. It's presented as a queer perspective on heterosexuality. You can see more and more books in which homosexuality is incidental.

RC   Though it's not true of all gay-themed writing.

DP   But the others just reproduce this historic Capote–Williams–Ethan Mordden dynamic of camp and subterfuge. Gay fiction will continue to be sociologically interesting, as a reflection of what gay people think about themselves. But primarily it's closed now. It's gay people speaking to each other, or offering straight people a glimpse of themselves.

Aesthetically, Gary Indiana is doing all kinds of things in his books— almost too many. Some are interesting, some not. He's always worth watching. Dennis Cooper used to be. Now he's in major retread mode. Before, he wrote more than just "autofiction." Rebecca Brown's one of my favorite living American writers. She's doing all sorts of fabulously interesting things. And then there's me, to blow my own awful horn.

Formal innovation isn't hot right now. People are far more concerned with the irrelevance of literature generally. Novels aren't the most important mode of cultural expression, and haven't been for some time. People don't generally care anymore. So it's like trying to build a better gasoline-powered car when electric cars are the future. You're innovating for your own sake, and for the few who care. But a lot of writers are wrestling with a false project instead—how to make novels the most important thing again. I don't think they ever will be, or should be. I was drawn to fiction precisely because it was shabby and overused, dusty and irrelevant. I wanted to hide—I'm shy. When I started writing, it was very much for myself. Only after I was published did I ever think of myself as a public or historical figure. When I did, I gave into the fantasy big time. I decided that, if possible, I was going to be considered among the great writers of my time. That kind of vainglorious thinking informs what I do.

I don't know that I'll always be a novelist. I'm more and more drawn to film. I'll probably hop into movies seriously at the point when they too have passed—when computers are the real art. I see civilization almost withdrawing into the Internet and ending there, as the natural world is destroyed. People will almost wholly live fantasy lives. They're already starting to, with cybersex and what's called "fan fiction" on the Web. These huge, on-line communities never see or hear each other. They communicate solely through text. It's the most exciting reading going on. Literary artists aren't interested because it's not about the author. It's purely receptive.

RC Is yours purely a spectator's engagement?

DP I don't have a Web page. I find the Internet erotically stimulating. But the other things on it are fascinating too—enormous Web sites devoted to fans of the *X-Files*, *Xena*, or whatever. People spin out incredible narratives with themselves as characters. Or they steal the characters and make them do what they want. There's a special name for it when you write fan fiction just to have sex with the character—"Jenny fiction," I think. It's dominated by women and is fascinating intellectually. Unfortunately, content-wise, all you get are Mulder and Scully from the *X-Files*. Who cares? Obviously zillions of people do. The stories themselves are unreadably dull. But the huge aura of intellectual energy being projected and received—that's incredible.

⋆   ⋆   ⋆

RC   Tell me about John Greyson's film of *The Law of Enclosures*. Could you talk a little about the experience of cowriting the screenplay? It's such a literary novel.

DP   It's a very insular novel—so methodical, so deeply embedded in language. Not a lot happens. There was a little streamlining of the narrative, and a lot of transplanting locations—just to have them in different places for the sake of giving the film a more interesting appearance. We did a little layering of the narrative too to make it more symmetrical. Initially I resisted that, but ultimately came to like it.

RC   What did you do with the autobiographical center?

DP   I told them before we started that wasn't in the package. It was never going to be part of the movie. It was written just for me; it was about my parents. John Greyson wanted to put it in in some form, because obviously it's a big part of the novel. It's often why people like the novel. But in the end there was no way you could have included it anyway. It would have added a lot of minutes—which means more money. There was already a lot of distillation.

One thing the experience brought home to me is how incredibly impoverished film is in terms of being an information-containing medium. You can pack a lot of visual stuff in there, but hardly any facts. There's so little space.

RC   You joked about one day moving into film.

DP I'm still interested in film. But I dare say the experience made me less interested. If you have anything to say, fiction is just a lot richer as a medium for a writer. Film is wonderfully evocative. You can fill it with emotion. But it can't contain complex paradigms.

RC Is the film still awaiting distribution?

DP Yes. It's been finished a couple of years now.

RC I want to ask about the inspiration for your short stories. What possessed you to write "Making Book," in which a pubescent kid is forced by his parents to watch a video of them having sex in order to conceive him? It's hilarious.

DP I do instinctively seem to know which ideas are going to work in which format. I couldn't tell you why—why some things feel long and others short. A lot of it may have to do with when the idea comes. If I'm already working on a novel, and I get an idea I really want to work on, I probably make it a story. That's the only way I get to work on it.

RC Do you work on the two simultaneously?

DP No. I use the stories as punctuation—to take a breather from a novel. I probably only write two stories a year. In large part, I've talked myself out of doing them. They're so uneconomical. They take a long time to write—you'll probably spend two months on a story, and then be really lucky to get paid a grand. But there are things you can do in a story that you can't in a novel. I started out writing short stories; I do really love them. To me *Martin and John* is fundamentally a book of short stories, not a novel. That was the point—that the individual pieces worked separately as well as together.

RC Do you plan to collect them some day?

DP That's the goal. My next book of fiction after this current novel will probably be a book of short stories. I've been working on them for a while. As with most things I do, I've ended up trying to create some sort of wacky system. The collection is going to be called "Twelve Caesars." The idea is that the twelve Roman emperors had very fixed characters. But they were all tyrants in different ways. They did to the empire what my characters end up doing to each other. It struck me that my characters generally behave in love rather similarly to the ways the emperors behaved to their empire. So I conceived of writing short stories in which the characteristics of the emperors appear in the characters in my stories.

Funnily enough, "Making Book" is one of the stories that won't be in the collection. Some older stories will go in after I've revised them. Others won't fit the paradigm. "Bliss" will be in there, and "The Law of Diminishing Returns" from *Granta*. There's also a second half to that story that'll go in, and then a bunch of new stories.

RC You finished the fourth book in the series—"The Garden of the Lost and Found"—in 2000. But the other forthcoming project you just mentioned is something else, isn't it?

DP Yes. It's not part of the novel series. It's called *What We Lost*. It's based on a real place—Greenville. That was the original title. I haven't decided whether to call it a novel or biography yet.[1] It's about a year and a half in my father's life. He was thirteen and fourteen, living in Greenville, at a really defining time in his life. It wasn't so much when he became who he was, as when he felt a lot of choices got closed off. There were a lot of people my father might have been in that year, and it was the last time in his life that would ever be the case.

Writing the book was based on all kinds of things—not least the fact that I had enormous difficulty selling "The Garden of the Lost and Found." Career choices and money problems can change the direction of your writing. "The Garden of the Lost and Found" might follow *What We Lost*, though it probably won't. It all comes down to business. My current editor has never seen "The Garden of the Lost and Found," which is a good thing. On the other hand, he can't help but notice that it wasn't taken up by those who did read it. Meanwhile, I'm with a new publisher,

---

1. *Author's note:* It was finally called "a work of creative nonfiction"; see the bio-bibliographical introduction.

Houghton Mifflin. They're taking a wait-and-see attitude with me. They're not buying anything else until *What We Lost* is published. For the next year, I can't get anything else published. So in the intervening time, I'm going to keep working on the stories.

I'm also doing some minor revisions to "The Garden of the Lost and Found" to make it reflect New York in the wake of September 11th. Weirdly, that event fits the book very well. The novel's about two people living together who are ostensibly best friends and help each other out. But because they never touch each other—love each other—one collapses. That leads to the other's collapse. So the images of September 11th fit eerily well. They're very illuminating.

I have very little to say about September 11th otherwise. I'm not particularly interested in making art about it. But I feel you can't publish a book about New York now that's set before September 11th—one that doesn't reflect the event.

RC You've spoken elsewhere of trying to read all the reviews of your work, and of taking criticism seriously. At the same time, you've developed something of a "rottweiler" reputation as a reviewer yourself—on people like Philip Roth; most recently on Rick Moody. The opening line of that review has become rather notorious: "Rick Moody is the worst writer of his generation." What would you say to the charge that that sort of attack isn't constructive?

DP It depends on what people think my motivation for writing the review was. Some people seem to think I wasn't sincere, that this was just agitprop. But I meant it. I thought his book was incredibly horrific, and if my piece persuaded Rick Moody never to write another book like it, I'd be delighted. I'm not trying to destroy his career by saying people shouldn't publish his books. But I had to point out why people shouldn't read them.

I write these reviews because—like a lot of people—I think literary fiction isn't on the right track. People keep writing books which are deliberately obscure and difficult, or which deliberately refuse any notion of harmony, of aesthetic consolation. A lot of novelists keep returning to the models of Pynchon, of Gaddis, of Barth—writing which was a little interesting forty years ago, but even then not that interesting.

It's like punk. People who claim they enjoy listening to real punk—

unharmonious, ugly punk—are missing the point. It's not supposed to be enjoyable. I think of postmodernism the same way. What we've done is learn to love the enemy. We've decided these books were pretty and meaningful—because we thought art was supposed to be both. But these books were not.

For me, this lesson was very much bound up in reading Thomas Bernhard, one of my favorite writers of all time. For a long while I thought Bernhard's style was difficult but would be inviting once you'd cracked the code. It's not true. Bernhard's style is meant to be difficult and to repel the reader. It's a test. Bernhard's trying to drive away people who don't care about literature. If you stay with his books, there are enormous beauties contained within them. But Bernhard was a deeply unpleasant personality, and they're deeply unpleasant books.

For the longest time, I thought you should learn from Bernhard. But learning from him didn't mean imitating him. Bernhard was at the end of a very small, obscure line of literature that I don't want to be anything like—from Knut Hamsun, through Kafka and Beckett. It's tremendously important work. I still find traces of Bernhard in my work. But now I know I don't need to imitate him. It's often said that imitation is the greatest form of flattery. But it's not necessarily the best homage. "Like me" doesn't mean "Be like me."

Finally, this has to do with my idea that the notion of generations isn't being followed in literature now—the idea that a new generation of writers will react to the previous one. We have an entire generation of fiction writers in America engaged in imitation—whether it's Jonathan Frantzen imitating DeLillo, or David Foster Wallace imitating Pynchon. There's a lot of talent in these writers. Part of the reason I got so offended by Rick Moody's books is that there are still incredibly heartrending moments you can pick out of them, especially from *The Ice Storm*. They're about his sense as a preppie white American that he's not allowed to feel pain. That's a great subject. But I wish he'd stop dressing that up. There's a huge amount of identity-based guilt instead—about the entitlement of suffering, the idea that: "Gosh—my daddy sat at J. P. Morgan's desk, so how can I possibly have problems?" Well, you're as allowed to have problems as any person.

RC   On that note, thanks very much for your time.